DADDY

DADDY

BY
Loup Durand

TRANSLATED BY
J. Maxwell Brownjohn

Villard Books
NEW YORK

For my son, Jean-François

DADDY

ONE

THOMAS THE YOUNGER OPENED HIS EYES. SEPTEMBER 18, 1942, his eleventh birthday, had dawned. It couldn't have been more than five o'clock. He peered out of the window. Fiery shafts of light were transfixing the sky and plunging into the sea. A leaden silence hung in the air, which was already stiflingly hot.

An unnatural silence.

Thomas scanned the motionless countryside without detecting anything or anyone to explain why he'd waked up so abruptly, why the machine in his head had sounded a sudden alarm, or why he'd darted to the window in three swift strides. It was illogical—he should still have been dead to the world. He'd sat up very late rereading the whole of Valentine Williams's *Man with the Club Foot*, which he liked as much as L. J. Vance's *Lone Wolf*, if not better, so it had been well past midnight when he went to sleep.

Nothing to be seen.

He swung his legs over the windowsill and sat there with his feet dangling. He was eleven now—awfully old, and he hadn't done much with his life yet.

All right, so he was kidding—eleven wasn't *that* old. He examined the contents of his mind. Nothing wrong there: the machine was functioning smoothly, sifting every detail, scouring the countryside millimeter by millimeter for the smallest detail that wasn't as it should have been. He could trust it not to overlook a thing. He treated himself to a rest and daydreamed for a moment or two, then climbed back into his bedroom and got dressed. He put on some espadrilles—one of the hundred and twenty pairs *She*'d brought him from Spain two years ago, on the last of Her surreptitious visits. Not knowing exactly how big his feet were but foreseeing that he would grow, She'd bought a dozen pairs in each of ten assorted sizes.

He knew perfectly well what he was going to do now, provided everything was as it should be outside. A boy didn't turn eleven every day of the week.

It was two years since he'd seen the Hispano. He always obeyed Her standing orders, but today was a special day. She would surely have said yes, especially as She knew that he'd known for the past four days that She wouldn't be there on his birthday.

He missed Her terribly, so much so that he felt quite sick with disappointment.

Enough of that, he told himself—stop it. There was no point.

No point at all.

TWO

THOMAS THE ELDER, HANS THOMAS VON GALL, DIED ON JULY 11, 1934, when he threw himself out of a fifth-floor window in Munich. The only extant photograph of him had been taken—without his knowledge—by the Gestapo. A tall, distinguished-looking man whose appearance belied his seventy years, he was snapped as he got into the back of a Mercedes while a liveried chauffeur, cap in hand, deferentially held the door for him. Visible in the background: a bank in Zurich's Paradeplatz.

The photograph predated his death by only six days.

On July 5 he was abducted on Swiss soil and spirited off to Germany for questioning. For the first few hours his interrogators treated him with chill courtesy. An eighth-generation banker, he was on close terms with such influential figures as Krupp von Bohlen, Fritz Thyssen, Albert Vögler, Georg von Schnitzler, Otto Wolf, and Baron Kurt von Schröder, the last being a fellow banker from Cologne. The tone of the interrogation changed on July 6 with the arrival on the scene of one Reinhard Heydrich, recently appointed head of the SD, the Security Service of the SS. Certain threats were put into effect, but Thomas the Elder stuck to his guns: if he had contrived to transfer large sums of capital abroad, he had done so only in compliance with current German legislation and at the express request of his clients. There could, of course, be no question of his disclosing the identity of those clients or the destination of the said funds. What was more, the figure

of one hundred million marks mentioned—or rather, bellowed at him
—by Herr Heydrich was absurdly wide of the mark. It was ludicrous.

No, he insisted, shaking his head at their ignorance of the routine,
none of the employees at his bank in Cologne had any knowledge of
these transactions. He had effected them entirely on his own.

He further stated that, having foreseen more than six years ago that
he might one day find himself in his present predicament, he had made
all the requisite arrangements in accordance with a long-matured
plan. Of his few surviving close relatives, there were none resident in
Germany on whom pressure could be exerted. Herr Heydrich could
deprive him of his personal fortune, his bank, even his life, but at his
age such things were of little . . .

He cracked, but only after one hundred and ten solid hours of
interrogation throughout which he had been compelled to remain
standing stripped to the skin. He was beaten with sundry lengths of
rubber hose, mainly on the lower part of the abdomen and the kid-
neys. For some obscure reason, Reinhard Heydrich was most anxious
to know whether or not these beatings resulted in a discharge of blood
into the urine, so the old man's interrogators presented him with an
enamel bucket after every session. When he pleaded an inability to
urinate, they administered two-liter doses of boiling water every four
hours.

At long last, being unable to speak, he consented to write. He was
given some paper and permitted to sit down. For nearly two hours he
churned out columns of names, numbered accounts, and complicated
access codes. Then he collapsed from sheer exhaustion. It happened
while the thirty-three scrawled sheets were on their way to Heydrich:
assumed to be only semiconscious, at death's door, and quite incapable of moving, old Gall sprang to his feet, ran to the window, and
launched himself into space. He crashed to the ground five floors below, preserving a courageous silence throughout his final descent.

It soon dawned on Heydrich that he had been hoodwinked: none of
the names listed was authentic. The old banker had concocted a series
of fanciful surnames with the aid of the letters composing the words
Dummkopf (blockhead) and *Blödsinn* (nonsense) repeated over and
over again, in acrostic fashion. Worse still, just before he stopped writing and feigned collapse, Hans Thomas von Gall had noted down
some only too authentic names complete with brief personal particulars: those of Adolf Hitler ("hysterical house-painter"), Paul Joseph
Goebbels ("unsuccessful novelist"), Hermann Göring ("obese drug

addict"), Horst Wessel ("pimp"), Heinrich Himmler ("chicken farmer"), and Reinhard Heydrich ("blond Jewish fiddler").

The very last words he scrawled before committing suicide were: "The exact sum in question amounts to seven hundred and twenty-four million marks."*

* The approximate equivalent today would be $350 million.

THREE

THE IDEA WAS HEYDRICH'S OWN. IN JANUARY 1935, AT A MEETING attended by Göring, Himmler, Gauleiter Dr. Robert Ley of Cologne, and Hans Frank, the young and brilliant head of the Party's legal department, it was decided to set up a *Sonderkommando*, a special task force, charged with recovering the vast sum by all and any available means. The first code name suggested for this operation was Sesame, but Heydrich preferred Schädelbohrer, literally "skull-borer," the instrument with which a surgeon pierces the cranium to expose the brain beneath.

Thanks to the stupidity of run-of-the-mill Gestapo sleuths unequal to Thomas the Elder's diabolical cunning, the entire four ensuing years were wasted. Inquiries were vigorously pursued in Switzerland, but they came to nothing. The Association of Swiss Bankers had had a forty-seventh article added to the federal banking law, its express purpose being to guarantee their depositors absolute secrecy and thereby thwart any Nazi investigators. In the autumn of 1938, Heydrich furiously instituted a complete reorganization of Schädelbohrer. He entrusted its direction to two men whose talents he considered complementary. One was Joachim Gortz, a lawyer specializing in international finance. The other was Gregor Laemmle.

Himmler was adamantly against employing Laemmle. It struck him as a bizarre and even decadent idea to enlist the services of a professor of philosophy who wasn't a member of the National Socialist Party, who had no experience of police work, who had evaded military service on the grounds of an alleged cardiac malformation, who had already published rather effete poems and a novel, and whom he, Himmler, detested on sight because of the undisguised insolence that smoldered in the man's yellow eyes.

But Heydrich had insisted and taken personal responsibility for the appointment. Gregor Laemmle was an exceptional man, he said. In order to get the better of a wily old fox like Thomas von Gall they needed a fox of equal cunning, and Gregor Laemmle was the most intelligent man in the Third Reich—"our beloved Führer and ourselves excepted, of course." Heydrich believed what he said, even if he didn't say all he knew. He had rescued Gregor Laemmle on two separate occasions: recently from the potential consequences of a disgusting lecture on Nietzsche he'd delivered to his students at Freiburg University, but, more important, earlier by doctoring Laemmle's papers to obliterate the fact that he had a Jewish grandmother.

Such things formed a bond. There was nothing like doing a man a favor to create a kind of permanent affinity and sense of responsibility for him.

Reinhard Heydrich got his way. Gregor Laemmle assumed command of Schädelbohrer in November 1938.

The hunt was really on at last.

THOMAS THE YOUNGER DESCENDED THE STAIRS AND CROSSED THE hall, tiptoeing in a dead straight line as if walking an imaginary tightrope suspended above Niagara Falls. He redoubled his precautions while passing the kitchen. He could smell coffee brewing, so Grandpa Allègre must be up already, but he made his exit unheard and unseen. Once outside in the oily, lukewarm residue of the night, so soon to be sucked up by the Mediterranean sun, he skirted a tall thorn hedge smothered in white blossoms and made his way around to the front of the villa. Crossing the terrace, he walked down the palm-fringed drive for twenty yards or so. Although he could see nothing on the road beyond the gates, he had an inexplicable sense that "someone" was out there. He hesitated.

Finally he put on his beret and retraced his steps, convinced that the invisible watcher was a figment of his imagination. He returned to the rear of the house, where the rose beds had been replaced by a kitchen garden in conformity with wartime restrictions, just as the tennis court was now occupied by a henhouse.

"Down, Adolf!"

Adolf was the dog employed to guard the hens. There was no love lost between Thomas and Adolf, but they tolerated each other, and at least the silly animal didn't bark. It followed his progress with a mobile eye, muzzle resting on forepaws, body motionless, as he slipped through the shrubbery. A cross between a Pyrenean sheepdog and a Mechlin, Adolf tipped the scales at a hundred pounds and loathed everyone in the world except Grandma Allègre, to whom the stupid mutt was insanely devoted.

Beyond the shrubbery lay a rough track and a dry-laid stone wall. Thomas made for the shelter of the pinewoods. He didn't turn around till he'd gone a couple of hundred yards. He was already higher than the villa's roof, and at this altitude the view was unobstructed. He could make out the cove of Port-Issol, Ban Rouge Point, a stretch of the road from Sanary, and the sea as far as the Embiez Archipelago.

Still nothing untoward.

He set off again and climbed higher, expecting any moment to feel the sun hit him in the back as it rose from the sea. Instead, just as he reached the white rocks at the summit, he sensed a human presence. Thomas owed the sensation to what She had one day laughingly called his "rat's instinct." He focused his gaze on a pine tree somewhat bigger than the rest, twenty yards away to his right. Positive that there was someone concealed behind it, he took another three steps. The man came into view, leaning against the trunk with a spuriously casual air: an immensely tall, dark-haired man with a big hooked nose and a lugubrious face. One of his huge, gnarled hands, the left one, had lost the little finger and the ring finger. He wore a cap and a black leather jacket, and cradled in his arms was a rifle.

REINHARD HEYDRICH HAD BEEN RIGHT. WITHIN A VERY FEW months, Gregor Laemmle and Joachim Gortz were on the right track. Gortz had managed to reconstruct the old Cologne banker's maneuver in its entirety. Thomas the Elder had not been content merely to salt away the enormous sums entrusted to him in Swiss banks. Foreseeing that Switzerland's neutrality might not be respected if war broke out, he had transferred the money to the other side of the Atlantic, either via Switzerland or by other routes, and deposited the bulk of it in the United States. Better still, the old fox had allowed for the possibility that the authorities in Washington might, in the event of a generalized conflict, invoke the terms of the Enemy Act and block all foreign assets. Gortz was well aware that others had been just as farsighted, notably the Dutch investment firm of Philips. He even became convinced that Gall had copied the Dutch, if not anticipated them. The old man would have deposited everything in America, not in ordinary accounts but with investment trusts, doubtless in the highly accommodating state of Delaware—institutions whose structure would enable them to escape the Enemy Act if it was applied. Although they were officially administered by American nationals, the true ownership of these companies was defined by highly secret trust deeds.

Gortz thought it more than probable that Gall had gained entire control of these trust funds before his death—that he was the general trustee of the whole extraordinary financial complex. But how would his clients be reimbursed? Here again, Gortz thought he knew the answer. A Herr Müller or Herr Bernstein who had entrusted the banker with, say, five hundred thousand marks would undoubtedly have received precise instructions: once outside Germany, the said gentlemen were to travel to Montreal, Mexico City, or Panama—anywhere, in fact. There, by coupling their request with a certain access code, they would be issued with a false passport belonging to a nonbelligerent country, instructed to present themselves at a given bank, and repaid their money in full, complete with interest, either in U.S. dollars or in the currency of their choice, at any place on earth that suited them.

Gortz, being a true professional himself, not only admired this high-precision system but obtained confirmation that his theories about it were correct. Gregor Laemmle, the former professor of philosophy from Freiburg University, turned out to be a formidable manhunter. He unmasked six of Thomas von Gall's mysterious clients, only two of whom were Jews. Four of them were induced to reveal the system whereby the transferred funds could be retrieved. In March, Gortz traveled to Philadelphia in America, and from there he visited Montreal, Toronto, and Mexico City. Equipped with four sets of false papers and the access codes of the four detainees, who had been tortured into revealing them, he passed himself off as the owner of each deposit account in turn. The result was identical in every case. The poker-faced lawyers or bankers he approached would request a forty-eight-hour delay, then confront him with the same icy response. What money? They had no idea what funds he was referring to. Who was this Herr von Gall or Müller or Bernstein on whose behalf they were alleged to be holding such and such a sum? As far as they were concerned, the secret codes produced by Gortz meant absolutely nothing.

Gortz was undeceived by these denials, especially after being compelled to wait for two days each time. He realized that although he had managed to pick nearly every lock in Gall's security system, he was ignorant of the final barrier, thus temporarily unable to breach it.

He returned to Germany early in May. Reviewing his hand on board the Hapag steamship *Hamburg*, he discovered that it contained only one remaining trump, a high card, but extremely difficult to play: Thomas the Elder, who had thought of everything, must necessarily have made allowance for his own death, natural or not, and thus for his replacement as trustee. He would surely have nominated one or more persons to succeed him.

These residuary trustees, as they were known, might be anyone and anywhere in the world. Although their identification would have solved everything, it seemed an altogether impossible task.

It was not until he landed that Gortz heard the news: his peculiar colleague Gregor Laemmle had, in fact, achieved the impossible.

He knew the identity of Thomas the Elder's successor.

"BUENOS DIAS, JAVIER," SAID THOMAS.

"*Hola, qué tal?*" said the man with the rifle and the leather jacket.

"*Buenos dias*, Miquel," said Thomas to another man on his left, who was so effectively concealed that only the toe of one shoe and the tip of his rifle barrel could be seen.

"*Hola, buenos dias*," replied Miquel the Invisible. Neither of the two lookouts had budged an inch. Thomas passed between them and breasted the summit of the hill. The sun appeared, bathing everything in a dull white glow. He turned for a last look at the ocher villa. It was well below him now, and the view had expanded still more to include Cride Point, Bandol, and the Embiez Islands. Thomas briefly debated whether or not to tell Javier about the funny feeling he'd had since waking up. He decided against it. Javier Coll could be relied on not to miss a trick—nothing ever escaped his notice. He and Miquel were already on the alert, their rifles ready for use, and Tomeo and Juan would not be far away.

Thomas made his way along the undulating crest for a while, the sun continuing to climb behind his back, the dry heat becoming more intense at every step. The little soil that clung to the white rocks was baked to the semblance of fine ash after so many weeks without rain. The brooding silence was such that the smallest twig snapped beneath his feet with a sound like splintering bone. He came to an expanse of open ground studded with metallic-looking thistles. Facing him stood a cottage, but he ignored it and headed for the rock face on the left. Biting into the rock was a big double door made of ill-fitting planks bleached gray by the elements and veined with black. The bolt was secured by a padlock that would have sprung open if a dragonfly had landed on it. Thomas peered cautiously in all directions, pried the two halves of the door apart, and squeezed inside the cave-cum-outhouse, taking care not to collide with the dusty, wicker-covered demijohns that lined the walls. He threaded his way between the cobwebs until he came to the far end. There, after pausing for thought, he deftly inserted his hand in a cavity in the rock and exerted downward pressure. With a faint click, the rear wall slid aside.

The car was still there, nestling like a jewel in the manmade grotto it had taken weeks to hew from the living rock. Thomas depressed a switch, and a naked bulb revealed it in all its incredible splendor. It was a Hispano-Suiza J-12 coupé type 68A with coachwork by Franay and a thirteen-foot wheelbase. The color scheme was silver-gray and black, the superb stylized stork surmounting the radiator cap cast in solid silver. Everything about the vehicle scintillated and shone. Even in the semidarkness, it seemed to have a life of its own.

GREGOR LAEMMLE FELT SURE HE WAS ON THE RIGHT TRACK. THIS certainty stemmed not only from his deductive powers but also from his burgeoning hunter's instinct, an instinct which was developing into a positive lust for the chase.

He was convinced beyond all doubt that the residuary trustee—to borrow Gortz's jargon—was a woman named Maria Weber.

Gregor Laemmle was a little man with sandy hair. When confronted by the tall, blond, stalwart young SS officers with whom Heydrich liked to surround himself, he tended to feel like a poodle frisking around in the midst of a pack of greyhounds. He believed in nothing on principle, and his sole interest in religions and political ideologies was that of a man who studied human idiosyncrasies as an entomologist might study the habits of the bee. His homosexuality wasn't a consuming passion. It was a simple matter of taste like a predilection for chocolates, and one from which he could have abstained indefinitely if need be. Now forty-six, he already knew—to the extent that it depended on himself—what form his death would take: he would calmly commit suicide. His indifference to the life and death of others was even greater. He had sought and obtained Heydrich's permission to visit half a dozen of the fifty concentration camps established from 1933 onward, including Dachau, Oranienburg, Sachsenhausen, and Buchenwald. The tour had interested him profoundly but left him quite unmoved.

Heydrich's offer of employment as head of Operation Schädelbohrer had come at an ideal moment. He had been on the point of resigning his chair in any case. Not because of the expulsion of Husserl, whose foremost pupil he had been (Husserl was of Jewish extraction), nor because of the oath of loyalty to Hitler demanded of all university professors (and duly taken by such luminaries as Heidegger), but because the Third Reich's education policy had condemned him to teach a bunch of morons, and, above all, because he wanted to devote himself to writing, relieved of any financial worries by a fortune inherited from his late lamented mother. He accepted Heydrich's offer partly to save argument, but also because, for the first time in his life, he was surprised at himself: usually so unmoved by anything or anyone, he found the prospect of Schädelbohrer fascinating.

Maria Weber. Laemmle picked up the threads of the investigation where the SD's agents had left them. Born in 1909, Maria was Thomas the Elder's granddaughter, the child of his only daughter's marriage to a French industrialist of Alsatian origin. She studied in Paris, where her ample means enabled her to occupy an eight-room apartment at 23 Rue Reynouard all by herself. In August 1931 she terminated the tenancy without leaving a forwarding address. There had been no further sign of life from her, either in Germany or in France. Basically, she had vanished into thin air. If dead she must have died under another name, because every possible register had been checked, but Gregor Laemmle didn't believe she was dead. He saw her disappearance in 1931 as the product of a plot between Thomas von Gall and his only living direct descendant.

Such was the line of inquiry on which Laemmle concentrated exclusively from the outset. He went off to Paris—his French was excellent—and interviewed all those who had known the girl as a law student. The picture he formed of her was not only clear-cut but intriguing: Maria Weber had been an exceptionally secretive person whose private life was a closed book. She was lovely to look at, made frequent visits to unknown destinations, spoke German, English, and Spanish as well as French, played tennis extremely well, had a passion for beautiful things and more than enough money to indulge it, liked Coco Chanel suits, tea roses, the best restaurants, jazz, and driving her Bugatti at a reckless speed. Her one brief allusion to home was made while dining at the Dôme in Montparnasse with a party that included Cocteau, Hemingway, and Gertrude Stein. When someone mentioned Suzanne Lenglen, she smiled "that mysterious smile of hers" and said, "I played her once on my parents' tennis court and took four games off her."

Maria Weber's parents were both dead. Her father, Pierre Weber, had been killed while leading his French infantry battalion into action at Verdun in 1916; her mother, Minna, née von Gall, had died in 1926. Neither their home nor any of Thomas the Elder's properties had ever boasted a tennis court, which seemed to suggest that Maria must have owned a house whose whereabouts she never divulged to anyone. Doggedly trying to retrace her steps eight years later, Gregor Laemmle spent four months compiling a list of one hundred and sixty-four persons who had known her in some degree or other: concierges, waiters, hotel porters, tennis partners, fellow law students. None of them possessed a photograph of her; several recalled that she had always shied away from cameras. "Lying low," Laemmle told himself. "She was already lying low."

Then a miracle occurred. Coco Chanel, to whom he was given an introduction by the designer Christian Bérard, reported that a woman had ordered eight or ten model gowns to be delivered to a suite at the Ritz. She had paid for them in cash and then disappeared. The reception desk at the Ritz had her registered as S. Lamiel, born in Grenoble in 1908. Gregor Laemmle's memory sounded the alarm: there was a Sophie Lamiel on the list of one hundred and sixty-four names—a Sophie Lamiel whom several witnesses referred to as Maria Weber's best friend, but whom Laemmle had failed to interview for the very good reason that she had officially died in a car crash in July 1931. The Sophie Lamiel who had stayed at the Ritz was a brunette like the dead woman but taller and more beautiful. She had gray eyes "as unforgettable as her smile," said the barman of the Ritz. "The kind of woman you don't see twice in a year." After checking out, she had vanished with the same virtuosity Maria Weber had displayed in August 1931. Their particulars tallied, their style and tastes were identical: the unknown woman had requested that her suite be adorned with fresh tea roses every morning.

Laemmle left immediately for Grenoble. He had no contacts there and conducted his inquiries with extreme discretion. Convinced that he was close to his objective, he had no wish to do anything that might alert his opponent, who had begun to obsess him. The Lamiels of Grenoble were a prosperous family who owned a country house (but no tennis court). They comprised a doctor, his wife, and their two children—there had been three, but the eldest daughter, Sophie, had died at the wheel of her Bugatti in 1931. For a second or two, the ex-professor-of-philosophy-turned-manhunter felt his heart pound at the sight of a young, dark-haired woman in a pastel summer dress walking ahead of him down the Rue Condillac. He thought for one moment that he had rediscovered Maria Weber.

But it was only Catherine Lamiel, one of the late Sophie's sisters. Her eyes were blue, not gray, she was only twenty-two, and she had certainly never set foot in the Ritz, however decorative she would have looked in such a setting.

Anxious not to give the game away by pursuing his investigation of her and her family too far, Laemmle decided to play his Spanish card. After all, hadn't he been told that Maria Weber was fluent in the language? He moved on to Spain, where the Gestapo's Madrid outstation placed itself at his disposal. It was a sheer waste of time. June went by, then July. Gregor Laemmle, now traveling on a Swiss passport, nonchalantly toured the French Riviera in quest of luxurious villas equipped with tennis courts. He'd started work on another novel but was exasperated to find that Maria Weber intruded between every line he wrote.

The alarm signal sounded on August 17: a Sophie Lamiel had checked into a big Lisbon hotel from New York and stayed there for three days before disappearing once more. The trail was already a week old.

Laemmle picked it up again himself. It occurred to him that she might have gone on to France and checked into another grand hotel. He caught the first available train but missed her at Biarritz by twelve hours. She had, in fact, stayed at the Hôtel d'Angleterre. Having devoted the morning, afternoon, and evening of August 26 to a number of mysterious meetings, she had asked for a typewriter, a large quantity of writing paper, and two hundred envelopes to be sent up to her suite. On the morning of the twenty-seventh she mailed the fruits of her labors in person. It was on this occasion that the head receptionist spotted one of her bodyguards—he used the plural because, in his opinion, there were at least two, if not more, "of obviously Spanish appearance." Their leader, who wore a black leather jacket, was "a very tall, gaunt man with a face like stone and eyes fit to chill your blood. A man with two fingers missing from his left hand."

She had quit the hotel, and doubtless Biarritz as well, on the morning of the 28th, but not without leaving two important clues behind. First there were the purchases she had made with the aid of directions given her by one of the Hôtel d'Angleterre's bellhops: an enormous box of chocolates from Dominique's and, more especially, a complete Meccano set from Biarritz-Bonheur. "It's for an eight-year-old boy with a mental age of fourteen or fifteen," she'd told the shop assistant with a smile. "If I know him, he'll turn up his nose at such a babyish present."

Then there was the car she'd boarded prior to her latest vanishing trick. Chauffeured by the man with the mutilated hand, it was an exceptional model, not to say unique: a twelve-cylinder Hispano-Suiza coupé with an engine displacement of 11.3 liters.

One or more Spanish bodyguards. More promising still, a car and a boy of eight. A boy who would have been born in 1931, the very year when Maria Weber left her Rue Reynouard apartment and vanished. A boy who might therefore be her son, who might be hidden somewhere in France—possibly at a house with a tennis court, why not?—and who would constitute a most effective means of persuasion if only he could be captured.

As for that magnificent car, every head must have turned as it sped past. Tracing it ought to be as easy as organizing a paper chase. Got her! thought Laemmle, trembling with an eagerness that surprised him. Got her! It's only a matter of hours—days at most. . . .

Then war broke out.

To Gregor Laemmle, the war seemed at first no more than an idiotic episode that compelled him to suspend Operation Schädelbohrer and threatened to ruin it altogether. As the months went by, however, he came to realize that he would now be able to enlist the support of the armies of the Third Reich, which were physically present and all-powerful throughout most of his hunting ground. He would rather have continued to operate alone, for the sheer beauty of the thing, but what could he do?

Besides, Heydrich was losing patience.

In September 1940 Laemmle entered Paris on the heels of the Wehr-macht. He did so in civilian clothes, even though Heydrich had in-sisted on appointing him an Obersturmbannführer, a lieutenant-colo-nel in the SS.

The hunt resumed at once.

A car and a child. . . .

THOMAS BEGAN BY CLIMBING INTO THE BACK OF THE HISPANO-Suiza, rediscovered the smoothness of the black leather upholstery, found he still couldn't put his feet on the footrest: they were several inches short of it, even after two whole years. He opened the walnut bar. The cut-glass Lalique decanters were there, and so were the glasses. He visualized Her pouring him a drink—lemonade—as the car glided majestically along the Promenade des Anglais, its twelve cylinders emitting an almost inaudible growl. She habitually addressed him in a low voice, confiding in him as if he were a grownup or, better still, Her sole companion and accomplice: "You've always been the only man in my life, Thomas, and you always will be." He shivered and shut his eyes, then opened them again. Although he'd heard noth-ing, he sensed that someone was there: Javier Coll had followed him into the rocky hideaway and was right beside the car, watching him impassively. Their eyes met. Then Thomas gestured to him and Javier opened the door, doffing his cap like a chauffeur with the rifle still in his other hand.

"Está muy limpio," said Thomas.

"We clean it once a month," Javier replied in French.

Thomas got in behind the wheel and felt for the pedals with his feet. He could operate them now. He played with the levers, the one that adjusted the shock absorbers and the other two, which enabled you to advance or retard the spark. He ran his fingers over the magnificent dashboard on which all the dials (the speedometer went up to two hundred kilometers per hour) were set in walnut veneer. The ignition key was there—he had only to switch it on and press the starter.

"I'm big enough to drive it now."

"Of course," said Javier.

"Today's my birthday. I simply had to come."

"I know. Many happy returns."

"Thank you," said Thomas, caressing the wheel.

Another exchange of glances, another silence. Javier quietly remarked that it wasn't the best of times to visit the hideaway. Thomas nodded, his gray eyes widening a little in the gloom. He could have asked if the red villa was under some kind of threat, as he'd sensed it to be since dawn, but that would have put Javier even more on his guard and made him insist on leaving the Hispano at once. He said nothing.

His eyes grew wider as he recalled that morning on the Grande Corniche two years ago. At Her request, Javier had parked the Hispano on the edge of a big drop. Javier got out and strolled off. The Citroën escorting them, with Miquel Enseñat at the wheel, had also pulled up and was almost concealed by a bend in the road. As soon as She was sure they were really alone, She'd asked him what he would like to do most in the world. He thought carefully before answering, as he always did, but only for a moment. Apart from living with Her all the time—not that this was possible, he knew—he yearned to drive the Hispano at least once in his life. She gazed at him for a long time, then nodded, looking very sad all of a sudden. "If that's what you want," She said, "you can try right now." They got out and took their places on the front seat, which was outside the passenger compartment. At this season of the year, the late summer of 1939, the black leather hood that shielded it from the elements was folded back. She said, "Take the wheel, Thomas." He did his best, but it was no use; his legs weren't long enough for him to work the pedals. She didn't laugh or make fun of him in the least, just went on gazing at him so tenderly and sadly that he wanted to cry. She said it was only a matter of time before both his wishes came true. Then She looked up and down the road to make doubly sure that no one was within earshot and asked if he remembered all She'd told him the day before, while they were walking side by side along the beach at Port-Issol. He concentrated as only he knew how, and it was as if a key had turned in his head: he repeated everything word for word, names, codes, figures, and all. It took a long time, so he smiled at Her when he'd finished, feeling not a little proud of himself, and that was when the strangest thing happened: instead of returning his smile, She began to weep. Very softly, with a total absence of sound and movement, but stricken by a sorrow whose irresistible intensity he recognized in a flash, because She didn't make a habit of crying. He would never, in fact, have believed Her capable of it.

He was petrified for a moment or two, imagining that it must be his fault—that his memory had played him false. But no, it was nothing of the kind, and he'd felt a savage hatred for the lousy world that was causing Her such distress. Again and again in the years that followed, like a never-extinct volcano, this scene on the Grande Corniche continued to erupt in his mind. He analyzed it repeatedly with surgical precision, recalling every word, every vocal inflection, every silence, every one of the minuscule tremors that had afflicted the face of his beloved mother.

And each time he experienced the same anguish, the same terrible remorse at having failed to tell Her that he understood and approved of all She'd had to do; that he was content to see Her only for brief periods, at long intervals, and in secret; that he didn't hold Her responsible for the mission She'd been entrusted with, which compelled Her to lead the life of a hunted beast and conceal the very existence of a son who might be used as a weapon against Her.

There were so many other things he would have liked to tell Her, too. For instance, how much he appreciated the unique complicity that had existed between them ever since he learned to speak, because She'd never treated him like a child and always asked his opinion on everything, doubtless for want of the husband She'd never had. "I only knew your father for a short time. He didn't count—he doesn't even know of your existence. If you want to make his acquaintance someday, the decision will be yours alone. . . ." Their complicity was underlain by a love that bordered on veneration. When he was away from her, his merciless memory would conjure up visions of Her hair, Her hands, Her lips, summon up the sound of Her voice and Her wonderful smile—even the fragrance of Her—with a clarity that rent his heart.

Javier Coll was speaking.

He spoke, and Thomas's mental film show ended abruptly.

"We'd better not hang around here," Javier repeated.

"Vamonos," said Thomas.

Obediently, he climbed out of the Hispano, made his way back through the cave, and emerged into the open air. It was broad daylight now. The rocks were already baking in the heat of the sun; the cicadas had started chirping. Thomas, who could still feel the dankness of the cave in his bones, was blinded by the glare, but the brutal transition had not impaired his "rat's instinct." His inexplicable premonition of danger returned in a flash, far stronger than before. He swung around, intending to catch Javier's eye and seek confirmation of his fears, but he had no time to complete the movement. A huge hand seized his arm and tugged at it.

"Muy pronto, Tomás! Date prisa!"

They broke into a run.

GREGOR LAEMMLE'S SOJOURN IN PARIS DURING SEPTEMBER 1940 was a waste of time. His reports to Reinhard Heydrich complained of his being hamstrung by the rivalry between the Wehrmacht and the Gestapo: the former claimed exclusive control of the occupied territories on Hitler's behalf, the latter had made a semiclandestine entry into the French capital.

Berlin replied in vague terms. Laemmle understood: Operation Schädelbohrer had already been pursuing its unproductive course for almost six years, so Heydrich would prefer him to be discreet to the point of invisibility. He was nonetheless to be assigned an office at 11 Rue des Saussaies, and a staff of ten. More to the point, he was to have all the French money he wanted, or almost all, because the Vichy government was making such astronomical monthly payments to the occupying power that no one knew what to do with them.

Laemmle never availed himself of the premises in the Rue de Saussaies—in fact, he never set foot there. Neither there, nor in the Hôtel Lutétia, nor in the Majestic, nor in any of the Gestapo's official domains. For his personal use he rented an apartment in the Rue de l'Abbaye off Saint-Germain-des-Prés, only a stone's throw from the Rue Saint-Benoît, where he'd spent three blissful years studying for his philosophy degree at the Sorbonne and completing his German doctorates with a degree in classical literature. If ever there was a moment when he was tempted to go to ground and play the forgotten sentry, rediscovering his old haunts and habits, this was it. He had always cherished a profound love for Paris, and his ambition to write in French had never left him. There was something miraculous about the opportunity he'd just been handed on a plate. He could easily have taken advantage of it and, in consequence, abandoned the hunt.

He did nothing of the kind, however. Not for patriotism's sake—he was totally devoid of that—but from intellectual curiosity: it would have been like leaving a game of chess undecided or a jigsaw puzzle incomplete. Perhaps, too, he was yielding to an obsession. There was no longer any question of his being in love with the mysterious Maria Weber. He saw or imagined her everywhere, that face he'd never seen but whose intelligence and willpower, chill deliberation and almost masculine strength of purpose, he could clearly sense. No, he would never rest until they were face to face.

Or rather, until he had her at his mercy.

Gortz joined him in November, having returned via Sweden from a trip to Canada, the United States, and Brazil, where he had set up raw-materials-purchasing agencies designed to go on functioning even if the war spread to America. Laemmle had raised his eyebrows at this. "You mean to tell me," he said, "that the warring nations will maintain their commercial links? That we frightful Nazis will continue to trade with the very countries we're fighting?" "Yes indeed," was Gortz's imperturbable reply. "Business is business."

Gortz, who took a very skeptical view of Operation Schädelbohrer, considered the matter closed. "Even if this Maria Weber of yours really is our residuary trustee, she'll have tucked herself away in America long ago. And if she really has a son she'll have done the same with him. Even if she left him behind in France and was caught napping by our lightning advance, the boy's bound to be in the unoccupied zone, and I don't see how you're going to trace him there. For instance, she may have camouflaged him years ago as the son of one of her girlfriends. What a lot of ifs!"

The ten men assigned to Gregor Laemmle had all graduated from the espionage school at Altenburg in Thuringia. Two or three of them spoke French well enough to disguise their origins, but the rest sounded as German as a brass band. Laemmle made them comb Paris and the occupied zone for four whole months. The least mediocre of these agents—an SS officer named Hess, not Rudolf but Jürgen—was sent to reconnoiter Grenoble in September. The Lamiels were no longer there: they had emigrated to Morocco six months earlier. Theirs seemed to have been a precipitate departure. Catherine Lamiel, the twenty-two-year-old girl whom Laemmle had momentarily mistaken for Maria Weber in the Rue Condillac in 1939, had broken off her medical studies just before embarking on her fifth and final year. Laemmle interpreted this sudden exodus as the result of a tactical ploy on Maria Weber's part. She had persuaded the Lamiels to go along with her assumption of Sophie's identity, then she removed them all from circulation before anyone could use them against her. A neat chessplayer's move. . . .

Hess returned from Grenoble bearing detailed dossiers, complete with photographs, on each of the four Lamiels—father and mother, son and daughter—and on the last two in particular, because rumor had it that Catherine and Frédéric Lamiel had left Morocco and were back in France. Another detail on file: Frédéric, Catherine's elder brother, who was studying architecture, had served with the International Brigades in Spain. How could Laemmle have failed to suspect a connection with the Spanish bodyguards accompanying Maria Weber at Biarritz?

The hunt for the Hispano was still in progress at the end of February 1942, under the direction of Jürgen Hess. His inquiries made it seem certain that the sumptuous car, after leaving Biarritz on the morning of August 28, 1939, had neither headed north nor crossed the frontier into Spain. That meant it must have headed east toward what was now the unoccupied zone, where it might still be based. Given that it consumed fifty liters of petrol every hundred kilometers when traveling at full speed, it must—unless it had gone to ground in the region of the Côte Basque—have stopped to tank up somewhere, and what garage attendant, even after an interval of thirty months, would have forgotten that two-and-a-half-ton monster with the black-and-silver paintwork?

Hess's men took up their positions on a starting line running from Libourne, northeast of Bordeaux, to Saint-Jean-Pied-de-Port on the Spanish frontier. Each member of his team was assigned a corridor ten to fifteen kilometers wide extending as far as the Italian border, and each was to conduct a systematic check on all the petrol pumps in his sector, one by one, whether or not they had been out of service since August 1939.

The agents crossed their demarcation line on March 2.

Gregor Laemmle was enchanted by the inexorable neatness of this procedure.

Except that it yielded nothing, absolutely nothing, for all of sixteen weeks. Either he'd been mistaken in his belief that the Hispano had headed east after leaving Biarritz, or—and this was the explanation he most readily accepted in his eagerness to conceive of an adversary at least as Machiavellian as himself—Maria Weber had prudently established some refueling depots in advance.

The fact remained that by the beginning of May, his beaters had reached the Marseilles–Saint-Etienne vertical without finding a thing.

Laemmle decided to change his tactics and recruit some reinforcements. If he drew on Gestapo personnel he would saddle himself with some more men of Hess's type, and that prospect didn't appeal to him at all, precisely because Jürgen Hess was no fool and had the effrontery to criticize him, Laemmle, to his face. He hadn't submitted a single report to Berlin for months, and the signs were that Heydrich and Himmler had forgotten his existence. He really couldn't see any point in jogging their memory—they might wind up Operation Schädelbohrer and, as he put it, "deprive me of my toy." After all, he was still drawing millions and millions of French francs, and no one seemed to care what use he made of them. In an emergency he could always fall back on his SS rank of Obersturmbannführer and his personally signed orders from Hitler and, with a modicum of persuasion, secure the assistance of an entire division.

He accepted a proposal Gortz had made him in February of the previous year. At a house on the edge of the Bois de Boulogne in Paris, a meeting took place between Laemmle and the director of the German purchasing agencies set up in France by Hermann Göring. This man, Otto Brandl by name, offered him the services of one of his protégés, whom he described as "a most exceptional person."

Brandl's nominee turned out to be a Frenchman who had recently been granted German nationality and the rank of captain in the Wehrmacht for services rendered, notably the dismantling of a Belgian resistance network. He was tall, massively built, and thoroughly masculine in spite of his strange falsetto voice. His self-confidence was absolute. He could personally vouch for all the men he supplied, fifty or a hundred or even more. Better still, his second-in-command was Pierre Bonny, generally reputed to be the finest detective in France.

He discussed terms in a charming and amiable manner: two hundred thousand francs for the recovery of the car, two million for the boy, ten million for the woman.

His name was Henri Lafont, alias Normand. Now that his finest hour had struck, he was known as Monsieur Henri. His offices were in

Avenue Pierre-I-de-Serbie, and he had just given a house-warming party at his new headquarters at 93 Rue Lauriston.

THOMAS AND JAVIER COLL SPRINTED ALONG UNDER COVER OF the pine trees, keeping to the hollows and gullies. The Hispano's hiding place was already five or six hundred yards behind them, the red villa considerably farther away than that. They passed Miquel Enseñat, who had flattened himself behind a rocky mound in such a way that only his eyes and the muzzle of his rifle were visible. Miquel withdrew as soon as they went by and broke into a run, turning ever and again to cover their retreat with his finger on the trigger—and no one, no one on earth, could shoot faster or straighter than Miquel.

Juan Llull was covering their left flank a little farther on. He had just straightened up and was trotting along with his eyes skinned. None of the bodyguards had uttered a single word as yet; they simply exchanged glances or gestures, and that was communication enough. Thomas marveled at their unerring precision, and he was filled with pride.

They came out on a narrow path hemmed in by holm oaks, arbutus, and other heavily scented shrubs. They had to make their way along it without a sound, without brushing against a single leaf. In places you could have sworn the path had come to an end, but no, you calmly ducked under a certain bush and there it was again. Thomas was no stranger to this procedure, having rehearsed it two or three times a month for months on end. Once, even, Javier had hauled him out of bed in the middle of the night—at three A.M.—and hustled him mercilessly along. They had followed the same route under the same sort of circumstances, with the other three armed Spaniards covering their retreat in similar fashion. They trekked west and north in turn, crossed the main road and the railway line, and spent the whole day hidden in a shepherd's hut on the slopes of the Gros Cerveau, not returning home until the following night, and then only after satisfying themselves that it had been a false alarm.

The path petered out. The main road was in sight. At a signal from Javier, the whole party froze. On previous occasions Tomeo Oliver had been stationed nearby as a lookout to watch the road and enable them to cross it unobserved.

This time he wasn't there.

MONSIEUR HENRI'S WHITE BENTLEY BREASTED SOME RISING ground. Moments later a small bay came into view on their left, a rocky cove adorned with a sandy beach.

"Port-Issol," said Monsieur Henri in his strange falsetto voice. "The villa is a little way beyond it on the right. They'll all be asleep— it's not even six yet. We weren't absolutely sure it was the right place until last night, when you were already on your way here by train. All the same, it had to be either this house or the one at Anthéor. There's a boy of around ten in both places, and they both have a tennis court."

The Bentley swung right onto a road that ran beside the sea.

"But the youngster at Anthéor definitely possesses a mother and a father, even if they are Jews. We've made a note of them for future reference—waste not, want not. The boy at the villa near Sanary is different. His name is Thomas, and he's supposed to be the grandson of the caretakers, Joseph and Alphonsine Allègre. They've put it about in Sanary that he's an illegitimate child their daughter Marthe gave birth to before her marriage. The records state that he was born on December 14, 1931, at Courthézon in the Vaucluse. We checked his birth and baptismal certificates. They're perfectly in order—quite impeccable. We almost gave up on him."

Gregor Laemmle was seated in the back of the Bentley with Monsieur Henri, who gave off an agreeably virile aroma of expensive *eau de toilette*, on his right. Laemmle's personal aide, a beefy but effeminate-looking young SS officer named Georg Soeft, was up front beside Eddy Pagnon, Monsieur Henri's chauffeur. Soeft had also been waiting at the station when Laemmle's train got in from Paris. The Bentley began to slow. Parked beside the road and visible through the windscreen was a black Citroën van.

"We almost gave up on him, but I persevered all the same. Instinct, you might say. We couldn't get hold of Marthe—she and her husband emigrated to Algeria years ago—so we went looking for the midwife who'd attended her at Courthézon in December 1931. We ran her to earth in Nice, where she's living in quiet comfort on the income from an apartment house she bought with a legacy someone left her. My nephew Paul and a couple of my men paid her a visit last night. They leaned on her a little and got her to talk. Marthe undoubtedly had a baby in 1931, but it was stillborn, and Joseph registered another child in its place—a child who was already two or three months old. That's point number one. Point number two: there are three or four Spaniards living on the hill behind the house, taciturn types, and one of them's short a couple of fingers. Ah, here we are."

A small group of men stood chatting beside the Citroën van. Gregor Laemmle already knew or was soon to know every one of the dozen men involved in the Sanary operation. Apart from Paul Clavié, Monsieur Henri's nephew, they included Louis Haré, Jean-Michel "Red-Nose" Chavez, Alfonse Menigault, Charles Cazauba, Abel "the Gorilla" Danos, one-armed Mohammed Begdane, Bernard "Girlie" Bonange, Dominique Carbotti, Adrien "Smiler" Estebeteguy, Georges Kaïdjian the Armenian, and Alex Villaplana, the former pro soccer player.

The Bentley pulled up and Paul Clavié presented his report. He'd been the first to arrive on the scene, having driven there straight from Nice. Sure enough, after thirty or forty minutes a boy had emerged from the house and crossed the terrace. He'd even started down the drive, only to turn on his heel and go inside again. "Can't think what he was up to at that ungodly hour. We were watching him from behind the hedge—we almost snatched him then and there, but I only had Adrien with me and we'd have had to jump the gate first. We were scared of messing things up. Besides, who knows how many of them there are inside the house?"

He went on to report that a team of five led by the Gorilla had set off for the main road beyond the villa twenty minutes earlier.

"They're bound to be in position by now."

Laemmle got out of the Bentley but refrained from slamming the door. He surveyed the red house as closely as its garden wall and dense privet hedge allowed. He was amazed at his own placidity, not to say indifference. The whole operation was doomed to fail, he felt sure, and he almost hoped that it would. Over to his left, Georg Soeft of the flaxen hair, girlish face, and bulging muscles had idiotically drawn his Luger and was trailing along behind the French pimps, thieves, and cutthroats who were on their way to besiege the villa. Would this bunch of repulsive thugs really succeed in capturing *her*?

Mechanically glancing at his watch, Gregor Laemmle saw that it was seven minutes to six on the morning of September 18, 1942.

IT WAS FOUR MINUTES SINCE ANYONE HAD MOVED AND THREE since Miquel Enseñat had gone off to reconnoiter in his silent, stealthy way. You turned your head for a moment and he wasn't there anymore. Thomas firmly believed that Miquel could have slipped through a bead curtain without displacing a single strand.

They waited. Thomas studied Javier's face, trying to read his intentions, but the face was its usual expressionless mask. Many people were as scared of Javier Coll as Grandpa Allègre, who often complained that the Spaniard sent shivers down his spine—many people, but not Thomas. Javier spoke little, or at any rate infrequently, and he seldom smiled. His dark eyes were on the wide side, and you felt the weight of his gaze when it rested on you. He was pretty old—forty at least—and thin as a rake, but watch out: he could lift a hundred-pound sack one-handed as easily as you could do the same with a bag of sweets, and he'd crack you a nut between his thumb and forefinger just like that. He always carried two knives, one that lived up his sleeve and sprang open with a click, and the other, a smaller one, in a flat leather sheath strapped to his left forearm. By the time you saw his hand move, the knife had gone whistling through the air and embedded itself in the trunk of a pine tree many yards away. Thomas wasn't the least bit scared of Javier, and anyway, he had Her assurance on the subject: "Javier is the only person in the world you can trust implicitly . . . except, of course, with our secret. . . ."

"Cuidado!" whispered Juan Llull.

There was movement on the road. Preceded by the sound of its engine, a car came into view, a black front-wheel-drive Citroën van. It was crawling along, and the two men in it were closely scrutinizing the verges on either side. Then it pulled up. The men got out, looking relaxed but alert. Each of them was carrying a submachine gun. In spite of Javier's heavy hand, which was clamping his nose to the ground, Thomas continued to peer through the undergrowth. His memory registered certain details: one of the pair had an arm missing, the other was a barrel-chested giant of a man. He studied their faces, their posture, their walk, until they were permanently imprinted on his mind. He would always recognize them from now on, even from behind.

Abel was the big one's name—the one-armed man had just called him that. Abel had jumped the ditch and was heading straight for them. He was fifty yards away at most, and the monumental nature of his physique became more and more apparent with every step he took. An idea popped into Thomas's head unbidden: he expected—or hoped, to be honest—that Javier Coll and Abel would fight like dogs. When you owned a dog that was tougher than all the rest and it came up against another dog of the same size, one half of you dreaded that they would spring at each other's throats while the other half yearned for them to do so because you knew in your heart of hearts that your dog would give the other one a hell of a hiding, or perhaps even kill it. Thomas felt rather ashamed of comparing Javier Coll to a dog, because he liked him a lot, but that was the way he was. If a thought like that popped into his head, he couldn't help carrying it through all the way.

In any case, there was no dogfight. Just as the huge man was starting to climb the mound that hid them from view, and had got to within thirty yards or so, a shot rang out on the left, far away in the Bandol direction. This first shot was swiftly followed by another, then several more, then a whole fireworks display. Miquel or Tomeo or both of them must have opened up, and some submachine guns had returned their fire. Abel and his one-armed companion ran back to the car, made a U-turn, and drove off fast the way they'd come.

At a nod from Javier, Juan Llull rose to his feet and went down to the road. He crossed it and signaled that the coast was clear. Thomas and Javier swiftly joined him on the other side. They were still striding out briskly twenty minutes later, having crossed the railway line. This time, contrary to Thomas's expectations, they headed northeast instead of making straight for the shepherd's hut. As he trotted along behind Juan Llull, precisely following his zigzag lead, Thomas was saddened but exhilarated by the certainty that he was leaving for good, that he would never see Grandpa and Grandma Allègre again—or their stupid mutt of a dog, though that was no great loss—and that his young life was about to undergo a vast and sudden transformation.

He'd just come to this conclusion when they reached the farm.

GREGOR LAEMMLE WAS STANDING IN THE MIDDLE OF THE BOY'S bedroom. He himself had touched nothing. He'd left that to Soeft, whose examination of various cupboards had disclosed the presence of sixteen Meccano sets in mint condition, a number of jigsaw puzzles, some comprising three or four thousand pieces—Laemmle, himself a great lover of such brain-teasers, immediately noted that they were special puzzles made to order by Symington & Travis of Manchester— and enough other toys to last a boy for years.

Oddly enough, another cupboard was found to contain no less than ten dozen pairs of espadrilles in assorted sizes.

As for books, they were everywhere—a whole army of them. Complete collections of *Masque* (thrillers in yellow hardback covers) and adventure stories in the *Emeraude* series rubbed shoulders with the complete works of Jules Verne, Louis Boussenard, Karl May, James Curwood, H. G. Wells, and Alexandre Dumas; Kipling, Paul Féval, and Gustave Aimard shared shelves with the adventures of Pistol Pete, Arsène Lupin, Rouletabille, Sherlock Holmes, and Fantômas. Odder still: Francis de Croisset's *La Dame de Malacca*, Malraux's *La Condition Humaine* ("At the age of ten?" muttered Laemmle, raising his eyebrows), and Hemingway's *A Farewell to Arms*.

The atlases—French, English, German—numbered at least a dozen and were all of superlative quality.

A terrible scream rang out downstairs—a woman's scream.

. . . all of superlative quality, though their maps were crisscrossed with pencil lines representing imaginary voyages of exploration. Soeft picked up the books one by one and thumbed through the pages, then tossed them unceremoniously on the floor. The hardbacks he slit with a razor blade to see if their covers concealed anything.

"Pointless, totally pointless," was Laemmle's wry and despondent verdict.

In his opinion, there wasn't a hope of finding any document of interest or value, let alone a photograph of Maria Weber. He turned on his heel, unable to endure the sight of books being dismembered in such a barbarous manner, and strolled into the room next door. It was a schoolroom and playroom combined. French, Spanish, German, and English grammars stood side by side on a shelf together with dictionaries and other reference books. There were no handwritten exercise books, but that didn't surprise him. Judging by the ashes in the big metal wastepaper basket, the boy had orders to burn anything that might provide a clue to his real identity.

A five-thousand-piece jigsaw puzzle lay spread out on a huge trestle table. It depicted an English cottage garden in full flower. Nearly half of it, including the borders, had been completed. The remainder of the pieces had been carefully sorted according to color and placed in shoe boxes. Very systematic. It was all Laemmle could do not to become engrossed in a search for some more of those carmine pieces forming part of the mass of blossom just below that dovecote, which had already been assembled with such skill and visual memory. . . .

He felt similarly tempted to sit down at the chessboard, where a game was in progress. White had the advantage and ought to win in five moves—no, six, unless . . . Well, I'll be damned! he thought. I didn't spot that black king's knight. What a diabolical trap!

He walked out into the passage and opened one door, then another. He knew what lay behind the third before he crossed the threshold. Just as he did so, another scream floated up from the ground floor. It conveyed even more pain and terror, if that was possible, than the first.

The room Laemmle entered was still redolent of Maria Weber's perfume, or so he imagined. It was a spacious room whose ultra-elegant décor centered on a four-poster bed draped in a white lace counterpane. Everything was bathed in the dawn light that flooded in through four windows overlooking the sea. Studying the ebony furniture more closely, Laemmle thought he recognized the style of Paul Iribe and Jacques-Emile Ruhlmann, both of them interior designers of his acquaintance. He took three or four steps and stopped short, almost suffocated by the sensation that he wasn't alone. He'd never before been so close to the woman he so desperately sought but had never seen. He could picture her in this very room—picture her relaxing after her duel on the tennis court with Suzanne Lenglen or burning the midnight oil as she tirelessly updated her residuary trustee's accounts.

The woman downstairs had stopped screaming. Her moaning and panting were suggestive of childbirth or copulation—nauseating, whichever.

Laemmle resumed his progress across the room. He sat down where she had undoubtedly sat, at the superb Mazarin bureau. Satisfied that he wouldn't find anything relevant to his quest in the drawers, he didn't even trouble to open them. His yellow eyes widened as he tried to suppress a little of the potent emotion that possessed him. He was still seated at the desk when Soeft came a few minutes later, having just ransacked the playroom-cum-schoolroom.

"Don't touch anything," said Laemmle, not bothering to turn his head.

"I could—" Soeft began.

"Get out of here!" Laemmle told him with a fury verging on hatred.

At last, some considerable time after the big blond SS man's departure, Laemmle tore himself away from the room and went downstairs. Silence had been restored, he noted: the woman was moaning no longer. He discovered the reason for this silence when he paid a visit to the staff quarters at the rear of the villa. The caretaker and his wife and dog had had their throats cut. Smiler, otherwise known as Adrien Estebeteguy, had decapitated the three corpses and made some minor rearrangements. The dog was adorned with the man's head, the woman with the dog's, the man with his wife's. Unmoved, Laemmle stepped over their remains and asked if any information had come to light.

The answer, it seemed, was yes.

JUAN LLULL ENTERED THE FARM ALONE WHILE THOMAS AND Javier Coll remained out of sight, concealed behind a windbreak of cypresses and yew trees bordering the narrow track that led to it. Thomas sat down on the sunbaked ground during this enforced wait. He was quite tired after their long walk.

"Will Grandpa and Grandma Allègre have a hard time?"

"It's possible," said Javier.

"They'll be asked questions about me, is that it?"

Javier nodded.

"About me and other people?" Thomas couldn't bring himself to say "Maman," and he hadn't wanted to say "Her."

"Probably," said Javier.

"Questions about you and Miquel and Juan and Tomeo, too?"

"Grandpa and Grandma Allègre know me," said Javier, "but they don't know Miquel or Juan or Tomeo."

"That's true." Thomas thought for a moment, and suddenly it all became clear—distressingly clear. *"Van a matarlos,"* he said. To his ears the statement sounded less brutal in Spanish than it would have in French or German.

"Who's going to kill them?"

"Lo sabes muy bien," Thomas said. "You know very well." And he turned away and gazed into the distance to disguise the fact that he was close to tears. It was then, as his eyes followed the line of the hills, that he registered something and automatically stored it in his memory without, for the moment, attaching much importance to it.

The sound of an engine broke the silence. A small gasogene truck emerged from the farmyard and drove past without stopping, but slowly enough for Javier to hoist Thomas into the back and climb in beside him. They stretched out flat, hidden from view by the slatted sides and a number of crates containing tomatoes. Thomas lay on his side on the hot, shiny steel floor. His eyes were still moist.

"Lo sabes muy bien," he repeated. "We ought to have brought them with us."

"They wouldn't have come," Javier said, very gently.

Too gently. It was obvious that he realized how sad Thomas felt and was doing his best to comfort him, though fortunately not to the extent of putting his arms around him. Thomas couldn't have borne to be hugged or comforted by anyone. He huddled up like a snail withdrawing into its shell.

"They couldn't have come with us in any case," said Javier. "It wasn't part of the plan."

"Let's not talk about it anymore," Thomas said.

"Vale," said Javier. "Have a tomato."

Thomas ate several. He was hungry, and it didn't do to discuss such things as hunger and thirst, sorrow or its absence.

"What about the Hispano?"

"Don't worry, they'll never find it."

Half an hour later the truck left the gorges of Ollioules and headed north, but just beyond Saint-Anne d'Evenos it turned right off the main road onto a very steep, unsurfaced track.

"You can sit up now," said Javier, sitting up himself.

Thomas followed suit. Two or three hundred yards behind them he spotted another small truck with two men on board. Tomeo was driving and Miquel, the top of his head just visible above the cab, was riding in the back.

The convoy drove on for a while. Then Javier rapped on the roof of the cab with his knuckles and Juan pulled up. They were in a kind of rocky defile, and there wasn't a house in sight.

"You're sure about the Hispano?"

"Quite sure."

The Spaniards got out and conferred in *mallorquín*, the sibilant and unintelligible Majorcan dialect they used when talking among themselves. Feeling excluded, Thomas went and sat on a boulder. He hadn't been worried at any stage by the possibility that She mightn't know where to find him after their abandonment of the red villa; Javier was bound to have done whatever was necessary. If the truth be told, now that he'd managed to banish Grandpa and Grandma Allègre from his mind, the Hispano was his main worry. All things considered, he shared Javier's certainty that "they" would never find it.

The trouble was, he longed desperately to see Her again. They wouldn't speak—they mightn't even look at each other—but at least they would be together, side by side.

It was two years since he'd seen Her. Two whole years. It was hard, never seeing your mother. Really hard.

"THE HOUSE IS OFFICIALLY OWNED BY SOME SWISS WHO—"

"I'm not interested in the house," said Laemmle.

Henri Lafont smiled. "I understand. The woman, then. The Allègres knew her only as Sophie Lamiel. One evening in October 1931, when Joseph Allègre was still working at the naval dockyard in Toulon, she pulled up outside their house in a Bugatti. Knowing that Marthe was pregnant and unmarried, she suggested that the girl should pretend to give birth to twins and said she would make all the necessary arrangements. Then she slapped two hundred thousand francs on the table."

"Irrelevant details. Go on."

"Very well. Until 1933 she and her son lived at the villa with the Allègres—she never told them he was her son, by the way, they merely assumed so. In 1933 she left, taking the boy with her. She didn't return for four years, but every year she paid the caretakers' fares so that they could visit their so-called grandson. The Allègres made trips to Switzerland, Italy, and Spain."

"Where in Spain?"

"Majorca, to be precise. A hotel in Palma. They only ever saw her in hotels, all of them five-star, so they never knew where she was really living. She brought the boy back to the villa in '37 and left him there. After that she began to stay away more and more often, sometimes for months on end. She always spoke German when she phoned the boy. He speaks German, Spanish, and English as well as French, plus quite a bit of Italian—he's as bright as they come, apparently. The Allègres tried sending him to school at Sanary, but it wasn't a success. The youngster refused to open his mouth, so they ended by having him do correspondence courses. He's three years ahead of schedule, if not more. In '39 a Spaniard turned up at the villa."

"The one with two fingers missing?"

"The same. Third and fourth fingers of the left hand. Taller than me, around six feet two."

"Any photographs?"

"Of him? None, nor of her either—none at all. In Switzerland one time, when old Allègre tried to snap the Lamiel woman and her son with his Box Brownie, a man swooped on him and ripped the film out of the camera. A man called Miguel or Michel."

"Not the Spaniard?"

"Another one. The Allègres only spotted him down here once, but they got the impression that he was prowling around the villa all the time, keeping out of sight."

"Who introduced the tall Spaniard to them?"

"She did—the Lamiel woman."

"Please don't refer to her as the Lamiel woman," Laemmle said quietly. "Just call her 'the woman.' "

"Very well." Lafont cocked his head and looked at Laemmle with curiosity. As he knew it would be, Laemmle's expression was blank, so Lafont simply continued with his history lesson. "It was the woman who introduced him to the Allègres. She told them that Javier Jiménez would represent her from now on, and that they were to follow his instructions to the letter."

"This was in '39, you say?"

"Yes, the end of '39. Nearly three years ago."

"Was Jiménez her lover?"

"Definitely not, according to the Allègres."

"Did they know the other Spaniards?"

"They never set eyes on them."

"And the Hispano-Suiza?"

"They didn't even know of its existence."

"Right," said Laemmle. "Drop me here."

The Bentley pulled up at a junction between the *route nationale* and an unsurfaced road. Bandol was visible on the left. Laemmle got out and adjusted the set of his panama. His cream tussore suit had been tailored for him in Savile Row some years before, when he was contemplating a little trip to Venice to reread Thomas Mann. Thanks to Operation Schädelbohrer, the trip had never come off.

"I admit our raid misfired a little," Monsieur Henri was saying, "but at least we located the house and unearthed the names of the Spaniard and the boy, Thomas—"

"Not the Hispano, though." Laemmle now treated Monsieur Henri to an amiable smile. Superb thighs, he thought, far from unattracted by the man.

"No," Monsieur Henri conceded, "we haven't found the goddam car, not yet, but we will, and the same goes for the woman, the Spaniards, and the boy. I've got plenty more friends I can call on."

"Crooks?"

"Good men, and all of them itching to do me a favor. I can put them to any use I like. They owe me."

"I'll think about it," Laemmle said benevolently.

He knew that in order to recruit his peculiar private army, Henri Lafont had personally visited Fresnes Prison in Paris and secured the release of twenty-five or thirty common criminals at one fell swoop, on no authority other than his own.

"Another thing: this is September 18, the boy's birthday. Discounting last year, Madame Lamiel—the woman, I mean—has always turned up to help him celebrate."

"She won't turn up this time," said Laemmle, still smiling. "There's no point in laying a trap for her. I'm convinced she won't come, and my verdict on your other proposal is also no."

Monsieur Henri burst out laughing. "I didn't know I'd made one."

"You were going to. You were going to point out that the bodies at the house will be found in due course; that the Spaniards, having disappeared, will be assumed to be the murderers; and that the French police, some of whom are friends of yours, will launch a full-scale manhunt for them."

"I do have a few friends in blue," Monsieur Henri said cheerfully.

"Times haven't changed much. *Flics* or not, some people always know which way the wind's blowing."

"I'm supremely uninterested," said Laemmle, shutting the door of the Bentley. Monsieur Henri was obliged to lower the window in order to complete their conversation.

"I don't want pay this time," he said. "No results, no cash."

"Your professional scruples do you credit."

"But I'm not beaten yet. I'll bring you those dagos' heads on a platter. As for the boy and the woman, you'll have them alive."

"I can hardly wait," said Laemmle.

"You really want me to leave you here in solitary state?"

"That's precisely what I want. I find the view delightful."

Laemmle watched the white Bentley until it disappeared into Bandol. Only then did he raise a chubby little hand, and moments later Jürgen Hess emerged from the side road at the wheel of a car with Geneva license plates. Laemmle got in beside him, removed his panama, and was disgusted to find the petersham sweatband slightly stained with perspiration. The sight sickened him. Physical cleanliness had always . . .

Jürgen Hess was spreading out a Michelin road map, talking as he did so.

. . . had always been an obsession with Gregor Laemmle. One of his few happy childhood memories was of daily baths administered by his governess, a gigantic Swiss with the huge, hard hands of a man. She used to wash—or rather, scour—him with meticulous care, turning his soft, tender little body over and over in the warm and fragrant water.

"That's where they are, to the nearest two or three kilometers," said Hess, indicating a small circle on the map to the east of Le Beausset. "The boy's in a gasogene truck laden with vegetables. Two men are with him, one of them the lanky Spaniard. Following them is a second truck with another two Spaniards on board, the ones who created a diversion by opening fire on Lafont's men. We've got the license numbers of both vehicles. They're heading northeast through uninhabited and very mountainous terrain. There are only three possible routes out: southeast toward Solliès-Toucas, north-northwest toward Signes, or due west in the direction of the Sainte-Baume massif."

"And you've got men covering all three?"

"I carried out your instructions," Hess replied stiffly.

"Our beloved Führer will be very pleased," said Laemmle.

Repugnant though he found his perspiring body, he couldn't repress a certain thrill of elation. Now that the interminable preliminaries were over, the game was getting under way at last. He himself had made the first move, and his opponent's response had taken precisely the form he expected. It was very gratifying.

His yellow eyes shone.

THOMAS TRIED TO GUESS THE TIME FROM THE SUN, BUT THERE wasn't any sun, just a dazzling white glow that flooded the entire landscape and relentlessly gobbled up every last morsel of shadow. The dusty whiteness and expanses of bone-dry rock reminded him of Spain. He was back in Spain with Her in the summer of 1937. They had just abandoned yet another house, the one in Murcia, and were heading north. She had called a halt and improvised a picnic. Juan Llull was driving and Miquel Enseñat was already there too, bleeding from the wound he'd received at the battle of Teruel. Javier hadn't joined them yet; he was still fighting at this time, the bomb had yet to fall on his wife and two sons, and he still owned his architect's office in Barcelona, his big apartment near the Plaza de Cataluña, and the beautiful white house at Sóller in Majorca where She and he, Thomas, had spent almost three months the year before. Javier's left hand was still intact and his back still unscarred by the frightful gash that had compelled him to trudge for miles—Thomas heard this later from Tomeo—holding his own intestines in place. Javier wasn't yet entirely dead inside; he could still weep for his beloved Spain, which was suicidally rending itself apart.

It was on that day, while She and Thomas were seated on the running board of the Voisin C24 Carène, that She told him he was to return to France and resume his official status as Grandpa and Grandma Allègre's grandson—in other words, that he wasn't going to live with Her any longer. "Please don't cry, *chéri*. I'm not too brave myself, and if *you* cry *I* shall start crying too. . . ."

The sky had been the same dazzling white and the heat just as oppressive as it was now, while Thomas sat waiting for Javier and the other three to finish their confabulation in *mallorquín*.

When it finally ended, Javier came over and sat down beside him on the boulder. It was awhile before he made up his mind to speak, which signified that he had plenty to say.

"The first point," he said at length, "is that they found you. I don't know how they managed it, but they did—that's all that matters. What about your room?"

"I didn't leave anything important behind," Thomas said. "They can search the place for a hundred years."

"*Muy bien*. You saw those two men on the road?"

Thomas nodded.

"So you'll know them if you see them again. Now, Thomas, I want you to think hard—I want you to recall everything that happened this morning from the moment you woke up."

Thomas marshaled the various facts, taking his time. He knew what Javier was driving at.

"'I made two mistakes," he said. "One was to go outside and walk across the terrace and down the drive when I felt something was wrong; the other was to keep that funny feeling to myself. I was so keen to see the Hispano again, I didn't tell you about it."

"*Muy bien*," said Javier. "Do you understand why I'm making you acknowledge your mistakes? Think carefully."

"I already did," Thomas said. "From now on, everything's going to be different. They nearly got me and they'll never stop looking for me wherever I go. They know I exist and what my name is and what I look like, so I can't afford to make another mistake, not ever."

Javier bowed his head for a moment. There was a trace of melancholy in his dark eyes when he looked up again. He's thinking of his two dead sons, Thomas told himself. He's comparing me with them and wondering what they might have become if that lousy bomb hadn't killed them, and he's awfully unhappy.

"You're a very intelligent boy, Thomas—incredibly intelligent. It almost frightens me sometimes."

Thomas noticed out of the corner of his eye that the other three Spaniards were also on the move. Miquel, with a casual air, was edging slowly sideways like someone in search of shade, but that couldn't be his true intention. He was obviously about to do one of his vanishing tricks. Miquel was like a wisp of smoke that disperses in a flash, leaving no trace.

Javier said, "One doesn't usually say such things to a little boy— one doesn't pay him such compliments in case he gets a swelled head. I don't think there's any risk of that with you, but it doesn't stop me worrying about you. It's difficult to live, as you do, with a well-oiled machine ticking away in your head night and day. In your case it could be very dangerous. You might become overconfident and assume that the people hunting for you are easily deceived. You understand?"

"I understand," Thomas said with a smile. He couldn't recall ever having heard Javier speak at such length except once, years ago, when She and he and Javier had been at the house in Majorca, but that was in another age and another life. Javier had been the soul of gaiety then. Thomas yearned to tell him how sad he was about his two sons, the ones that had died in the air raid, but it wouldn't have helped. The less you said about things that really saddened you, the better. It was the same with Grandpa and Grandma Allègre: you stopped talking about them and buried their memory as deep as possible inside you—there wasn't any other way.

"I'll be very careful," Thomas said.

"Muy bien," said Javier. *"Vale."*

He rose. All the Spaniards were now standing in front of Thomas as he sat perched on the boulder with his beret on his head and his legs dangling, like a solitary prisoner in the dock.

All the Spaniards save one. Almost without perceptible movement and certainly without a sign or sound, Miquel had melted into the landscape and disappeared.

"Thomas," said Javier, "when Miquel and Tomeo covered our escape by opening fire, Miquel spotted someone in the distance: a tall, fair-haired man. He was busy watching the whole operation through binoculars from a hilltop. There was another lookout over toward Bandol."

Thomas had a lightning recollection of the detail he'd automatically filed away in his memory while waiting for Juan to pick them up in the truck.

"A man on a motorbike, at least a kilometer away. He had a pair of binoculars too, I think."

A man whose presence he should have reported at once, but he'd been wrestling with his grief at the thought of Grandpa and Grandma Allègre, and—

"Don't worry, Thomas," said Javier.

"That was another mistake I made."

"We won't discuss it anymore."

"Vale," said Thomas.

"Instead, let's discuss the reason why those men were there. If you were an ordinary little boy we wouldn't involve you in such matters. We'd tell you what to do and you'd do it because we're responsible for you, even though we've made some serious mistakes ourselves. But you aren't an ordinary little boy, so you know what the presence of those men signifies, don't you?"

Again Thomas paused for thought. Then he nodded.

"There are two groups," he said. "One was supposed to storm the house and capture me, the other simply shadows us. Maybe there are two men in charge who don't see eye to eye. Or else . . ."

"Go on," said Javier.

"Or else there's only one man in charge, but he's very cunning. He guessed the first group wouldn't capture me because of you, so the wisest policy was to let us think we'd escaped and try to follow us. Maybe so as to be sure of capturing me later, or maybe . . ."

"Go on."

"Or maybe . . ."

Thomas broke off again. Everything had become transparently, frighteningly clear to him.

"Or maybe to compel someone to come looking for me and capture *them.*"

He still found it impossible to say "Maman."

"Muy bien."

Javier's voice was muffled, almost constricted. Alone of the three men facing Thomas, Tomeo gave him a warm, friendly smile. Tomeo was the youngest and most cheerful of his four bodyguards. Eighteen and a half and illiterate, he made ideal company when Thomas had enjoyed reading a book and wanted to share his pleasure with someone. Tomeo would spend whole afternoons listening enthralled to Thomas's imaginatively embroidered versions of the adventures of Rouletabille or Pistol Pete. His present smile was that of an elder brother proudly congratulating a younger on having passed a difficult examination with flying colors.

Thomas smiled back, but the wheels in his head went on turning: the torment persisted. He had reexamined his line of reasoning and found it logical—inescapably so. He could also see that Javier endorsed it. Javier didn't need him to explain these things; he simply wanted him to arrive at the same conclusion. Thomas stared at the ground between his feet.

"Was She supposed to be coming for my birthday?"

"Yes, especially as she didn't make it last year."

"Is She in France?"

"I don't know yet—I've no idea where she is. I was supposed to hear today."

"What if She went to the villa?"

Javier shook his head. "No danger of that, thank God. I was to take you to her, not the other way around."

"Except that it's impossible now," said Thomas, heartbroken at having reached precisely the conclusion Javier had meant him to reach.

"Except that it's impossible now," Javier repeated. The other two turned away looking equally disconsolate. Tomeo almost had tears in his eyes.

"They mustn't capture Her," Thomas said, as if he were announcing his own death.

"No, they mustn't."

"Then I'd rather not see Her."

Thomas felt his throat tighten as he uttered the words; every syllable was a drop of blood. His head was spinning and he wanted to be sick. He clung despairingly to the boulder beneath him. For someone who had been counting the months, weeks, days, and hours till he saw Her again, to say what he'd just said had been the hardest thing in the world.

"It would be wiser not to, I think. You've made a very brave decision, Thomas, but *I* shall somehow contrive to reach her without being followed. She must be very anxious to see you too—so much so that she may risk everything."

"You must tell Her I don't want to see Her, and that She isn't to come looking for me. Be sure to tell Her that from me."

Javier simply nodded; it was clear that he, too, found speaking an effort. Periodically broken by a hiss or splutter from the gasogene truck's charcoal burners, the ensuing silence was so awkward that everyone felt relieved when a faint sound intruded. A tiny pebble came bouncing down the track, not dislodged by chance but propelled by some human agency. It was a signal.

Thomas was about to look up when he noticed that none of the other three had even glanced in the direction of the rocks from which the pebble had undoubtedly come. He froze. Javier was looking at him and talking, but not to him. He had switched to *mallorquín*. Although Thomas didn't speak the language, it was close enough to Castilian and French for him to get the gist. There was no doubt about it: Javier and the unseen Miquel were discussing a man on a motorbike. A man who was watching them through binoculars from several hundred yards away. A man who was about to die. . . .

I hope, Thomas thought with savage hatred, I hope they hurt him before they kill him!

GREGOR LAEMMLE OFTEN DEBATED DURING THE YEARS THAT followed—quite casually, to be sure—how else the affair might have turned out if the tactics he'd employed at Sanary had been different. It seemed clear that if he'd reinforced Monsieur Henri's men with those of Jürgen Hess, let alone enlisted some other French mercenaries, he could have besieged the villa and seized the boy on September 18, 1942—always assuming that Javier Jiménez, the man with the missing fingers, hadn't had some other tricks up his sleeve.

The matter would have been settled in a very short space of time, and he, Gregor Laemmle, having wound up Operation Schädelbohrer to the entire satisfaction of those sinister knuckleheads in Berlin, would have been given some idiotic new assignment. They might even have compelled him to sport one of those grotesque black SS uniforms, which would have looked as incongruous on him as a gingham apron on a Tirolean cow.

No, he never doubted that he'd made the right decision, and he was already convinced of it now, thirty hours after the raid on the red villa. He was at Bandol, a place he'd never visited before but found extremely congenial. The echoes of the war were almost inaudible there. He'd dined last night on a *bourride*, a form of bouillabaisse for which the restaurant had charged him an exorbitant sum, and had been tactful enough to speak French with the strong Vaudois accent proper to someone traveling on a Swiss passport. The experience had delighted him. The locals took him for a fool, but it was a rare plea-sure to be taken for a fool by fools. In the morning, woken by the chirping of crickets, he'd risen early and taken his potbelly for a stroll along the beach. There he encountered some very pretty women, who left him completely cold, and some tanned adolescents, who stirred certain half-remembered emotions. Now he was walking down the Boulevard Louis-Lumière in another of his Savile Row suits, his feet encased in some admirable two-tone moccasins from Celestini of Milan, his head adorned with an elegant white panama encircled by an egg-yellow band. He listened patiently as Jürgen Hess reported on his latest failures.

"We've lost them," Hess was saying. "I had a man breathing down their necks on a motorbike, but he's vanished—they must have killed him. His machine was found abandoned outside the Toulon station. One of the trucks has also been found on a forest track some kilometers off the main road between Le Camp and Signes. We could mobilize the French police through Lafont. If only you'd authorize me to call them in, we—"

"No," Laemmle said blandly.

"It would at least enable us to trace the owners of the two vehicles."

Laemmle shook his head. "They'll have thought of that, I'm sure, so the owners' identity is quite irrelevant. Try again."

He was cogitating hard himself. He'd been striving for over thirty hours to explore that rarest of phenomena, the mind of a woman whose intelligence was equal—though not, of course, superior—to his own. It was a fascinating battle of wits. In Maria Weber's place he would have anticipated the raid on the villa, the caretakers' capture, and their admissions under duress, so he wouldn't have entrusted them with any information of vital or even secondary importance. He would have ensured that once they were forced to abandon the red villa, the boy and his bodyguards could swiftly retire to some long-prepared haven outside France. Before spiriting them out of the country, however, he would have accommodated them in a halfway house, a staging post. Somewhere snug, somewhere nice and quiet. Being as intelligent as he and Maria Weber were, where would he have chosen?

"They can't have escaped by sea," Jürgen Hess was saying. "A policeman friend of Lafont's has been keeping an eye on anything that floats, ships bound for Corsica included. The checks have been even tighter since yesterday morning. On your authority, I've offered a reward of one million francs for the man with the missing fingers and two hundred thousand apiece for the other Spaniards."

"Excellent," said Laemmle.

If he was Maria Weber, he would have chosen a fall-back position not too far from Sanary. Traveling was difficult these days. Trains and buses were not only overcrowded but subject to frequent police checks, if only because of the black market, so he would have opted for somewhere within, say, a hundred kilometers of the red villa. A boy escorted by four sinister-looking Spaniards would hardly pass unnoticed. That was the first point. In the second place, he wouldn't have installed them in a secluded house in the country. That was all right while the boy was thought to be immune from discovery, but no longer. An isolated house was insecure: the surroundings might seem completely deserted, but there was always some yokel around to note your comings and goings and the size of your underpants hanging on the clothesline. In a town, by contrast, you could live next door to someone for ten years without knowing more about him than the name above his bell. Ergo, while waiting to extricate them from France and the clutches of its vile Nazi visitors, he would temporarily have housed the boy and his bodyguards in some town less than a hundred kilometers from Sanary.

"I've also alerted our networks in Rome, Madrid, and Geneva," Hess announced, "just in case the Spaniards try crossing the border right away."

If he were Maria Weber, thought Laemmle, he'd have chosen between Marseilles, Aix, and Avignon, or Toulon, Cannes, and Nice, all of them places less than half a day's drive from the red villa—places where a person could go to ground very quickly and melt into the urban crowd before his pursuers could get organized.

"The postman from Sanary was surprised to see no sign of life at the villa this morning," Hess went on, "so he went inside, found the bodies, and called the police. The latter's suspicions have fastened on Jiménez. I thought it advisable to let the gendarmes know that there were four Spaniards living in the neighborhood, not just one."

"Splendid, Jürgen," said Laemmle. "Devilishly subtle of you."

He resumed his mental impersonation of Maria Weber, which took the form of an unspoken monologue.

Being Maria and knowing myself as well as I do—even though I've never set eyes on myself—I've installed my son in the middle of a town. In an apartment house on several floors, of course, not an isolated building. In an apartment, but a very sizable one—I certainly wouldn't imprison my beloved son in a two-roomed flat, and anyway, where would I put the Spaniards? I'm a wealthy woman with a taste for nice things, so the apartment is a luxurious place—rich neighbors tend to be less inquisitive and more unsociable than the common herd. There are plenty of books, too: my son couldn't live without them, especially if he has to spend days on end cooped up without putting his nose outside. And here's an interesting thought: *the apartment was already occupied when my son got there*. Naturally it was! Without someone there to prepare the ground in advance, the apartment's sudden invasion by four armed Spaniards and a little boy would have attracted attention. It was occupied by a self-styled uncle or aunt, or both, or—why not?—by another brace of grandparents like the ones at Sanary.

"Quiet a minute, Jürgen, I'm thinking."

As for the town itself, I'd choose somewhere known to me in my carefree bachelor-girl days before the war. . . . Cannes? Yes, Cannes would be nice—not Marseilles, anyway. I detest Marseilles. It's full of fat women with tufts of hair under their arms. Cannes, then . . . or Nice?

Or Aix?

I would surely have been to Aix as a girl. Just like that cultured and intelligent individual Gregor Laemmle, I would have browsed among its many antique shops and bookshops. Like him, I may even have dreamed of making an academic career down there, of teaching philosophy to Provençal skeptics and flooring them with my devastatingly brilliant arguments, of living in some house in the neighborhood of Tholonet, within sight of Cézanne's Sainte-Victoire.

Why not Aix? One has to start somewhere, after all.

As for the gendarmes mobilized by Jürgen Hess, I don't give a damn about them. They haven't a hope of capturing the Man with the Missing Fingers—he's far too smart for them.

The Man with the Missing Fingers . . . what a splendid title it would make! Anyone would think this was a film by Fritz Lang. . . .

THOMAS TOURED THE ROOMS ONE BY ONE. THE LAYOUT OF THE big apartment was unusual, being semicircular. He opened each door in turn, glanced inside, and walked on. Three successive rooms contained books, but the books were shut away behind grilles or, worse still, panes of glass. Prisoners, all of them.

Left, right, left . . . After opening each door and closing it again, Thomas resumed his progress along the passage that formed the apartment's curving backbone, an expanse of uncarpeted, creaking boards.

"I hate this place, I hate this place . . ." He came to the drawing room. Light was issuing from the half-open door, together with a whiff of pipe smoke. Thomas sidestepped and slunk along the far wall so the lousy floorboards wouldn't creak so much. He'd just tiptoed past the luminous rectangle when a voice stopped him in his tracks.

"Thomas?"

He froze.

"I'm glad you've decided to leave your room at last."

He waited. The man's tone was gentle, kindly, and concerned, but its kindly concern was just what infuriated him. He didn't want to be consoled, not by anyone.

"Won't you come in, Thomas? I'm told you play an excellent game of chess."

Thomas experienced another spasm of fury. He's going to challenge me to a game, he thought, just to lure me inside. He set off again, no longer caring how much noise he made.

"Give me a pawn and I might be a match for you," called the colonel, his new grandfather. "I could try, anyway."

At least he didn't suggest giving *me* an advantage, so he isn't stupid enough to think he can beat me, Thomas told himself, briefly smitten with remorse, but he kept going. Ten yards farther on the passage swung left and he came to a big door he'd noticed the previous night. He hadn't opened it then—the latch had made a devil of a row when he tried it in the dark—but this time he did so and found himself confronted by a flight of stairs. He climbed them. The door at the top was equipped with two bolts. They slid back easily. A moment later he was standing beneath a night sky ablaze with stars. After four days of self-imposed confinement, he was greedy for fresh air. Three strides took him to a stone gutter running between two mansard roofs. A tepid breeze enveloped him, laden with the scent of pantiles warmed by the preceding day's sun. His eyes quickly accustomed themselves to the steely, starlit gloom. Although his downward view of the town was obscured, he could see a whole jigsaw puzzle of roofs so tightly inter-locked that it was hard to believe in the existence of streets below them. He could also distinguish the figure of a nearby lookout hugging the lee of a chimney stack so closely that man and brickwork were almost one. Above all, he could see the big hexagonal tower of Saint-Sauveur Cathedral beyond the spidery iron summit of the bell tower.

He was in Aix-en-Provence.

GREGOR LAEMMLE WAS LESS THAN TWENTY YARDS FROM HIS quarry. He didn't know it, but he had a kind of presentiment. He had reexamined his Bandol calculations twenty times, and eighteen times out of twenty he'd found them flawless—entirely unproven but logically irrefutable and quite in keeping with what he knew of Maria Weber.

Anyway, what choice did he have? He could either obey his hunter's instinct or put his faith in Jürgen Hess, Henri Lafont's mercenaries, or, more ridiculous still, the French police.

He'd spent most of the previous seventy-two hours touring the local bookshops. Assuming an air of timidity and embarrassment, he'd posed as a penniless refugee from Paris eager to dispose of his sole remaining asset, a collection of old books. He even hinted, when this seemed advantageous, that he was Jewish. The product of this elaborate masquerade was a list of local people who owned substantial libraries. He'd already ruled out 50 percent of these bibliophiles for various reasons, notably the fact that their homes were swarming with children. I, Maria Weber, would never have subjected my brilliant loner of a son to the company of ordinary little brats. All else apart, they might talk about him. . . ."

Only four names were left by the evening of Laemmle's third day at Aix, and two of these failed to fit his theory because they belonged to people residing outside of town.

His latest conference with Jürgen Hess that afternoon had taken place, at his insistence, in the privacy of a hotel room. He had no wish to be seen in the company of his second-in-command, who spoke impeccable French but looked too Teutonic to be true.

Hess opened the proceedings with an interminable account of events unrelated to the matter in hand: the course of the war, the fighting in progress in Russia and North Africa, Himmler's plans for the British once the Wehrmacht landed in England. Just as long as they don't gas my old Jewish tailor, thought Laemmle, who was quite indifferent to any other aspect of these cataclysmic developments. He never listened to the news or read a newspaper—apart, of course, from the art and book reviews.

At long last, however, Hess brought his war communiqué to a close and got down to business. Consumed with hatred—"They're savages, those people!"—he reported that the Spaniards had killed the motorcyclist who'd been trailing them. After slitting his throat, they'd wedged his body into a cleft in the rocks with the aid of some stones. Hess went on to announce that he'd reinforced his contacts with the underworld of Marseilles and the Côte d'Azur. The hunt for the Spanish fugitives was in full swing and would inevitably result in their death or capture.

"Excellent," said Laemmle, for once without a trace of sarcasm. He still hadn't told Hess anything about his own vague theories or discreet inquiries. The man thought him crackbrained enough as it was.

But there was another reason for his silence—one that had occurred to him while walking along the leafy tunnel of the Cours Mirabeau on his way to this rendezvous at a small hotel near the station. It was accompanied by one of those periodic lurches of the heart and head which left him feeling disgusted with life in general and himself in particular. He'd never entertained the slightest doubt about Operation Schädelbohrer's unmitigated stupidity. The sum in question had always struck him as inordinate. If Thomas the Elder, on the verge of suicide, had jotted down the figure of seven hundred and twenty-four million marks, it seemed blindingly obvious that he had done so purely to rile his tormentors—to cock a final snook at them, so to speak. Only a knuckleheaded Nazi could have failed to see that. Still, Schädelbohrer had at least had the merit of granting him a relatively enjoyable three years, the more so since he'd developed such a peculiar passion for this game, this battle of wits with an unknown woman.

Quite suddenly, though, he felt fed up with the whole affair—sickened by it, even. He answered Jürgen Hess noncommittally, with the result that he acquiesced in a plan of campaign which he would doubtless have rejected in the ordinary way: a systematic search was to be launched for the Hispano-Suiza, using all available resources. This entailed a semi-concerted operation by the French police, the French Gestapo under Henri Lafont and Pierre Bonny, and the Marseilles underworld. Reward: two million francs, or twice that sum if the car's discovery led to that of the boy and ten times as much if it resulted in the woman's arrest.

Leaving Jürgen Hess, Laemmle made his way back to the Cours Mirabeau via the Quartier Mazarin, a checkerboard of silent and deserted streets lined with elegant town houses. He dined, atrociously, at a restaurant in the Rue Lacépède, where the headwaiter clearly mistrusted him and refused to take his money on the evident assumption that he was a black-market inspector.

His depression and disgust became more pronounced. This wasn't the first such mood he'd had, and it probably wouldn't be the last, but its intensity and persistence were reviving his old obsession with suicide in a far less pleasant way than usual.

After dinner he repaired to the terrace of the Deux Garçons for an ersatz coffee. It was deserted, perhaps because the university hadn't reopened yet—if it ever did so in this insane wartime world. He left the Deux Garçons having distinctly overheard, but deliberately ignored, a waiter's surreptitious comments on him. Undeceived by his Swiss camouflage, the waiter had taken him for a German. For the first time in his life, Gregor Laemmle experienced a brief but violent spasm of hatred. Being referred to as a dirty Boche was fine with him; on any other occasion it would have tended to make him smile. What really enraged him was the notion that an illiterate Provençal with grimy fingernails could for one moment think him incapable of understanding such an insult when his own French was a hundred times better. He could almost have wept.

He decided to return to his hotel, which was next door to the thermal baths, by way of the old city's maze of narrow streets. It must have been ten o'clock by now. Reaching an intersection, he instinctively turned left instead of heading straight for the town hall. The reason for this impulse eluded him at first—he was still seething with rage—but fifty yards farther on he discovered what lay behind his change of direction: he came to a charming little square with a fountain in the center. Then he remembered. This was where one of his two remaining book collectors lived, an octogenarian colonel named Apprinx. Tomorrow, he told himself, I shall check to see if, by some miraculous coincidence, the colonel has acquired a grandson or great-grandson in the last few days. . . .

The thought of tomorrow titillated him. So he was going to survive the night and postpone his own execution after all; ever since that moronic waiter had succeeded in infuriating him, he'd doubted it.

Laemmle surveyed the moonlit square and the front of the house. He was about to look up when something stopped him. Eyes down, he commanded himself. If the woman has him hidden here, his Spanish bodyguards can't be far away. They'll be keeping watch. One of them is bound to be stationed on the roof or peering through the shutters. There will also be another on the far side of the street behind me or in the building opposite, where he can watch people coming and going. If so, strange as it may seem, I'm probably under observation at this very moment. Wouldn't it be paradoxical if they killed me just when I've postponed the date of my suicide!

He could almost feel a dagger burying itself beneath his left shoulder blade.

He turned on his heel and set off again, having got over his mood and concluded an armistice with himself.

The hunt was on again.

THOMAS LAY STRETCHED OUT ON THE WARM TILES, BELLY DOWN, watching the movements of the man in the square some forty feet below. A portly but dapper little man in a pale-colored suit and hat and matching shoes, he'd entered the square from the right and paused for two or three seconds, glancing at the fountain and possibly the house as well. Now he was walking off in the opposite direction.

He soon disappeared down the dark side street, and the sound of his footsteps grew fainter.

"Miquel?" Thomas said in a low voice.

"Yes, Thomas?"

"Did you and Javier kill the man on the motorbike?"

"One doesn't ask such questions."

"I didn't hear your rifle. It doesn't make much noise, but still. Javier must have killed him with his knife, that's my guess. All the better."

No reply.

"I mustn't talk about it, right?"

"Right."

The footsteps had died away. Absently, Thomas wondered if the little man had meant to look up in his direction and thought better of it at the last moment—he'd certainly detected an odd little movement of the head. Obedient to his "rat's instinct," he filed the fact away in his memory just in case. The street was deserted now. Thomas withdrew a few inches, his skinny little shoulders wedged between two courses of tiles. The night sky was very beautiful. He'd always loved climbing onto roofs at night and gazing up at the sky. One time very long ago—four or five years at least—he'd tried to imagine infinity and failed dismally. He'd almost wept with rage.

"I'd like to talk, Miquel."

Miquel was visible only as a vague shape. He appeared to be standing with his back to the stonework. The rifle in the crook of his arm was vertical, and his hands would be limp and relaxed like those of all who could shoot with the utmost speed and accuracy.

"I'm a good listener," he said.

"How soon will Javier be back?"

"No sé."

"Do you know where he went?"

"No."

"Would you tell me if you did?"

"No." There was a trace of sadness in Miquel's voice.

Thomas nodded. He moved again, and this time managed to settle one shoulder and his hip in a groove between the tiles.

"Tomeo says I'm wrong to have shut myself up in my room and refused to speak to my new grandfather since we got here," he whispered, staring into the darkness.

"I think so too."

"Tomeo says my new grandfather is a very nice man."

"Lo creo también."

Thomas nodded again. The truth was, he'd been crying for the last few seconds, very gently and without a sound. Big tears were welling out of his eyes. He'd held them back for days and days, but now he couldn't any longer.

"Grandpa Allègre was nice. Grandma Allègre was very nice too, and now they're both dead—I'm sure they're dead. What's the point of loving nice people when you know they're going to die because of you?"

A long silence. Then, "I really don't know the answer to that, Thomas."

"But you're a grown-up."

"I'm only twenty-two. That's not very old."

"You're twice as old as me, though, and you've killed people."

"Twenty-two isn't old. As for killing people, it isn't good to shoot men like rabbits—it makes you feel sick. I'm not very intelligent, either. You're a whole lot more intelligent than I am."

Here we go again, Thomas thought bitterly. Everyone's always saying how intelligent I am, but what's the good of being intelligent? You may understand things a bit quicker and better, but the better you understand them the more complicated they become and the unhappier they make you. Who wants to be intelligent?

He was weeping hot tears now. The dam had burst, and they poured down his cheeks like a cataract. He even found it impossible, or almost so, to see himself weeping from the outside: a small boy lying on a roof in Aix—one roof amid a patchwork quilt of a thousand similar roofs. If he did succeed in escaping from his body and projecting himself into the stars, it was only for moments too brief to serve any useful purpose. Even that device had ceased to work.

He cried for two or three minutes, and then it was over: the machine resumed its habitual task of sifting and dissection. He noticed that Miquel hadn't moved and was grateful to him for simply standing patiently in the gloom, for realizing that he didn't want to be comforted.

Not even by Her, if She'd been there. By Her less than anyone. That would really be the worst thing of all: that She should see him crying and imagine for one moment that She couldn't depend on him.

His head was entirely clear now. He'd recovered most of his frightening, abnormal lucidity. Gazing up at the vast expanse of darkness overhead, he addressed it in a deliberately conversational tone. His choice of German was equally deliberate.

"I'm just a boy of eleven who's very sad because he's separated from the mother he loves more than anyone or anything else in the world, but who had to say he didn't want to see her even though he'd been counting the days for two whole years. Since I'm supposed to be so intelligent, it had to be me that decided not to see her, so I did: I said what I was expected to say. The only trouble is, I'm terribly sad and unhappy. I'm sad about Grandpa and Grandma Allègre too, who must be dead or they wouldn't have hidden the newspapers from me. I'm also sad for my friend with the missing fingers—I won't say his name because you'd recognize it, Invisible Man. I'm sad because he's gone to see my mother and may not come back—they may already have killed him as well, just as they'll almost certainly kill you and your friends, Invisible Man, and everyone else who protects me, including my new grandfather. That's why I've been thinking more and more about running away on my own. I can't see any other solution—there isn't one, and anyway, I'm suffocating here. I'm too unhappy, and if I go away I may feel less unhappy and they'll stop killing the people who love me. . . ."

Silence.

Thomas lowered his wide gray eyes and fastened them on the shadowy form beside the chimney stack.

"I don't speak German," said Miquel's voice. "I didn't understand a single word—*ni una palabra*."

"I know," said Thomas.

HE CAME DOWN FROM THE ROOF AND MADE HIS WAY BACK ALONG the central passage. At the far end, Tomeo emerged from the lobby that had been his guard post since their arrival in Aix. His round face conveyed a mixture of concern and distress as he watched Thomas approach. He'd been trying to rouse the boy from his lethargy for nearly five days. Tomeo's short, thick arms hung limp at his sides, and the bulge of the pistol in his belt was clearly visible beneath his jacket.

"Ahora va bien," said Thomas. "Everything's fine now."

He smiled at Tomeo. The half-open door of the drawing room was on his left, still emitting the same rectangular shaft of light. He knocked, was invited to enter, and went in. His new grandfather had a white mustache and bright blue eyes, and his face was smooth and pink. His knees were enveloped in a red-and-blue-checked rug despite the warmth of the night, and the upturned book beside him suggested that he'd been reading.

"I've come to apologize," said Thomas, standing very straight and speaking in the calm, clear voice he modeled on Hers. "I shouldn't have refused to leave my room. I hope you'll forgive me for behaving like this."

They eyed each other without a word. Then they transferred their gaze to the chessboard on a low table on the colonel's left.

"You can be white," Thomas said. "What should I call you?"

The colonel bowed his head in thought. "Grandfather?" he hazarded.

"If you don't mind," said Thomas, "I'd sooner call you monsieur."

"Why not? That's what I used to call my own father and grandfather. Have you played chess long?" The colonel moved his king's pawn.

Thomas followed suit. "Ever since I was very little," he said. He concentrated really hard for the first few minutes, not knowing how strong his opponent's game was.

It was strong but not exceptionally so. Unless he's faking, thought Thomas, which is always possible. Maybe he wants to let me win because he thinks it'll make me feel better. That would really get my goat!

Thomas debated this possibility for another few minutes until he was sure: no, the colonel was definitely not a really strong player. He checkmated him in twenty-three moves.

"Whom do you usually play?"

"Myself," said Thomas. "I usually play by myself."

During the second game his attention strayed more and more often from the ivory chessmen. He glanced at the row of curtained windows, which obviously overlooked the square and the fountain. Juan Llull generally took up his position on the second floor of the building across the way, where he could watch the front of the house. Tomeo was in the lobby and Miquel on the roof. According to Tomeo, Miquel slept in a room in the house next door, but one with a window from which he could climb out onto the roofs anytime he liked. Everything was as it should be.

He concentrated on the colonel again. It was true: he was a nice man—awfully old and clumsy and even a little shy around him, but nice for all that. In time he was sure he'd come to like him a little—it shouldn't be too hard. He could like the old man for four or five days without making things too dangerous for him, because then he'd be off his hands.

Why? Because his mind was made up: he would wait another four or five days and then, if Javier still wasn't back, he would take off. It was Wednesday night now. He would wait until the early hours of Monday morning.

Not even eagle-eyed Miquel would see him go. He knew how to slip away without being seen, just as he knew where to go and why.

Thomas won the second game even more easily than the first. He checkmated the colonel in eighteen moves, and even then he spun things out a bit to give himself time for thought.

GREGOR LAEMMLE SPENT THE NEXT THREE DAYS SATISFYING HIM-
self that his hunch had been well founded. With infinite care, he veri-
fied his hypotheses one by one, reproaching himself for having fool-
ishly ventured near the apartment house where Colonel Apprinx lived,
even—or especially—at night. It had been the height of carelessness.
He might have been spotted, and perhaps he had been.

That said, he was dazzled and delighted by his own discoveries.
Although the philosopher in him found hunches and other feats of
intuition profoundly suspect because all such irrational certainties
merited rejection on principle, every last one of his assumptions, however ambitious, had proved correct. He had postulated that a lookout
would normally be based in one of the apartments opposite. Well, so it
had turned out: five days ago, or some thirty-six hours after the raid
on the red villa, a commercial traveler named Juan Llop had taken a
three-room second-floor apartment whose windows afforded a perfect
view of the old colonel's front door. What was more, the self-styled
Monsieur Llop hailed from French Catalonia like the self-styled Javier
Jiménez. But that wasn't all. On the very day that Llop moved in, a
man named Michel Boyer had turned up from Toulouse and rented an
attic room nearby. It was quite separate from the Apprinx apartment,
needless to say, except that anyone surveying the premises through
binoculars from the clock tower, as Laemmle had, could see at once
that the window of the said room provided an easy access to the
neighboring roofs.

Better still: Colonel Apprinx, who had hitherto lived alone with a
cook-housekeeper almost as elderly as himself, had radically altered
his way of life overnight. A grandson from Dijon having come to stay
with him, the colonel had engaged a young man of about twenty to
assist the old housekeeper. Reputed to be a distant relative of hers, this
youth was called Thomas Vidal and spoke French with a strong Cata-
lonian accent.

It wasn't until Saturday that Laemmle summoned Hess and ap-
prised him of his discoveries, with all the smug satisfaction he'd expected to feel. While gendarmes, crooks, and SS plainclothesmen had
been scurrying hither and thither, he, Gregor Laemmle, sitting on his
plump little backside and using nothing but his abundance of gray
matter, had solved the problem all by himself.

His self-congratulation was tinged with regret, however. He was
putting paid to his game of chance. Once the boy was caught, compel-

ling the woman to give herself up would be a mere formality, and that would inevitably spell the end of Operation Schädelbohrer.

She'll have to come to me, he reflected. If she needs any further convincing, Soeft will amuse himself by slicing off her beloved son's ears. She'll come sure enough, and I'll hand her over to Gortz or Heydrich or Himmler or whoever else requests custody of her through official channels. I shall see her at last, that's the main thing . . . but I'm bound to be disappointed. After all, how could she possibly measure up to my mental picture of her?

Jürgen Hess, who favored an immediate assault, claimed that it would take him only a few hours, thanks to his contacts with the Marseilles crime bosses, to recruit a far more efficient raiding party than the one that had handled the Sanary operation. He proposed to hire twenty or thirty men—forty, if need be—and split them up into three groups: one to deal with the Spaniard in the building opposite, one to exterminate the lookout on the roof, and the third, commanded by himself, to besiege the apartment and capture the boy. He could go into action that very night, Saturday night. To postpone the raid for too long would be risky. The fourth Spaniard, the man with the missing fingers, had not been found. It was probable that he commanded the bodyguards, so his reappearance would signify that the boy was about to be moved again, this time with a view to spiriting him out of France.

Laemmle also thought it wise to attack while the fourth Spaniard was still away, hence his decision to swallow his misgivings and speak to Hess, but speed wasn't synonymous with impetuosity. An ill-prepared offensive didn't suit his plan, and twenty-four hours more or less would make no difference. He settled on very late Sunday night.

The mistral had sprung up that Saturday morning, bringing a chill to the air and repainting the sky above the plane trees in its true color, a startling Prussian blue. After winding up his staff conference with Hess, Laemmle forced himself to go for a walk. He abhorred physical exercise, but it was one way of suppressing his fierce temptation to haunt the environs of the apartment, which he had also forbidden Hess to reconnoiter: "Those damned Spaniards have got eyes in the back of their heads. They'd spot you at once—you above all, with your unforgivably Aryan looks." The most he had authorized was long-range surveillance, and then only by Hess's French mercenaries.

He left Aix by the Tholonet road. The very fact that he'd just covered three kilometers on foot—a considerable distance by his standards—provided a sudden indication of the extent of his own uneasiness. It wasn't the imminence of bloodshed that worried him. He'd blithely ordained that no one was to be left alive—apart, of course, from the boy—and sanctioned the execution of the retired colonel and his housekeeper as well as the three Spaniards. No survivors, no witnesses. In the unlikely event that the boy escaped capture yet again, anyone tempted to shelter him would know what fate to expect.

No, what Laemmle found a far more compelling argument was that this latest massacre would give Maria Weber food for thought, if the slaughtered couple at Sanary hadn't already convinced her. She would be psychologically undermined.

Gregor Laemmle's habitual indifference to the death of others had done the rest. He'd even briefly considered taking advantage of the massacre to ordain the murder of the waiter who had so enraged him at the Deux Garçons. He had only to spin Jürgen Hess some yarn or other, for instance that the man was spying for the Spaniards. What an intoxicating sensation it was, even for a philosopher like himself, to wield the power of life and death. He smiled at a female passerby, an elderly crone, haggard-looking and none too clean. She didn't return his smile. If the fancy took me, he reflected, I could have her killed too. I would probably be doing her a favor.

The mistral was tousling his hair and would have blown his panama away if he hadn't taken the precaution of carrying it in his hand. He walked on, still thinking of Maria Weber. They would soon be face to face. He already resented the disappointment she was going to prove and bore her a grudge for destroying his dream.

I really am a complex character, he told himself, but only fools are straightforward. Besides, they're unreliable. . . .

THOMAS WAS NOW ROULETABILLE IN *LE CHÂTEAU NOIR*, EXTRIcating himself from the clutches of Kara Selim. It had taken him some forty minutes to leave his room, tiptoe along the interminable passage without making a single floorboard creak, lift the latch, climb halfway up the staircase leading to the roof, turn off to the right into the little low-ceilinged attic, crawl across it with infinite care, and finally reach the tiny window. It was so small that no grown-up, male or female, could have squeezed through it. Thomas could, but only just. His hips brushed the sides.

Then came a void. All the more terrifying because it was pitch-black and apparently bottomless, it created the impression of a claustrophobic tomb filled with cobwebs and creepy-crawlies. "God, am I scared!" breathed Thomas, with all the sincerity in the world. Only the lower half of his legs remained inside the window; the rest of him overbalanced into the two-foot gap between two buildings at least forty feet high. He saved himself from falling only by bracing his shoulders against the opposite wall with all his might, as if trying to push the two buildings apart.

I really *am* scared. . . .

He withdrew one foot and applied it to the wall facing him. All went well: he didn't fall. He withdrew his other foot and placed it beside the first. No doubt about it, he could support his own weight.

He could even progress downward, inch by inch, moving one espadrille-shod foot at a time. Absolutely delighted at first by the ease of this procedure, he thought what fun it was to be a fly. It happened just as he was nearing a transverse wall which he planned to cross. Behind it was a drainpipe which he would have to descend in order to reach another roof, and another, and another, and a second skylight through which he—

It not only happened, it happened almost instantaneously: first a terrible, uncontrollable rasping in his throat, which Miquel couldn't fail to hear, then a tremor in his legs and thighs, which cramped up, then the sound of Miquel's light, stealthy tread, then the furtive footsteps of men running, then a scuffle.

Then the first shot, swiftly followed by other shots.

GREGOR LAEMMLE WAS SITTING IN THE BACK OF A CITROEN 15 CV with Soeft at the wheel and another SS man, Greifer by name, beside him. They were only waiting for Hess to turn up with the boy before speeding north toward the demarcation line between the occupied and unoccupied zones. Once across it, they would make for the nearest German garrison headquarters.

Until the very last moment, Laemmle had racked his brains in search of one good reason, just one, for postponing the operation indefinitely. He failed to find one. The Man with the Missing Fingers hadn't yet rejoined his companions, as far as they knew. No doubt he'd gone to report what had happened. He might well have seen the woman and received his orders. As soon as he returned he would act on them and take the boy to a place of safety beyond their reach, so it made no sense to wait any longer. A pity, but still . . .

A shot rang out. Three more shots followed in quick succession.

"Two A.M. precisely," said Soeft.

The Citroën was parked in one of the streets parallel to the Cours Mirabeau, only a hundred and fifty yards from the raiders' objective. Laemmle had watched Hess's troops move up to the front line and lay siege to the peaceful neighborhood. At least thirty strong, they had stealthily but self-confidently converged in small groups for this Provençal version of the Night of the Long Knives.

More shots, muffled by reason of their having been fired inside buildings, were quickly followed by others. Sounds of running feet could be heard, and then, with the crisp incisiveness of sailcloth ripped apart in a single movement, the scream of a man hurled off a rooftop. Scattered lights began to appear in nearby windows. Laemmle got out of the car.

"They won't be long," said Soeft, meaning Hess and the boy.

He also meant that it wasn't advisable to stray too far, because whatever happened, he would have to drive off fast at a moment's notice. Without replying, Laemmle strolled a few steps down the street. A strange silence had descended on the battlefield. Not more than a minute had elapsed between the first shots and the last, but that, in theory, should have been enough. There should now be five corpses—those of the three Spaniards, the retired colonel, and the housekeeper—plus a few additional ones if the Spaniards had had time to retaliate before being overwhelmed by numbers.

Laemmle strolled a little farther. Looking left at the next intersection, he could see the Cours Mirabeau at the far end of the street. There seems to have been a minor hitch, he told himself. A strange but exhilarating sense of relief came over him. Then he heard hurried footsteps, not from the left, where Jürgen Hess should by now have materialized, but from the opposite direction. A uniformed gendarme, out of breath and puce in the face, came pounding along the street. He caught sight of Laemmle and skidded to a halt.

"Sounded like gunfire, didn't it?"

"You could be right," Laemmle replied in a noncommittal tone.

He gave the gendarme a benevolent smile to disguise what he was thinking: If Jürgen Hess turns up now, *mon brave*, you've had it. Maybe I should tell Soeft to shoot you anyway, just because you've seen me. But the man was already cantering off on his stubby legs, clumsily attempting to draw the absurd little popgun that was all he carried in the way of a weapon. For no precise reason—for no reason at all, in fact, other than his hunch that the whole affair had somehow gone awry—Laemmle also set off for the Cours Mirabeau. He was all the more inclined to dissociate himself from the proceedings because a backward glance told him that Soeft, too, had got out of the car and was waiting grimly for Hess to turn up with a child in his arms. Without knowing why, or rather, without wanting to know, Laemmle sniggered to himself.

Whistles began to shrill in the rudely awakened town as more gendarmes hurried to the scene. Laemmle sighted four of them pedaling valiantly toward the Cours Mirabeau on their bikes. To avoid them he turned off down the first alleyway he came to. A world of silence and darkness enveloped him. The din of battle hadn't carried this far, and the only light visible issued from a low window, hardly more than an air vent, at the base of a bakery wall. Through the grimy pane, Laemmle could see the baker and his apprentice removing a batch of long French loaves from the oven. He paused to listen.

The wind had abated since nightfall. The whirling gusts were separated by intervals of calm, and the silence in these sudden lulls was total. Laemmle could hear not only his own breathing; he caught the sound of someone panting hard—someone approaching at a run. Instantly visualizing some fugitive from the battle, most probably a Spaniard, he just had time to secrete himself in a doorway. Fortunately for him, it was deeply recessed and very dark. He congratulated himself on his luck. It really would have been a ridiculous quirk of fate if, having quietly abandoned the theater of operations, he'd bumped into a killer whom his killers had failed to kill.

Thanks to the glow emitted by the bakery window, his hiding place afforded an excellent view of the alleyway. He didn't have long to wait: a figure came into view—a small, frail figure in short trousers and a beret. It paused and hesitated for a few seconds, peering in all directions. There was no fear in the startlingly gray eyes; on the contrary, they were cold and keen and penetrating in the extreme. Laemmle's impressions of this moment were incredibly strong, and he never forgot them. Their potency was not due merely to the miraculous coincidence that had brought the hunter face to face with his quarry just when the hunt seemed irretrievably lost, nor yet to the temporary isolation of someone who had thirty or forty men at his disposal and could mobilize ten times that number, nor even to his bittersweet belief that the hunt was up at last.

No, he was quite simply fascinated. Later on, having reread Thomas Mann's novella five or six times, he was to amuse himself by picking out the traits he shared with the central character of *Death in Venice*. For the moment, his reactions were instinctive and almost unconscious. He was moved by the frailty of the childish figure, by the set of the head on the slender shoulders, by the slow pivoting of the body, and, above all, by the eyes that must beyond doubt be a perfect replica of the woman's. . . .

He followed at a discreet distance when the boy set off again. It never for one moment occurred to him to round up Jürgen Hess and his pack of hounds—or if it did, he discarded the idea at once.

THOMAS HAD SCRAMBLED FROM ROOF TO ROOF AND BUILDING TO building, squeezed through several skylights too small for anyone larger than he to negotiate, and stripped off his shirt and trousers rather than tear them. On two or three occasions men had crunched across the tiles within a yard of him. He'd even tiptoed through a bedroom, unseen by its occupants because they were busy gawping out of the window and wondering what all the rumpus was about. Three of his attempts to reach street level by climbing down drainpipes had been thwarted by the presence of lookouts and cars below, but he finally made it and got dressed again. Once safely down, he was forced to keep to dark alleyways. In one of them, which was dimly lit because a baker was already hard at work there, he'd been brought up short by the sensation that someone was watching him. He'd seen nothing, though, even in that dark and cavernous doorway where someone might well have been hiding. In any case, a lurking enemy scout would have jumped him at once.

So he set off again. His knowledge of Aix being limited to descriptions given him by the colonel and his housekeeper, Thomas had to zigzag several times before reaching his first objective, the cloister of Saint-Sauveur Cathedral. He slipped inside and made for the darkest

corner facing the entrance. There he hunkered down to wait, taking
care not to dirty his clothes, until the first rays of dawn began to light
up the statue of Saint Peter, a primitive sculpture with disproportion-
ate hands and feet. He had three twenty-franc pieces in the right-hand
pocket of his trousers, a thousand more francs in hundred-franc notes
in the other, and twenty thousand in a rubber pouch suspended from a
thong around his waist. After counting his money for the umpteenth
time, he made his way down to the station to catch the first train to
Marseilles.

From there he caught the ten fifty-three for Lyons, though it took a
bit of bravado and imagination to get past the ticket clerk and the
gendarmes at the barrier. Having surveyed the huge, seething throng
in Saint-Charles Station, he carefully selected an old woman whom he
characterized at long range as his grandmother. Apart from being
very lame, he announced, she was mourning the simultaneous demise
of her son and daughter-in-law. "In other words, my papa and
maman. If I don't look after her, who will?" So saying, he invested in
two first-class tickets.

He invited the old lady to join him in a first-class carriage, but not
before moving her to tears with his description of how he'd just lost
his poor papa, for whom the second ticket had officially been destined.
She was bound for Tarare, not far from Lyons. At Lyons she took him
to a bakery owned by her nephew and treated him to a delicious snack
of real white rolls topped with chocolate. "Poor little boy, you can't
leave empty-handed. Take this shopping bag and this loaf and a few
slices of sausage. Food's scarce these days—one has to manage somehow. Whereabouts in Lyons are you staying? With your uncle? Very
well, first have a bite and then my nephew will drive you to your
uncle's in his delivery van."

He escaped through the lavatory window and made his way back to
the station, where he repeated his Marseilles tactic, this time on a
priest bound for Grenoble.

Except that it didn't work, partly because he'd again bought first-
class tickets. The priest was uncooperative enough to disown him. As
for Thomas, he fastened his gray eyes on the gendarmes and addressed
them calmly.

"Traveling alone? Who's traveling alone? Not me."

The priest, that uncharitable soul, had scuttled off down the platform and disappeared into a third-class carriage. The gendarmes, seeing no one within a mile of Thomas, commented on the fact.

"What about my uncle?" Thomas demanded. "He's sitting in the compartment at the far end of this carriage. He's short and fat, with ginger hair and yellow eyes, and he's wearing a cream-colored suit and black-and-white shoes. He did have a hat to match, but he chucked it into the gutter at Aix. He may be crazy, but he's still my uncle. You can't choose your relations."

"BUT OF COURSE I'M HIS UNCLE," GREGOR LAEMMLE ASSURED the gendarmes. "I'd have thought the resemblance obvious. I don't mean the eyes, of course, or the face or the hair or the general appearance, but there's a definite family resemblance. He's my nephew Aloysius."

"I've never been called Aloysius," Thomas said distastefully.

"His real name is Otto, but he's always hated it . . ."

"I'm not called Otto either," said Thomas. "I'm called Otto even less than I'm called Aloysius, if that's possible."

"He's my sister's son," Laemmle explained. "He inherits his love of contradiction from her. My sister's such a contrary person that if you drowned her in the Rhône at Arles, her body would float upstream to Switzerland."

He smiled at the gendarmes, whom he'd addressed in a Swiss accent so broad as to be almost unintelligible.

"Anything else I can do for you, gentlemen?"

"No," the gendarmes told him rather hesitantly. They'd already spent a long time scrutinizing his papers, which identified him as a Swiss employed by the International Red Cross. When they finally left the compartment, one of them turned back before disappearing down the corridor.

"Did you really chuck your hat into a gutter at Aix-en-Provence?" Laemmle didn't flinch.

"Certainly I did," he replied. "I always do that when something annoys me. Once, at Lausanne, it was my trousers. We Swiss are more temperamental than people give us credit for."

This time the gendarmes left for good. Thirty seconds after they quit the carriage, the Grenoble train pulled out.

"YOU THINK I'VE BEEN TAILING YOU EVER SINCE AIX?"

"Yes. You didn't dare follow me into the cloister, it's true, but you hung around outside the entrance all the time I was there."

The train was well under way now.

"Did you see me?"

"I spotted you before I went in, and you were still there when I came out."

Thomas's choice of words was guarded and deliberate. He'd decided on his tactics: he must seem intelligent but not too intelligent—not too innocent either.

For all that, he found the yellow-eyed man a peculiarly disconcerting person to deal with, and intriguing to the point of fascination. In compelling him to intervene when those lousy gendarmes were making a nuisance of themselves, he hadn't at all been acting on impulse; it was a carefully considered move on his part. He'd been waiting for just such an opportunity to test the man who'd been tailing him for the past seventeen or eighteen hours. As someone who tended to think in terms of chess, he generally favored a knight for a trial move of this kind, because it progressed across the board in a zigzag, erratic fashion. You moved it for no good reason, just to see whether your opponent would be taken aback or grasp that it was merely a ruse—in short, to gauge his reactions.

When confronted by the gendarmes his opponent had not only reacted swiftly and correctly but responded with an erratic move of his own. He was a strong player, really strong.

"You were still following me when I got to the Aix station," Thomas went on. "That was when you got rid of your hat."

"Why should I have got rid of it?"

"A thing like that? Because I'd have spotted it from five hundred kilometers away, that's why."

"That 'thing' was a panama of the finest quality. I discarded it with the greatest reluctance."

"Unnecessarily, too, since I'd already spotted you."

"I could have been hiding from someone else," the yellow-eyed man said smoothly.

Thomas thought it over, then nodded. "Maybe, but you were also hiding from me."

"Perhaps I wasn't hiding from you at all. Perhaps I was hiding from some other people who were tailing us both—perhaps I simply didn't want them to see us together."

Thomas thought again, very calmly. "Yes," he said, "that's another possibility."

The train stopped at a station and pulled out again.

"Did you hear some gunfire at Aix?"

"I heard a lot of bangs, if that's what you mean."

"Those men were shooting at one another on your account."

Silence. *The game has really started now,* Thomas told himself. *I can't afford to make a single mistake.*

The yellow-eyed man said, "I could be on the same side as those who want to harm you."

"You probably are," Thomas replied. He leveled his gray eyes at the yellow ones once more, then turned away and feigned an intense interest in the countryside gliding past the window.

"Of course I could be on their side, but in that case, why should I have spent hours waiting for you to emerge from the cloister instead of going to fetch reinforcements? I could easily have done so."

"Perhaps you were afraid I'd run off while you were gone."

"I had several hours in which to solve that problem. People passed by. I could have asked them to take a message for me."

Silence.

"But I didn't, I simply waited for you to come out again. Doesn't that prove I mean you no harm?"

"Not necessarily."

The train slowed, stopped, and got under way again.

Thomas could have bitten his tongue off. "Not necessarily" was an invitation to the yellow-eyed man to inquire what other reason he could have had for taking no action while Thomas was holed up in the cloister, awaiting daybreak and the first train to Marseilles. Sure enough, he did just that.

"So why, in your opinion, didn't I try to capture you?"

"Perhaps you hoped to win a medal by capturing me all by yourself."

The yellow-eyed man burst out laughing.

"I think you're pulling my leg, Thomas."

He knows my name, thought Thomas. *He knows it and it didn't slip* out by accident. He said it on purpose. He's an awfully good player. . . .

For a few moments Thomas was close to panic. It was the first time he'd ever come up against someone as good as himself. Or possibly even better.

All that saved him was an ancient recollection of Her, dredged up from the depths of his memory. He'd been four years old or even younger when She taught him the rudiments of chess. They played fifty or a hundred games together. Toying with Her black-and-silver cigarette holder and watching him with a smile in Her eyes, She beat him cold time after time, mercilessly hounding him from square to square until he broke down and wept with rage at his own incompetence. Then She told him that life was like that, that no one would ever do him any favors, that he must learn to keep calm under all circumstances, that he must remain lucid and cool-headed even, or especially, when he felt cornered, trapped, and beaten, because that was when a person's true mettle showed. "Oh, *mon chéri*, my darling, *mein Schatz*," She used to say, taking him in Her arms and weeping too, "how else can I prepare you for the life you're going to lead thanks to me?" Little by little he began to hold his own against her, then to beat Her, occasionally at first, then every other game, then two games out of three, then invariably, reducing Her to tears—but tears of joy this time—with the merciless accuracy of his play. And when he felt remorseful for having beaten Her so soundly, it was She who consoled him with that wonderful, infectious laughter of Hers.

"You still haven't answered my question, Thomas, not really. That business about the medal was amusing, but it was a ploy, not an answer. You were inside that cloister and I knew you could only leave the way you'd come. You remained in there for hours, yet I neither sent for help nor tried to capture you myself. Why, Thomas?"

The rotten, yellow-eyed swine, thought Thomas. He's chasing me all around the board with his queen, his rook, everything he's got, but he's not going to get an answer out of me. I'm going to keep my mouth shut. Answering him just to show how smart I am would be the worst mistake I could make. I'll play the poor little sleepy-head. He may not be taken in completely, but he won't know for sure. It'll prevent him from finding out how strong my game is, and that's the best I can do for now. . . .

Anyway, he was genuinely tired. He couldn't have slept for more than two hours last night, so he didn't have to pretend. His eyelids felt heavy, and even the machine in his head was slowing down. It was still functioning, though, or had done so pretty well till now. For instance, it had finally supplied him with an answer to the question the yellow-eyed man kept asking. The answer was simple and straightforward. He didn't jump me in the cloister or send for reinforcements, just shadowed me, because it isn't me he wants. He thinks I'm on my way to join Her, and it's Her he plans to capture. He's acting like Pistol Pete when he tailed the bandit's horse, which led him to the secret cave behind the waterfall, so he was able to arrest the whole gang. Except that I'm a good bit smarter than a horse!

That was one answer. There was another: it was just conceivable that the yellow-eyed man had been sent by Her, unbeknown to the Spaniards, as a new and additional form of protection, but that he believed as little as he believed in the guardian angels and fork-tailed demons poor Grandma Allègre used to tell him about while peeling potatoes in the kitchen at Sanary.

He felt awfully sleepy but was afraid to doze off at such close quarters with the yellow-eyed man. The train kept stopping. At one station their first-class carriage was invaded by a platoon of moronic youths in big, floppy berets, most of them wearing shorts. They were a ludicrous bunch, and even Yellow Eyes shot Thomas a look of sarcastic complicity at the sight of them. Clustered around a government minister who appeared to be suffering from menopausal symptoms, these senior members of the Chantiers de Jeunesse, or Vichy youth movement, struck Gregor Laemmle as ultra-French, in other words, undersized, hirsute, slovenly, loudmouthed, and convinced that the world revolved around them. They preened themselves and struck poses, unintentionally burlesquing their counterparts in the Hitler Youth.

Thomas, who had heard Grandpa Allègre describe these overgrown fascist Boy Scouts in unflattering terms, hated them on sight but welcomed their reassuring presence. He surrendered to his exhaustion and was sound asleep when the train pulled into Grenoble.

GREGOR LAEMMLE ALMOST TREMBLED AS HE GAZED AT THE sleeping boy. The two of them were seated facing each other in the window seats of the first-class compartment. The fascination that had overcome him in that shadowy doorway at Aix, looking out at Thomas's childish figure illuminated by the glow from the bakery, was as intense as ever.

After meeting his eye half a dozen times or so, the boy had spent the rest of the time with his forehead pressed to the windowpane. Laemmle couldn't make up his mind whether this was a ruse, a sign of complete indifference, or simply the effect of physical fatigue on an eleven-year-old exhausted by a sleepless night and a long train journey. The worst of it was, he wondered if it was a deliberate ploy calculated to keep him guessing.

Night had fallen outside. Looking at Thomas, he was seized with a strange and unwonted feeling of shyness. I'm simultaneously in love with a woman and her son, he thought. To me, they're a single person. It's an absurd and unusual situation, and its absurdity is heightened by the fact that I'm hunting them down with the sole intention of destroying them. I've always known I was an exceptional person, but this time, honestly, I'm excelling myself. . . .

The train was pulling into Grenoble.

I'll end by making mincemeat of them—it's inevitable. I know myself too well—my natural sadism will prevail. The whole thing's going to end in tragedy, I'm sure it is. . . .

The train came to a stop.

I'll have to kill them both, but not until I've played with them like a cat. Each man kills the thing he loves, as dear Oscar so aptly said, and I—well, having always known that I would kill myself, why should I be squeamish about others?

The train had been stationary for three or four minutes at least. The Vichy minister, who was evidently on an official tour of inspection, had disappeared with his knobby-kneed acolytes in tow.

"Thomas?"

He really was asleep.

"Thomas? We're here."

They emerged from the station, an unlikely pair whose destinies were linked from now on. Linked for the worse, too. That was one point on which Gregor Laemmle entertained no doubts whatever.

FOUR

HIS NAME WAS DAVID JOHN QUARTERMAIN. ON THE DAY WHEN he entered the complicated and deadly game being played by Thomas and Gregor Laemmle, he had absolutely no knowledge of Thomas's existence, still less of what had happened at Sanary and Aix-en-Provence or Grenoble. If the truth be told, he was almost indifferent to current events in France and Europe, though the fall of Paris twenty-seven months earlier had mildly depressed him for a day or two.

Vermont in the fall was the pleasantest and most tranquil place imaginable. Quartermain, having arrived there an hour ago, had left his bags in the car and was strolling through a maple forest incandescent with leaves that glowed red in the Indian summer sun. A tall man in his mid-thirties, immensely casual in manner and gesture, he strode lithely along despite a slight and almost imperceptible limp which he'd acquired in 1936; in a collision with another car, he had simultaneously smashed up his Duesenberg and his pelvis.

Life in the past few weeks had been particularly hectic. Accompanied by his cousin Emerson and Joe Sowinski, who headed the foreign department of the family bank, Quartermain had gone on an extremely tedious trip to Venezuela and Buenos Aires, where most of the conversation had been devoted to crude oil, tin, and other raw materials. Returning to New York just in time to attend an even more tedious board meeting of MOMA, the Museum of Modern Art, founded by the Clan and Aunt Abbie in particular, he'd promptly left for Chicago and St. Louis, there to simulate a keen interest in the investments which Cousin Larry had persuaded him to make in Eastern Airlines and the aircraft factory founded by an Arkansas Scot named James S. McDonnell. Notwithstanding his total lack of interest in business matters of all kinds, he'd ended by signing two checks, one for a hundred and fifty thousand dollars and the other for eight hundred thousand. This made him the second-largest stockholder in both concerns—second only to Cousin Larry, of course. Larry was the eldest of his seven cousins, which meant that he would become the richest man in the world once Uncle Peter kicked the bucket.

Taking advantage of the fact that Quartermain already had his checkbook out, the Clan had prevailed on him to write sundry other checks including one for eight hundred and twenty-five thousand dollars payable to ASAP, the Association for South American Progress. ASAP's president was—who else?—Cousin Henry, and its objective was to rid Latin America not only of German and Italian commercial interests—being at war with those folk, why not profit from the fact? —but of British and French interests as well. When U.S. corporations and capital were at stake, even allies were fair game. "At least let's get something out of that damnfool war in Europe," said Cousin Henry, who dreamed of moving into the White House someday. "The British portfolio in South America contains some useful investments, so why not pocket them right away? It's time we put an end to all this British colonialism, and besides, Lend-Lease is costing us a packet. . . ."

David Quartermain had redeployed a total of nine million dollars at the Clan's behest. He always followed the Clan's directives. Even though he didn't bear its name, being a cousin on his mother's side, he belonged to it by birth, by tradition, by a multiplicity of dynastic marriages, by social status and personal wealth. When he was a child, hardly a summer Sunday went by that he didn't go to play with Cousins Larry, James, Emerson, Henry, Michael, Winthrop, and Rodman at Uncle Peter's stately home on the banks of the Hudson, a country mansion set in the midst of a hundred-acre estate. He'd received fourteen million dollars in 1934—*only* fourteen million, he overheard Winthrop scoff—when Roosevelt's New Deal legislation compelled his mother to split the family fortune between herself, David's two sisters, and David himself. Where money was concerned, he had to admit— and laughed at the admission—that he'd never made a single decision of his own. He'd been content to follow the advice of Uncle Peter and his cousins, and he hadn't done too badly out of it, either. His original capital had more than doubled.

He went to Princeton, of course, and surprised everyone by majoring in philosophy. Then came Harvard, but only for three semesters—law bored him to death. He wasn't married. For more than ten years now he'd evaded all the many matrimonial traps laid in his path; no one could tell if his current bachelor state was attributable to his diabolical cunning or natural laziness reinforced by utter indecision. He knew it was a combination of the two, along with the simple fact that he preferred the fun of absolute freedom.

Last night he'd signed the last of the checks demanded of him: three hundred and twenty thousand eight hundred and one dollars for a variety of philanthropic causes to which every member of the Clan was expected to make an ostentatious contribution. That done, he headed north alone by car for the little Vermont farm he'd purchased four years earlier in the strictest secrecy, unbeknown even to his tax advisers, as a private haven for his fleeting and entertaining affairs with chorus girls, the occasional hatcheck girl, and, most recently, a quite beautiful starlet who had just left to hit it big in Hollywood. That was how he came to be strolling through the woods within sight of Lake Champlain, not even having stopped to remove his bags from the trunk of the Packard V12.

When walking palled, he made his way back to the rustic love nest where Ginny of the long legs—or was it Tessa?—no, Ginny—Tessa was the brunette—would be joining him as soon as she and her fellow dancers had completed their too lengthy pre-Broadway tour.

He entered the house and, in so doing, the story.

Two men were waiting for him inside. Two men he'd never seen before.

THE YELLOW-EYED MAN OBTAINED SOME ROOMS AT THE HÔTEL-Trois Dauphins, overlooking Grenoble's Place Grenette. The premises were occupied, in every sense of the word, by some Italian officers, but that little problem had soon been sorted out at a meeting attended by the Italians, the manager of the Trois Dauphins, and Yellow Eyes himself. Thomas, hovering in the background, was the target of the latter's smile throughout this conference, which ended in their being given an entire suite.

Yellow Eyes had given his name as Pierre Golaz-Hueber, a representative of the International Red Cross from Lausanne. He produced a Swiss passport, various documents in French and German, and pocketfuls of high-denomination banknotes. He even got the hotel to serve them dinner in the sitting room between their bedrooms. The room was lit only by candles in silver candlesticks, though, Thomas observed, there was no power failure in progress, and the meal comprised foie gras, roast duck, three kinds of vegetables, four sweets, and champagne.

"No champagne for me, thank you," said Thomas.

"Ever had any?"

"No."

It wasn't true, but Thomas would have died rather than tell him how She had once made him drink a glass of Dom Pérignon at the Palace Hotel in Saint Moritz. It had made him feel quite dizzy. The restaurant started lurching and swaying in the oddest way, and they'd danced together, She in a black-and-white gown trimmed with lace. His head really swam after that—the machine refused to function properly—so She bore him off to Her room, and that night he fell asleep in Her arms, delirious with happiness and lulled by the sound of Her voice: "I love you, Thomas. You're my son and my man, *mein Schatz*—you're my second self. The very fact of your existence lets me live twice over. Don't look at me that way, sweetheart. May God protect you from your own intelligence. You're growing up equipped with all the weapons I can give you—too many of them, perhaps. I'm almost afraid of what I've made of you, what I've done to you. What I've made you do. Come closer, my darling son. There, there, everything's all right. . . ."

"Try a little sip," said Yellow Eyes.

"I'm not old enough."

"You've never been young, Thomas. At least try some."

"No, thank you," said Thomas.

He picked up his half-filled glass, turned it upside down, and calmly went on eating. He was awfully hungry.

Having locked the recollection away in his mind and set the machine in motion, he debated what to do now that Yellow Eyes was dogging his every step. If that man's name is Golaz-whatever, he told himself, mine's Maurice Chevalier. Maybe I should have run for it at Marseilles while all those people were crowding aboard the trains. Maybe, except that there could have been twenty or thirty of them tailing me. If so, he deliberately let me see him in that silly hat and that tropical suit like something out of *African Explorers*, so I'd think he was alone and pay no attention to the other thirty. . . . But there's another thing: I used him to get on board that train and stay on board—to send those lousy gendarmes packing and get me across the demarcation line, quite apart from the fact that I'm still using him now, because I wouldn't know where else to eat and sleep in Grenoble. It's an awful nuisance, only being eleven. . . .

"I beg your pardon for spilling that champagne," he said.

"The tablecloth and I accept your apology."

Thomas sat up very straight, elbows tucked in, wielding his knife and fork as She had taught him to. Yellow Eyes said nothing, just watched him interminably.

Thomas was prepared for the questions he was bound to be asked at any moment: why had he come to Grenoble, what did he plan to do there, who did he plan to see?

All right, he said to himself, fire away.

QUARTERMAIN WASN'T PARTICULARLY SURPRISED TO FIND THE farmhouse door unlocked. Mrs. Annacone, his caretaker and cleaning woman, must have forgotten to lock up or thought it pointless. After all, burglars were few and far between in the depths of Vermont.

He went inside. The house consisted of three rooms plus a bathroom, a kitchen, and a pantry. The biggest of the rooms was a living room, whose salient features were a piano and a stone fireplace.

That was where the men were waiting for him.

One of the two, who were both in city suits, was nursing a leather briefcase. The other introduced himself as Geoffrey Hobson, an attorney with a Boston law firm, and produced documentary evidence of his identity. He apologized to Quartermain for invading his privacy.

"We were compelled to tail you, Mr. Quartermain—I believe that's the conventional term. I'm not in the habit of playing the private eye, but you left New York just as we were about to contact you. I must say, you drive extremely fast . . ."

Quartermain eyed Hobson's companion. He was a shortish man of about his own age, Latin in type, with dark and inscrutable eyes.

". . . and that completes my part in this affair," Hobson was saying. "With your permission, I'll leave you two together."

The business card he deposited on the table before making his exit was found there three days later by Virginia "Ginny" Kendall, Quartermain's weekend tryst, on her arrival at the deserted farmhouse. It was forwarded to the Clan's inquiry agents. They found Hobson quickly enough, but he hid behind his oath of professional secrecy for two whole weeks. The consequences of this delay were far-reaching.

Watching through the window, Quartermain saw Hobson make for a black Chevrolet parked behind a screen of elms, where it was almost invisible from the house.

"You speak Spanish?"

"No, just a bit of French," Quartermain replied, turning to face the man with the briefcase. "Who are you?"

"I have a communication for David John Quartermain. My instructions are to deliver it to him personally."

Quartermain grinned. "I can show you my driver's license."

"You lived in Paris in 1930. Where, exactly?"

"Rue de Lille."

"Which floor, please?"

"The third." Quartermain grinned again. "There was a marble dining table in the room on the right and a big drawing room on the left with two black leather sofas in it. Like me to describe the bedrooms?"

"Only the one you used to sleep in, please. What was hanging above the fireplace?"

"A painting by Mondrian. The subject was a forest of red trees."

"Here's the letter," said the Spaniard, and held it out.

"THAT REALLY WON'T BE NECESSARY, THOMAS," SAID YELLOW-Eyes.

He was obviously referring to the knife which Thomas had purloined from the supper table and was tightly clutching beneath the bedclothes.

"Good night, Monsieur Hubert Golaz."

"Golaz-Hueber. Good night, Thomas."

It was quite a while before Yellow Eyes finally left the room. Thomas heard him sit down and pour himself some more champagne —the clink of bottle on glass might have been deliberate. Minutes dragged by. Thomas strove to breathe as slowly and steadily as possible. Eyes closed, he forced his memory to reconstruct, in every detail, the culmination of the third game between Capablanca and Alexandre Alekhine in London in June 1926, when, after the twenty-third move, Alekhine had moved his king's rook to KR5 and checkmated in six. Playing the white knight in defense like Capablanca, he abruptly turned on his side with the little grunt that Grandpa Allègre used to make when dozing off after a heavy lunch. To snore, he thought, would be overdoing it. His right hand, which was holding the knife, emerged from the covers; his fingers relaxed their grip on the handle.

Another minute went by. What was he waiting for?

Success at last. Yellow Eyes got up and came in, very quietly. Tiptoeing over to the bed, he whispered, "Give me the knife, boy."

He'd said it *in German*.

Thomas didn't move a muscle. He controlled his breathing admirably, even when Yellow Eyes removed the knife from his limp fingers—even when he heard the faint click of the door closing.

Why? Because it was quite possible that Yellow Eyes had only pretended to go out. He might still be there, only a foot or two from the bed, watching and waiting in the darkness.

Thomas played Alekhine's next move: QBPXP . . .

Then the five succeeding moves, each time visualizing the ivory pieces on the board more vividly than if they'd actually been there in front of him. He checkmated Capablanca and still nothing happened. Then, fighting off an unwelcome urge to sleep, he played the return game in which Capablanca had launched his famous whirlwind attack, sixty-one moves in succession. The machine was still functioning, thank goodness, and functioning remarkably well.

The latch.

The latch of the communicating door between his bedroom and the sitting room had clicked. It clicked twice: once when the door was opened and again when it was very softly closed. He's really gone this time, Thomas told himself, but wait a little longer just the same. . . .

He played Alekhine's thirty-second move, then the two thirty-third moves, and turned over—slowly.

The room was empty.

He sat up in bed and, for the second time that day, was gripped by incipient panic. He didn't know exactly how long he'd taken to run through those two games of chess, but it had to be half an hour or so. Half an hour, and Yellow Eyes had watched him all that time, just to see if he was really asleep! Patience of that order was an almost frightening phenomenon, a measure of the strength of his opponent's game.

He may well have guessed what you plan to do here, Thomas told himself. No, he *must* have guessed. It's going to be awfully hard with him on your heels, him and the others. He isn't operating on his own, you bet. . . .

Thomas got out of bed and tiptoed over to the communicating door just in time to hear the outer door close. Yellow Eyes had gone downstairs. He'd been right to wait.

He could always make a run for it—or try to, anyway—but for the moment that was out. It was out for the reason that had become clear to him during those long hours of waiting in the cloister at Aix: he *had* to stay with the man, even—no, especially—if he was being followed purely as a lead to Her. It was the only way to keep Her safe.

THE SPANIARD HAD LEFT THE FARMHOUSE, BUT HE HADN'T joined Hobson in the Chevy. He waited outside, surveying the landscape with an air of curiosity. It was three in the afternoon in Vermont.

Quartermain poured himself a beer, sat down facing the unlit fire, and read Maria Weber's letter again.

David, I wouldn't be getting in touch with you unless the circumstances were quite exceptional. By writing this letter, I'm infringing all the rules that have governed my life to date.

She reminded him, albeit in language as frigid as an autopsy report, of the affair they'd had between August 1930 and February 1931. She recalled their life in Paris, the exact sequence and dates of their jaunts to Taormina, Seville, and Zermatt, and those few wintry days in February when she'd driven them off in the Bugatti for what was to be their last trip together.

The fact is, I was pregnant by you. Don't misunderstand me—I wanted that child more than anything else in the world, but I broke with you precisely because you'd fathered it on me. Although I've no idea how you remember me after twelve years, you may recall that I never lied to you.

His name is Thomas. He was born at Lausanne on September 18, 1931, at the Grand-Chêne Clinic, and registered as Thomas David Lamiel, father unknown. Subject to certain conditions, the bearer of this letter will acquaint you with the reasons for the secrecy surrounding the birth of my son. Because of them, and thanks to me, he's now in such mortal danger that I no longer feel justified in depriving him of the help which you may be able to provide, and which I implore you to give him.

She signed herself simply *"Maria,"* just that.

Quartermain was to be invaded by other recollections in the days, weeks, and months to come, but nothing comparable with the mesmeric few minutes it took him to read her letter—nothing as cruelly traumatic as this resurrection of his past in the peaceful depths of Vermont. He was with her again beside the Mediterranean, after one of those crazy joyrides that were her specialty. Right at the end of the Côte Varoise she parked the black Bugatti so that its huge wheels were touching the water. It was awhile before she switched off one engine and broke her silence. "We've only got another four days together, David. I could have waited until the last moment or written you, but that would have been pure cowardice on my part." Then she told him that they would never see each other again. "I want to be sure you'll make no attempt to find me. It's very important, David. I want you to give me your word."

No explanation. There had always been a mutual agreement, ever since they met, that each of them would remain entirely uncommitted to the other. They spent the next four days at a big, secluded villa on the far side of Sanary, near the mouth of the road to Bandol. Owned by some Swiss friends of hers, so she said, it was an ocher-colored two-story house with a tennis court, a handsome drive flanked by twenty-four palm trees, and staff quarters occupied by a couple named Allègre. At about two o'clock on the third night, Quartermain woke up without knowing why. Discovering that he was alone in the four-poster bed, he got up and went to look for Maria. He found her in front of the half-dead fire in the drawing-room, weeping as though her heart would break. He stoked the fire and got it going again, then turned on her furiously. He could swallow the fact that she proposed to break off their affair without a word of explanation—he could even overlook all the mystery in which she'd cloaked herself throughout the seven months they'd known each other—but that she should refuse any form of help was unpardonable. He could mobilize the entire Clan on her behalf. He could marry her—God knew, he'd already proposed half a dozen times.

He sat down facing her and watched her cry, determined to get the truth out of her at last, but his resolution wavered when she held out her arms to him and buried her face in his chest, sobbing convulsively. All her barriers were down for once, but not for long. Next morning she had recovered her habitual, diabolical self-possession. She repeated her demand: he must never under any circumstances make any attempt to find her.

They agreed that he should take the Blue Train back to Paris without her. Early that afternoon she drove him to the Marseilles station in the Bugatti, dropped him at the foot of the steps, and drove off. He climbed a few steps, then turned to look. Following the Bugatti in another car were two keen-eyed, alert-looking men. Their swarthy faces were familiar. He'd spotted them a couple of times, once in Paris and another time in Sicily, watching Maria from a distance.

"They could easily have been Spaniards like yourself."

The messenger made no response.

"Where is she?" Quartermain demanded.

"I've no idea."

"Are you acquainted with the contents of this letter?"

"The main essentials, yes."

"Where's the boy?"

"In the South of France, or he was when I left Europe."

"Is he really in danger?"

"Yes." The Spaniard raised one hand, palm outward. "I'm not at liberty to answer any more questions, Mr. Quartermain."

"Meaning what?"

"You must decide first."

"Whether or not to try to help the kid?"

"Yes."

"How long do I have to make up my mind?"

Silence.

"I see," said Quartermain. Still holding the letter, he made for the door. His mother and the rest of the Clan were used to his sudden disappearances. It would be a couple of weeks before they started worrying about him. He gave a rueful glance at his fishing tackle. There was Ginny to be considered too, but he could always leave her a note.

"What's he like, the boy?"

"Exceptional," said the Spaniard.

JÜRGEN HESS'S DISEMBODIED VOICE SAID, "WE ELIMINATED TWO of the Spanish bodyguards. The third got away, but we may have wounded him."

"You're sure the other two are dead?"

"Quite sure," Hess replied. Yes, he realized that his orders had been to capture at least one of them alive, but he'd had no choice. The one inside the apartment had fought back with incredible tenacity. Even when his limbs were riddled with bullets, he'd kept coming, gone on firing. Three of the raiding party had died at his hands. "I had to finish him off—I had no option."

"Your own demise would have been no great loss, my dear Jürgen. You failed to carry out my orders. What *are* you good for, anyway? If the Third Reich bites the dust one day, you'll have a lot to answer for."

Gregor Laemmle, closeted in a phone booth in the lobby of the Hôtel Dauphine, rocked with silent mirth under the puzzled gaze of a party of senior Italian officers seated not far away.

"What about the residents?"

He meant the retired colonel and his housekeeper, but he wasn't going to mention any names over a hotel phone. Hess replied that they were both alive. He'd had them transferred to a secluded house for interrogation, so far with little success. They didn't seem to know much, but the colonel would talk sooner or later.

"And the man with the missing fingers?"

Not a sign of him anywhere, said Hess. He proceeded to describe his efforts to locate the man, then suddenly went over to the attack. Laemmle's disappearance from Aix had taken him by surprise—he'd had no word from him for twenty-four hours and resented being kept out of the picture like this. Anyway, he'd got in touch with the Gestapo in Paris and—

Laemmle hung up on him and emerged from the booth. He ordered a glass of Chartreuse and toasted the Italians, two or three of whom continued to regard him curiously. Here I am with a mutiny on my hands, he reflected. The worthy Jürgen is within an ace of thinking for himself. Nazism certainly isn't what it was. . . .

He set off across the lobby. For a moment he considered joining the Italians, if only to brush up his knowledge of their language. Instead, carrying his Chartreuse as gingerly as if it were nitroglycerine, he made for the revolving door and gazed out at the Place Grenette with unseeing eyes. He was feeling decidedly odd—almost on the verge of one of those moods that induced such a profound disgust for himself and the world at large.

He was just taking another sip of liqueur when he caught sight of tall, blond, handsome Georg Soeft seated in a parked car with two of his men, waiting for a signal that would set him in motion. They were not alone, of course. Other men were similarly posted in the neighborhood of the hotel and throughout Grenoble. Men . . . the chess analogy was inescapable. The white queen and the black queen are both in Grenoble, Laemmle thought. I'm the black queen, of course, protected on all sides by my bishops and rooks, knights and pawns, but who is there to protect the poor little white queen in short pants?

The phone rang. It was for him. Joachim Gortz's voice announced that he was in Paris and willing to carry out the redeployment Laemmle had requested, though he had little idea of its purpose.

"That makes two of us," Laemmle replied. Still speaking, he instinctively transferred his gaze from the Italians to the staircase that led to the rooms above. He'd seen no one, not the smallest sign of a small boy in shorts, but he'd sensed something. Or had his optic nerves retained the image of a shadowy form in a darkened bedroom? He smiled. To think the little imp had feigned sleep for over three-quarters of an hour. . . .

"If the boy's so smart," said Gortz, "why hasn't he tried to give you the slip? Who's protecting him?"

"An excellent question. Good night, my dear Joachim."

He hung up once more and knocked back the rest of his Chartreuse, only regretting that his tongue wasn't long enough to reach the bottom of the glass. Then he started up the stairs.

He paused on each landing and waited with a faint but delicious thrill of anticipation for the man with the missing fingers to jump out and slit his throat from ear to ear, but nothing happened.

The boy was fast asleep, or so it seemed.

QUARTERMAIN TURNED FOR A FINAL LOOK AT THE HOUSE through the Chevrolet's rear window. His twelve-cylinder Packard was still parked outside.

"I never even had a chance to unpack my things." A sudden thought struck him. "Damn, I forgot to leave a note for my girlfriend!"

"We'll go back if you like," said Hobson.

"No," Quartermain told him, "it doesn't matter. Keep going." He could buy any clothes he needed en route. After all, he'd be back within a week. . . .

He settled into the corner of the seat. The Spaniard, who was sitting on his left, had produced a passport describing himself as Juan Vidal, born at Palma de Mallorca in 1905, which made him thirty-seven. Occupation: bank director.

The car crossed the Canadian border soon afterward and reached Montreal an hour and a half after that. Hobson picked up a couple of air tickets for Zurich, handed them over, and took his leave.

"How does one get into France?"

"Zurich's in Switzerland."

Quartermain laughed. "That much I do know." The man had a banker's sense of humor, all right. "How do we get to Switzerland, then?"

"We fly from here to Shannon, then Shannon to Lisbon, Lisbon to Madrid, Madrid to Zurich. It'll take us three days at most. Do you know Spain?"

Quartermain had been once to Madrid and once to Pamplona in the company of that madman Ernie Hemingway, who'd unsuccessfully tried to infect him with his craze for bullfighting.

"You should visit Majorca someday."

No longer constrained by Hobson's presence, the Spaniard became a trifle more talkative. He disclosed that he'd already done business with the Clan, or at least with its representatives in Spain.

"I once attended a dinner at Barcelona in honor of Mr. Joseph Sowinski . . ."

"If there's anything that interests me less than my family's business activities, I'd like to know what it is," Quartermain said lightly.

The Spanish banker smiled for the first time. The four-engined plane had just taken off and was heading for its first port of call, Gander in Newfoundland. Night had fallen. A mere six hours ago, Quartermain had been looking forward to a peaceful three days of fishing followed by a week-long tête-à-tête with five feet six inches of fragrant pink flesh. Even as he cursed himself for being aboard this plane, he surrendered to an almost childish, but undeniably exhilarating rush of excitement.

It had been a long time since he had done something just for love.

THE RAIN THAT BEGAN TO DELUGE GRENOBLE DURING THEIR second night had persisted ever since. Gregor Laemmle was obliged to walk the streets beneath a gigantic black umbrella of the kind favored by shepherds and country clergymen. He hated this implement almost as much as he hated the ghastly clothes he was wearing, which he'd purchased in Grenoble because his luggage—Jürgen Hess deserved the firing squad for that piece of negligence alone—had yet to arrive from Aix. Above all, he loathed the form of physical exercise to which he'd now been subjected for two days in succession: trudging around Grenoble while the boy strode blithely ahead of him.

The whole thing had started the day before. It couldn't have been later than six o'clock when Laemmle was roused from his slumbers by a brisk and repeated knocking sound. The more he ignored it, the more insistent it became. He swathed himself in a bedspread and staggered out of his room, only to be shot at point-blank range, so to speak, by a serene gaze from two gray eyes. Already dressed, his dark hair still moist and spiky from the shower, Thomas was seated at the breakfast table tapping the edge of a plate with his knife.

"I'm sorry if I woke you, monsieur."

"You certainly did, and it isn't even six yet."

"I'm awfully sorry, really I am."

"I'm sure you are," said Laemmle, who'd had three hours' sleep at most. While browsing through the hotel's little library the night before, he'd come upon a copy of Stendhal's *Henri Brulard* and read nearly three hundred pages of it before dropping off.

"Thank you for accepting my apology, monsieur," Thomas said gracefully. "I usually have coffee for breakfast," he added.

And rolls.

And butter.

And apricot jam—not strawberry. He didn't like strawberry jam because the pips got in your teeth.

Laemmle had to sally forth into the corridor, walk to the lift, ride it down to the kitchen, order breakfast, and extract a promise from the cook—in return for twenty francs—that it would be served in the next five minutes. All this he did while draped in his bedspread like some Roman senator of old, half asleep but strangely titillated by the pleasure it gave him to submit to the boy's importunate demands, which seemed a mark of budding intimacy. Once back in his room he hurriedly washed and dressed. For once in his life he dispensed with a long, hot bath and contented himself with a shower. Worse still, in default of a change of clothes, and underclothes in particular, he had to put on those he'd worn the day before, shuddering with distaste.

Meanwhile, breakfast had been served.

"I'm awfully hungry, Monsieur Hubert Golaz."

"Golaz-Hueber. If you're hungry, eat."

"I'm used to having my rolls buttered for me."

The gray eyes never wavered. Laemmle set to work, conscious that his leg was being pulled but enjoying the sensation.

"Another one, Thomas?"—"Yes please. I don't want to be rude, but . . ."—"Yes, what is it?"—"Well, you aren't very good at it. Look at all those holes."—"I'm doing my best, I assure you. Anyway, you're exaggerating. There aren't any holes."—"I don't mean the rolls, I mean the way you're spreading them. There *are* some holes, look, you've left gaps in the butter, see for yourself."—"I'll try harder, Thomas. There, that one's not too bad, is it?"—"Not too bad, monsieur, but it could be better."—"You don't want another one, surely?" —"Well, I *am* a bit hungry still."—"But you've already had seven!"

Laemmle did his utmost to make a masterpiece of the eighth roll. He watched Thomas sink his teeth in it.

"Well?"—"This one's fine, honestly."—"I'm glad I've succeeded after only seven attempts."—"Except that my coffee's cold. Could you ask them to bring me some more, please?"

And now Gregor Laemmle was walking the streets of Grenoble beneath his hateful black umbrella. This second day had begun like the first: the same crack-of-dawn awakening, the same ritual with the rolls and jam, the same exodus from the hotel at around seven-fifteen.

And the same ridiculous traipsing around.

Thomas led the way. After three or four hundred yards he disappeared into a baker's shop and joined the queue of housewives inside with Laemmle lining up behind him. The women bent a faintly hostile gaze on this ill-assorted pair of strangers to the neighborhood. The boy seemed unobjectionable, but the man in the cream suit smiled too much for their taste. When Thomas finally got to the counter, he addressed the baker's wife as follows: "I don't want any bread, madame—I don't have a ration card anyway. All I've got is a message for you to give your husband. Tell him that the dog belonging to the man with the clubfoot has got scarlet fever. That's all: the dog belonging to the man with the clubfoot has got scarlet fever. *Au revoir*, madame."

So saying, he walked out of the shop, which Soeft and his Gestapo men had discreetly surrounded.

But that was only a modest beginning. Two streets farther on, Thomas entered a bar. This time, the proprietor was no less flabbergasted than the baker's wife when told that Sherlock Holmes had sent Thomas to warn him that the elephant's trunk was growing feathers.

And so on ad infinitum.

The first day had taken them to no less than thirty-seven establishments of various kinds: shops, department stores, and public buildings, including a post office, where Thomas had insisted on informing the postmaster, in the strictest confidence, that Bulldog Drummond had lost his false teeth.

The second day had followed an identical course. They'd now been trudging through the pouring rain for five whole hours. Twenty-five messages had already been delivered, some to places visited the day before, others to new addressees. There was no discernible pattern to this endless perambulation through Grenoble. They would pass such-and-such a hardware store and completely ignore it, only to return an hour later and deliver a message even more whimsical than the itinerary that had preceded it, for instance, "Arsène Lupin has sold his trousers again." Alternatively, they would walk past the church of Saint-Joseph five times before notifying the astonished verger that he had a rendezvous with Davy Crockett in an hour's time.

"Anyone would think he was broadcasting coded messages to the Resistance from London," Laemmle muttered to Soeft, overcome by a multitude of conflicting emotions. These included exasperation, admiration, an urge to laugh hysterically, and loving pride. The adorable, eagle-eyed youngster was leading them all a dance: himself, Soeft, and their team of sleuths. Poor Soeft was going crazy checking all those addresses, while he, Laemmle, was beginning to crack up too in his efforts to memorize all the ridiculous messages Thomas had delivered like a postman going his rounds.

Which was, of course, the boy's main aim. Why? Because one of the contacts he'd established in the town must have been a prearranged channel of communication with his mother.

"Aren't you hungry, Thomas? It's half past twelve."

Thomas's gray eyes slowly detached themselves from the window of an antique shop—which might or might not have been his next port of call—and homed in on Laemmle's face. Not a word was spoken, but the significance of the look was unmistakable. He's waiting for me to beg for mercy, thought Laemmle, momentarily furious. The little brat's got eight or ten men trailing around after him, me included. He not only knows it, he's laughing up his sleeve at me, when I've only to say the word and bring the whole damned farce to an end. I could have him seized and made to talk by any and every means—that's what Hess and Soeft recommend, and even Joachim Gortz thinks so too. He ought to realize that I alone stand between him and the rest. I and my eccentric ideas are his sole protection. He—

Wait a minute. "Who's protecting him?"—wasn't that what Gortz asked me on the phone the other night? The answer's obvious: *I* am— I, Gregor Laemmle!

Thomas now had his nose glued to the window of a Category A restaurant (wartime menus from thirty-five to fifty francs, the legal maximum, consisting of a cold first course not including eggs or fish and one main dish containing neither butter nor sugar, the whole meal to be accompanied by not more than one-fifth of a liter of wine and obtainable only on production of the requisite coupons).

Laemmle continued to brood on his latest realization. The boy knows that I'm waiting for him to lead me to his mother, or that his mother will try to get him away from me. Anyone else in my position would pluck out his eyes to make him talk, whereas with me he stands a chance. He realizes that and he's defying me—challenging me. It's like a game of chess. . . .

"Come on, Thomas, let's go somewhere else—somewhere where you can eat as much as you like."

I'll give him another three days—no, four. Till Monday night. Then Soeft can try his hand. Not Hess. Hess would spoil the youngster's looks. . . .

YELLOW EYES TOOK THEM TO A BLACK-MARKET RESTAURANT
where they lunched on Parma ham with melon followed by braised
lamb and beans. Thomas had already stuffed himself. He wasn't as
hungry as all that, but—as Grandpa Allègre used to say—it always
paid to stoke up while you could.

"Another slice of lamb, Thomas?"

"No, thank you, monsieur. Really not."

"I thought you were starving."

"Not anymore, monsieur."

Thomas felt singularly tired, and not only in the legs. Preparing a
jigsaw puzzle took time, especially one with four or five thousand
pieces. You had to find the edges and sort out the colors before you
could even start on it.

Well, he'd done his sorting out by calling at all those shops. Javier's
instructions had been followed to the letter. "If ever anything goes
wrong, Thomas," Javier had told him, "if we ever become separated,
make your way to the greengrocer's shop in Grenoble. You have his
address, but be careful. . . ."

"Couldn't you find room for something sweet, Thomas?"

The question, which was couched in German, almost took him by
surprise. He hadn't been concentrating hard enough—that was how
you lost at chess. He stared, feigning incomprehension.

"I asked if you had room for something sweet," said Yellow Eyes,
this time in French.

"For something sweet, yes. I'm very fond of those little batter balls
in chocolate sauce."

"Be careful, Thomas," Javier had said. "If you get to Grenoble and
have a hunch, even a hunch, that you're being followed, don't go to
the greengrocer direct. Go there in such a way that the people who
may be following you won't guess at our arrangement with him, understand? I can suggest a way, but you won't always have me around.
I'd prefer you to think one up by yourself. Take your time—we'll have
another talk about it tomorrow. I'm curious to know if you'll dream
up something really smart."

Thomas had tackled the question in the same way as he approached
a chess problem: with total concentration. Going back to Javier that

same evening, he explained what he would do if he found himself alone in Grenoble with enemies watching his every move and no one there to help him but Barthélémy, the greengrocer in the Place Saint-Claire—Barthélémy, who was a Majorcan from Sóller like Javier himself. He would go into fifty or sixty shops, if not more, so the people shadowing him wouldn't know which was the right one, and spout a whole lot of gibberish like the BBC's coded messages to the Resistance —"Auntie's got a toothache," et cetera. That would make fifty or sixty shops or even more—why not two hundred, while he was about it?— which his pursuers would have to check, and they'd go crazy puzzling over those messages, all of which would be meaningless except the one designed to let the greengrocer know that he needed help, and fast.

Thomas emerged from the restaurant at the yellow-eyed man's heels, gleefully noting that the latter's feet were hurting him. Outside he spotted another three men in addition to the first four he'd seen. One of them was the tall, fair-haired man who'd been parked outside the hotel the first night. His name was Soeft, or something of the kind —he couldn't be Hess, because Hess had been telephoning from elsewhere at the time. That made seven of them, anyway. Maybe there weren't thirty after all, but seven were more than enough, even discounting the ones that had so far escaped his notice.

"It's still raining, Thomas," remarked Yellow Eyes.

"Fancy that," Thomas replied casually. Don't overdo it, he told himself—don't be too damned clever.

"It's very chilly, too. I wouldn't want you to catch cold."

No, thought Thomas, but you wouldn't mind slicing me up like salami. Aloud, he said, "I'm not the least bit cold, monsieur, really not. I'm nice and warm, thanks to the overcoat and shoes you kindly bought me."

Yellow Eyes was obviously getting sick of traipsing around Grenoble, he thought as he headed for the Place de Verdun, a square whose name was familiar to him because he'd already passed it seven times. Picking a shop at random—a dress shop, as it happened—he darted across the street and ran inside. The consequences of his sudden dash were gratifyingly reflected in the shop window: his pursuers had also broken into a run. That got a rise out of them, he told himself.

"Ali Baba dislikes cheese sandwiches," he informed the shop assistant.

"I don't understand," she said, just as Yellow Eyes hurried into the shop.

"Pay no attention," he told her. "My nephew's a mischievous little fellow."

Thomas docilely allowed himself to be led outside.

"Are you going to be much longer?"

Take care, he's getting really annoyed. "I'll soon be through, monsieur—for today." Thomas's tone and expression were carefully gauged. He couldn't afford to seem flippant.

The next establishment he visited was a restaurant, where the chef was informed that Coco the Clown had a wart on his bottom. Then came a haberdasher's, a crowded café, another haberdasher's, a funeral parlor ("Tarzan wants his coffin by Friday"), a bakery, a shoe shop (for the third time), a hotel reception desk, two more cafés in succession, and a butcher's shop.

After yet another trek across the Place de Verdun, Thomas and his retinue called at a café full of tipsy Italian soldiers, a hardware store, a shop selling fruit and vegetables (the first such), a grocer's, a furniture store, a tax office where he queued up and stood on tiptoe to inform a baldheaded clerk that Mandrake the Magician was behind with his taxes, another furniture store ("Biggles has crashed his plane"), a church he'd passed before, but going in the opposite direction, another café, and a school.

Zigzagging at random, so it seemed, he slowly but surely drew nearer the Place Saint-Claire.

There it was at last.

He went inside and, quite as naturally as on any previous occasion, came out with another nonsensical phrase. He did so even though he'd recognized Barthélémy, the Majorcan greengrocer, from the description Javier had given him, and even though he felt a strong and almost fatal urge to hurl himself into the man's arms.

"Moby Dick has lost his tail."

The greengrocer was picking over some lettuces. He didn't turn a hair. Two or three seconds elapsed before he raised his head and stared blankly at Thomas. Then he turned to Thomas's constant companion with an uncomprehending frown.

"Don't mind my nephew," said Yellow Eyes. "He's too fond of practical jokes."

Not very imaginative of him, thought Thomas. He's already used that explanation thirty times at least. If I can think up something new every time, so could he. . . .

Grenoble Cathedral had already tolled five o'clock, and the streets were filling up with children homeward bound from school. The light was fading fast. Thomas called at nine more stores, shops, and offices in quick succession. His legs were aching dreadfully now.

I can't go on, he thought—I really will have to call it a day. Let's hope the greengrocer understood and did what he's supposed to do. Unless I spoke to the wrong Barthélémy . . . maybe it was his brother or his cousin—maybe they all look alike in his family . . .

Stop it! You're getting wound up for nothing. Only another five stops. . . .

He surveyed the street ahead of him. It was the turning on the right, he'd memorized it.

Three more stops including yet another haberdasher's—how many *were* there in this town? It was really dark by now, and terribly cold. Thomas felt frozen stiff. The confounded rain seemed to be stopping—or was it giving way to snow? God, how cold and tired he was!

Only two more, but what to say? He was running out of ideas.

"Time to go home, Thomas, don't you think so?"

Yellow Eyes stood rooted to the pavement, seemingly reluctant to take another step. It was obvious that he, too, had had enough, and the exasperation in his voice sounded ominous. Thomas, who'd been on the point of entering a wood and coal merchant's shop, turned and stared at him. He still hadn't budged. Beyond him Thomas caught another glimpse of the fair-haired giant—Soeft, or whatever his name was—and his six companions.

No, dammit, there were seven of them. That made nine in all.

He was about to enter the shop, when suddenly—oh God, this must be it!—they were waiting for him: three boys of whom one at least was familiar to him from his visit to Barthélémy's establishment.

Javier's voice: "Their names are Paul, Michel, and Jacques . . ."

Yellow Eyes: "That's enough, Thomas!"

It was now or never.

Another few steps took him past the coal merchant's and into a café he'd visited before. A dozen beefy-looking men stood propped against the bar drinking white wine and watching a hand of cards in progress at the table beside them. Just as he'd done the time before, Thomas made his way along the counter toward the proprietor, who was sitting behind his till. A glance at the mirror on the wall confirmed that Yellow Eyes had paused in the doorway, looking thoroughly disgruntled. Halfway along the counter Thomas stopped short and insinuated himself into the group at the bar. Tugging one of the drinkers by the sleeve—he purposely chose the one with the reddest face and loudest voice—he fixed him with a wide-eyed, innocent gaze and addressed him in a piping voice.

"Please help me, monsieur," he said breathlessly. "That man's been following me ever since I got out of school. He tried to touch me—he asked me to do dirty things with him."

Still out of earshot, Yellow Eyes seemed intrigued and faintly perturbed by this unexpected development. He edged closer.

"You mean that pink pussycat who just came in?" demanded Thomas's newfound friend.

"That's him. He put his hand down my trousers."

"You don't say?" The big man squared his shoulders like a mountain on the move—Thomas congratulated himself on his choice—and his boon companions followed suit.

Yellow Eyes cleared his throat. "I think there's been a slight misunderstanding," he said suavely. "I happen to be this little boy's uncle, and—"

"His *uncle*?"

Thomas didn't wait for any more. He slipped out through the back room, which opened onto a courtyard with wine casks stacked against the walls, and dived down the covered way he'd noticed during his reconnaissance the day before.

It came out in a narrow street. As he was sprinting along it, a diminutive figure beckoned to him and a boy's voice called, "Turn right at the end!" He did so without slackening his pace. Another thirty yards or less, and he was hailed again.

"This way, Thomas!"

He knows my name, Thomas thought briefly. Then it was along a passage, up a flight of stairs, through an apartment uninhabited except for some cats, out of a window, onto a roof, across the roof, and in through another window.

A youth closed the window behind him. "I'm Michel Barthélémy. Follow me."

They made their way through an apartment where two old ladies sat knitting and pretending not to see a thing, then out onto a landing and down some stairs.

"Can you ride a bike, Thomas?"

"Sort of."

Another door, another street. They sauntered along it, turned down an alleyway, and entered a carpenter's workshop by the back door.

Three men were at work inside, but none of them so much as glanced up. The three wise monkeys had nothing on them.

A passage. Then they were in a cobbler's shop with a glass door opening onto the street.

"Now we wait." Michel smiled, his eyes sparkling with glee. "Fun, isn't it?"

"Terrific fun," said Thomas.

He remained on his guard, poised to run like lightning even though instinct told him that all was well—that his headlong dash was temporarily over. A minute or two went by.

"Don't worry, Thomas, the others'll be here soon. We didn't know for sure which way you'd come, so we had to cover the whole block. Lucky there are three of us."

The other two turned up at last. They pushed open the glass door and came in. The younger boy was the one who had told Thomas which way to go.

"My brothers," said Michel. "The big one's Paul, the other one's Jacques. Get those clothes off, Thomas—coat, shorts, sweater, beret, everything. And your shoes. Come on, hurry!"

Thomas changed in the cobbler's workshop. He put on some different shorts, which were too tight for him, a fur-lined jacket, which more or less fitted, a pair of shoes with wooden soles, a red-and-blue balaclava, and some woolen gloves. They all belonged to Jacques, who exchanged them for some clothes from a bundle Paul had brought.

"What about my own things?" Thomas asked.

"Paul will take care of those—Papa said to hide them. Come on."

Thomas found himself outside in the street with Michel and two bicycles, each of them attached to a small two-wheeled trailer made of plywood. The trailers were filled with vegetables, mostly wilting lettuces.

"Quickly, Thomas, but remember, you're called Jacques now."

Michel had already mounted his own bicycle and was urging Thomas to do likewise. Thomas got astride the saddle and strained at the pedals. The trailer was surprisingly heavy, but he managed to get it moving at last.

They rode off.

"Who are all those lettuces for?"

Michel laughed. "The goats, of course."

QUARTERMAIN'S THOUGHTS OF MARIA PERSISTED WHEN HE reached Lisbon. It had never occurred to him that she could become pregnant and have a baby like any other woman, but he'd been only twenty-two at the time: a fledgling member of the Clan still nesting in the youthful unsophistication from which he wasn't sure he'd yet emerged. From their very first encounter in the Rue de l'Estrapade onward, she'd seemed to him to have lived ten lives; he had been a boy, she a woman to her fingertips.

The slow resurgence of memories had continued as the propellers of successive aircraft laboriously churned the air for hours on end. It was a chaotic process devoid of order and logic, a bittersweet process that culminated in melancholy, because the pain of losing her had also returned. Quartermain thought he'd relegated their affair to the realm of youthful flings, but was mistaken, and it surprised him. The fact was, he'd left Vermont at a moment's notice in response to a mere letter. He found his behavior almost inexplicable. Was he a romantic at heart after all?

He hadn't been frightened of her—that would be an exaggeration—but she certainly used to alarm him at times. When he told her, "I love you," with all the rapture appropriate to such a statement, she simply laughed and said, "You may be growing up, David, but you've a long way to go yet." She was extraordinarily emancipated. Once, in Sicily in September 1930, she'd swum and sunbathed in the nude regardless of some fishermen nearby. Maria never wore a bra, and her breasts used to bob deliciously beneath her Chanel blouse. Equally uninhibited when it came to making love, she would tell him quite bluntly what she expected of him in bed. She was dazzlingly intelligent, frighteningly perceptive, and constantly alert, yet given to sudden, inexplicable silences so brutal and complete that they resembled a total cessation of life, as if she'd been abruptly recalled to a different and cruel reality. Quartermain had even supposed her to be suffering from some incurable disease and hectically living out her last few months in the shadow of death, but that theory proved untenable. Besides, it didn't explain the omnipresence of those mysterious bodyguards, or whatever they were.

Quartermain was getting ready to leave for Madrid, where he was to catch a Lati flight to Zurich the following day.

"Won't you be coming with me?"

Juan Vidal shook his head. "I'd be no use to you in Switzerland, Mr. Quartermain. Madrid is as far as I go. In any case, someone will meet you in Geneva at the rendezvous I gave you."

"How will I recognize him?"

"Don't worry, he'll recognize you."

At no stage in their long journey had the Spanish banker disclosed the nature of the "exceptional circumstances" to which Maria's letter had alluded. He'd talked a great deal, but only about his beloved Majorca, Quartermain's membership in the Clan—which profoundly impressed him—and the Clan's substantial business interests in Europe. Quartermain had turned a deaf ear to the last subject, though the man seemed to suggest that his family's influence might prove useful in the present affair. As if he would dream of telling Cousin Larry about it, let alone Uncle Peter!

"Is there anything else you're supposed to tell me?"

"Absolutely nothing."

Quartermain's initial excitement was still as intense. Having four hours to kill, he spent them exploring Lisbon. He strolled along the Tagus waterfront, sipped an appropriate glass of white port at a café bordering the Rossio, Lisbon's main square, unexpectedly found himself in the Rua do Ouro, and went for a ride in the Santa Justa lift designed by Gustave Eiffel. He would be seeing her again: that was his overriding thought.

He returned to his hotel to find Juan Vidal waiting for him in one of the cane chairs in the lobby. The Spaniard handed him a sealed envelope.

"I was supposed to give you this in the States, but it only just reached me."

Quartermain slit the flap. Inside were some photographs of a boy of ten or so. He recognized the eyes at once: they were hers. The resemblance was almost uncanny.

"I'VE NEVER ACTUALLY SEEN A GOAT," SAID THOMAS.

"Aren't there any goats where you come from? Where *do* you come from, anyway?"

"A long way off," said Thomas, instantly on his guard again.

Still towing their trailers, the two boys left the ancient walls of Grenoble behind them and pedaled on. Michel talked incessantly. His father was a Majorcan, he said, but his mother originally came from Savoy. He could speak a little Spanish but was more fluent in the Majorcan dialect.

"How about you, Thomas?"

"I don't know either," Thomas replied, still on his guard.

Their destination proved to be a suburban house with goats grazing in the garden. The goats, which looked rather unintelligent, fell upon the wilting lettuces as soon as Michel unloaded them. He was still talking—he wanted to be an engineer and build bridges—when they entered the house. It was very warm and peaceful inside. Thomas was suddenly overcome with weariness and relief: he'd made it—he'd given Yellow Eyes the slip. He was going to see Her again.

He could hardly remember having supper with the greengrocer and his wife and three sons. It distressed him a little not to be able to tell them how much he appreciated their kindness, but he was half asleep.

"Come on, youngster." Barthélémy picked him up bodily and bore him off to a bedroom. "You've had it, haven't you? Get some sleep. No one's going to bother you here."

He relaxed for the first time in days. It was awfully nice to have someone to take care of you. Hours later he awoke with a start, terrified out of his wits, to find Michel patting him soothingly on the shoulder.

"It's all right, you were having a bad dream. One day we'll go to Majorca, the two of us. We'll go to Sóller—Papa always says it's the finest place on earth. Like me to tell you about it?"

An extraordinary feeling of tranquillity stole over Thomas as he drifted off again. In the morning someone gently woke him: Madame Barthélémy had brought him his breakfast in bed. "You can get washed afterward," she told him, "but mind you don't leave anything out!" The words were accompanied by a smile that might have made him cry if the machine in his head hadn't reprimanded him first. That's right, it said, let yourself go, lower your guard, and the next thing you know you'll be sunk. Hasn't She told you a thousand times never to trust anyone? Even the nicest people can harm you without meaning to.

The burly-looking man who turned up an hour later had a smile as broad as a barn door. He turned out to be Uncle Mathieu, Barthélémy's brother, who was to smuggle him into Switzerland.

"It's child's play, *muchacho*—you won't be the first or the last to sneak across this way. I've got a truck, you see, but not just any old truck: there's a trapdoor behind the cab with a hidey-hole underneath. Grown-ups have used it before now, so you'll fit inside nicely. Ready to go? Don't budge an inch if I have to stop—you can breathe, but that's all. If you hear me singing, though, you can knock on the partition. Then, if the coast is clear, you can climb out and stretch your legs a bit."

Once they were under way, Thomas fell asleep again. He woke up on the four or five occasions they stopped, but the truck drove on each time. At last, hearing Uncle Mathieu break into song and wanting to relieve himself, he knocked on the partition. The truck pulled up almost immediately. Climbing out, he saw snow-covered mountains close at hand. Uncle Mathieu joined him beside the road for a pee.

"You speak Spanish, don't you?"

"No," said Thomas. The man had addressed him in Castilian.

"*Qué va! Entiendes muy bien.* According to Javier Coll, who's from Sóller like us, you can speak Castilian as well as the Generalissimo himself."

"Javier Coll? Who's he?"

Uncle Matthieu laughed heartily and shook his head. "I don't blame you for being careful, Thomas. After all, it's the Germans who are after you, not the Italians. The Italians can always be fixed, but the Germans . . ." He shrugged. "Except that we're safely past all their checkpoints. You can ride up front with me now. Like something to eat and drink?"

Thomas would sooner have stayed in the hidey-hole—it seemed risky to show himself—but Uncle Mathieu was already replacing his load of tires and car batteries on top of the trapdoor.

Not long afterward they reached a small town. "Annemasse," said Uncle Mathieu. The truck drove past a Catholic school of some kind. A priest standing outside removed his beret and scratched his head. "That means everything's all right, Thomas. We can go inside." Uncle Mathieu swung the wheel over and drove back to the school. This time he turned into the courtyard itself. *"Adiós y suerte, muchacho. Give our regards to Javier."*

Thomas was shown into a small room by the priest in the beret, who introduced himself as Father Favre. The window overlooked a garden bounded by a stone wall. "Switzerland lies just beyond that wall," said Father Favre, pointing to it. "I'll bring you something to eat in a minute. Is there anything else you'd like? Something to read, perhaps? There are plenty of books in the room next door. You'll be crossing the frontier tonight."

Everything's going too well, thought Thomas; it's all too easy. But that again was the voice of the machine in his head, and for once he didn't want to listen. His one thought was of Her, his one certainty that She would be waiting for him on the other side of the wall.

Father Favre brought him some food on a tray, but he hardly touched it. He tried playing a game of mental chess to calm his nerves, but he couldn't concentrate sufficiently. He borrowed a Gustave Aymard from the little school library next door and read two hundred pages of it with the lightning rapidity that had always astounded Grandpa Allègre.

Don't think of him, he commanded himself. Neither of him, nor of Grandma Allègre, nor of the colonel at Aix, nor of the greengrocer, nor of the greengrocer's wife and sons. Forget them—forget them all. There's no point in thinking about people you'll never see again. It only hurts. . . .

By nine o'clock that night he was outside in the garden. Father Favre signaled to him to keep still. Two Italian sentries strolled slowly past and disappeared around a bend in the wall.

"Now," said Father Favre.

Thomas started up the ladder. Only then did he discover that he had company: seven or eight men and women were crossing the border with him.

"Be quick!" the priest hissed.

One of the men helped Thomas over the wall by prodding him in the back. He jumped down and landed on the other side. The rest of the party followed suit and swiftly set off into the darkness. All at once, lights blazed and soldiers armed with rifles appeared from nowhere. "It's all right," said one of the fugitives. "They're Swiss, thank God."

But the voice inside his head had risen to a shout. The man who had shoved him over the wall gripped his shoulder. "We've done it, boy.

We're in Switzerland—we're safe at last!" Thomas brusquely shook off his hand and broke into a run. A ditch yawned in front of him after thirty yards or so. He went sprawling, picked himself up, and made for some trees barely visible in the gloom. Plunging into them, he was about to emerge on the far side of the copse when he saw three soldiers with flashlights dead ahead. He cowered down in the undergrowth and froze. The soldiers didn't appear to have seen him.

A truck drove up, illuminated by the glare from some other vehicles' headlights. Thomas saw his recent companions start climbing aboard. I'll wait till they've gone, he told himself, and then . . .

And then it happened: the man who had just congratulated him on his good fortune, a little man with a bald head, buttonholed one of the frontier guards and pointed in his direction. "Come on out, little boy," he called. "There's nothing to be scared of anymore—we're in Switzerland!" Flashlights were trained on his hiding place, soldiers converged on him, a hand seized him by the arm and led him to the truck.

He clambered aboard in a blind rage, only to find himself alongside his baldheaded betrayer. "But I did it for your own good, my boy. You've no need to be frightened any longer." The worst of it was, the poor man couldn't have been more sincere. Thomas trembled with murderous hatred. The truck drove off. The naked bulb dangling from the canvas roof revealed two soldiers seated beside the tailgate. Escape was out of the question.

The entire party was deposited in front of a brightly lit building situated beside some tram tracks. There was even a tram with Geneva lettering on it.

Half an hour later Thomas was ushered into an office. The man behind the desk said, "Would you by any chance be Thomas David Lamiel, born at Lausanne?"

He knew the answer and was only feigning uncertainty, Thomas could tell.

"Go and wait in the room next door," said the man. "Someone's coming to collect you."

These words kindled a tiny little spark of hope in Thomas's heart, but he knew it was a delusion. She would have been there by now if circumstances had permitted; if not, Javier Coll or someone else would have come in Her place.

He waited in a bleak room guarded by a stolid Swiss soldier who never took his eyes off him. A very long time went by.

Then he heard footsteps and voices speaking German. He caught a few words like "many thanks," "much appreciated," and "very helpful."

The door opened, and in came a smartly dressed man with white hair, pink cheeks, and blue eyes. He was smiling broadly.

"Good evening, Thomas," he said. "We've been expecting you ever since you left Grenoble. My name is Gortz, Joachim Gortz."

AT ZURICH, WHERE HIS PLANE LANDED, QUARTERMAIN HAD scarcely passed through customs and immigration before a man accosted him. He introduced himself as Fernando Valdez and, to prove that he really was a messenger from Maria, mentioned the Mondrian painting that had adorned the Rue de Lille apartment twelve years earlier.

"Is that good enough for you, Mr. Quartermain? I can amplify my credentials if you aren't satisfied."

Although Quartermain didn't doubt the man's identity, sheer curiosity prompted him to ask for some additional proofs, if only to discover what Maria still remembered about him.

"A hotel in Zermatt where you broke a cut-glass vase, a restaurant in the Rue de l'Estrapade where you asked the waiter what a *gibelotte* of rabbit was, a double puncture on the road to Seville. That's all I know."

Quartermain grinned. "It'll do."

Valdez conducted him to a small private plane, which flew them to Geneva. The lake and the darkening sky had almost merged by the time Quartermain was installed in a hotel overlooking the Quai Wilson.

"That completes my mission," Valdez told him. "You're to remain here in the hotel, though not necessarily in your room. Shall I keep you company for a while, or would you prefer to wait alone?"

Quartermain politely chose the latter, and Valdez took his leave.

Six hours elapsed before someone tapped quietly on the door. The man who entered was as tall as Quartermain, but he radiated a physical strength that made his stature even more impressive. In spite of all the intervening years, Quartermain recognized him at once.

"My name is Javier Coll. Thank you for coming."

He spoke French with a singsong intonation reminiscent of

Perpignan or Narbonne. I'm glad he's on my side, thought Quartermain. He'd kill me if we got into a fight.

"But I'm afraid your journey was a waste of time," Coll went on.

"Where's Maria?"

"Not in Switzerland. I was referring to the boy, Mr. Quartermain. The Germans pulled off a coup tonight, only a few kilometers from here."

Coll had closed the door behind him but was still standing just inside the room with his back to it.

"The man in charge calls himself Golaz-Hueber, though his real name is Gregor Laemmle. It seems odd that a former professor of philosophy from Freiburg University should be leading such a manhunt, but he's a formidable opponent for all that. He tracked Thomas down against all the odds. We rescued the boy and planned to smuggle him into Switzerland, where Maria wanted him handed over to you, but Laemmle beat us to it. I couldn't get anywhere near the French border. There were checkpoints everywhere—I almost got myself arrested."

"So where's the boy now?"

"Back in their hands again. I could do nothing to help him."

Javier Coll leaned back against the doorframe and shut his eyes.

"What about the Swiss police?" asked Quartermain.

"Call them. They'll tell you that no small boy named Thomas Lamiel has crossed the frontier tonight."

"Did you try, at least?" Quartermain regretted the words as soon as he'd uttered them. Coll's dark eyes snapped open and fastened themselves on his face. "I'm sorry," he went on quickly. For the first time since his involvement in the affair, its serious or even tragic nature had become truly apparent to him. "Is there anything I can do?"

The big Spaniard's gaze was unwavering. "She wrote you that letter on her own initiative," he said at length in his slow, rather husky voice.

"Is she accountable to you in any way?"

"No."

"Who are you?"

"Just an old friend."

"Did she tell you what we were to each other?"

"Yes."

Silence fell. Then Quartermain said, "Where is she?"

Coll's reply was preceded by another silence. "There's nothing she wouldn't do to extricate her son from his present predicament."

"Does that include giving herself up?"

"Yes."

"The Maria I knew would never have given up on anything."

"She had no child in those days."

"So where is she, Coll? I'd like to talk with her."

The dark eyes hardened. "To do that you'd have to go to France."

Quartermain had a stroke of intuition. So that's it, he thought, and for some moments he imagined a whole series of Machiavellian maneuvers designed to lure him first to Switzerland and then to France, where he would be used as a hostage because of his membership in the Clan—what else, since he wasn't worth much aside from money? Was she capable of doing such a thing?

"Where in France?"

"The unoccupied zone." Javier Coll stared out of the window. The lake was as black as pitch. "If she'd consulted me about calling you in, I'd have advised her not to. I don't know how much she told you in her letter."

"She told me that Thomas is my son," Quartermain said. It dawned on him that this might be the question he really wanted answered—the question that underlay everything else.

"I know nothing of her private life."

"I'm not obliged to believe you."

"You're not obliged to do anything, Mr. Quartermain. As far as I'm concerned, you can go back to America and forget the whole thing. It was she who asked me to bring you Thomas. I failed and I came to tell you so."

That stung Quartermain. "What'll happen to the boy?"

"They'll take him off to Germany, if they haven't already done so, or more probably to France. They know she'd be more likely to agree to an exchange in France."

"An exchange?"

"Herself for him. It's her they want." The towering figure left the window and walked past Quartermain to the door. "And there's nothing you can do about it. Absolutely nothing."

Coll's hand was already on the doorknob. Although he realized how naive it sounded, Quartermain said, "How was she the last time you saw her?"

Coll paused. "At the end of her rope," he said. "She's a desperate woman."

He went out. Quartermain walked to the window and peered down, waiting for him to emerge from the hotel entrance, but he saw no one. Whether deliberately or not, the man had said just what was required to persuade him to go to France, to intervene, then vanished into the night like a wraith. As if he *could* do anything, except write a check . . . as if he had *ever* done anything except write a check.

He called room service and ordered himself a drink. It was half past midnight by now. A waiter appeared with some whiskey and ice. "A desperate woman." Premeditated or not, the phrase moved him more and more with every passing minute. Coll's veiled animosity toward him might also have been attributable to the Spaniard's own love for Maria or his fierce conviction that he alone—"an old friend"—had the power to protect her.

Which was probably true. He, Quartermain, would be intervening in a years-long struggle of which he knew nothing and for which he was totally unprepared.

Around one in the morning he called the reception desk and asked if there was any way of getting into unoccupied France from Geneva. Yes, he was told. He would have to take a plane and fly to Marseilles via Spain.

Be honest, he told himself, you haven't made up your mind yet. . . .

He'd just fallen asleep when the telephone rang. It was Valdez with a brief suggestion for him: in the event that he decided to visit France and stay at the Hôtel Noailles on the Canebière in Marseilles, someone would make contact with him there.

In the event that . . .

JOACHIM GORTZ SHOOK HIS HEAD AND REPEATED THAT HE DIDN'T agree. He was all for taking the boy to Germany.

"My dear Joachim," Laemmle said, and his smile was as bland as his voice, "but for me you wouldn't even know of the boy's existence. What's more, I'm still in charge of this operation. Responsibility for it was given me by the late lamented Reinhard Heydrich, who can't fail to go down in history as one of the most humane and charitable men to have trodden this earth. Has anyone revoked or countermanded his orders? No? In that case, thank you for returning Thomas to me."

"It wasn't easy. We didn't know exactly where he'd cross the frontier, and—"

"I trust that my own efforts didn't escape your notice, Joachim. We all played our part. Who was waiting for him in Switzerland?"

"The Swiss intercepted a man who was trying to get past one of their checkpoints. They arrested him, in fact, but he put three frontier guards out of commission and escaped. I need hardly add that he was a tall man with two fingers missing from his left hand."

"So he hasn't been recaptured?"

"No, it looks as if he contrived to get out of Switzerland. That Jürgen Hess of yours has failed to track him down."

"He isn't *my* Jürgen Hess, Joachim. I didn't choose him any more than I chose Adolf Hitler, if you get my meaning. Poor Jürgen couldn't find me a cathedral if I sent him to Chartres."

Laemmle bent over the bed. Back in his old room at the Hôtel Trois Dauphins in Grenoble, Thomas was still under the effects of a sedative injection administered before his involuntary recrossing of the Franco-Swiss border. His sleeping face conveyed unalloyed peace of mind. No hint of distress marred the delicate line of his slightly parted lips.

"What now?" asked Gortz.

The little hands were relaxed, the fingers almost fully extended, the sounds of breathing regular. It wouldn't be long before he awoke.

"What now?" Gortz repeated.

"Now she'll come to me," Laemmle replied at length. "His mother, I mean. She'll come to me somehow or other. Why should I have to explain such things to you?" He pulled up an armchair and sat down beside the bed. "She'll come, Joachim, and I'll trap her as one traps a lioness robbed of her young." He was not only fascinated by the boy but filled with pity for himself. "And it'll all go terribly wrong, you mark my words. Be prepared for the worst."

THOMAS GAVE HIS DAMP HAIR A BRISK COMBING AND EMERGED from the bedroom. Yellow Eyes was seated at the table in the sitting room next door. Although he couldn't have failed to hear Thomas moving around for the past hour, he continued to sit there motionless, feigning intense concentration.

Thomas walked over to the door: sure enough, there was a man standing guard in the passage. He went to the window and looked out. Rain was spattering the cold cobblestones. There were three cars parked outside, each with two men in front, and a truck containing still more men. Others could be seen in doorways, at windows, and on the roofs of the buildings opposite.

He'd cried when he woke up, burying his face in the pillow and wanting desperately to die. But it didn't last. The machine had re-started: it hurt if you lost a game, but you forgot everything except the blunders you'd made so as to avoid them the next time around. He shouldn't have put his faith in Uncle Mathieu, nice fellow though he was. He'd known that everything was going too smoothly, too easily— he ought to have made the crossing on his own.

He returned to the table. Yellow Eyes, who was seated in front of the white pieces, had played the first three moves by himself: pawns at Q4 and QB4 and a knight at KB3 for white, pawns at K3 and QN3 and a knight at KB3 for black. He doesn't know how to open the conversation, thought Thomas, so he thinks a game of chess will do the trick.

The machine was functioning well. He gave it an order and it set to work on the chessboard.

"My real name isn't Golaz-Hueber, Thomas, it's Laemmle—Gregor Laemmle. You still say you don't know German?"

Thomas shrugged. "I didn't have time to learn it in Switzerland." He sat down at the table feeling thoroughly ferocious and determined to give the man a hiding, not quickly but nastily, by slow degrees.

Yellow Eyes made his fourth move for white, P–KN3.

"Who's the man with the missing fingers, Thomas?"

"I only know the man with the clubfoot."

He was really concentrating now. Yellow Eyes could talk all he liked, he couldn't care less. He almost moved his bishop to N2 as usual, but decided against it at the last moment. Instead, he tried out an idea he'd been contemplating for at least three years and played it on R3. Yellow Eyes may advance his queen to R4 and his bishop to N2 and then castle, he told himself. That would be the normal thing to do, but then I'd have the advantage. I'd be in a better position, unless . . . No, if he's as good as I think he is, he'll play QN–Q2. . . .

The white Queen's knight duly landed on Q2.

"Did you see those men outside, Thomas?"

Keep talking. . . .

"Yes," said Thomas, "there must be at least fifteen of them."

"Many more than that."

If I play P–B4, he'll be bound to play B–N2 and then castle—if he's really good, and I hope he is. It'll hurt him all the more when I thrash him. . . .

"What about the roof?" Thomas asked.

"There's a whole bunch of them up there," said Yellow Eyes. "I doubt if your Spanish friends have the slightest chance of getting to you."

"What Spanish friends?"

He castled just as I knew he would. Me, I'm still waiting. I can afford to wait—I've got a triple defense. He's good, though, really good. So much the better. . . .

Unbroken silence reigned for fifteen minutes. Thomas had ceased to see his opponent. He'd forgotten the lookouts and Javier, who might be prowling in the vicinity. He'd even forgotten Her, who hadn't been waiting for him on the Swiss side of the wall. He was concentrating like mad now, cheeks flushed, ears deaf to the sounds outside. The machine was running flat out.

"You're a really strong player, Thomas. Was that a deliberate move, I wonder?"

What did he think it was? He's trying to put you off, get under your skin. . . .

The twenty-third move did it: white's position was completely off balance. Thomas and Yellow Eyes had lost the same number of pieces, but that was immaterial.

I could have beaten him twice already, but that would have been too quick. He'd have put it down to luck or a blunder on his part, and I want to beat him hollow. His king's isolated. Even if he spots that, it'll be too late. . . .

"You realize, of course, that your mother will be forced to come out of hiding?"

Don't listen to him!

"She'll have to, Thomas. She knows where I am, so she'll get in touch with me. I'm waiting for her."

"Check," said Thomas.

This is it—he's caught on at last. Has he deliberately allowed me to maneuver him into his present position? No, remember what She always says: Never look at an opponent's eyes, only at his hands. Well, his hands are trembling a little. He's growing edgy. He's caught on at last, but it's too late. He realizes that his game was weighted on the queen's side. He'll move his king out of check, but it's too late. Mate in . . . *No!* I don't want to checkmate him, I want him to resign!

"Check," said Thomas, advancing his knight to KB7.

"I've been waiting for her for a very long time, Thomas, a very long time indeed—years, in fact. Shall I tell you something? I suspect that you have her eyes, and that you're very like her to look at. I suspect that—"

"Check," said Thomas. "My queen."

In a minute he's going to have to take my pawn on Q7 and expect another attack from my queen. . . .

"I suspect that my meeting with your mother will be one of my life's greatest moments, Thomas. I suspect that she's turned you into a fascinating machine."

"Check."

"I may have a solution to your problem, yours and hers. She need only give Herr Gortz what he wants and you can both go free, I give you my word. I can protect you, Thomas."

My rook to QB3. He'll have to counter the threat from there, and another six moves should do it. . . .

"I shall do my utmost to see that nothing happens to you, Thomas."

Another four checks. He's cracking. He'll try defending with his queen, he can't do anything else. Another two moves and I'll counter with my queen—no, with my rook to Q1, and he'll have to withdraw his rook. . . .

"Did you hear what I said about your mother, Thomas?"

Now for my pawns. . . .

"I heard you, monsieur."

"But you don't believe me?"

"It would be very rude of me not to believe you. Your move, monsieur."

Silence. Check, check, check.

I'm slaughtering him. . . .

The telephone rang. Yellow Eyes stared at Thomas before answering it. He said "yes" several times in German, then, "Those weren't the orders I gave you."

He hung up and returned to the table, but he didn't sit down. He gave Thomas another long look.

"You didn't answer my question, Thomas. Did you hear what I said about your mother and yourself?"

"I've put you in check eleven times, monsieur. Do you want to play on?"

"I resign, Thomas."

"In that case, you must lay down your king."

Yellow Eyes complied.

"I've lost—you're too good for me. You played extremely well."

"Perhaps you'll beat me the next time."

"You think I'm capable of beating you, Thomas?"

"No, I'm afraid I don't, monsieur. I apologize for being rude. You resigned after the sixty-third move."

He held the yellow eyed gaze without flinching.

"I thought we might go for a drive, Thomas. A boy your age needs all the fresh air he can get."

"Thank you for the invitation, monsieur," said Thomas. "I'd like that."

QUARTERMAIN WALKED INTO THE U.S. CONSULATE IN MAR-seilles, an offshoot of the embassy to the Vichy French government, and gave his name. Within a remarkably short space of time he was shown into the office of the consul himself, a man named Callaghan.

"Mr. Quartermain?"

"In person."

"Mr. David John Quartermain? Unless I'm much mistaken, you're the nephew of—"

"I am," said Quartermain, "and there are times when I wonder if it's such a good thing."

He spent the next few minutes studying the photo portrait of Franklin D. Roosevelt above Callaghan's desk and replying with his habitual nonchalance to a series of questions about the health and well-being of Uncle Peter and Cousins Larry, James, Emerson, Henry, Michael, Winthrop, and Rodman.

Likewise of the President, with whom Uncle Peter had dined a week earlier.

Likewise of the Secretary of State, who'd recently spent a weekend as the Clan's houseguest.

Quartermain said yes, thanks, he was pretty well himself.

A career diplomat, Callaghan had been an expert on French affairs ever since crossing the Atlantic in the cabin next to Maurice Chevalier's. On top of that, he knew the words of "Auprès de ma blonde" by heart.

"I'm impressed," said Quartermain. "With you around, our national interests are obviously in good hands."

Callaghan inquired the purpose of such a flattering visit. Quartermain replied that he had dropped in *en passant* and would appreciate a little information. For instance, who was this elderly marshal whose picture one saw everywhere, what were the political, geographical, and economic differences between the occupied and unoccupied zones, and could an ordinary U.S. citizen make a little tour of the latter, taking care, of course, not to cross the famous demarcation line?

"You wouldn't have a map of it, I suppose?"

Callaghan made him a present of a Michelin road map on which he carefully penned the demarcation line in black ink. He stressed that no state of war existed between the Vichy government and the United States.

"As an American citizen you're free to come and go as you please, but I wouldn't recommend it. Our relations with Monsieur Laval's government aren't exactly . . ."

Callaghan, who positively insisted on acting as Quartermain's guide, took him to lunch at a restaurant in the Vieux Port. Afterward they repaired to a garage, where he handed over the keys of a Ford with French license plates and a diplomatic badge. It was his own car, he said. "The tank's full and there are three twenty-liter cans in the trunk. Gas is in short supply these days—you could have trouble finding it."

Quartermain thanked him as warmly as courtesy prescribed, pleaded a date with some friends, and got rid of him. He devoted the next half hour to loitering nostalgically outside the restaurant where he and Maria had last dined together.

He returned to the Hôtel Noailles around five o'clock to check that no one had left a message for him. Then he went out again. He walked the length of the Canebière and the neighboring streets, overcome by the strangest sensation. He knew he was extraordinarily ignorant of world affairs, but why had France been bisected in this curious way? The country had always surprised and puzzled him, it was true. He found it delightful and exasperating by turns, and all the more exasperating for being so delightful.

Almost mechanically, he made his way back to the hotel and headed for the bar on the left of the lobby.

He froze.

The girl was standing with her back to him, poised on a pair of very high-heeled shoes. Her figure was slim and graceful, her suit by Chanel, and there was no mistaking the quality of the fur coat draped casually over the back of the chair beside her. Quartermain held his breath for at least five seconds, rooted to the spot by a sudden influx of memories.

Then he caught the look she gave him in the mirror of her powder compact. The eyes were blue, not gray. She turned, walked straight up to him, and kissed him full on the lips.

"Don't say anything," she murmured in English.

She kissed him again, smiling like a woman reunited with the man she loves.

Which was all right with Quartermain, except that he'd never seen her before.

"SHALL WE GO?"

The yellow-eyed man whose name was Gregor Laemmle indicated the open door of the car. Thomas got in. The fair-haired giant he guessed to be Soeft was seated behind the wheel with another man beside him.

"We'd like a breath of country air, Soeft, this young man and I."

A second car preceded them and a third brought up the rear. The convoy crawled along so slowly that the lookouts on either side of the street had no difficulty keeping up.

"Very amusing, Thomas, the way you managed to escape the other day. You're an artful little devil."

"I didn't escape, I got lost."

Laemmle laughingly instructed Soeft in German to follow "the pre-arranged route." This turned out to be a repetition of Thomas's movements when he'd trailed from place to place.

They eventually reached the Place Sainte-Claire and pulled up, not outside the greengrocer's but on the opposite side of the square.

"Would you care for some fruit, Thomas?" Laemmle tapped the driver on the shoulder. "Go and buy us some, Soeft."

There was silence in the car as Soeft got out and walked across the square. Thomas, feeling the yellow eyes upon him, found it terribly hard not to move, to sit there without even turning his head, or only an inch or two, as if quite uninterested in Soeft and the men surrounding the car.

Two minutes went by, then Soeft returned with a bundle wrapped in newspaper. He handed it to Laemmle.

"Apples and nuts," he said in German. "That was all they had."

"Shall we drive on, Thomas?"

"If you like, monsieur."

"Unless you'd prefer to stay put? We could take a stroll around the square. You might care to visit a shop or two, or perhaps you'd sooner have bought the fruit yourself?"

Thomas desperately racked his brains for a reply. At length he said, "I thought we were going for a drive in the country."

Another silence, then, "Drive on, Soeft."

The car left the Place Sainte-Claire, precisely retracing Thomas's steps of three days before: first the café, then the covered way, then the street on the right, then around the block to the carpenter's workshop and, just next door, the cobbler's shop where he'd swapped clothes with Jacques, the youngest of the greengrocer's sons.

"You enjoy riding a bicycle, Thomas?"

"Yes."

"I could buy you one."

"No, thank you, monsieur, I don't like it all that much."

"Drive on, Soeft."

The three cars hadn't really stopped. They twisted and turned until they came to the avenue flanked by the house with the goats in the garden.

"How do goats appeal to you, Thomas?"

"What goats?"

"Any goats—goats in general. I only ask because I caught sight of some in a garden back there. Are you fond of animals?"

"Not German shepherds," said Thomas. If Yellow Eyes thought he could scare him, he had another think coming.

Still crawling along in convoy, the three cars entered a park outside the city walls.

"This'll do, Soeft."

The men on foot caught up and fanned out to form a circular cordon.

"How about that stroll, Thomas? Coming?"

Nearly all the lookouts wore black leather overcoats and kept their hands in their pockets, a sure sign that they were armed. Thomas walked at Laemmle's side, shielded from the rain by his big black umbrella. As they progressed, so the cordon moved too.

"Some nuts, Thomas?"

"No thank you, monsieur."

"An apple, then?"

Thomas raised his head and looked into the yellow eyes. An idea struck him—a crazy idea, he knew, but awfully tempting. Not just yet, though. . . .

"I'd like an apple," he said. "Thank you, monsieur."

Laemmle gave him the umbrella to hold while he carefully selected two apples from the bundle he'd been carrying since they left the car. He polished them thoroughly with a silk handkerchief, handed one to Thomas, and took the umbrella back.

"Were you fond of Monsieur and Madame Allègre when you lived at that house near Sanary?"

Play for time. . . .

"Where's Sanary?"

Play for time, even though you know what's coming. . . .

Thomas got ready to sink his teeth into the apple. All at once he felt frightened, terribly frightened. He pretended to be searching for the best place to bite into.

"How fond of them were you, Thomas? Did you like them as servants or love them like a grandson?"

"I don't know what you mean, monsieur."

"They're dead, Thomas, both of them. They died in agony because we had to persuade them to talk—to tell us all they knew about your mother. Grandma Allègre made a lot of noise before she died. She wasn't afraid, mark you: she screamed and cursed us like the courageous woman she was. Grandpa Allègre died bravely too, though he didn't cry out much—very little, in fact. After we'd killed them one of my men amused himself by cutting off their heads—he even planted the dog's head on the old woman's neck. But you aren't eating your apple, Thomas. Is there something wrong with it?"

Laemmle stroked Thomas's hair, then took his arm and gently propelled him along. The bundle of fruit and nuts had fallen to the rain-sodden ground.

"And now there's the greengrocer, his wife, his three sons, and the goats. You know, of course, that the greengrocer is of Spanish origin? He moved to France some twenty years ago. His wife is French, but he comes from Sóller, a small town on the island of Majorca, just like Javier Coll Planells, a Majorcan architect who was practicing in Barcelona at that time. The Allègres knew him as Javier Jiménez. Javier Coll Planells is a very romantic figure, Thomas. His wife and children were killed in an air raid during the Spanish Civil War. He himself was gravely wounded—indeed, it's a miracle he's still in one piece, or almost: all he lost was a couple of fingers on his left hand. You know *who* he is, Thomas. Do you know *where* he is?"

Thomas did his best, but it was no use: he'd started crying. He disengaged his arm from the hand that was holding it and spurned the shelter of the big black umbrella. Rain mingled with the tears streaming down his cheeks. It would soon be dark, and swaths of gray mist were stealing through the trees. Nobody moved.

"You want me to kill the greengrocer and his family, Thomas? We could swap their heads with those of the goats for variety's sake—there'd be plenty of heads to go around."

Thomas was revisited by the crazy idea. It took root in his mind and refused to budge.

"Listen, Thomas. What happens to the greengrocer and his family depends on you and what you tell your mother. I explained it all while you were beating me at chess, but you didn't appear to be listening. To repeat: I want to see your mother, speak with her, meet her face to face. It'll be quite sufficient for me if she gives Herr Gortz the information he requires, which doesn't interest me in the least. All that interests me is you and your mother. I won't harm either of you. You're an exceptionally intelligent boy, Thomas. I'm sure you can tell when someone's lying to you, especially if you pause for thought as you always do. Your mother has trained you wonderfully well—she's made a little monster of you, but I happen to like little monsters. I'm very fond of you, Thomas, so I'll never do you any harm. I believe you realize that, or you wouldn't have remained with me from Aix onward —you knew I'd protect you. I want your mother, though. Not to kill her, just to talk with her and get to know her. I'm sure she's as exceptional as you are—the kind of woman one doesn't meet twice in a lifetime. I know almost everything about her, but I don't know her face or the sound of her voice."

Thomas could have flung himself down on the ground and wept. He wanted to curl up like a frightened hedgehog, but the feeling gradually subsided. He began to feel a little better.

Why? Because of the Idea.

So it was crazy, but who cared?

He looked first at the apple in his hand, then at the city walls some two hundred yards behind him. Going over to a small heap of twigs, he selected one and tried to break it.

"Please could you help me, monsieur?"

Sure enough, a glint of curiosity appeared in the yellow eyes. With a puzzled half-smile, Laemmle took the twig and broke it in the requisite place.

"Like a slingshot," Thomas explained, making a V in the air with his fingers.

Laemmle was looking amused now. "You want me to remove the leaves as well?"

"If you would, monsieur." Thomas waited. "It's got to have three prongs, two at the top like a V and one pointing downward. Can you snap them off? Not too short at the bottom, please."

"But we don't have any elastic," Laemmle objected with an airy laugh.

"That doesn't matter, it's only a pretend one. Now could you hold it up in front of your face?"

The yellow eyes twinkled at him between the two arms of the V.

"Like this?"

Thomas almost shivered. It was terribly hard not to move at this stage, but that would have been crazier still. Soeft and the others were only yards away. . . .

"Now could you stick it in the ground?" He pointed to a spot midway between them. The end of the twig went in with ease, thanks to all the rain. "That's fine, monsieur. Thanks a lot."

He tried to wedge his apple in the fork but it wouldn't hold; it was too big, too heavy and round, so he trimmed it into shape with his teeth.

This time the apple stayed there.

"Watch carefully, please."

He raised his arm and counted: one, two, three.

Then he lowered it.

The apple exploded into a thousand fragments. Microseconds later, a shot rang out.

Crrrack!

Thomas treated Laemmle to a cold stare.

"That twig was in front of your face just now. If I'd given the signal then you'd have a nasty great hole between your eyes. What's more, you'd be dead."

He experienced a fierce thrill of triumph, but he didn't turn to look at the city walls from which Miquel the Invisible had opened fire.

"My name is Catherine Lamiel," the girl told Quartermain. "All I had to help me recognize you was this snapshot of you she took at Saint Moritz."

She held it out. He recognized it, or recognized himself at least, clowning around on skis with a ridiculous woolen pompom hat pulled down over his eyes. He laughed.

"You're some physiognomist. My own mother wouldn't know me."

"She also described you and told me about your car crash."

"That happened years after we split up. How did she know?"

The girl shrugged. "No idea."

Jesus, so she'd followed his progress at a distance for years. . . .

The bar of the Noailles was too public for a private talk, the girl decided, so they left the hotel and set off down the Canebière. Quartermain studied her in profile. He felt there was something vaguely familiar about her, but she shook her head.

"You've never seen me before, but I think you met my sister Sophie —Maria assumed her identity when she died in 1931. I don't have a car, do you?"

"Why, are we going somewhere?"

"Not right away, but I'd prefer to drive around for a while. We can talk better in a car."

Night was falling, and the two old sea forts guarding the Vieux Port were tinged with pink. It was a fine evening—chilly because of the wind, but fine. They got into the Ford. For want of any precise instructions, Quartermain took the coast road.

"It's a long story, Monsieur Quartermain . . ."

"David."

A long story doomed to end in tragedy if nothing was done: such was the conclusion she came out with a good hour later, as they sat in the car parked a little way off the road to Cassis. Her account had covered everything from the abduction and death of Thomas von Gall to Maria's assumption of his responsibilities, the birth of her son, the raid on the villa near Sanary, the massacre at Aix, and the abortive attempt to smuggle young Thomas into Switzerland.

Catherine Lamiel fell silent. The Ford stood facing the sea. There wasn't another living soul in sight.

"Where is Maria now?"

"I don't have the faintest idea. Maybe here in France, maybe not."

"When did you see her last?"

An almost imperceptible pause. Quartermain was intrigued by the girl's hesitation and made a mental note of it, just as he had noted her mounting agitation and apprehension. Her nerves were clearly on edge.

"In Barcelona the day before yesterday," she said at length. "She'd just received a telegram from Javier Coll informing her that Thomas had been recaptured. She was even against my coming here to meet you—I had to insist. It's hard to believe when you know her, but she's willing to do anything—anything at all, and that includes giving herself up. After all these years, she's finally surrendered."

Once again he detected an odd little break in her voice. He put it down to nervous tension.

"You mean she intends to contact this man Laemmle?"

"She's determined to."

"When?"

"She may well have done so already."

"YES, MADAME, GREGOR LAEMMLE SPEAKING. . . ."

His voice had never been more mellifluous than it was now, as he purred into the telephone. A mere ten feet away, Thomas sat absolutely motionless in an armchair in the sitting room between their sleeping quarters at the Hôtel Trois Dauphins. He held his breath. Although he couldn't hear Her voice, She was somewhere at the other end of the line.

"I quite understand, madame," said Laemmle. "Meeting you at last will be a pleasure and privilege long denied me."

She must now be setting out the conditions governing their exchange. Thomas wished he were dead—if he were, that would solve everything. Ideas flashed through his mind one by one. He contemplated various ways of killing himself right now, while She was on the phone—almost beside him, so to speak. She would know he was dead and grieve for him, naturally, but at least She wouldn't have to talk to Yellow Eyes anymore, wouldn't be soiled by contact with him, wouldn't have to accept his conditions, wouldn't have to take orders from that rotten, yellow-eyed swine. There had to be a way. He studied the problem coldly. He could strangle himself with his scarf, for instance, or swallow his tongue and suffocate, or slit his throat with one of the knives on the table—except that Yellow Eyes had grown wary and replaced them with round-ended knives too blunt to cut a boiled potato. Or he could throw himself out of the window—except that Soeft was watching him like a hawk and would be bound to catch him by the leg, even if he managed to crash through the windowpanes and the shutters beyond them. He yearned to die. . . .

"That's that, then," Laemmle was saying. "So it's all settled, madame. I couldn't be more delighted, believe me."

A brief pause, then:

"But of course, I'll get him for you. Thomas? Would you come and have a word with your mother, please?"

Thomas shut his eyes.

"Thomas?"

He still didn't move, both hands gripping the arms of his chair. If I don't talk to Her, if I refuse to talk, She'll think I'm already dead. She'll think that Yellow Eyes has already killed me, that he's lying and there wouldn't be any point in giving Herself up. She'll get away—they won't be able to catch Her. . . .

"Thomas!"

Laemmle's voice had risen almost to a shout, but he hurriedly moderated it.

"Bring him here, Soeft."

Still with his eyes shut, Thomas was pried away from the chair to which he'd been clinging so desperately. Laemmle's voice was very close now.

"Madame? I suggest for everyone's sake that you persuade the boy to talk to you."

Soeft twisted his arm with an iron hand. It hurt terribly, but no matter. He gritted his teeth. Maybe Soeft would kill him without meaning to. All the better.

Except that someone had clamped the receiver to his ear.

Except that he could hear Her voice.

It was no use trying not to listen, none at all. A tide of tenderness and affection flowed over him, immersing him, drowning him. He burst out crying—he couldn't help it, the urge was too strong. He knew She would hear him, but what could he do? She was speaking, imploring him to say something, because the lives of Barthélémy and his entire family were at stake—because he must trust Her implicitly and let Her do what had to be done.

Because if he maintained his silence, She would really think him dead and, deprived of any further reason for living, die Herself.

It was this last argument, more than any other, that finally breached his defenses and induced him to surrender.

"Maman," he sobbed, though not quite as wildly as before. "Oh, Maman!"

She asked him to recall a specific request he'd made Her one day on the Grande Corniche, and he realized that She wanted some proof of his identity—a guarantee that he wasn't just some small boy whom Laemmle had plucked from the streets of Grenoble and put in his place to fool Her.

"Do you remember what you asked me, *mein Schatz*?"

"I told you I wanted to drive the Hispano."

And then he heard Her crying too. That was the worst thing of all —it sent him into a paroxysm of fury. He struggled, lashed out with his fists and feet, punched the two men as hard as he could. Soeft picked him up, holding him at arm's length, carried him into his room, and locked him in. He promptly hurled himself at the door, pounded on it, kicked it, clawed at it.

"Until the day after tomorrow, then, madame. . . ."

A momentary silence. Then the key turned in the lock and the door swung open.

There was an odd expression in Laemmle's yellow eyes as he gazed at Thomas. Soeft had now been joined by another three men, who must have heard Thomas hammering on the door and hurried in. They all stood motionless, staring at him.

Very deliberately, he spread his thumb and forefinger in the shape of a V and aligned them with Laemmle's face as though taking aim. His voice trembled with rage and hatred.

"I'll kill you, do you hear? I'll kill you!"

Laemmle was still wearing that odd expression. He smiled, but it wasn't a real smile. He nodded.

"I could wish for nothing better, Thomas."

THE FORD HAD BEEN STOPPED AT A POLICE CHECKPOINT ON THE outskirts of Marseilles, but Quartermain's papers and the diplomatic badge on the car—more especially the latter—had proved sufficient to get them past it.

They'd been driving for some minutes before Quartermain spoke.

"I'm certainly no businessman, still less a banker," he said. "If I had to define myself, I'd say I was someone who'd inherited a lot of money and done his best to live it down."

"What an apt sense of humor," Catherine Lamiel said coldly. "It must be pleasant to be able to take everything so lightly."

I'm getting dumber by the minute, thought Quartermain. If I go on this way I'll wind up on a funny farm.

"All I meant was," he said aloud, "a team of lawyers and bankers could have taken over from Maria—relieved her of the responsibility."

"A brilliant idea," she replied with weary sarcasm. "After all, why worry about enemies capable of hounding an old man to death and chopping off a head or two? A good lawyer would have stopped them in their tracks. He'd have threatened to file a suit and they'd have slunk off with their tails between their legs. Why didn't we think of that?"

They were heading toward Aubagne along a valley pervaded by the sickening stench from a soap factory, Quartermain remembered the identification papers she'd produced at the checkpoint.

"What's your real name?"

"The one I gave you. Pagnan was my husband's name."

"Was?"

"He was killed."

"In the war?"

Dumb question.

"Yes."

And yet, why did he get the feeling something was wrong?

"I'm sorry."

"There's no need to be. It wasn't your fault."

Her flippancy was a pose, he could have sworn it, but why should she put on an act for his benefit?

"Where are we really heading for?"

"A house near Toulon."

"Will Maria be there?"

No reply. He studied her out of the corner of his eye. Her face would have been enchanting but for its inherent tension, or rather, its lifelessness.

"Yes or no?"

"She told me she'd decided to do a deal: Thomas's freedom in exchange for herself and the banker's codes in her possession."

"She isn't the type to give herself up without a potential escape route in mind. What is it?"

"I've no idea."

Another silence.

"Why do I get the feeling you're lying to me?"

Her eyelids flickered briefly, that was all, but she did deign to look at him.

"Maria and I have been through some pretty hard times in the past few months."

"Where will the exchange take place?"

"Somewhere between Menton and Marseilles. The German, Laemmle, will be in a car with Thomas and one other man. He'll leave Menton at eight A.M. the day after tomorrow and drive west. Maria will meet him somewhere along the way."

"It's insane."

"She won't be alone—Javier Coll will be with her—and she won't show herself until she's quite satisfied that Laemmle has kept his word and only brought a driver."

They passed through Aubagne. Not long afterward, Quartermain sighted two truckloads of steel-helmeted policemen parked beside a winding road just short of Cuges.

"Gardes Mobiles," Catherine Lamiel explained.

"Which side are they on?"

"Neither. This business doesn't concern them."

"Laemmle kidnaps a child, slaughters any number of people, and it doesn't concern the French police?"

"Maria isn't even his mother, officially. She took every possible precaution. She still can't fathom how Laemmle found the boy."

"She could still go to the police."

"Not all French policemen love the Germans, it's true. Some of them are Gaullists, in fact. Knowing which are which, that's the problem. Laemmle has at least one Toulon policeman working for him."

"Have you met him?"

"I called at the villa on the afternoon of the raid. I was the one who found the bodies and notified the police."

The feeling persisted. She was either lying to him or withholding part of the truth.

"And that's the only reason she didn't call them in? One pro-Nazi policeman?"

"Maria wouldn't hear of it. She doesn't trust anyone."

"Not even you?"

"My sister Sophie was her best friend. I and my family have helped her for years. She could never have borrowed Sophie's identity without our consent and assistance."

They started to descend. A road sign read "Toulon 24." On two occasions, after emerging from a long series of hairpin bends, Quartermain had spotted the headlights of a vehicle that seemed to be keeping pace with them. The stretch behind them at this moment was long and straight. He looked in the rearview mirror but could see nothing. He was getting paranoid, he told himself. Why should anyone be tailing him?

"What if I went to the police and told them the whole story?"

"Thomas stands more of a chance with Laemmle than he would with the ordinary Gestapo. If Maria wants to take that gamble, it's up to her."

Quartermain found this line of argument rather obscure. However, what right had he to question the judgment of a woman who'd been fighting a solitary battle for years on end?

He asked about Javier Coll and was surprised when Catherine Lamiel seemed never to have heard of him. Maria employed Spanish bodyguards, that was all she knew.

"Maria lived in Spain for quite a while. She often came to visit us in Casablanca."

"Us?"

"My parents, my brother, and me."

They were nearing the end of the long descent to Toulon. The question was on the tip of his tongue, but he didn't ask it.

"When we reach the outskirts, take the first turn on the left and keep going straight uphill."

He eventually turned off along an unsurfaced road flanked by pine trees. There was a house at the end.

"Here we are. You can leave the car where it is."

Five small rooms at most.

"We'll have to share a bathroom. That's my bedroom—you can have the other."

Quartermain dumped the two suitcases, Catherine's and the one he'd bought himself at Geneva. The living room's sole attraction was a bay window overlooking Toulon harbor, or so he guessed. They'd dined before leaving Marseilles, and it was already past eleven.

"Hungry?"

"No, thanks. How long do we have to stay here?"

Catherine had already disappeared into her own room. She emerged with some clothes over her arm, evidently in the process of unpacking.

"Maria's rendezvous with Laemmle is fixed for the day after tomorrow. If all goes well I'll deliver the boy to you here."

"And then?"

She stared at him. Her hesitation was very pronounced this time, but she went back into her room and came out with an American passport. He took it from her and opened it. It was made out in the name of Thomas David Quartermain, born September 18, 1931. Place of birth: Clamercy.

"I thought he was born at Lausanne."

"Clamercy is a small town in the north of France. The town hall and records office were completely destroyed. No one on earth could prove he wasn't registered there."

"And you'll bring him here?"

"All being well."

"So I've got over thirty-six hours to kill."

"You've wasted a lot longer than that already. Why worry about a few more hours?"

Her manner was more than edgy, it was tormented, but he put that down to the general situation.

"How long have you known Maria?"

"Years and years." She shook her head. "I know what you're going to ask, but don't."

He just looked at her.

"If you're wondering whether Thomas is your son," she said, "I don't know any more than you do. I was a girl of fourteen when he was born. I honestly don't know."

"Who does?"

"She does. No one else."

GREGOR LAEMMLE'S FIRST CONSCIOUS ACT ON WAKING WAS TO make sure that Thomas was still there, cocooned in blankets on the backseat of the car. He was, though all that could be seen of him was a lock of dark hair and half an inch of forehead.

Very gingerly, so as not to wake the boy, Laemmle draped a blanket around his own shoulders and got out. It was past two A.M., somewhere in the wilds of the Alpes de Provence. In addition to Soeft, Thomas, and the driver, Laemmle had an escort including Jürgen Hess and an impressive array of men and vehicles. Most of the former were cowering inside the latter—not surprisingly, in view of the temperature.

They'd left Grenoble on time, or almost, because Joachim Gortz had turned up just as Laemmle was about to give the order to move out. Looking a trifle morose, Gortz had condemned the idea of an exchange on the road between Menton and Marseilles as rash, to put it mildly, because it left so much to be desired from the security aspect. "You'll risk losing the boy *and* his mother, Gregor. What's more, you have every chance of getting yourself killed."

This irritated Laemmle, who was eager to be off. Had Gortz forgotten what feats of intelligence, Machiavellian cunning, and cold-blooded treachery he, Laemmle, had already performed? Thanks to him, they were at long last on the point of capturing the woman who held all Thomas von Gall's secrets; in other words, of winding up Operation Schädelbohrer to the general satisfaction and greater glory of the Fourth Reich—or was it the Third? He'd never had a head for figures.

"You dislike my idea of a mobile rendezvous on the Côte d'Azur? What's wrong with it? I'm disappointed in you, Joachim. Of course the exchange must take place in the unoccupied zone. Where else in Europe *could* it take place? Do you believe for one moment that she would have consented to cross the demarcation line and venture into territory swarming with your gallant German comrades? Eh? Yes, of course you're right, they're my comrades too, I tend to forget that. Whenever I see those field-gray uniforms tramping around the streets of Paris I feel personally invaded and occupied, but don't tell Adolf, he might take offense. No, seriously, my dear Joachim, can you really see her agreeing to a rendezvous in Paris? Why not Berlin while you're about it?"

Laemmle had pooh-poohed Gortz's misgivings in a daze of elation. He was still savoring the sound of her voice on the phone, the prospect of seeing her in the flesh. He trembled, partly with excitement at the imminence of the triumph he'd looked forward to for so long, but partly with monstrous self-loathing because of what he'd done to the boy. This he found inexplicable. He would have made mincemeat of the greengrocer, plus family and goats, without turning a hair. He would have witnessed—and probably would witness, the way things were going—the almost total annihilation of the human race, or at least of the Europe he loved, with equal equanimity. Yet at the same time he'd wanted to kill Soeft, his alter ego in so many respects, simply for twisting the boy's arm and causing him severe physical pain—so much so that he'd really meant what he said in answer to Thomas's threat to kill him: that he could wish for nothing better. That would not only be in the nature of things; it would prove that Thomas loved him a little. Or would it? Laemmle sometimes wondered if his thought processes weren't a little too complex even for his own devious mind to unravel.

"Some coffee, please, Soeft."

He left the Delage, a stationary speck in the rugged alpine land-scape, and headed for a small slab of rock far enough away from the car to be out of earshot of the boy in case he woke. Beckoning to Jürgen Hess to join him on this makeshift bench, he sat down and sipped some coffee from his vacuum flask. He drew the blanket a fraction tighter around him, wishing he'd brought two. His poor little feet were like blocks of ice.

"Well, Jürgen, bring me up to date on world affairs. How goes the war?" Hess was always more amenable if encouraged to talk about the things that interested him most.

Hess needed no second bidding. He launched into an account of the Russian offensive that was desperately trying to relieve Moscow now that the victorious armies of the Third Reich—So it *is* the Third, thought Laemmle—were in sight of the Kremlin's gilded onion domes.

"I take it for granted," said Laemmle, "that this pathetic effort on the part of the red muzhiks, inferior beings that they are, will be mercilessly crushed?"

"It's only a matter of hours," Hess assured him.

"I'm overjoyed to hear that, Jürgen. What stirring times we live in! Anything else?"

Laemmle listened patiently to another battlefront communiqué, but with only half an ear. The boy had waked up, possibly roused from his slumbers by their prolonged immobility, possibly alerted by the animal instinct for danger that seemed to be part of his makeup. Whatever the reason, Laemmle caught sight of a thin, pale face behind the misted glass of the car window. Let's get to the point, he thought. I don't want to spend all night here.

"Tell me, Jürgen, what's this army of yours?"

He pointed to the line of cars and their sinister-looking occupants.

"I've got fifty-four men at my disposal," said Hess, "but I can get more—our tame policeman in Toulon has promised to lend me a few of his friends. We can have two hundred men on the ground by the day after tomorrow."

Laemmle buried his nose in his mug of very sweet coffee.

"No, Jürgen."

Hess stiffened and squared his shoulders. "We can't afford to let her get away," he said.

"What's my rank?"

"Oberführer," Hess conceded.

"And yours?"

"Hauptsturmführer."

Laemmle could recall Heydrich's conferring some kind of rank on him, but he couldn't for the life of him remember which. What was more, he seemed to have been promoted in the interim. If he didn't watch out he would wake up one morning and find himself Führer plain and simple, and tens of millions of little Jürgen Hesses would weep with rapture at the very sight of him. It might be an amusing experience, but it didn't appeal to him in the least. He would have to yell into a microphone, and his throat had always been delicate.

"That makes me your superior officer, Jürgen, and I'm giving you an order. While I think of it, why not pay a flying visit to Moscow?

How long would it take you to capture the place? Two days? Sure you wouldn't like to see some action on the Russian front?"

Hess glared at him, but Laemmle stared him down. What was it they said in the army? Ah, yes . . .

"Atten-shun! Now, Hess, here are my orders. You'll get rid of all but thirty-five of these men, let's say. You'll take eight of them, drive to Menton, and assemble them in front of the casino by eight-fifteen A.M. At eight-fifteen you'll set off along the coast road to Marseilles. Maintain a speed of sixty kilometers an hour. Not fifty-nine or sixty-one: sixty precisely. If it becomes necessary to amend these instructions in the meantime, I'll call you. By the way, what name are you using these days?"

"Marcel Magny."

"You don't have the face for a Marcel. A Marcel would wear a peaked cap and baggy trousers and tour the local dance halls on a bicycle, but never mind. I'll call you at the first bar on the right along the street facing the casino—the Avenue de Verdun, I think it is. Wait there. If I haven't called you by eight-fourteen, you leave a minute later on the dot."

"What about the rest of the men?"

"Thirty-five plus one, that's you, makes thirty-six. Less nine, makes twenty-seven. Send eight of them to Nice . . ."

Laemmle went on to dispatch another eight to Toulon. The remaining eleven, split up into three groups, were to hold themselves in readiness at Cannes, Fréjus, and some appropriate point on the main road halfway between Hyères and Sainte-Maxime.

"But they're not to intervene without a direct order from me, Hess. As for you, unless you're keen to conquer the Russian Empire single-handed, down to the last Siberian snowflake, you'll obey my instructions to the letter."

Laemmle smiled. He obviously couldn't rule out a potential excess of zeal on Hess's part, nor did he, and it worried him intensely. He ought to have removed his crazy underling from the scene long ago, but he wouldn't have known whom else to turn to under present circumstances. Heydrich's recent death at the hands of a Czech terrorist had deprived him of his principal backer. He was operating in isolation now, his sole asset being that Hess hadn't realized it yet—at least, he hoped not.

He studied Hess's face but could detect little save a kind of sullen obstinacy. All would be well, he told himself. Wherever she turned up

—and he guessed it would be somewhere between Toulon and Marseilles—Soeft and his ten or fifteen men would be on the spot before Hess and his private army. All would be well. . . .

"Carry on, Hess."

He watched Hess's convoy move off, then tipped the dregs in his mug onto the frozen ground. He had a vague desire to be sick, not on account of the atrocious coffee but because the elation he'd felt at Grenoble, while conversing with Gortz, had been succeeded by another of his "moods." He'd recently noted with clinical detachment that each such mood was more severe than its predecessor. There had been a time, many years ago, when he'd hoped to be able to hate someone or something more than he hated himself, but that hope had long been extinct.

He walked back to the Delage and got in again, wrapping himself in two extra blankets.

"Not asleep, Thomas?"

No reply.

"Drive on, Soeft."

It was quite miraculous that he should have managed to sleep at all since leaving Grenoble, and he didn't expect to repeat the miracle now. The Delage drove on through the moonlight. Looking down at the sleeping boy, Laemmle temporarily yielded to the feelings of tenderness that were, for him, such an utter novelty.

And, he suspected, such an invitation to disaster.

DAWN HAD BROKEN, AND THOMAS WAS BREAKFASTING BESIDE the road in beautiful but deserted surroundings. Just before they stopped he'd seen a road sign marked Saint-Paul-de-Vence. He had no idea of their whereabouts. The scenery reminded him a little of Provence, so maybe that was where they were.

"Tell me about your invisible sniper, Thomas."

Thomas went on eating. He was hungry. So far, he felt a whole lot better than he'd felt last night. He must trust Her to do what had to be done—that was what She'd said on the phone. She wouldn't let Herself be captured by old Yellow Eyes—she must have worked out a plan, a trick of some kind. Silly of him not to have thought of that before. All he had to do was wait and keep cool.

"You aren't very talkative, Thomas."

It was at least ten minutes since the white Delage had pulled off the road. Soeft and the driver had got out and unloaded a portable stove, together with some milk, Swiss chocolate (it said so on the packet), rolls, butter, and German jam. The driver even spread a cloth on the bonnet, which was still warm, and Thomas and Yellow Eyes had got out too. Now they were having breakfast. It was like a regular picnic.

"That friend of yours who shoots so well, Thomas—you honestly think he's managed to follow us? Personally, I doubt it very much. I think he's lost track of us. We've been twisting and turning all night long. Think for a moment. He's on a motorbike, that's my guess, but we've kept a special lookout for motorbikes and failed to spot a single one. Where can he be, I wonder? Still in Grenoble?"

Thomas peered around as if genuinely looking for Miquel. He wasn't, of course, and for two reasons: first because he felt positive that Miquel wasn't far away, and second because it would have been pointless. You saw Miquel only if he wanted to be seen, not otherwise.

"Shall I butter you another roll, Thomas?"

"Yes, please, monsieur."

They were the first words he'd spoken since telling Yellow Eyes that he was going to kill him.

"I'm becoming quite an expert at buttering rolls, you've got to admit."

"Yes, monsieur, you do it very well now."

. . . that he was going to kill him. He'd meant it, too. He even knew how—not when, but how. When the Three Musketeers wanted Milady killed—though Milady was a woman, Athos's wife—they'd got the executioner of Lille to do it for them. Well, he'd got someone like that—he'd got Miquel. Yesterday in the park . . .

"Might I have a little more chocolate, monsieur?"

. . . yesterday in the park he could have got Miquel to blow the man's head off, but that would have been stupid. If he had, Hess would be guarding him now, and Hess was another kettle of fish altogether. No, the apple was a far better idea. What a scare it had given old Yellow Eyes! He knew Miquel existed now, of course, but that didn't matter. It was all to the good, in fact. . . .

"I want to talk to you, Thomas."

Why was Yellow Eyes speaking so softly, as if he didn't want Soeft and the driver to overhear—as if he were on the same side? He must think him, Thomas, an utter fool. He was scared by the knowledge that he, Thomas, could have him killed at any moment, that was all. . . .

"Tomorrow, my boy, you and I have an appointment with your mother. She dictated how and where we were to meet, and I accepted her conditions. As long as no one else interferes, all will be well. I've done my best—I wanted you to know that. Do you believe me?"

Don't answer right away, Thomas told himself. He hung his head and screwed up his face as though he were on the verge of tears.

"Thomas?" The voice was strangely gentle. "I hope you believe me, Thomas. If I don't do what I'm in the process of doing, others will, and you and your mother . . ."

Yellow Eyes left the sentence unfinished. This time it was his turn to look tearful. Thomas stared at him as he took the proffered roll and butter. I'll tell Miquel not to kill him straight off, he thought, but very slowly, so it hurts for ages and ages. . . .

"I never got my chocolate, monsieur," he said.

"I'D SOONER YOU DIDN'T GO OUTSIDE," SAID CATHERINE LAMIEL. "Your clothes look too foreign—someone would spot you."

"Who, for instance?"

"Oh, no one in particular." She summoned up a smile. "Sorry, I'm rather jumpy this morning." The bedroom door closed behind her.

It must have been around nine o'clock, and sunlight was streaming in through the bay window overlooking Toulon harbor. Quartermain stood there sipping his second cup of coffee. He hadn't slept much. At some stage during the night he'd got out of bed and paced around the kitchen and living room until the tiled floors chilled his feet, as they very soon did. He almost knocked on Catherine's door but resisted the temptation. Quartermain had always been shy with women—in fact he could scarcely recall an occasion when he'd gone to bed with one on his own initiative. It was usually they who made the first move.

Hearing the door open behind him, he turned in time to see Catherine emerge wearing a plain, almost dowdy coat and a hat perched on her upswept hair. Her cork-soled platform shoes were equally devoid of chic. She said she had to go out and wasn't sure if she'd be back for lunch.

"There's some bread and a cold chicken."

"That'll do for me. What if the phone rings?"

"Nobody knows I'm here. Let it ring."

She set off down the dirt road. Just before the pine trees hid her from view she half-turned her head. The almost imperceptible movement struck Quartermain as odd. Had she been afraid he might be following her? Perhaps. Disorientation, that was his trouble. He'd not only switched continents; he was involved in an affair of which everyone had told him as little as possible, and precious little at that.

He explored the house for a while. There were few personal touches apart from some books on a shelf and three or four framed photographs. They showed Catherine in the company of sundry unknowns, the face that recurred most often being that of a man of thirty or thereabouts, broad-shouldered and quite good-looking, with slicked-down hair and a ready smile. Her husband, perhaps.

Quartermain opened some drawers with the perverse pleasure of a burglar violating someone's private domain. He found some more photographs, most of them in a cloth-bound album. They depicted a much younger Catherine, almost a child, together with a teenager who was almost certainly her sister Sophie. The backgrounds were North African, and he recognized the Hotel Mamounia at Marrakech.

There was no picture of Maria anywhere, but then she'd never let him take a snap of her in the old days.

He ended by searching Catherine's room, though not before he'd locked the front door, salving his conscience with the near certainty that she'd lied to him nonstop, if only by omission, ever since their meeting in Marseilles.

Nothing.

Nothing either, discounting a change of clothes, in the suitcase she'd brought with her last night. Apart, perhaps, from a 1:200,000 road map of the area between Toulon and the Italian frontier. It was folded so that only one section was visible: the coastal region between Hyères and Fréyjus, with the Corniche des Maures and the big peninsula between Sainte-Maxime and Cavalaire at its central point. If that was a clue, thought Quartermain, it was a pretty slim one.

One hour went by, then another. He spent them seated beside the bay window and regretting the lack of binoculars that prevented him from taking a closer look at the huge vessels in the harbor. It seemed bizarre that so many warships should be riding peacefully at anchor there when the country they belonged to had lost the war.

Impatience overcame him. He was seized with an urge to take the air, go outside, do anything rather than remain cooped up in this cramped little house, but he couldn't hope to pass unnoticed in Toulon wearing his London-tailored overcoat. Then he remembered seeing a raincoat in one of the cupboards. It was a bit too short for him, but at least it would make him look a trifle more French.

He got into the car.

It was precisely because he was on the lookout for Catherine Lamiel that he noticed the movement in his rearview mirror. Just as he turned out onto the main road, he thought he saw a man dart across it. A minute later, while driving down into Toulon, his suspicions seemed to be confirmed: two men were following in a black Citroën saloon.

He parked at random in a small square with a bandstand in the middle. The two men did likewise, though their manner was so natural that he wondered, yet again, if he was suffering from a touch of paranoia. His doubts were reinforced when he failed to spot them following him through the narrow streets. It so happened that his haphazard route took him past a shop selling marine equipment of all kinds. Going inside, he bought the most powerful pair of binoculars in stock. The proprietor raised his eyebrows at the fat wad of hundred-and thousand-franc notes he produced when paying for his new acquisition. He really was doing all he could to make himself conspicuous, he thought ruefully. Wrapping paper was unobtainable, he was informed, so he bought a small canvas satchel to accommodate the binoculars.

"American?" the proprietor asked in an undertone as he handed Quartermain his change. Quartermain hesitated for a moment, then nodded. "Well done," said the man. "Bravo!"

Still wondering why he deserved to be congratulated on his nationality, Quartermain made his way down to the naval dockyard but didn't dare take out his binoculars for fear of being arrested as a spy. He strolled back to the city center. Feeling hungry, he sought out a restaurant in a broad boulevard lined with cafés and cinemas. The waiter demanded some food coupons. He hadn't any, he said—he was a foreigner. How did a man get to eat in France if he wasn't French? The waiter's shrug conveyed that that was Quartermain's problem, not his. He gave up and walked out. A few yards farther along the boulevard it happened again: someone caught up to him and fell into step beside him.

"I heard you in the restaurant just now, monsieur. Are you by any chance an American?"

"Is it a criminal offense?"

The man flung his arms around him and, despite their difference in height, enfolded him in a warm embrace.

"I wanted to congratulate you!"

"Really?" Quartermain said uncertainly.

"You're looking for a place to eat? Go to Mado's, Place Puget, and ask for Mado herself. Coupons or no coupons, she'll feed you like a king."

The man gave him two or three more slaps on the back and walked off. Bewildered by his new popularity, Quartermain asked a woman the way to Place Puget. She beamed when she heard his accent and pointed him in the right direction. His bewilderment grew. He couldn't remember his accent arousing such enthusiasm the last time he'd passed through Toulon.

Mado was five feet tall and almost as much around the waist. "*Venez*," she said. "Come with me."

She towed him into her restaurant kitchen, cleared one corner of the cluttered table, and sat him down.

"I have a *filet mignon* and some *ratatouille niçoise*, and I make you some *frites*, okay?"

"Sounds great." Quartermain thought he must be dreaming.

"*Je parle anglais*, I speak English very good. How often you can come here?"

"Every day, if you insist."

She gave him a friendly dig in the ribs. "*Agent secret*, eh? Here, have some *ratatouille*."

All was explained when she told him that an Anglo-American expeditionary force had landed in North Africa during the small hours of that very day, November 8, 1942.

Calm and unflappable by nature though he was, Quartermain would have expressed some surprise if his mouth hadn't been so full. He wasn't unduly perturbed by this latest development, however, and saw no reason why it should affect his personal business. He finished his meal and attempted to pay, but Mado brushed his money aside. While trying to find his way back to the car he came to a big square dominated by the Préfecture Maritime. Just as he reached it, a convoy of gleaming cars adorned with pennants drove off. They were filled with German officers. His premonition of danger suddenly grew. He asked the way to the nearest post office and telephoned the U.S. Consulate in

Marseilles. Callaghan was out, but a man named Pillsbury took the call.

"Mr. Quartermain? Bob Callaghan was hoping you'd get in touch. I've a message for you. Diplomatic relations between Washington and Vichy will be broken off in the next few hours. All American diplomatic personnel have been instructed to leave French territory for Spain. Bob suggests a choice of three rendezvous. Either be here at the consulate by nine A.M. tomorrow or find your way to the Hôtel Cheval Blanc, Place des Arènes, in Nîmes. Alternatively, drive straight to the frontier post at Boulou. Bob insists on your coming with us."

Quartermain decided not to ask the obvious question—what would happen to him if he remained in France?—because it was irrelevant. He wasn't leaving. He had to wait till Maria's situation was resolved. Besides, he should still have time to wrap the whole thing up. The rendezvous, if it came off at all, would take place less than twenty-four hours from now. He would still have time to get to Nîmes or, in a pinch, the frontier post.

He found his way back to the Ford. The suspect Citroën and its occupants had disappeared. Obviously, he must have been imagining things.

The house in the hills was deserted, nor was there any sign that Catherine Lamiel had returned in his absence. He would long remember those hours he spent at the bay window overlooking Toulon harbor, reading or idly playing with his new binoculars. He also conducted an intermittent argument with himself, though not in any very serious way. He already knew what he was going to do.

Catherine turned up toward seven, well after nightfall. Hearing the sound of a car, he slipped outside in time to see her emerge from a black Peugeot parked some distance from the Ford and facing the main road. He hurried back into the house, attributing his childish suspicions, as he thought of them, to an overdose of the Simenon thriller he'd been reading to pass the time. Catherine came in and removed her coat. The strain in her face was, if anything, even more pronounced than before. "I'll make us something to eat," she said.

Quartermain followed her into the kitchen. "Can I help?" he asked. He expected her to comment on the fact that he hadn't touched his lunch, but she was so preoccupied with whatever was troubling her that she didn't seem to notice.

"Are you sure there's nothing you'd like to tell me?"

"Quite sure."

She mechanically made them an omelette without thinking to look in the oven, where the cold roast chicken still languished. They ate in silence. He helped her to clear the table and, for the first time in his life, prepared to do the washing up as well. She told him not to bother —a cleaning woman would be coming tomorrow. Everything about her conveyed nervous exhaustion.

"So it's all settled?" she said. "You'll wait here till I bring the boy?"

He nodded. She lingered in front of the bay window for a while, then asked him to excuse her: she would have to be up very early in the morning.

"Just pretend I'm not here," he told her.

He himself retired to bed soon afterward, leaving his door open. He woke up once at around two o'clock but managed to get off to sleep again after half an hour, most of which he devoted to pondering the obvious question: Catherine must have heard about the Allied landing in North Africa, so why hadn't she mentioned it to him?

Because she found it secondary to the matter in hand?

That was one possible answer, but he could think of another. If he hadn't made up his mind already, it would have tipped the scales.

Quartermain waited for her to leave the house next morning—she set off on foot, but he slipped out in time to see her drive away in the Peugeot. Then he spent two or three minutes getting his things together. He pocketed his passport and all the money he had with him: some forty-five thousand U.S. dollars, a little over thirty thousand Swiss francs, and about two hundred thousand French francs acquired while he was in Geneva.

Although the traffic was light at this hour, a few cars were already on the road. Quartermain drove for several hundred yards without spotting anything suspicious behind him, and his strange nocturnal misgivings began to subside.

That was when his rearview mirror picked up the black Citroën with two men inside. It drove past, thirty seconds after he'd rounded a bend, made a sharp right down a side street, screeched to a halt, and jumped out.

It was the same car and the same men. He just had time to register the surprise and dismay on their faces as they passed the mouth of the street: their quarry had unaccountably disappeared. The Citroën drove slowly on, then picked up speed, presumably because the driver thought he'd been outdistanced.

Quartermain got back behind the wheel and made a three-point turn. Instead of taking the Marseilles road he headed east toward Hyères and Fréjus. He'd decided to stake everything on the folded road map in Catherine Lamiel's suitcase.

It was eight-fifteen.

HAVING LEFT MENTON AT EIGHT O'CLOCK PRECISELY, THE WHITE Delage had covered sixty-three kilometers in—Gregor Laemmle consulted his watch for the umpteenth time—fifty-nine minutes. It was now entering Cannes.

"We're slightly ahead of schedule, Soeft. We can pull over and wait —no, not here, a little farther on. The Croisette will do. Stop outside the Majestic."

Besides, thought Laemmle, I want to make sure that Jürgen Hess has obeyed my orders instead of flouting them with his usual effrontery. I wouldn't put it past him to follow me at a distance of half a kilometer instead of the fifteen I stipulated—given, of course, that sixty kilometers an hour really is the equivalent of one kilometer per minute. As I was saying only yesterday, I'm a dunce at mathematics. . . .

He was seated in the back of the Delage with Thomas on his left. The door handle on Thomas's side had been removed at Soeft's suggestion. Soeft himself, who was driving, had armed himself as heavily as some Mexican general preparing to issue a *pronunciamento*. He had a monstrous automatic on his lap, a submachine gun concealed beneath a newspaper on the seat beside him, and a third gun propped against the door on his left. He also had a few grenades tucked away somewhere. Laemmle smiled to himself. If he'd let him, Soeft would have brought a field gun along too. He was a conscientious youngster.

The Delage drove along the Croisette and pulled up outside the Majestic. The doorman advanced, but Laemmle waved him away with a smile. He was feeling distinctly odd, almost feverish, not that this was surprising in someone eager for the sight of a silver-and-black Hispano-Suiza with a woman at the wheel—a woman he'd been hunting for four long years.

"Keep the engine running, Soeft."

He turned and looked back along the dead-straight, palm-fringed expanse of the Croisette, half expecting to catch sight of Jürgen Hess and his three dozen thugs, but no.

It wasn't just a strange, vivid dream, he told himself. His quest was at an end, or would be in the next few hours. Either he would see her at the wheel of the Hispano, or she would have found some means of killing him before young Soeft could kill her son. If he survived he would see her face to face, a prospect made daunting by the despair that ensues when any dream comes true.

He was still surveying the Croisette through the rear window. A gasogene van had pulled up some three hundred yards behind them, but the driver got out and delivered a package to a nearby villa. Could Jürgen Hess really have obeyed orders? If so, it was a miracle.

"Three minutes," Soeft announced.

Laemmle abandoned his surveillance—it was giving him a neck ache in any case—and transferred his attention to Thomas. The boy was sitting motionless, both hands resting limply on his bare knees, veiled eyes gazing out to sea.

"Let's go, Soeft."

The Delage drove off again. Fifty-two minutes later it had passed through Saint-Aygulf and was less than twenty kilometers from Sainte-Maxime. They had now reached one of the points on their route where Laemmle thought something might happen. The Maures massif seemed a better bet than that of Esterel because its secondary roads would present the Hispano with a wider choice of escape routes. Having mistakenly expected her to materialize in Menton itself, however, he now thought her more likely to favor the stretch between Toulon and Marseilles—in other words, the vicinity of Sanary.

She *would* materialize—of that he was absolutely convinced—at some stage or other in their leisurely progress along the coast from the Italian frontier to Marseilles. It was a route that offered hundreds of possible means of access and escape, not excluding the sea itself.

Although he didn't dare turn to look, a sidelong glance revealed that Thomas's demeanor had undergone a change: the tension in the boy's small frame was mounting with every minute that passed.

She'll come—he knows that too. . . .

IT WAS ALMOST TEN O'CLOCK WHEN QUARTERMAIN FINALLY caught up with Catherine Lamiel.

He'd driven like a madman since leaving Toulon. He shot through Hyères like a bullet and did the same through the next built-up area—La Lande or La Londe, he was traveling too fast to be sure of the name. Then he came to a fork. If the Peugeot had passed this way, would it have gone left or right? For no immediately discernible reason, he chose the road on the right.

And that was how he found himself driving along the Corniche des Maures, his head filled with thoughts of Maria. Of course! They'd driven this way together in the old days—he remembered now, and his motive in taking the right-hand road seemed less obscure.

At one point a small road ran off to the left, presumably in the direction of the Dom Forest. He glanced at it mechanically for a split second, no more. Another split second later he braked so violently that the Ford slewed halfway across the road. He applied the handbrake, left the engine running and the driver's door open, and ran back up the road for thirty or forty yards.

It was Catherine Lamiel's black Peugeot.

The car was parked in the driveway of a white villa. Quartermain started up the side road, his long strides slightly hampered by the limp that never left him. Conjured forth by a November sun more worthy of May, summery scents of vegetation rose to his nostrils as he picked his way through some undergrowth on the far side of the road until he was within a few yards of the house. Peering through the foliage, he saw Catherine in the company of a tall blond man. The man was addressing her with cold self-assurance. "You're coming," was all Quartermain could catch. "You have no choice."

Then she turned and he saw the look of anguish on her face. Car doors slammed. Quartermain sprinted through the pine trees and down a path that led back to the road. He jumped into the Ford and drove off. Three or four hundred yards farther on he found what he was looking for: a narrow track with a convenient bend in it. Once around the corner and out of sight, he glanced at the map. Catherine and her unknown companion could go either of two ways: up into the mountains along a minor road dotted with hairpin bends, or past him along the road he'd just left. In the latter case, he would hear them and be able to follow. But why, he wondered, did he have such a premonition of disaster?

Two minutes passed in silence. They must have taken the mountain road or, worse still, turned right in the direction of Hyères. Quartermain slammed the Ford into reverse.

Then he stopped dead: a car was coming at last. It passed the mouth of the track, heading east. He counted up to twenty before backing out onto the road and setting off in pursuit.

A minute later he was cursing himself for being too quick off the mark. Rounding a bend, he remained in full view of the Peugeot for several seconds—long enough for him to see that Catherine Lamiel and the fair-haired man were not alone in the car. Another two men had joined them.

They passed through Le Rayol, then Cavalaire. Quartermain reduced his speed still further because the slightly less tortuous road compelled him to put more distance between himself and the Peugeot.

Just as he emerged from the village of La Croix-Valmer he overtook a big truck laden with balks of timber. It was a little after nine o'clock by now. The sky was blue and cloudless, but a stiff sea breeze had sprung up.

Three kilometers farther on—the timber truck seemed to have put on speed and was keeping pace with the Ford some three or four hundred yards behind—Quartermain sighted a road junction. According to the signpost, Saint-Tropez was to the right, Cogolin to the left, Sainte-Maxime and Fréjus straight on.

That was when another two trucks entered his field of vision. Both were identically laden with big, rough-hewn balks of timber. Somehow, he didn't like the look of them. Anxiety was steadily eroding his veneer of calm, though his overriding emotion was one of curiosity.

The Peugeot reached the road junction and drove straight on. Quartermain did likewise. Moments later, screened by a convenient reed hedge, he skidded to a halt: the Peugeot had pulled up only half a kilometer ahead. Also stationary but facing in the opposite direction, having evidently driven west to meet it, were another three cars. The terrain was sparsely wooded and almost flat.

Quartermain opened the driver's door and got out. He leveled his binoculars. Ten or fifteen men had gathered around the tall, fair-haired man, who appeared to be their leader. He was addressing them with his hands thrust into the pockets of his double-breasted jacket, and something about his pose conveyed contempt.

The binoculars swung left and picked up Catherine Lamiel. She was leaning against the Peugeot a few yards away, weeping.

Quartermain lowered the glasses, then put them to his eyes again and scanned the surrounding country. The map indicated that there was another road junction a kilometer farther on, but he couldn't see it; his view was obstructed by rows of cypresses and more reed hedges. The three trucks behind him had reached the first road junction and pulled up too. There were two men in each, and each was guarding one exit.

A fourth truck could be seen on the left, a fifth on the road beyond the fair-haired man and his companions. Quartermain made out at least two more inland, far up the mountainside and almost concealed by the trees in which they were lurking.

There might even be others. More by luck than judgment, he'd discovered the site of the ambush.

Another look at the map, and it all seemed as clear as daylight: the invisible road junction was that of Saint-Pons-les-Mûres, which gave access to a whole network of minor roads and forest tracks traversing the heavily wooded Maures massif. Anyone wishing to sneak in or out could choose between eight or ten different routes. Equally, anyone could use this network of escape routes as a feint designed to camouflage a getaway by sea.

Just a minute!

He moved a few yards to his right and leveled the binoculars again, this time at the little bay marked on the map as Saint-Tropez: sure enough, there was a motor launch moored there. It looked quite capable of twenty or thirty knots, a speed that would whisk it safely out to sea and out of sight in a matter of minutes.

He hadn't the vaguest idea what to do next. Nor, for that matter, was he entirely convinced that he wanted to do anything at all.

He trained his binoculars on the wooded slopes inland, which rose to an altitude of a thousand or twelve hundred feet. Although they looked pretty impenetrable, he decided to head for higher ground, possibly just above Grimaud or a little farther north.

He got into the car, made a U-turn with a minimum of noise, and drove back to the road junction. There he turned right for Cogolin.

No reaction from the men in the stationary truck: they simply watched him go by.

He took the next turning on the right.

It was nine fifty-three A.M.

"THERE'S THAT VAN AGAIN," SAID SOEFT.

Turning to look, Laemmle recognized the vehicle he'd already seen on the Croisette and dismissed as harmless. The driver seemed to be alone, but there might be other men concealed in the back. If so, who were they—Jürgen Hess's scouts operating in contravention of his orders, or a reconnaissance patrol working for the other side—*her* side?

The Delage had just passed through Saint-Maxime and was heading southwest with the sea on its left and some heavily wooded hills on its right. According to the map on Laemmle's knees the next two villages they came to would be Beauvallon and Saint-Pons-les-Mûres. After that they would have to turn left toward La Croix-Valmer and the Corniche des Maures, of which Laemmle preserved fond memories. Twenty years ago he'd spent a whole sun-drenched month at Le Rayol with his beloved mother.

He was still studying the map and fondly reminiscing when a sudden discharge of adrenaline made his hands tremble. Surely he wasn't frightened? That would be a quite unprecedented phenomenon.

No, of course not. It must be something else—the thrill of the chase, for instance, stimulated by a sensation unwonted in someone as rational as himself: an awareness of his ignorance of what he actually expected to happen. In short, he yearned for her to appear while simultaneously hoping that she would remain a myth.

And then he realized what had made his pulses race: *this* was where she would appear!

Why hadn't he spotted it before? The map made it look so patently obvious: an ideal combination of roads flanked on one side by the funnel-shaped bay of Saint-Tropez, and on the other by a densely wooded wilderness offering countless potential escape routes.

He looked up just as Soeft pulled out to overtake a big truck laden with balks of timber.

"Keep your eyes peeled, Soeft. We're getting warm."

The Delage passed the truck and pulled in again. A sprinkling of houses showed up in the distance. Laemmle was feeling positively feverish.

Seconds ticked by.

"Behind us!" Soeft shouted suddenly, reaching for his submachine gun one-handed.

Laemmle swung around in his seat again: two hundred yards to their rear the enormous truck had smashed into the gasogene van and crushed it like an eggshell.

"I knew it! This is the place!"

The road veered inland. They were approaching an intersection.

"Look at that!" cried Soeft.

It was a spectacle whose impact transcended all Laemmle's dreams of the past four years. He could hardly believe his eyes.

But there it was—there couldn't be another like it. Standing motionless at the mouth of a narrow forest track, its paintwork glinting in the sunlight, the silver-and-black Hispano presented a picture of majestic, almost vibrant beauty: a jewel in a casket of green leaves and ocher soil.

QUARTERMAIN WAS DRIVING VERY SLOWLY NOW. HE DIDN'T know his exact whereabouts, only that he was somewhere above Saint-Pons. The road forked after another hundred yards. The sign pointing to the left said Plan-de-la-Tour, the other—

He braked hard. A man had appeared from behind a bank, rifle in hand.

Five seconds dragged by. Then the man raised the muzzle of his gun and beckoned.

Quartermain inched forward. When the Ford was level with him, the man peered closely at the diplomatic badge and waved it on.

Quartermain bore left. He could see in his rearview mirror that a second man, also armed, had joined the first and was staring after him. Moments later a bend hid the pair from view.

He drove on, then pulled up again, feeling very unsure of himself. It all seemed so pointless.

He got out and made his way back to the junction on foot. There was no one in sight now. He surveyed the other road, which was completely unsurfaced. It was less of a road than a mule track, but tire marks could be detected in the reddish soil. They were still fresh.

There's really no point, he told himself. You'll get yourself picked off like a rabbit for no good reason, and they'll go crazy back in the States, trying to figure out how you managed to bite the dust in France in November 1942. . . .

After a final look around to satisfy himself that the sentries had disappeared, he set off along the mule track. The gradient steadily increased as it wound downhill through the forest, which was pervaded by a dreamlike hush. One bend succeeded another until, quite suddenly, the trees gave way to an explosion of light and color.

Quartermain froze. The coastal plain below him, only another three or four hairpin bends farther down the track, presented a stupefying spectacle.

A white car, a Delage, was just pulling up. Facing it only twenty or thirty yards away, a silver-and-black Hispano-Suiza glittered in the brilliant sunlight.

But it wasn't merely this confrontation between two cars that rooted Quartermain to the spot; he was fascinated and appalled to see, closing in from all directions, a small army of men and vehicles. There was something reptilian about their slow advance, and their point of convergence was the Hispano-Suiza.

The binoculars showed a dark-haired woman, visible only from behind, seated at the wheel with her gloved hands resting on it. Beside her sat a man with a hawklike profile and a gun in each of his big, gnarled fists. There was no mistaking Javier Coll.

Quartermain transferred his attention to the Delage. The driver, a man with a girlish face, he ignored. It was his first glimpse of the boy that fascinated him. Even as he watched, the small figure stiffened and gripped the back of the front seat with both hands, the gray eyes widened to their fullest extent, the mouth opened.

He heard the cry and shivered, but its effect was that of a prearranged signal. Scattered shots rang out.

"I'M GETTING OUT, SOEFT," LAEMMLE HAD STARTED TO SAY. HIS hand was on the door handle even before the Delage came to a halt.

He depressed it, noticing out of the corner of his eye that Soeft had turned and put the muzzle of his automatic to Thomas's forehead.

"Don't kill the boy—not unless I get it first."

The door swung open and he got out. Mechanically smoothing away any creases his cream suit might have acquired during the trip, he walked toward the Hispano with a sense of exaltation which nothing could be allowed to disrupt. He did so like a spectator of his own actions. He saw himself—and would see himself again and again in time to come—walking toward the car with his hands outspread to show that he was unarmed. He'd already covered ten or fifteen of the yards that separated him from the woman whose face he could only vaguely discern through the glare of the sunlight on the windscreen, but which he'd so often pictured in his waking dreams. He couldn't fail to hear the commotion around him—the metallic sound of car doors slamming, the hurried footsteps, the shouts, the words of command—nor could he fail to realize what they meant: Jürgen Hess had not only disobeyed orders, he'd known where the rendezvous would take place.

I'll have Jürgen's hide for this, he told himself, but he shelved the thought in the same way as he relegated certain other things to the fringe of his consciousness: Thomas's first cry, the first shots, and the steadily converging figures of a rabble whom he quickly identified as the thugs whose services he'd refused in the mountains two nights ago.

The truth was, he thought he could still control the situation. It was a simple matter of logic: however stupid and fanatical Hess might be, not even he would forget that the woman must be taken alive. No, it was time to nip this foolishness in the bud.

He was nearly there now. He smiled, already formulating the exquisitely courteous phrase he intended to utter by way of introduction. He took another step, as serenely indifferent to a bullet that whistled past his head as he was to one that kicked up the dust at his feet.

Another step. He rounded the front of the car with a connoisseur's appreciation of its beauty, half tempted to pause and run his fingers over the solid silver stork adorning the radiator cap, but his main attention was reserved for the woman. He gazed at what he could see of her, telling himself that it was understandable that she should shake her head in such a despairing way. Not even the fact that the man beside her had begun to fire back, not even the bullets that were perforating the bodywork, shattering the headlights, puncturing the tires, holing the radiator, starring the windows—none of these seemed of any consequence. He was going to stop this ridiculous fusillade.

Level with the massive fender and a foot from the silver-trimmed casing that held the spare wheel, he smiled. His big moment had come at last.

Except that the car was moving, backing away from him, gaining speed.

"Come back!" he shouted, scenting disaster. "I'm your only hope!"

The worst of it was, she must think he'd broken his word to her.

He started to run, something he hadn't done for thirty-five years at least, but the Hispano, even traveling in reverse and hampered by its shredded tires, outpaced him with ease. Twenty yards away it slewed around and prepared to head for the hills.

Before it could complete its turn, men loomed up on the left. One of them threw something. Instantly, the Hispano became a sunburst of huge yellow flames and stopped dead. From it, transformed into a living torch, leaped a figure terrifying in its seemingly superhuman stature. Bellowing like a wild beast, a gun blazing in each of his massive fists, Javier Coll withstood the hail of bullets that pierced his body in a dozen places—withstood it for an eternity of seconds before he fell. Laemmle bellowed too, in a paroxysm of fear and despair that took him back forty years to the nocturnal terrors of his childhood, but he overcame it sufficiently to run to the driver's door and grasp the hot metal handle. He wrenched at it vainly, weeping as he watched the woman inside turn to look at him with terrible deliberation, her big gray eyes dilated: a woman being consumed alive by the flames that were licking at her shoulders and dancing in her dark hair.

QUARTERMAIN HAD STARTED TO RUN TOWARD THE TWO CARS, which seemed to be quietly communing in the midst of the pandemonium around them, but he was deflected by a near collision with two or three men who were also hurrying to the scene. He swerved like the college football player he'd once been, oblivious of the pain in his hip, sprinted across one farm track, then another, and found himself within fifty yards of the inferno which the Hispano-Suiza had become.

He stood transfixed with horror as the scene etched itself into his mind: the blazing car, the motionless figure in the driver's seat, the human torch that could only be Javier Coll, still firing back as the bullets thudded into him. He also saw a little sandy-haired man in a cream linen suit and a panama hat—a man whose face he was never to forget. Yelling inaudibly, his voice drowned by the roar of the flames and the rattle of gunfire, he was dancing like a dervish beside one of the Hispano's doors.

Quartermain saw other men too, one in particular, who caught sight of him, raised his gun, took aim . . .

And fell over sideways with blood oozing from a hole in his temple. Quartermain stared uncomprehendingly for a moment. Then he set off again, only to see another man draw a bead on him and collapse.

And another.

Someone was carving out a route for him. Someone, somewhere, was eliminating anyone who barred his path. He broke into a run again, trying to locate this unknown friend as he went.

That last shot had definitely come from the left, from the hills.

He ran toward the white Delage. The engine was ticking over and the man with the girlish face was still at the wheel, one hand gripping the boy by the collar, the other holding an automatic pistol to his head.

As he neared the car, Quartermain caught sight of a leather-jacketed figure perched on a rock some two hundred yards beyond it—a young man, from the look of him, armed with a sniper's rifle. He was gesturing urgently with the barrel of the gun, waving Quartermain toward the Delage.

As if in a dream, Quartermain headed for the driver's door. The man with the girlish face turned out to have a downy mustache. He said, "Come any closer and I'll kill the boy."

"Try it," Quartermain retorted in a kind of trance, "and I'll murder you." And he thrust his hand through the open window and seized the barrel of the gun, not even aware that it had swiveled in his direction. He wrenched at the driver's arm, heard a shot but disregarded it, and hauled the man bodily out of the window, gun and all. Hitting out in a paroxysm of rage and hatred, he knocked the man senseless and heaved the inert body aside like a sack of potatoes.

He glanced at the sniper on the rock and saw him make another gesture. Its meaning was unmistakable.

Quartermain got in behind the wheel and gunned the engine. The car shot forward and headed straight for the nearest armed men. One-handed, he grabbed the submachine gun lying on the seat beside him, propped the barrel on the window ledge, and squeezed the trigger, experiencing a fierce thrill of pleasure at the sight of bullet-riddled bodies dropping in his path. Figures leaped aside as he raced through a swirling cloud of black smoke heavy with the stench of charred flesh. Still accelerating, the Delage tore up the mule track with dirt and stones spurting from its tires.

Quartermain's trancelike state persisted until he reached the fork. He pulled up and got out.

"Come on, kid, let's go!"

There was absolutely no reaction. The boy might have been deaf. His eyes were fixed and staring like those of a corpse. Quartermain opened the rear door and picked him up. He was quite unscathed.

The Ford was still where Quartermain had left it. He sprinted the hundred yards with the boy in his arms, laid him on the rear seat, and set off again.

For the next few minutes he drove as he'd never driven before. The road was tortuous but completely deserted. He didn't even glance at the map. His one burning desire was to get away as fast as possible, and in any case, he was far too preoccupied with keeping the car on the road as it skidded round one hairpin bend after another. An eternity later he reached the main Aix-Fréjus road. For some reason which he couldn't explain, he turned neither right nor left. He waited until the road was empty in both directions, then crossed it and drove north at the same reckless speed.

His head began to clear a little. Easy, he told himself, you'll kill yourself this way. What's more important, you'll kill the boy.

He slowed and glanced over his shoulder. The boy was still stretched out on the rear seat. He had the disarticulated look of a puppet, and his eyes remained as wide and unseeing as ever.

Accelerating again, Quartermain drove through a series of remote and scattered villages with names like Lorgues, Salernes, and Aups. Still instinctively heading north, he came to an arid, mountainous district that might have been situated in the heart of Arizona or New Mexico.

They were utterly alone.

Quartermain took the precaution of stopping the car at the foot of a small gorge. He switched off the ignition and allowed the car to coast for the last few yards until it fetched up against a boulder and stopped. A sudden tremor ran through him. He got out, feeling sick as a dog.

"Oh, my God . . ."

He vomited interminably, then walked back to the car. The boy hadn't stirred.

"Thomas?"

Not an eyelid flickered.

He opened the rear door and got in beside him.

"Thomas?"

He shook the boy gently and tried to sit him up, but the little body was quite inert. He took him in his arms, rested the head against his chest, and something inside him snapped: tears rolled down his cheeks.

He wept for a minute, maybe longer. Finally he said, "I'm an American, Thomas. My name is David Quartermain. I loved your mother very much."

QUARTERMAIN WAS NO LONGER ACTING ON IMPULSE BUT CARRYING out a preconceived plan. His mind was made up: he would head for Nîmes on the off chance that the American diplomatic mission was still there, as it should be if that was where all the personnel from Marseilles, Vichy, and elsewhere had assembled. If not, he would catch up with them at the Spanish frontier.

He clung to this objective for want of anything better. He'd temporarily debated whether to make for Switzerland, but he didn't fancy his chances of getting across the demarcation line, and anyway, he doubted if the Swiss frontier was all that easy to negotiate.

The fact was, he hadn't entirely recovered his composure. He was still reeling under the impact of the recent horror and experiencing the same sensation of incredulity. Had he really seen Maria burn to death? Again and again, with the stubborn inexorability of waves breaking on a shore, he was revisited by mental pictures of which the secondary, imaginary ones were more harrowing than those that derived from what he'd actually seen: fire consuming Maria's white belly and breasts, flames licking her rosy lips, penetrating her mouth, incinerating her tongue . . .

Stop it, he told himself. Anyway, what about *him*?

The boy had shut his eyes at last and seemed to be asleep—Quartermain hoped so, at least. Several times while driving through villages he'd wondered whether to stop and buy a sedative or knock at the door of some doctor who could have given the youngster something to alleviate his state of shock, but he'd ended up doing nothing. Rightly or wrongly, he'd thought it more important to show himself as little as possible and stay ahead of the pursuers who must surely be after him by now.

"Thomas?"

Still no response, but the boy had sat up very straight, both hands flat on the seat on either side of him. His eyes were shut, his cheeks waxen.

Quartermain's watch said one-thirty. He was maintaining his breakneck speed, but the tank was almost empty and he would have to stop soon. He blessed Callaghan for being prudent enough to carry three spare cans of gas. The road was deserted. According to the map they were somewhere between the Durance and a small mountain range called the Luberon. That put them about a hundred kilometers from Nîmes. He slowed to a stop.

"I'm going to fill up the tank," he explained.

He was just refilling the tank when he heard the rear door open and the boy got out. The sight of him jolted Quartermain: the gray eyes were so reminiscent of Maria's that he couldn't suppress a start.

"Don't go too far," Quartermain said gently. "We'll be leaving right away."

Thomas jumped the ditch and walked off across a field of blackened stubble. Quartermain, anxious not to spill a drop of his precious gas, found the boy's calm demeanor reassuring. Fifteen or twenty seconds elapsed before he looked up again.

"Thomas!"

But Thomas had broken into a run. He was already a hundred yards away and sprinting like a hare.

"Thomas!"

Quartermain nearly dropped the can. Instead, he deposited it carefully on the ground. He wasn't really worried yet, feeling sure that Thomas would run until he dropped—run the misery out of his system and give free rein to his tears. He jumped the ditch himself and set off in pursuit. The distance between them had now increased to a hundred and fifty yards. At first he simply kept up with the boy, still expecting him to stop after a couple of minutes, but he was wrong. The gap between them widened, even though the small, bare-legged figure was scrambling up a slope. Quartermain put on speed, forgetting or trying to forget the pain in his hip. He pounded across the remaining stretch of stubble and started up the hill, putting as much of his weight as possible on his left leg. Immediately beyond the summit lay a hollow planted with vines, but the slope beyond that was rugged and steeper than the first. Thomas had already reached it and was climbing from rock to rock.

He's getting away, Quartermain thought despairingly. If anything happens to him I'll never forgive myself. . . .

He spurted through the vines and hurled himself at the second slope. The gap seemed to have narrowed to fifty yards, but this was an illusion created by the lay of the land. He wasn't gaining on the boy at all.

"Thomas!"

The pain in his hip was almost paralyzing. He'd torn a fingernail on a spur of rock, halfway down to the quick, and despite the icy wind he was sweating under his coat, but he continued to climb, foot by foot, mesmerized by the sheer vitality of the figure ahead of him.

He really planned to escape, he thought. He tricked me quite deliberately. . . .

Then Quartermain gained a slight advantage. Confronted by a rocky shelf the height of a man, Thomas made several time-wasting attempts to scale it before giving up and going the long way around. Quartermain hauled himself up it with ease and so gained fifteen yards. He opened his mouth to give another shout, but he couldn't muster sufficient breath. Thomas had disappeared over the crest by now. Without warning, a shower of stones came hurtling through the air. One of them struck Quartermain on the shoulder.

The short downhill slope beyond the crest ended in a line of trees. Thomas sprinted through them and out the other side. Everything depended on the next few seconds. Beyond the trees was a big, grassy plain bounded on the left by a dense strip of forest. Quartermain spotted the danger at once. If Thomas took refuge in that, he would be gone for good.

Miraculously, he ran straight on across the almost level expanse of grass, where the man's superior strength began to tell.

Forty yards, then thirty . . .

The boy didn't turn to look; he continued to run with his head tucked in, making little use of his arms.

Fifteen yards . . .

He tripped and fell. Before he could get up, Quartermain made a dive and grabbed one ankle. The other foot dealt him a terrible kick in the face, but he didn't let go; on the contrary, he consolidated his position by getting a grip on Thomas's knee. The boy struggled with almost preternatural ferocity, wide-eyed and open-mouthed but mute. Then, heralded by a shrill cry like that of a rabbit caught in a trap, the storm broke in earnest. More cries followed—cries of pent-up fury— and the little body twisted frantically this way and that. Quartermain strove to hold his kicking, punching, biting captive at arm's length for safety's sake. Thomas broke free for a moment, but Quartermain re-captured him with another headlong dive. This time he pinned him down by main force and kept him spread-eagled.

"Easy, Thomas, easy! Please! Hush," he cooed. "Quiet. Hush."

It was unbelievable: the boy refused to give up. He continued to struggle, yelling at the top of his voice. He even arched his body and succeeded in lifting Quartermain's hundred and eighty pounds off the ground a couple of times.

And then, at long last, it was over. He subsided into limp, panting resignation.

Quartermain got his breath back before rising cautiously to his feet. The boy's thin cheeks were chalky white, his lips dappled with blood where he'd bitten them, his eyes enormous.

"Are you okay?" Quartermain asked.

The only response was an expressionless stare. Quartermain stood there, poised to thwart another attempt at escape. His chest wasn't heaving so painfully now.

"Let's go back to the car."

He gripped the boy's coat collar and hauled him to his feet. They made their way back to the road.

"Got it out of your system?"

He reinstalled Thomas on the backseat.

"What do you want me to tell you? That I'm just as sick as you are? I loved her too, Thomas. I . . ."

Oh, hell, what *could* one say to an eleven-year-old boy in his posi-tion? Quartermain felt another pang of pity. He shook his head, at a loss for words.

He got in behind the wheel and reached for the ignition. Then he remembered that he hadn't finished refueling. He filled the tank up with the second can, watching Thomas out of the corner of his eye. The boy didn't stir. He got in again and drove off.

"Hating me is a waste of time and energy, *mon petit*. I'm on your side. I'll say it again: I'm an American—my name's David Quartermain. I'm only here in France because your mother wrote and asked me to come . . ."

He broke off. He'd been going to add, ". . . And because she told me that you're my son," but the words seemed ludicrously out of place.

"She asked me to take care of you if anything happened to her," he said, and promptly cursed himself for using such a stupid turn of phrase. He accelerated.

"It's more than likely they're after you. Me too, probably. They must know who I am." Feeling more at ease in this context, he went on, "Look, Thomas, my French isn't too bad, but anyone can tell from my accent that I'm a foreigner. I may need you. Those men will recapture you unless you help me."

He glanced around quickly, almost shyly, and was somehow relieved to see that the boy had shut his eyes again. Perhaps he hadn't heard a word.

They crossed the Durance half an hour later and headed due west along a road marked in yellow on the map. Thomas hadn't moved, but he wasn't asleep either, even though his eyes were still shut. He sat there in his original position, bolt upright, with his hands flat on the seat and his head back. The worst seemed to be over.

"We're going to Nîmes. Here's the address just in case: Hôtel Cheval Blanc, Place des Arènes. If I'm not with you, ask for a Mr. Callaghan, Robert Callaghan. He's a diplomat, if you know what that means. He works for the U.S. embassy."

They were on the outskirts of Arles.

"Give him this."

Quartermain fumbled in his pocket and produced the passport Catherine Lamiel had given him, made out in the name of Thomas David Quartermain. He reached back and balanced it on the boy's bare knees.

No reaction. They drove through the old town in silence for a while.

"That passport says you're my son, Thomas. Your mother got it for you specially."

Still no reaction.

Quartermain hesitated. He didn't feel hungry himself, but the boy would have to eat sooner or later. In the end, however, he decided against stopping. He felt instinctively that the sooner they crossed the Rhône, that formidable barrier between them and the west, the better it would be. Besides, Nîmes was only another twenty minutes' drive, and that, he felt sure, was where they would find the U.S. diplomatic corps.

Having come to this decision, he headed for the Rhône bridge. He approached it gingerly, half expecting to find it blocked by a dozen cars or a horde of armed men, but he saw nothing.

They were across. He ran up through the gears and flattened his foot. That was when the boy spoke for the first time since his mother had died.

"They saw us," he said.

"Who did?"

"Two men in a black Citroën. They saw us, and one of them ran off to telephone."

QUARTERMAIN DROVE ANOTHER FOUR OR FIVE KILOMETERS WITH one eye on his rearview mirror.

"Are you sure?"

Silence.

"There's no one behind us, Thomas."

He pulled up and turned off the engine. The surrounding country-side was absolutely flat and very sparsely wooded. He glanced around. Thomas had made no move to open the passport and was sitting there with his clenched fists resting on his knees, seemingly in the throes of some desperate inner conflict.

"Are you all right?"

If only the boy would cry, at least. . . .

"You're really positive you saw those men?"

A nod.

He would have to make do with that. For a few seconds he debated the possibility of returning to Arles. The plain truth was, he didn't know what to do. His strongest temptation was to put his foot down and drive like a maniac to Nîmes, now only twenty-odd kilometers away. He reached for the ignition.

Then he stopped and forced himself to think again. What about Catherine Lamiel? Rightly or wrongly, he was convinced that she'd betrayed Maria and divulged the location of the rendezvous to Laemmle. It didn't matter if he was mistaken; that was what he be-lieved. Why? Because Catherine knew him and had seen his car, because she or Laemmle knew what he planned to do, because he'd been followed at Toulon and kept under constant surveillance, because his call to that guy at the consulate, Fosbury or whatever his name was, had probably been intercepted. If his worst fears were justified, Laemmle must realize that he was heading for Nîmes and the protection of the diplomatic mission bound for Spain.

Except that he wouldn't bet a quarter on the mission's ability to protect him. Face facts, he told himself: he'd killed people. He might even be accused of having kidnapped the boy. Who would come forward to defend him against such a charge? Thomas's mother was dead, and so was that Spaniard he'd have been damned glad to have on his side at this moment.

Then another unpleasant possibility occurred to him. What if Laemmle had taken it into his head to notify the French police? That would be the last straw, but why not?

"Thomas?"

He suddenly noticed that the boy was shaking all over. His teeth were clenched, his muscles as taut as a bowstring, and his muffled cries resembled nothing that ever issued from a human throat.

"Easy, Thomas. *Calme-toi.*"

It was ten minutes before the paroxysm gave way to a torpor almost more alarming than the violence that had preceded it. The boy's body was icy cold, and so rigid that Quartermain had difficulty in laying him down flat on the backseat. He found some rugs in the trunk and wrapped him up in them. The moans of a beast in agony had given way to plaintive sobs and whimpers. Quartermain perched on the edge of the seat and tried, with a clumsiness that exasperated him, to allay the boy's terrible grief.

The body in his arms gradually relaxed, the whimpers became intermittent and were replaced by pathetic little sounds so soft as to be almost inaudible. To Quartermain's infinite relief, the boy was falling asleep. He felt utterly disarmed and thoroughly ashamed of himself for not having stopped to look for a doctor. Once more he considered turning back to Arles, but he dismissed the idea. Nîmes, then. What was he waiting for?

Thomas seemed to be sound asleep at last. Quartermain made a pillow of his overcoat and very gingerly inserted it beneath the boy's head. It wasn't just pity he felt, but a kind of tenderness as well. What did he know of children, after all? He had a couple of dozen nephews and nieces, sure, but he belonged to a family that employed platoons of nurses and governesses to look after them. He couldn't think of a single time when he'd had to cope with a child in distress.

He got in behind the wheel and studied the map again. The main road from Arles to Nîmes was marked in red, but he'd been careful to avoid it. He now believed that "they" would be waiting for him at Nîmes. Even though it was founded solely on what a grief-stricken little boy thought he'd seen at Arles and on some vague and ill-defined suspicions of his own, his certainty was absolute.

Quartermain set the car in motion, driving slowly so as not to wake his passenger. It was almost three o'clock in the afternoon. Apart from the fact that he'd wasted an awful lot of time, he hoped to hell he knew what he was doing.

He drove into Bellegarde as if venturing into a minefield, but the place was as quiet as the grave. Nothing conflicted with the peaceful impression he'd gained through his binoculars before entering the little town.

"I've nothing to sell you," the grocer told him.

Quartermain deposited five one-hundred-franc notes on the counter.

"I'm Swedish," he said. He was pretty sure the Swedes were still neutral. Not knowing how a Swede would speak French, he did his best to adopt a vaguely Germanic accent.

The grocer eyed Quartermain and the banknotes in turn. Finally he disappeared into his back room and returned with a sausage and some crackers in a big tin box.

"Another five hundred for the crackers," he said.

"Any chocolate?" asked Quartermain.

"In wartime, monsieur? You must be joking."

"Well, then." Quartermain peeled off another thousand francs. "I'll take anything you've got."

"Some hard-boiled eggs?"

"Fine, and some salt to go with them."

Half a dozen hard-boiled eggs joined the sausage and the tin of biscuits in the satchel Quartermain had bought for his binoculars.

"I'll make you a present of the salt," said the grocer, without a ghost of a smile.

Quartermain had turned to go when the man spoke again.

"An American," he said, "a tall American who walks with a slight limp, traveling in an American car with a gray-eyed boy of ten or so . . ."

Quartermain stopped dead, then swung around.

"Are you talking to me?"

The grocer nodded.

"They passed through here around midday, a whole bunch of them in half a dozen cars, heading for Nîmes. Some more came past a bit later—similar types. There was a tall, fair-haired fellow in the first group—spoke perfect French but wasn't a Frenchman. He had a word with the local gendarmes."

Quartermain pulled out his wad of French money again.

"The police station is on the outskirts, right alongside the road to Nîmes, but the gendarmes only have bicycles. Anyone who wanted to avoid them would take the Saint-Gilles road. That's on the right as you leave here."

Quartermain proffered some more banknotes. The grocer glanced at them impassively and shook his head.

"I sell groceries, that's all," he said.

"Thanks for the salt," said Quartermain.

"Don't mention it. It's good for business to make a gesture occasionally."

THOMAS OPENED HIS EYES AND SAW THAT THE CAR HAD STOPPED again, not on a long, straight road where anyone could see it, but in a narrow lane flanked by reed hedges. He sat up. There was no one else in the car, and the driver's door was open.

He looked through the rear window. The lane itself was deserted, but a glance through the windscreen showed him that the American was standing in the reeds some yards away. His arms were raised, and Thomas wondered for a moment what he could be up to. Then he moved a little and the binoculars he was holding came into view.

Thomas made a strenuous effort to concentrate on the American, on the car, on the lane, on the time when they'd driven through Arles and crossed the bridge, passing the two lookouts in the black Citroën. No other memories were permitted.

He knew that She was dead—yes, but that was precisely why he had to make this supreme mental effort. It was like walking along a very narrow plank that swayed beneath your feet and threatened to pitch you headlong into a black and bottomless pit. The American was part of that plank; so was the problem of how to prevent Yellow Eyes from recapturing him; so, also, were details such as the car, the reeds, his reason for being in this car with a stranger, their reason for lurking here in the twilight, and their present whereabouts.

He must concentrate very hard on these things and set the wheels turning in his head—and, above all, refrain from looking over the edge of the plank.

Be careful, it was all coming back!

An enormous Thing was looming up, coming closer, compressing his skull until it hurt terribly. He felt himself toppling into the pit. He could smell burning, see the color of the flames devouring Her in the Hispano. Javier Coll was in flames too, cut in half by a hail of bullets, and still She didn't get out. She sank forward with her hair on fire, and he, Thomas, was screaming, screaming at the top of his voice . . .

"Thomas, Thomas!"

The American was pinning him down very tightly. He wasn't in the car anymore. All he could see was a grassy bank and an expanse of water.

"Let me up, please."

"All right now?"

"Yes."

"You had another of your . . . fits. Sure you're okay?"

"If I say I'm all right, I'm all right."

The American got off him, but slowly, as if he was scared of something.

"You tried to throw yourself into the canal, Thomas. You won't try it again, will you?"

"No, it's over."

The American stood up. His hand was bleeding.

"You bit me."

"I'm sorry."

The American grinned. "This morning you nearly got my ear. You didn't miss this time."

"I apologize," said Thomas. "I'll be very careful from now on. I'm sorry I bit you, really I am."

"We won't talk about it anymore," said the American. "Can you get up?"

Thomas sat up, then got to his feet. His wrists and arms were sore, probably because the American had been gripping them so hard. He looked awfully tall—almost as tall as Javier, but less . . .

Don't think of Javier!

"Shall we go back to the car?"

"Yes."

They set off side by side. The car was two hundred yards or more along the lane. At one point the American stooped to retrieve his binoculars, which were lying on the ground. It was almost dark now.

"Where are we?"

"In the Camargue, according to my map, twenty kilometers from a place called Nîmes."

"Why are we hiding?"

"Because some men are out looking for us."

"Laemmle's men," Thomas said quickly.

"Whose?"

"Yellow Eyes said his name was Gregor Laemmle. He's the one that's looking for us."

They got into the car.

"Like something to eat?"

"I'm not hungry."

"You should eat something all the same."

Thomas ate a hard-boiled egg, then another, then a banana. He drank some lemonade. The wheels were turning smoothly now.

"Did you get these things from a shop?"

"Where else?" The American smiled. "There aren't many bananas growing on the trees around here. Come to that, there aren't many trees."

Thomas eyed him quizzically. "I don't know your name," he said.

"Quartermain—David Quartermain."

"Excuse me, it's very rude to forget a person's name. I remember now. But the shopkeeper will remember you too and say he saw you."

"Maybe, but we had to eat sometime."

"How far away are they, the men who are looking for us?"

"I saw a couple of them go by not long ago, out on the main road."

"Perhaps they've already spotted us," said Thomas. "They may be sneaking up behind us right now."

He didn't look around as he spoke. His aim had been to see if the American was nervous, but all he did was scare himself. He looked round sharply, feeling rather foolish.

The American didn't budge—he didn't even glance at the rearview mirror. Instead, he produced a road map and spread it out on his lap. The machine in Thomas's head registered this display of imperturbability.

"I think," said the American, "that they'll be waiting for us at Nîmes."

And he went on to explain that the embassy and consular staff from Vichy and Marseilles were quitting France for Spain. He also said he didn't think the ambassador and the consul would be much help to them. His theory was that Yellow Eyes—Laemmle—had stationed his men along a line running from a place called Aigues-Mortes, which was beside the sea, to Nîmes or even farther north.

"They didn't have time to take up their positions along the Rhône, which would have been the best place to catch us. All they were able to do, I guess, was post lookouts at each likely crossing point. Those men you spotted were two of them."

"So they know we crossed the river."

"Exactly."

"And the shopkeeper will tell them what time we passed through his town."

"They'll find out sooner or later, that's for sure."

"And now they'll be wondering why we haven't got to Nîmes yet, when we should have been there ages ago."

The American smiled. "You're right. They must be starting to ask themselves that question."

"Which is why they're looking for us between Nîmes and the Rhône. . . ."

Thomas pondered the problem. It was a pretty simple one, and there were only five possible solutions: lie low in the Camargue and wait for the hue and cry to die down; head straight for Spain and penetrate the cordon by driving through Nîmes or bypassing it, though it was easier to hide in a town than in the country; turn back east toward Marseilles and Toulon; stow away aboard a boat bound for Africa; or, last but not least, head north.

"I think we should head north between their cordon and the Rhône," he said. "May I get out, monsieur?"

"No one's stopping you."

"I won't run away."

"You've no need to—you're free to go anytime. I only chase after you when I'm afraid you're going to hurt yourself."

"I want to pee, that's all."

He got out and did so. It gave him time to think things over. The American had thought things over too, that was obvious. He agreed that going north was best, Thomas could tell, because it was the last thing Yellow Eyes would expect them to do.

He got back into the car. The American was still studying his map by the minuscule light from the glove compartment. He was neither dark nor fair but somewhere in between. He had big, bony hands with very long fingers, and he reminded Thomas of the hero in a cowboy film he'd once seen—Gary Cooper, that was it. The American certainly wasn't Gary Cooper—his face wasn't lean enough—but he definitely resembled him.

"What are we going to do, monsieur?"

"I don't know yet, Thomas, I'm still thinking. Which reminds me: what about that man in a leather jacket who saved my life—the one who's so good with a rifle? Do you know where he is now?"

"No."

"Do you know who he is?"

"I don't know that either."

Silence. Thomas could tell that the American knew he was lying.

"But you'd know how to get in touch with him?"

"How could I, monsieur, if I don't even know who he is?"

Thomas was sitting with his hands resting on the seat on either side of him, the way a well-brought-up boy was supposed to sit, but his hands defied him. They slid between his knees and clasped each other till the knuckles went white. He was fighting another battle with the Thing that lurked in his head. It almost beat him, but not quite. All he wanted to do was cry.

The night was so dark that they could barely see the reeds beside them. The American started the car and crawled along the lane without switching on his headlights. At length he came to an asphalt road and stopped. The engine turned over very quietly, almost inaudibly, while he explained what they were going to do—if Thomas agreed, of course.

"Can I rely on you, Thomas?"

"I'll watch out, monsieur. It won't happen again."

"I'm counting on you."

"All right."

A moment later the American switched on his headlights and turned left on to the asphalt road. He hadn't driven far when they saw a road sign reading: "Nîmes 7."

GREGOR LAEMMLE REACHED MARSEILLES EARLY ON THE AFTER-
noon of November 9, 1942, having recovered from his initial shock
and abandoned the idea of fleeing to Italy and taking refuge in his villa
at Fiesole. He booked into the Noailles—quite coincidentally, the hotel where Quartermain had stayed before him. From then on, events
went their own sweet way. Progress reports flooded in from the members of Soeft's team, though "progress" was a misnomer, because all
such reports proved negative. They did, however, disclose that Jürgen
Hess and his gang were following a trail identical to their own.

Laemmle received his first definite lead in midafternoon:
Quartermain's Ford had been sighted while crossing the Rhône, a
strong indication that the American was heading for Nîmes. He'd sent
for Quartermain's file, which included some photographs taken with
Catherine Lamiel at Marseilles and a brief memorandum based on
information extracted from her. Laemmle studied the American's face
closely in an attempt to detect resemblances to the boy. He failed to
see any, but that proved nothing. He had, he told himself, a very
suspicious mind.

Soeft turned up at dinnertime, nursing a badly bruised face and
bearing two fresh items of news. The first was that Jürgen Hess had
stationed his forces at Nîmes, the second that Hess's friend in the
Toulon police had precipitated a general alert by claiming that his
investigation of the massacre at Saint-Pons-les-Mûres pointed to its
having been organized by an American with the help of a gang of paid
killers.

"Really?" was Laemmle's response to this development. "I may
even recommend dear Jürgen for a medal from the Führer's own
hand. I never dreamed he had such a perverted imagination."

Laemmle thereupon retired to bed, convinced that he would be
unable to sleep. He was right: the telephone continued to ring with
maddening persistence.

On the morning of the 10th, insomnia notwithstanding, his depression gradually receded. Hadn't he always sensed that things would go
wrong? Well, they had, so why be surprised? Anyway, he reflected
with almost sarcastic belligerence, if he left Jürgen Hess to organize
the manhunt alone, he would never see Thomas again.

He devoted a long time to his bath that morning. He'd received confirmation that the American and the boy were still at large. Quartermain hadn't turned up at Nîmes, nor had anyone seen him try to contact his compatriots in the U.S. diplomatic mission at any point along their route. The lookouts on the Aigues-Mortes–Alès axis were unanimous in stating that no Ford of the relevant type had been sighted, and the roadblocks set up by the French police had also drawn a blank.

After his bath Laemmle played chess—or, at least, he set out the board, white in front of him, black in front of the empty chair on the far side of the table in his sitting-room at the Noailles. He conducted the game aloud.

"White opened with P–Q4, black played his knight on KB3; then P–QB4 and P–K3; then N–KB3 and P–QN3. Then I played P–KN3 . . . and that was when he sprang his first surprise by moving his bishop not to N2 as I expected him to—and as is conventional, what's more—but to R3. Why?"

Soeft, glued to the phone, said, "The American mission has just left Nîmes."

"Just suppose he'd played his bishop on N2, which he didn't. If he had, I'd have . . . Aha! That explains it. At the seventh move, white would have gained an advantage—only a slight one, but still . . . And the little imp spotted it!"

Soeft was on the line to someone else now. "That Ford they found belonged to a man named Callaghan, the American consul at Marseilles . . ."

"Shut up, Soeft," said Laemmle. He resumed his monologue. "And if I'd played my queen on R4?" Thinking hard, he rose and sat down on the black side. "No, whatever I did, he'd have found his way back into that triple fork he so skillfully constructed. There's no doubt about it, my friend: he beat you fair and square, and that's not a privilege granted to many. The artful little devil!" He felt almost proud.

Soeft again: "Herr Gortz is on his way."

"Tell him I've just left for Patagonia!"

Joachim Gortz turned up an hour later, having driven all the way from Basel. He'd had to spell his chauffeur at the wheel of his new Mercedes Benz, a 540K.

"Which I'm not too happy with, incidentally—the car, I mean, not the chauffeur. I preferred the roadster of five years back, or even the

500. The increased displacement isn't anything to write home about, nor the fifth gear, and why the devil have they modified the bodywork?"

Laemmle, who'd been taking his twentieth phone call of the morning, hung up and told Soeft to leave them alone. The door closed behind his faithful minion. He embarked on a game of solitaire.

"I detest that mustache of his. I shall instruct him to shave it off pursuant to an order of the day issued by the Führer's supreme headquarters." Laemmle smiled. "My dear Joachim, I can't conceive of anything that interests me less than the displacement of your Mercedes."

"Apart from the peregrinations of Adolf's armies?" Gortz said dryly.

"True. Coffee?"

"I'll help myself." Gortz did so in silence. Then he said, "What happened down there on the coast, Gregor?"

"Jürgen Hess submitted a report, I presume?"

"Yes, he did. It's your version I'd like to hear."

"Are you under orders to interrogate me, my dear Joachim?"

Gortz clicked his tongue. "You're prickly today. I've never seen you like this before."

"Prickly isn't the word. Our good friend Jürgen knew in advance where the rendezvous would take place but neglected to inform me. Maria Weber turned up as arranged, but so did Jürgen's thugs. She saw them and tried to escape. They opened fire. She was killed, and so was that big Spaniard with the missing fingers."

Laemmle shuffled his cards and laid them out in seven graduated columns.

"According to Hess," said Gortz, "he gave you such information as he had, but you refused to make use of it. You were determined to do things your own way—you were obsessed with some obscure kind of aestheticism . . ."

"Aestheticism? Our good friend Jürgen doesn't even know the word."

"What's more, he says, you deliberately allowed the boy to escape."

"Bravo," said Laemmle, who had just freed his ace of clubs.

"Do you know where Hess got his information from?"

"I didn't, but I do now. It seems that the Paris Gestapo arrested a woman named Catherine Lamiel, whose hobby was a game called Resistance. They kept her in a cellar in the Rue de Saussaies, where they applied sulfuric acid to certain parts of her anatomy. Her father, mother, and brother, all experienced players of the same game, were arrested as a result. They were shot this morning, contrary to a promise Hess gave the said young woman to persuade her to help him a little. She's been a trifle unhinged ever since, I'm told." Laemmle paused. "Why exactly did you come, Joachim?"

"Do you know where the boy is?"

"Why not ask Hess?"

"Does he have a hope of capturing the boy?"

Laemmle smiled as he put the queen of hearts on the king of spades. "None whatever."

"He's got the French police and militia helping him."

"An amusing thought," said Laemmle.

"I'll repeat my question: do you know where the boy is?"

"Why bother to repeat it? I heard you the first time."

"Look, Gregor," said Gortz, "you've been in a pretty bizarre position since Heydrich's death. You exist without existing, so to speak. There *is* a man named Gregor Franz Laemmle, promoted to SS Oberführer in March of this year, but he's never received an official assignment. Stranger still, he's never drawn any pay. How have you been managing, Gregor?"

"On the astronomical sums of money that were placed at my disposal in October 1940."

"In French francs—I know. They represented a tiny fraction of the indemnities paid to us by Vichy since our occupation of France. In your case they were meant as a margin for maneuver. How much do you have left?"

"More than I know what to do with."

"And that's not counting your personal assets, which have always been substantial. But you haven't received a single mark from the German exchequer or the German military authorities. Hess has been doing his utmost for weeks to get you taken off the Gall case. He's failed so far, if only because you can't be deprived of an assignment that was never officially given you in the first place."

"The other reason being that you, dear Joachim, are watching over my interests." Laemmle's tone was thoroughly flippant. "Are they going to send me to the Russian front?"

"Hess is working on it. By the way, I know you don't smoke, so I brought you some Swiss chocolates instead."

"My eyes are moist with gratitude. Why did you come at all, Joachim?"

"Perhaps you can guess."

"You realize that Hess is an idiot and you're counting on me to get the boy back. You're asking me without asking but asking all the same, am I right? Would it be possible to send Hess to the Russian front?"

"I'm afraid not—not for the moment."

"You're asking a dear, delightful, intelligent, house-trained little pedigreed poodle—that's me—to team up with a dirty great slobbering boneheaded Doberman whose sole instinct is to sink its fangs in anything that moves. That boy will run rings around the Doberman, but I'll try. . . ." Laemmle freed his ace of diamonds. "You realize, Joachim, that I never even managed to see her face while she was burning to death in that car." He got out all the diamonds up to the queen. "I'll try not to let the Doberman get in my way too much. Why else did you want to see me?"

"Quartermain."

"I don't follow you."

"You follow me perfectly. Quartermain's worth a great deal more than the boy."

"Because of his family and your connections with his family?"

"Please don't kill him, that's all."

"These chocolates are excellent."

"Don't kill him, Gregor. He's worth a thousand times more than the boy, not that the boy's worth much now his mother's dead."

Laemmle, munching with gusto, smiled. He'd come to the conclusion that he hated Gortz a little, though "hated" was something of an exaggeration: to hate him, Laemmle would have had to be able to hate someone other than himself, which wasn't the case. He had as little in common with Gortz as he did with Hess, but Hess at least displayed all the qualities he found so amusing: he was stupid, fanatical, predictable, and capable of reconciling patriotism with mass extermination—in short, he was a typical man in the street. Gortz was another matter. In the first place, he was a born survivor—the sort of man who tours a corpse-strewn battlefield and calculates its value per acre now that it has been freshly fertilized. Secondly, Laemmle had disliked Gortz's references to the boy. Gortz seemed to suggest that his only motive in pursuing the inquiry was to recover the object of his affections by slaughtering its vile seducer, namely, Quartermain. A pleasing idea in one respect, but all the more irritating because it contained a germ of truth. He did, in fact, cherish the hope of eliminating Quartermain, especially as he was coming to believe that the American was Thomas's father and, thus, possessed of certain rights over the boy. If it hadn't been for those delicious chocolates, he might have ground his teeth.

"Am I to assume that Operation Schädelbohrer has been wound up, Joachim?"

"It has lost its priority, let's say. Is Quartermain with the boy?"

"Yes."

"Do you know where?"

"That's hard to say."

"According to Hess, they've already succeeded in leaving France. He thinks they must have slipped through his cordon on foot. Did you hear where the Ford was found?"

Laemmle had won his game of solitaire. He shuffled the cards and started on another, far more difficult game of Marie Antoinette. Hers was a name of ill omen, poor woman, but he wasn't superstitious.

"You obviously know," Gortz went on. "The car had been hidden near Nîmes, less than two kilometers from the outskirts of the town. There was that phone call too, but you know all this, Gregor. I must have the American alive, and he must be arrested on French territory. What do you want in return?"

No reply.

"All right," said Gortz, "you can have the boy, but I'll need a good reason to convince the Gestapo. And Hess, for that matter."

Poor Marie Antoinette must have had a brain the size of a snuffbox, Laemmle reflected. Her solitaire game was quite idiotic—a chimpanzee would enjoy the game, but only if mentally retarded.

Should he play his trump card now? By so doing he would be condemning the boy to death, or to torture at the very least, and that would break him completely. His mother's cremation must have had an appalling effect on him. The spectacle would haunt him to the end of his days—indeed, he might never recover from it. For some time to come he would be like a human bomb, ready to explode at any moment, especially as he had reached that critical age at which social conventions had yet to extinguish or redirect the natural cruelty of youth. What was more, his mother's training had multiplied an already exceptional intelligence tenfold. And yet, thought Laemmle, and yet . . . If he didn't play his trump card, Hess would delight in killing Thomas, either from sheer stupidity or because he knew how much the boy meant to him, Laemmle.

"I've got a very compelling reason," he said.

Gortz smiled. "I knew you'd think of one. What is it?"

"The boy knows everything his mother knew. From Operation Schädelbohrer's point of view, he's as valuable as she was. All those banker's codes and other amusing little secrets that interested you so much before you became obsessed with Quartermain—he carries them all in his head."

It was awhile before Gortz spoke. "You wouldn't be trying to bluff me, Gregor, would you?"

"That remains to be seen," Laemmle said blandly.

"How long have you known this?"

"I think I knew it from the outset. It was a logical assumption, based on what the woman had made of her son. If I hadn't already been convinced after my train ride in his company, our game of chess would have clinched the matter. He beat me cold, did I tell you?"

The telephone rang.

"Don't worry," said Laemmle, "you'll have your American. *Au revoir*, my dear Joachim."

DURING THE NIGHT OF NOVEMBER 9–10, QUARTERMAIN HAD ventured as far as Nîmes on foot, leaving Thomas and the Ford concealed near a deserted hunting lodge. His expectations were fulfilled as soon as he reached the outskirts: the sparse traffic was filtering through a roadblock manned by a vanful of gendarmes, and other vehicles and motorcycles were parked beyond it. Not content with this preliminary sighting, he crawled nearer and surveyed the scene through his binoculars. Sure enough, there were a number of less-official-looking cars drawn up across every road in sight.

Finding a telephone took time. He skirted the police cordon at a distance of several hundred yards. Its extent impressed him. One or two gaps could be seen, but he mistrusted them. They could be traps, he told himself, marveling at his own subtlety. Another twenty-five or thirty years of this, and he would make a first-class spy.

At last he spotted some telephone wires issuing from the town and leading out into the country. He followed them. They took him across some wasteland, over a series of embankments and ditches lined with concrete, and around an artificial lake, which turned out to be a reservoir. The sight of it gave him an idea.

Still following the telephone wires, he came to a large farmhouse. Through the windows, which were ablaze with light, he saw a party in progress—a wedding party. He even glimpsed the bride and bridegroom at the head of the festive board.

Another two kilometers brought him to within sight of another farmhouse, this one in total darkness. He was in luck—the owners had probably been asked to their neighbors' wedding. He tried the front entrance. The gates looked as if they led to a large inner courtyard, but they were locked. A complete tour of the premises made him curse the Gallic mania for treating any home like a castle under siege. In the end, however, he discovered a loft window that not only lacked bars but had one shutter gaping open. It was twelve or fifteen feet from the ground, but he propped a cart against the wall and shinnied up one of the shafts.

From the loft he made his way to the ground floor, where he found some candles and lit them. The look of the interior surprised him. He wasn't in a farmhouse so much as a country house in which agricultural implements, pitchforks and so on, were used for decorative purposes only. The place abounded in books, knickknacks, and canned food—a staggering amount of it. The cellars were crammed with provisions, the passages lined with them. More cans were stacked in every cupboard and beneath the kitchen table.

There was also a study. A search of this room revealed that the owner of the house, a certain Francis-Henri Maurel, was a senior official at the Ministry of Supply—and making the most of his job, too, thought Quartermain. The telephone was on the desk, but he resisted the temptation to use it right away.

He completed his inspection of the ground floor and went out into the courtyard. Nearly all the erstwhile barns and stables had been converted into living quarters. The one exception was a garage, and tucked away inside it was a car shrouded in a tarpaulin. It proved to be a well-maintained Chenard-Walker. The battery had been removed and placed on a bench near a power outlet, to which it was connected.

Quartermain reinstalled the battery. The engine started on the first try. The tank was three-quarters full.

Filled with a sudden sense of urgency by the thought of Thomas waiting alone in the dark, Quartermain set to work. It took him several trips to load the trunk of the car with all he needed in the way of canned food and boxes of crackers. He also purloined half a dozen blankets, a can opener, a knife, a couple of flashlights, a coil of rope— it might come in handy some time—and a whole sheaf of ration cards.

He paused in front of a rackful of shotguns, wondering whether to help himself, but finally abandoned the idea. Then he hurried back to the study and pocketed the bunch of spare keys he'd found there.

The moment had come.

He picked up the receiver. The operator took an age to answer.

"*Je non parler bien français,*" he said. "*Je suis suédois, demande me pardonner. Je vouloir parler police, vite!*"

A minute or more elapsed before a man's voice announced that this was the gendarmerie and asked what the trouble was. Quartermain launched into another effusion of fractured French mingled with made-up words resembling the singsong gutturalities of the Swedish actress with whom he'd spent a delightful weekend at Palm Springs last year. He explained that his name was Svensson, and that he'd just been assaulted by a man who'd tried to steal his car. The policeman at the other end of the line pricked up his ears as soon as Quartermain described his assailant. Had the man by any chance been accompanied by a small boy with dark hair and gray eyes? "*Ya, ya,*" Quartermain said eagerly, "*petit garçon dans petite voiture.*" Could he describe the little car in question? *Ya, ya,* it was a Citroën Trèfle—he'd even taken its number.

He gave the license number of a car belonging to one of the wedding guests at the neighboring farm, announced that he himself, Gustav Svensson from Stockholm, would be in Nîmes first thing in the morning, and promised—*ya, ya*—to report to the police station without delay.

He hung up. The rest of his chores would have to be completed in double-quick time. He drove the Chenard out of the courtyard and locked the gates behind him. Five minutes later he pulled up near the first farmhouse. The guests were now singing lustily. He got out and made for the Citroën Trèfle. He didn't start the engine until he'd pushed it some way down the lane. Then he drove to the reservoir. Not far from the water's edge he switched off the headlights, jammed the throttle with a stone, put the car into first, and jumped clear.

The Citroën was almost too light and buoyant. It took two interminable minutes to settle and sink below the surface.

Quartermain hurried back to the Chenard. He thought he'd made a mistake when he reached the hunting lodge: the Ford had disappeared —it wasn't where he'd left it. He got out and played a flashlight over the surrounding area. The hunting lodge, a modest hut, was empty. Could the boy have driven off? Then the beam of the flashlight picked up something metallic. The Ford had been backed into some undergrowth.

"Thomas?" He should never have left him on his own. "Thomas? It's me, Quartermain."

"I'm here."

Almost at his feet, Thomas emerged from beneath a kind of little trapdoor made of reeds and foliage. Quartermain could have come within a yard and failed to spot him, even in broad daylight. The boy inspected the Chenard.

"Where did you get it?"

"I stole it."

"One more reason for the gendarmes to come after you." Thomas's tone was serene rather than sarcastic.

"Give me a hand, would you?"

Quartermain went over to the Ford and fetched the two remaining cans of gasoline, one of which was partly empty. He tipped the remainder of its contents into the Chenard's capacious tank and stowed the other can in the trunk. The boy watched him without moving.

"Were the gendarmes waiting for us at Nîmes?"

"Yes."

"And the others?"

"Yes."

"Did you make that phone call?"

Quartermain felt surprised at himself. He was reporting to the boy —*reporting*, that was the only word for it. He said, "Hop in, Thomas."

"That was pretty smart of you," said Thomas. "I mean, calling the police and telling them that lie. Not *very* smart, but quite. Yellow Eyes won't be taken in, even if the others are."

"What others? I thought Laemmle was in charge."

"He wouldn't be dumb enough to use gendarmes, let alone set up roadblocks you can see for miles. That must be Jürgen Hess. He's a fool."

"You can tell me about this Hess guy in the car. Get in."

Instead of complying, Thomas retreated three or four steps.

"That depends where you're going."

"I know damn well where I'm going. Don't waste any more time."

"If I ran away now, you'd never catch me."

"I already caught you once today."

"I don't remember, but if you did I must have been in a state. I'm not in a state anymore."

Quartermain sighed. Coming on top of what had preceded them, the last two hours had exhausted him. "I see," he said. "So you want me to discuss our destination with you."

"It would be better if you did."

"They're lying in wait for us at Nîmes and probably for tens of kilometers on either side of the place. They'll be checking all the boats along the coast and watching the bridges over the Rhône. We'll head north, keeping the Rhône on our right. We won't turn south toward Spain until we're across the Cévennes."

"But that's just what Yellow Eyes will expect us to do. He'll leave Hess and his gendarmes to take care of Nîmes and the Rhône bridges and the boats while he goes north and waits for us there. He's awfully smart."

"Smarter than me, you mean?"

"He could beat you anytime," Thomas said, but he sidled toward the Chenard and finally got in. "All right," he said, "we'll go north."

"Okay, boss," said Quartermain, "but why, if you're so sure that's where Laemmle will be waiting for us?"

"Because I'd sooner bump into him than Hess. Hess is crazy." Quartermain started the car. "Almost as crazy as Laemmle," Thomas added.

"You think Laemmle's crazy too?"

"Everyone's crazy. It just depends how crazy, that's all."

"Does that go for me as well?"

"I said everyone, monsieur." The boy slowly turned and looked at him, then pulled the door shut. "I'm sorry," he said, "that wasn't very polite of me. We'll leave as soon as you like."

THOMAS AWOKE TO FIND THEIR NEW CAR DRIVING ALONG A ROAD so narrow that the leaves of the oak trees flanking it rattled against the body from time to time. He didn't move. The Thing was sneaking up on him, and it was all he could do to hold it at bay.

The Thing persisted, so he pretended to stir in his sleep and rested his forehead against the door. That enabled him to open his eyes unobserved, which helped a little. Besides, the other Thomas—the one that made the machine work and played chess—kept telling him he'd get over it.

And he did. It was terribly difficult, but he did. The worst part was when you shut your eyes and the other Thomas went to sleep and the wheels stopped turning.

It was over now.

He sat up and looked at the American, who glanced at him and smiled but said nothing. The American looked awfully tired. He seemed a nice enough man. Of course, he might be pretending to be nice just to get him, Thomas, to give away the secrets She'd confided in him, complete with instructions on where and how to pass them on.

Not necessarily, though. Maybe he was simply being nice for no special reason. People were like that sometimes, so She'd told him, but very seldom.

Be on your guard all the same. . . .

He'd examined all the papers the American had left in his overcoat when he went off to reconnoiter. They included the American's passport, the passport containing his own photograph, various documents of no interest, photographs of unknown people, and the letter. It was the letter that had stuck in his mind, of course. He hadn't understood it all, but he'd grasped its main essentials. He'd also recognized her signature. *David, I wouldn't be getting in touch with you unless the circumstances were quite exceptional. By writing this letter, I'm*—a word he didn't know—*all the rules . . .*

He didn't know the word "pregnant," either, but it wasn't hard to deduce its meaning from what followed: *Don't misunderstand me—I wanted that child . . .*

Therefore, "pregnant" could only mean *enceinte*, and "that child" was himself.

In other words, the American was his father.

Unless the letter was a fake and they'd forged Her handwriting.

Maybe, maybe not. He thought hard for a moment.

There was another possible explanation. Perhaps She'd genuinely written the letter but told the American a pack of lies, just to get him to come to Europe.

It didn't matter anyway. Yellow Eyes would kill the American sooner or later—he would tell Soeft to kill him and that would be that. It was no use taking an interest in people who were going to die. You started to grow fond of them and you got them killed. It was pointless, especially if he had to use the American like a knight or a rook and sacrifice him to lay a trap for Yellow Eyes. When sacrificing a piece was the only way to win, you couldn't afford to hesitate.

"All right, Thomas?" said the American.

"Yes, monsieur."

"You managed to grab a little sleep, didn't you?"

"Yes, monsieur. You're a really good driver, monsieur."

"Thank you, Thomas. You don't have to call me 'monsieur' all the time, you know."

"I know," said Thomas.

IT WAS NEARLY FOUR IN THE MORNING WHEN QUARTERMAIN decided to call a halt. He was so exhausted that his leaden eyelids had drooped disastrously, twice in quick succession. All that woke him was a crunch of gravel the first time and a violent blow on the right fender the second. The fender was so badly buckled that it was rubbing against the wheel and he'd had to lever it out with the jack handle.

Most of the countless minor roads he'd taken were marked in white on the map. According to the latter he was in Ardèche, which wasn't altogether unfamiliar to him. To keep himself awake he recalled the cycle tour he'd made there fifteen years ago with Cousin Larry, initially accompanied by Babe, a girl cousin of theirs. Babe had complained so bitterly of all the ups and downs that they finally banished her to the Rolls in which Watson, the chauffeur-bodyguard wished on them by Uncle Peter, was following on behind with their baggage. With Babe out of the way Cousin Larry had been overcome, for the first and only time in his life, by a thirst for freedom. At Quartermain's instigation they gave Watson the slip by pedaling madly off across a field and losing themselves in a maze of little byroads. They absconded for four whole days, sleeping in barns and eating at country inns. One night they mingled with the revelers at a village dance—the crowning glory of their escapade, in the view of Cousin Larry, who kept rubbing his hands with glee like a naughty schoolboy. Having rounded up two girls and coaxed them into a hayloft, Quartermain goaded Larry into playing doctors and nurses with one of them

and personally ensured that the game was brought to its logical con-
clusion. They ended their escapade in police custody because Uncle
Peter, suspecting that they'd been kidnapped by a gang of goddam
Frogs, had initiated a nationwide manhunt for them by alerting the
State Department, the U.S. Embassy in Paris, the President of the
French Republic, and the Minister of the Interior.

Well, here he was, back in Ardèche again with the Cévennes range
on his left, and if he didn't stop soon and get some sleep he would
wrap the Chenard around a tree.

He turned off down a sunken lane, his headlights illuminating an
archway of foliage overhead, and followed it for forty or fifty yards.
The moon had disappeared, visibility was nil, and the air streaming
through the half-open window was bitterly cold. The boy was asleep,
sound asleep now, not stirring restlessly as he had since they left the
vicinity of Nîmes. Three hours ago he'd briefly waked up after a long
succession of plaintive little whimpers interspersed with muffled words
in German or French—it was hard to tell which. Quartermain had
smiled at him and said something, but all he elicited was a monosyl-
labic reply and a look from those big, startlingly luminous gray eyes.

Quartermain eased the door open and, in spite of his aching hip,
conducted a thorough tour of inspection. He had no wish to wake up
at dawn beneath the windows of some house he'd failed to spot in the
darkness, but the sunken lane petered out into a number of rough
tracks that didn't seem to go far. There were no lights to be seen, no
telltale whiffs of smoke, no signs that the lane was regularly used by
farmers. The only tracks in the mud at the mouth of the lane were the
Chenard's, and those Quartermain obliterated with the aid of a
branch. He scraped the loose soil together with his feet and hands,
then scattered and smoothed it over with his makeshift broom. Although he was so tired he could hardly stand, he didn't return to the
car until he'd carefully erased his own footprints. He really was getting paranoid, he told himself.

One more thing remained to be done. He picked up the sleeping
boy, transferred him to the backseat, and wrapped him up in four of
the blankets from the farmhouse. The gray eyes snapped open at his
touch and gazed at him with the cold, dispassionate intensity of an
owl watching a fieldmouse.

"You'll be more comfortable there, *mon petit*—you can stretch out.
Go back to sleep, everything's okay."

Quartermain settled himself in the front as well as he could, what

with the steering wheel, the gap between the seats, and the length of
his legs. His hip was hurting like hell. He swathed himself in the two
remaining blankets and turned his coat collar up. The silence was
absolute. Listening for a moment, he could tell from the boy's rhyth-
mical breathing that he'd gone to sleep again.

*I wanted that child more than anything else in the world, but I broke
with you precisely because you'd fathered it on me. Although I've no
idea how you remember me after twelve years, you may recall that I
never lied to you. . . .*

He fell asleep too, imagining—quite wrongly, he felt sure—that he
was being watched by a pair of owlish eyes.

To GREGOR LAEMMLE, THE TWO ENSUING DAYS AND PART OF
the one after that seemed to crawl by.

True, he'd received word early on the afternoon of the 10th that the
stolen Citroën had been recovered following a report from a self-styled
Swede who claimed to have been attacked by a man fitting
Quartermain's description. Laemmle hadn't for one moment believed
in this mysterious Scandinavian, whom he promptly identified as
Quartermain himself, and his rather vague mental picture of the latter
at once began to assume definite shape. The man was ingenious and
might even possess a sense of humor. He'd certainly been imaginative
enough to dream up a hoax that had kept Hess and his gendarme
friends guessing throughout the night of the 9th and 10th.

Laemmle had been equally doubtful that the American was heading
west via Nîmes or making for Spain via anywhere at all—not directly,
anyway. If that was true he would have had to concede that the man
was as stupid as Hess, and that the boy was still too shocked by recent
events to contribute to their joint plan of action. "And that I'm just as
reluctant to believe, Soeft. Our young friend is incredibly resourceful.
I'll bet his precocious little brain has already started humming like a
turbine again."

The next theory he dismissed was that the pair had turned about
and headed back across the Rhône—an unexpected maneuver, to be
sure, but fraught with danger. An escape by sea? Either it had been
planned in advance, in which case they were already bound for the
Balearics and well beyond reach, or it was impractical. Even Hess had

thought to keep watch on Saintes-Maries-de-la-Mer, the only place they could have sailed from. No, that only left the northern route.

"How long have your men been in position, Soeft?"

Soeft reported that he'd dispatched them at eleven-thirty on the morning of the 9th. According to him, his first line of lookouts was in place by nightfall. The second cordon had stationed itself farther north, more precisely, in the Ardèche area, at about ten-thirty P.M.

"The little Citroën was stolen between seven and ten P.M. the same evening. The Swede made his telephone call at nine twenty-three P.M., and the call came from the immediate vicinity of Nîmes. Correct so far, Soeft?"

"Yes."

"They abandoned the Ford and pretended to steal a Citroën. That means they must have got hold of another vehicle. Has anyone reported the theft of a car or a motorcycle?"

"No."

"That leaves us with two possibilities, Soeft. Either some good Samaritan or accomplice gave them a lift, or they borrowed a car whose theft has not yet been reported. Q.E.D. Shut up, Soeft, I'm not asking for your opinion—you're my one-man Greek chorus, that's all. What's more, they penetrated your first line of defense—no, don't contradict me! Nobody spotted them, and that proves it."

Soeft said that his first line of lookouts had noted the license numbers of every northbound vehicle from six P.M. on the 9th onward, and that they were continuing to do so.

Laemmle called Krug von Nidda, Germany's consul-general at Vichy, who was an old friend of his, and implored him to use his influence with the French authorities to obtain the owners' names and addresses.

No news on the 10th.

Nothing definite on the 11th either.

Nothing at first on the 12th.

He'd lost them! Stupor was succeeded by genuine despair. Coming on top of Maria Weber's tragic death, Laemmle's growing conviction that he'd lost her son as well seemed unendurable. He was reeling from one disaster to the next with an inexorability worthy of a Greek tragedy. He took out the photographs of Quartermain and studied them again. Could this cowboy—well dressed, it was true, and not bad-looking, he had to admit—could this cowboy *really* have robbed him of the boy? To his own amazement, he was suddenly overcome with rage. Had he finally found someone to hate apart from himself?

On the evening of the 10th he decided to call Paris and consult Monsieur Henri Lafont.

Some preliminary information came in on the morning of the 11th. Among the vehicles listed by Soeft's first line of lookouts was a Chenard-Walker belonging to a senior government official at Vichy. He hadn't reported its theft because he hadn't known about it. His name was Maurel, and he owned a country house near Nîmes.

The said Chenard, with one fender buckled, had been sighted in the area east of the Cévennes during the night of the 10th and 11th. Traveling at a reckless speed, it had zoomed past one of Soeft's second-line lookouts.

Positive identification of the American and his passenger followed on the morning of November 12, when they were sighted crossing the Rhône bridge at Valence, heading west.

The hunt was on again.

QUARTERMAIN DREAMED THAT HE WAS TAKING A SHOWER. OPENing his eyes, he found that cold, torrential rain was driving in through the Chenard's open window.

"Hungry, monsieur?"

A few seconds of stupor, then memory reasserted itself. He was in a stolen car—the second one he'd stolen. Uncle Peter would have a heart attack if he knew! More than that, he was being hunted by French police and German secret agents in the company of a boy whose false passport described him as his son.

"Hungry?"

Thomas was munching an enormous ham sandwich with his beret pulled down over his ears and the rest of him enveloped in a dark blue cape. Hooked over his shoulder was a gigantic black umbrella with a handle in the shape of a duck's or goose's head.

Quartermain came to at last.

"Where did you get those things?"

"I brought the umbrella for you."

"I asked you a question."

Thomas's nonchalant manner was belied by the look in his eye.

"There's a farm over there. It's awfully good, their ham." He took another gargantuan mouthful. "So is this butter. They've got plenty of coffee, too."

I'm still dreaming, Quartermain thought. He sat up behind the wheel. His hip transmitted spasms of pain to his leg and the whole right side of his body, which ached all over. He kneaded his eyes.

"Don't tell me you went to a farm! Did anyone see you?"

"There were eleven of them around the kitchen table. If they didn't see me they must be blind. Coming?"

Quartermain reached for the ignition.

"Get in, we're off."

The boy shook his head, clearly disappointed by Quartermain's lack of perception. "They've got three British airmen hidden in one of their barns," he said with his mouth full, "not to mention a submachine gun and some rifles—I saw them with my own eyes. I'd be very surprised if they went and told the gendarmes—in fact, I'm positive they won't. Besides, if you leave now you're bound to be spotted by the people in the farm across the way. *They'll* tell the police all right—they're Pétainists." He paused to swallow his latest mouthful. "Well, do you want some breakfast or don't you?"

A minute later Quartermain found himself walking through a wood composed largely of chestnut trees. The downpour had redoubled. From time to time he stepped on a chestnut husk and winced, imagining that he'd crushed some small creature underfoot. He was limping worse than ever. Looking at his watch, he saw that it was well past nine o'clock. That meant he'd had nearly five hours' sleep—a lot, considering the uncomfortable conditions. Although his initial torpor had almost worn off, his sense of unreality, heightened by the spectral appearance of this dripping, mist-enshrouded wood, was growing ever stronger. Vermont seemed very far away.

"How long have you been up, Thomas?"

"I haven't got a watch. An hour, maybe."

Quartermain could hardly believe that a farmer's family would have been lazing around the breakfast table at eight o'clock in the morning. The boy must have been up since dawn, if not before.

"An hour or two," Thomas amended casually.

"And you actually saw these British airmen?"

"Yes."

"Complete with their airplane, I suppose?"

"They were wearing French clothes, but they stuck out like a sore thumb. They all had great big mustaches and were talking in English."

"Did you speak to them?"

"No."

No, said Thomas, he'd simply watched them. He was only six feet away but they hadn't noticed him. They might be good at dropping bombs, but they were pretty dumb in other respects. They were bound to get caught, what with their mustaches and the row they made.

"At least *I* don't have a mustache," Quartermain said defensively.

"No, thank goodness."

Thomas walked on ahead for half a kilometer or so. He threaded his way through the dank, dark trees with an unerring sense of direction, following a series of almost invisible paths that seemed to lead nowhere but always came out somewhere. The trees soon thinned, and beyond them Quartermain glimpsed a rectangular group of stone buildings with wet and glistening roofs.

The boy paused and turned to him.

"Monsieur Cazes told me to be careful from here on. We mustn't let the Pétainists see us, nor those British airmen. They're so stupid they might start cheering if they saw an American. We're to wait here."

"For what?"

"For Émilie. She's got German measles—that's why she isn't at school. Me, I've already had them, so I can't catch them again. Besides, she's better."

He might be talking in code, thought Quartermain. German measles he could understand, but the reference to Pétainists was more puzzling. They sounded like a hostile local tribe.

"And another thing," said Thomas, eyeing him expressionlessly. "I told the Cazes family you were my father."

Quartermain saw a diminutive figure appear around the corner of one of the farm buildings and beckon to them.

"Your father?" he said.

"I had to tell them something or they'd wonder what we're doing together. See that row of little sticks in the ground? Stay close to them —it's the only way of getting there without being seen from the farm opposite."

THOMAS LEFT THE AMERICAN EATING IN THE KITCHEN UNDER the supervision of Madame Cazes and slipped outside. He liked being out in the rain, especially in this nice warm cape. Everything smelled of the country and moist earth. Émilie was waiting for him at the prearranged spot.

"Let's go."

They dodged from building to building in single file. Once in the woods at a distance of several hundred yards from the farm, they started climbing.

"He's tall, your father," said Émilie. "Really tall. How come he's American?"

"Because he isn't Spanish," Thomas retorted.

"Oh, I thought there might be a more complicated reason."

They continued to climb, though the going became harder and harder because the hillside was steep and slippery with wet leaves. Besides, wooden clogs were heavy. They might be fine for walking through mud, but not for climbing hills. Émilie climbed like a mountain goat, which rather annoyed Thomas, who was encumbered with the binoculars. She seemed quite at ease and never slipped, whereas he'd already fallen twice and smeared his hands and face with rotting leaves.

"Ever been to America, Thomas?"

"Lots of times."

"How many is lots?"

"Seventeen."

"In a ship?"

"No, I swam—what do you think?"

"Is it nice there?"

"Not bad," said Thomas. He was all out of breath, whereas she kept skipping on ahead and turning around to wait for him. He produced the binoculars from under his cape when they reached the top of the first hill, but he couldn't see much because of the trees.

"Can one really see everything from the place you said?"

"Everything."

They followed the crest of the hill, which dipped a little before climbing again. Thomas estimated that they'd been gone an hour when they finally reached the rocks. Émilie scrambled up first and showed him the way to the top. One quick look around convinced him that she was right: you could see an awfully long way. There was a river some five or six hundred feet below, but that was purely inciden-

tal. He focused the binoculars and a little village appeared—twenty or
thirty houses, not more—with a crossroads in the middle. He consulted the American's map: all four approach roads were marked in
white or yellow.

All he had to do now was find the lookout, who could only be there,
nowhere else, because of the crossroads. Yellow Eyes was bound to
have guessed what the American would do—and what he had done—
since leaving Nîmes: head north, sticking to the little white and yellow
roads. That meant he would have posted his lookouts at the points
where those roads intersected. It wasn't such a difficult proposition—
he didn't need a whole army of lookouts. If there were only eight or
ten such crossroads, he could keep watch on all of them with eight or
ten men.

"Seen any Red Indians in America?"

"Masses."

"With feathers?"

"Masses of feathers."

"How old are you?"

"Eleven and a half." He nearly said twelve to make himself sound
older, but eleven and a half wasn't bad.

"I'm older than you are. I was twelve in April."

"That's really old. You ought to settle down and get married." Still
peering through the binoculars at a range of fifteen hundred yards,
Thomas scrutinized the houses and the gardens behind them, one by
one.

"Are you teasing me?"

"You're quick."

There he was!

The lookout was there all right. He'd thought the man would be
hiding somewhere, but not at all. The silly fool was sitting in a car
beside the crossroads. Thomas couldn't distinguish his face clearly. He
could only tell that he was alone and looked as if he'd been waiting for
a long time.

"You aren't very big for eleven and a half. I'm taller than you are."

"That's because I don't want to grow up."

"Why not?"

"I don't want to, that's all. When I do, I will."

Of course, he might *not* be one of Laemmle's lookouts. It wasn't a
certainty, and you couldn't make a move like that unless you were
certain. If only a car would come past. . . . He trained his binoculars

on the two right-hand roads. If the American hadn't stopped to sleep, they'd have bumped right into him.

Yellow Eyes must have stationed a first line of lookouts farther south as well. If so, the American must have driven past them while he, Thomas, was asleep. They would have noted the number of the car, which was easy to recognize with its damaged fender, and would now be trying to trace its owner. They might even know by now that it had been stolen.

All right, so they knew, but they didn't know where the car or its occupants were. If the man down there was really a lookout, he must belong to the second line.

"You can kiss me if you like," said Émilie.

"In a minute," said Thomas.

The lookout would also make a note of their number and report it by phone. Yellow Eyes would guess which way they were heading, but he wouldn't bank on it. He would bar their route in the east as well as the west. That way he would be sure of catching them wherever they made for, Switzerland or Spain. That was what he'd done, Thomas felt sure.

He continued to watch the roads on the right.

"You aren't in a hurry to kiss me, I must say."

He abandoned his surveillance long enough to glare at Émilie for a moment or two, convulsed with sudden rage. He almost felt like pushing her over the edge and into the river below. As if he wanted to kiss *her*, after *Her!*

He crouched down, gripping the binoculars very tightly, and commanded himself to concentrate on Yellow Eyes, nothing but Yellow Eyes and how to beat him. How to kill him, and Soeft, and Hess— how to kill them all. He mustn't, *mustn't*, think of anything else. . . .

"Are you all right?"

He raised his head and found that the binoculars weren't there any longer. Émilie was holding them—she'd taken them without his even noticing and was looking at the village.

"I've got a headache," he said. "It hurts a lot."

"I spoke to you but you didn't listen, you just stared at the ground."

"I've got a really bad headache, that's why."

"What were you looking at just now?"

"Nothing special. I like looking at things."

He gently relieved her of the binoculars. Just at that moment a bus came into view on one of the right-hand roads. Now he would see whether or not the man was a lookout.

He watched him get out of his car and stand there as though waiting to catch the bus. When it stopped he boarded it and walked to the back, then got off again as though he'd changed his mind. Returning to his car, he noted something down.

That proved it.

"We'd better go home now," said Émilie, "especially as I've had German measles. Besides, it'll soon be lunchtime."

Thomas lowered the binoculars, then raised them quickly. This time a car was coming along the other right-hand road. The lookout sat up sharply when he saw it.

"Did you hear, Thomas? Maman will give us a good telling-off, and that includes you."

"You go on ahead."

The lookout had binoculars too. He leveled them for a moment, then jotted something else down: obviously, the registration number of the approaching car, which turned out to contain a man, a woman, and two little girls. It drove past him and out of sight. Thomas, still watching the lookout, saw him get out and walk across the road to the local café.

He was going to telephone, but he could still watch the road from inside. No one could drive past without being spotted.

Fine, Thomas thought contentedly. As long as I know for sure.

"Race you to the bottom," he said to Émilie.

This time it was Émilie who came a cropper. She grazed her knee and started crying, by which time he was at least four or five yards in the lead. He stopped and waited for her, pulling on his clogs. He'd removed them to help him run faster.

But I'd have won anyway, he told himself. He never liked losing—not one little bit.

MADAME CAZES WAS A SMALL, ACERBIC WOMAN IN HER FIFTIES, with very white skin and a birthmark on her left cheek with three black hairs sprouting from it. If she'd ever been pretty, that fact had long been forgotten, even by her.

"Stay put and don't show yourself at the window," she told Quartermain as she conducted him to one of the upstairs rooms. "The Pétainists might see you—they're always spying on us. I'll bring you something to eat."

No sooner said than done. She returned with a plate of ham and eggs and some coffee.

"And stay away from those Englishmen, whatever you do. They should have moved on last night, but it seems the trains are being very closely watched. That means we'll have to keep them here for a while longer, and it's no rest cure, I can tell you. They're crazy. They play *le rugby* in the barn and jabber all day long. They don't understand a word of French either, the barbarians. At least you're the quiet type. Is that leg of yours hurting? Your son told us—it was bad luck, landing on top of that train by parachute. Those stupid *rosbifs* were luckier. When their plane was hit they floated down to earth like feathers. Some of our people had a tough time smuggling them across the Line and bringing them here, and now they're complaining because they aren't in Spain already. I told them to take the Blue Train next time, but they didn't get the joke. Your son calmed them down a bit, thank goodness, but it would be better if they didn't see you. Your son's all right—he can pass for French—but not you, and if they were caught they'd probably talk. Here, I thought you might like a book to read. This is all we've got in the house. Your son's back at last, by the way. He and Émilie went for a walk—a walk in this weather, I ask you, when she's just had German measles! Émilie's my youngest daughter. She's a pretty girl, though God knows where she got her looks from. The boy'll come and see you when he's eaten—he wanted to eat with us, if that's all right. You should be proud of him—he's as bright as a button. Would you like some soup as well? I'll get your son to bring you some as soon as the others have gone back to work."

QUARTERMAIN LOOKED UP AT THOMAS.

"What's the soup like?"

"Terrific. Don't let it get cold."

"Where did you go?"

The gray eyes were totally uncommunicative.

"Here, I brought your binoculars back. They work extremely well."

He put the binoculars on the bed beside Quartermain. Extracting a sheet of paper and a pencil from his pocket, he drew a cluster of little squares with four double lines radiating from it.

"That's the village and those are the roads. If we'd kept going last night we'd have come along this one and bumped into the lookout— see, I've marked him with a cross. He's all alone, but maybe they take turns and he's got a partner asleep inside somewhere. When a car passes by . . ."

He described the lookout's procedure and his own conception of Laemmle's system for catching them: one lookout posted at every minor intersection in the area.

"It sounds like a lot, but there aren't that many crossroads, see for yourself. He'd have had to put one there, one there, one there . . ."

He made a number of crosses on the road map.

"So what's your idea?" Quartermain asked in English.

No reply.

"You understood me perfectly well," Quartermain went on. "Why didn't you tell me you spoke English?"

"You never asked me."

"You read that letter, didn't you?"

"What letter?"

Quartermain just looked at him.

Thomas stiffened a little. "You left the letter in your coat on purpose, I suppose, and you left the other papers with it because the letter would have looked odd on its own." He paused. "Yes," he said, "I read it."

"Did you understand it all?"

"Yes." The gray eyes were as inscrutable as ever.

"What did you think of it?"

"Nothing."

"That's not an answer, Thomas."

"I don't want to talk about it."

"But I do. I came over from America just because of that letter and what your mother told me in it."

"I don't believe you're my father."

The statement was so abrupt and unexpected that Quartermain was temporarily at a loss for words.

"You don't believe it, or you don't want to believe it?"

"I told you, I'd rather not talk about it."

"Do you have some reason for not believing it? Tell me the truth."

"No."

"What does that mean?"

"I don't have a reason."

"You mean you think she was lying to me?"

"I'd rather you didn't call her 'she.' "

"So you think she—your mother—lied to me? You don't think I'm really your father?"

"That makes two questions."

"Yes, and I'd like an answer to both of them."

"I don't think it was true, what she said in her letter, and I don't think you're my father."

"But you don't have any reason for thinking either of those things?"

"I don't *want* you to be my father, that's all."

Quartermain winced. He'd asked for that.

"Why do you think your mother would have lied to me?"

"Because she was worried about me. Because you're an American and very rich and you have connections in Germany."

"But you don't need anyone's help?"

"No."

"You think you can give Laemmle the slip all by yourself?"

Thomas didn't reply at once. Then he said, "I can beat him at his own game, yes. Your soup's cold."

Quartermain reminded himself that he couldn't treat Thomas like an ordinary youngster. Ordinary he'd never been, even before he saw his mother burn to death. Quartermain's forefinger was still between the pages of the book he'd been reading, a dog-eared edition of *Les Misérables*. He put the book down and rose, remembering just in time not to show himself at the window.

He said, "But I could be useful when it comes to getting past these hypothetical lookouts of yours?"

"If that means you don't think they exist, you're wrong."

"Okay, let's assume they do. Can I help you to get past them?"

"Yes, if you like."

"Glad to be of *some* use, at least."

Quartermain instantly regretted the words. He turned his back on the boy and remained like that until his resentment had subsided. He was taken aback when he turned around again. Thomas was sitting on the bed, but not with the complacent air of one who has won an argument, nor even in his usual characteristic pose: body erect, head up, hands on thighs. Instead, he seemed somehow to have wilted. With one shoulder resting against the brass bedstead and his head slightly bowed, he was staring strangely, fixedly, at his hands as they clasped and unclasped each other.

Quartermain's lingering annoyance vanished. A great surge of affection engulfed him, mingled with sorrow and pity.

"Thomas?"

The boy's chin sank deeper onto his chest. His lips contracted and an almost imperceptible tremor flitted across his pale face. I don't believe it, Quartermain told himself. He's actually going to cry, the poor little devil.

"Thomas?" he said. "Listen, I'd be interested to know how you aim to get past those lookouts without being nabbed. Like to tell me about it?"

There was no reply, but the tremor became more pronounced.

"Thomas?"

At long last, the boy nodded.

I ALMOST CRIED JUST NOW, THOMAS THOUGHT. IT'S ODD—I don't know what came over me. I haven't cried since She . . . I've tried but it's no use, I can't. I'm all dried up inside like a riverbed in summer. Either the Thing grabs hold of me and sends me crazy, so I don't know where I am or what I'm doing, or the machine starts up and drives the Thing away. All I can think of is Yellow Eyes and how to beat him.

Except that it isn't just one or the other. There's something in between. The American isn't the Thing and he isn't the machine either. I shouldn't care what he thinks, but I can't help it. He's nice and kind, sure, but that's just the trouble. He's a piece to be sacrificed. I'm going to lose him, and I need to lose him if I'm going to win. A person would have to be pretty silly to get fond of a piece on a chessboard.

He's nice, but he's clever as well. I thought he was a lot less clever than Yellow Eyes, but I was wrong—he isn't that much less. He's different, which isn't the same thing. For instance, when he asked me to tell him how I plan to get past the lookouts, he only did it because he saw how sad I was. He understood at once—that's why he said something that would stop me from feeling sad, or make me feel less sad, at least.

It's funny having someone around who looks into your eyes and

knows when you're feeling sad and why. Not even Javier could do
that. With the American, we look at each other and there's no need to
say much. That means I'm not alone anymore. He was right to alter a
couple of things in my plan when we talked about it. The new plan—
the one we've worked out together—is a pretty good one.

Then he told me about himself when he was young and the way his
own mind worked when he was eleven or twelve like me. That was
something else he did on purpose, telling me stories to calm me down
and take my mind off things. Funny that he should have had the same
ideas as me. Pretty much the same, anyway. Like when you hate the
whole world, or when you look up at the sky at night and feel like
crying because it goes on forever and it makes you mad, not being able
to imagine what infinity's like. He used to get that feeling too. It's a
funny thing. . . .

I'm sorry I had to meet him now, just when he's got to die. Really
sorry. That's why I told him I didn't want him to be my father. I was
telling the truth: it's the last thing I want.

He's just a piece to be sacrificed, that's all. If he was anything more
than that it would be awful. . . .

IT WAS STILL RAINING WHEN MONSIEUR CAZES CAME TO SEE
Quartermain halfway through the afternoon.

"It's set in for days, this rain. When the mountains look like this
you'd better start building your Ark, as we country folk say."

Monsieur Cazes, who was wearing a big fur-lined jacket with a
rabbitskin collar, halved his bulk by taking it off. He seemed a vigor-
ous, determined man, and his every gesture confirmed that first impression. Not much taller than his wife but sturdily built, he walked
with his arms slightly bent at the elbow and his hands in a permanently pincerlike position. He might have been mistaken for a Mongol,
with his big, drooping mustache, but his eyes were very blue. He
sputtered rather than spoke, and Quartermain suspected that his con-
versations with Madame Cazes must sound like a machine-gun duel.

"Must have a word with you," he said. "Got some news."

Monsieur Cazes had turned up with a bottle of wine and two
glasses, which he promptly filled. He took a more than generous pull
at his own glass and smacked his lips.

"Listen," he resumed at length. "Hiding British airmen is one thing, even if they're as dumb as the three in the barn out there, and they don't come any dumber than that, but you and your son are another kettle of fish."

"Don't worry," said Quartermain, who had taken to Monsieur Cazes on sight, "we'll be gone by morning."

"Drink your wine. It's good, we make it ourselves. My sister's husband is the local postmaster, my sister's the telephone operator, and a cousin of my wife's runs the local bus company. Well, I went to see them—them and a couple of other people—just to make sure you and your son weren't spinning us a yarn this morning."

"About my son . . ." Quartermain began, but that was as far as he got.

"That boy of yours," Monsieur Cazes went on, ignoring the interruption, "he's got the cheek of the devil. I don't know how you raise them in America, but if they're all like him I pity the poor Indians. He watches my house, searches it while we're still asleep, and then he comes and tells me, bold as brass, that he's found three British airmen and some guns on my premises, and that it would be better for me and my family if you weren't arrested, the two of you, because if you are he'll tell the gendarmes all about us. That's what I call a nerve!"

"I don't know what to say," said Quartermain.

"Not to mention the fact that he spied on us. We were having breakfast in the kitchen, me and my wife and the rest, and up he popped like a jack-in-the-box. What's more, he'd overheard us talking about our neighbors across the way, those *foutus* Pétainists, and he had the gall to tell us so. Said it made everything just perfect."

Monsieur Cazes refilled his glass. Just then a loud clip-clopping sound made itself heard on the stairs, and Thomas entered in his beret, his cape, and the wooden clogs that had made all the clatter.

"Talk of the devil," said Monsieur Cazes. "If you were a couple of years older, my son, I'd tan your hide for saucing me and making our Émilie cry—and take those muddy clogs off when you come into the house."

"Yes, monsieur. I'm sorry, monsieur."

"Anyway," Monsieur Cazes went on, "I made some inquiries, and the boy turned out to be telling the truth. They're looking for you, all right—they've even called out the militia. Questions are being asked at every garage about a tall man who might have tried to buy or rent a car—a tall, blue-eyed man with an American accent and a limp, accompanied by a small boy with dark hair and gray eyes. It's like beating for game. They're moving up from the south—in fact, they'll be here by tomorrow at the latest. And listen to this: it's just a rumor, not official, but they're said to be offering a reward of half a million francs."

"Your clogs," Quartermain told Thomas. The boy removed his clogs and stood there holding them.

"And another thing," said Monsieur Cazes. "According to my sister, who always listens in on phone calls, there are a number of strangers in the district with foreign accents. They keep calling someone at the Hôtel Noailles in Marseilles—someone called Golaz."

Monsieur Cazes held his wine to the light and studied it for a moment. Then he caught Quartermain's eye.

"Now don't go offering me money, monsieur—I might get mad at you, really mad. And don't be a fool, either. We can hide you for a few more days—they won't find you. It's a pity we've already got those Englishmen, but it can't be helped."

"We'll leave tonight," Quartermain insisted, looking at Thomas with a recurrence of his newfound, almost agonizing affection for the boy. "We'll leave tonight," he repeated. "My son and I have thought of an idea, a plan that should enable us to continue our journey."

"You'll have to change cars. You wouldn't get far in that Chenard." Monsieur Cazes at last came out with a decision he'd obviously been mulling over for some time. He refilled his glass again. "I've got two of my sons downstairs—they'll help us. This miserable weather will come in handy, too. Want to tell me about your idea or not? If we can be of any use to you, just say."

"You can," Quartermain told him.

"That's settled, then. What do you think of this wine?"

"It's excellent," said Quartermain.

"The truth is," said Monsieur Cazes, "it tastes like horsepiss. You obviously don't know the first thing about wine."

IT WAS PAST MIDNIGHT WHEN QUARTERMAIN WOKE THOMAS AND accompanied him downstairs to the kitchen. By the light of a single candle—anything more might have alerted the suspicions of the Pétainists across the way—Madame Cazes made them drink some hot coffee and pressed a packet of sandwiches on them. It was better to be on the safe side these days, she said. Anyway, she couldn't stand arguments—they put her in a bad temper. "God be with you both, and now, push off."

Outside, one of the Cazes boys was waiting for them in the pouring rain. They made their way through the storm-lashed woods to where the Chenard was hidden. Monsieur Cazes and his sons helped to move the car out of its place of concealment—however much noise the storm was making, you never knew with all these snoopers around—and pushed it as far as the road, where Quartermain started it up.

The Cazes boys' two cars took the lead with a couple of hundred yards between them and the same distance between the second of them and the Chenard, though this depended on the road. The more bends there were, the smaller the interval. In an emergency—if gendarmes were sighted, for instance—the second Cazes son would switch his lights on and off three times and Quartermain would make himself scarce.

"Why did you tell them I landed by parachute? And on top of a train?!"

Thomas had just been reprimanding himself for not saying goodbye to Émilie. He ought to have kissed her too—why not, if it would have given her pleasure? She was a nice girl, and awfully pretty in spite of those spots.

"Why, Thomas?"

"I made it up, that's all."

"My eye," said Quartermain. "You aren't the type to say a thing for no good reason. I'm getting wise to you, believe it or not."

"There wasn't any reason."

"Maybe you wish, deep down, that I *had* come by parachute."

Thomas pondered this. All at once, a surprising thought struck him: the American might actually be right! He wasn't going to admit it, though.

"I don't know," he said.

"As a general rule," said Quartermain, "heroes turn up on white horses. Me, I came by parachute."

"That's silly," Thomas said fiercely.

They were driving north. The rain showed signs of stopping from time to time, only to start again with redoubled intensity. The wind was howling, and the whole scene—the road ahead, the swollen river beside it, even the mountains—was lit up as bright as day by intermittent flashes of lightning. Thomas felt genuinely furious. So the American fancied himself a hero now. What was worse, he thought *he* thought the same. Some nerve!

"Mad at me, Thomas?"

"No, not at all."

"I'm no hero."

"You don't have to tell me that."

"I don't want to be one, either. I just want to come out of this in one piece."

"Okay," said Thomas, but he was still seething. He wondered why he should get so angry when the American said something, whereas he wouldn't care two hoots if someone else said it.

They were going very, very slowly now. The road swung left, then right. Thomas recognized the bends: they were coming to the village where the lookout had been.

"I like the Cazes family a lot," Quartermain said. "At least, I like the ones I've met—Monsieur and Madame Cazes, I mean. I don't know Émilie. She's a good-looking girl, I gather."

"Let's talk about something else," said Thomas.

Quartermain shrugged. "Okay, but if this goes on much longer we won't have anything left to talk about."

"We don't have to talk."

"Except that we're traveling together—and being hunted together."

"It's me they're after, not you."

"You mean I don't have to stay with you?"

Thomas hesitated, feeling thoroughly put out.

He was still searching for a suitable reply when the car pulled up with a jerk. He just had time to see a pair of red taillights flash on and off repeatedly. Quartermain had already slammed the car into reverse and was backing fast.

TWIGS CLAWED AT THE CHENARD'S PAINTWORK AS QUARTERmain backed it into a thicket overhung by trees. He'd just backed at top speed for a hundred and fifty yards along an unlit road flanked on the left by the swirling waters of a flooding river. He made a mental note never to try such a thing again, especially at night.

He switched off the ignition and sat back. Only then did it occur to him that he hadn't doused his headlights, which were slicing across the road he'd just left. He hastily did so, cursing under his breath.

"Really smart of you," said Thomas, "forgetting to switch off your headlights like that."

"Save it."

A minute went by. All that broke the silence was the rain pattering on the roof. Then two vehicles passed in quick succession, one of them a police van.

"Why don't you flag them down next time?"

Quartermain suppressed a faint desire to laugh. It surprised him that he should have felt like laughing at all. No doubt about it, the little monkey would be a match for Uncle Peter himself. He lit a cigarette.

"Cigarette smoke makes me cough," said Thomas.

"That's your tough luck."

Quartermain wasn't feeling hilarious, exactly. He could think of any number of places and situations that would have been more conducive to hilarity, yet his sense of wild intoxication was such that he felt capable of toppling mountains and routing half a dozen German divisions—and all because of the presence, two feet away on his right, of a small boy whom he'd known for less than forty-eight hours, but who had only to look at him with *her* eyes to make him feel thoroughly foolish.

He stubbed out his half-smoked cigarette and flicked it into the bushes. Was it possible to fall in love, paternally in love, in the same way as you could be smitten with desire for an unknown girl at first sight? Why ask himself that question when he already knew the answer?

A long silence followed. The boy beside him didn't stir, perhaps because he, too, was aware of their changed relationship. Unless, of course, the machine in his head was grinding out another of his Machiavellian schemes.

It was half an hour before one of Monsieur Cazes's sons appeared, a shadowy figure toiling through the rain. Quartermain quickly wound his window down. They would have to wait a bit longer, he was told. Two vanloads of police had moved on, but one was still mounting guard over the intersection. Young Cazes shook his head, dislodging a shower of raindrops. "They're really after your blood, and no mistake." He waded off through the mud.

"Why are they so anxious to get you, Thomas?"

"I don't know what you mean."

Maria wouldn't really have confided those banker's codes to a little boy, would she? Or *would* she? Did he have the means to reach all that money? Did he know what she had known, what old von Gall had put in motion years ago? Why else would she have involved him, Quartermain, in this affair? There had to be some good reason for such a monumental manhunt. You didn't mobilize dozens if not hundreds of men to capture a youngster whose sole claim to fame was his status as Maria Weber's son.

Or his own. . . . Catherine Lamiel knew what Maria had told him in her letter, so Laemmle must know too. So what? If they were hunting Thomas because he was his son, or might be, capturing him, Quartermain, would be worth more to them—always assuming that he possessed some value, which was doubtful in the extreme. No, it didn't make sense.

Young Cazes reappeared.

"It's no use, the gendarmes won't budge. You could bypass them, though."

"And get past the lookout as well?"

"Yes. You'll have to drive without lights, and the track's so water-logged you may get stuck, but it's worth a try. I'll walk on ahead and you follow me in first gear."

Quartermain didn't enjoy the next few minutes. He crawled along the flooded riverbank for several hundred yards in almost total darkness. Then the Cazes boy reappeared beside him.

"There's a bridge on your left. Take it absolutely straight and you should just make it—and don't rev your engine too much. The *flics* are just around the bend."

Quartermain insisted on getting out and taking a look. The bridge was timber-built and had no parapet, and the condition of the planks left a lot to be desired. He didn't know if they would bear the Chenard's weight, but time would very soon tell.

"Get out, Thomas."

"In this rain?"

He leaned across and opened the passenger door. "No arguments. Go and wait for me on the other side."

Then he started across the bridge, obeying a series of prearranged signals. Several brisk taps on his left or right front fender meant that he was straying too far in one direction or the other, one good slap that he'd corrected the error and all was well. Young Cazes gave the hood a final slap and came to the window.

"You made it. Frankly, I wasn't too optimistic."

"Thanks for telling me now," said Quartermain.

Thomas got in again and they crawled through the darkness at a walking pace.

"How's your English, Thomas?"

"Not bad."

"How many languages *do* you speak?"

"French and English."

"How about German?"

"A bit."

"Spanish?"

"A bit."

"Italian?"

"No."

"Not a word?"

"Just a little bit."

"Say something in English for me."

"My mother's dead," Thomas said. "She was burnt alive."

Quartermain winced. Steadying his voice with an effort, he said, "We tend to say 'burned' in the States, but 'burnt' is quite correct too —the verb 'to burn' is regular and irregular at the same time."

"Thank you, monsieur. I'll make a note of that."

It was another ten or fifteen minutes before young Cazes reappeared at the window.

"You can switch on your parking lights now, but not your headlights. My brother and I will lead the way."

They speeded up a little. The muddy track skirted a darkened farmhouse and brought them to an asphalt road.

"You're on your own now," said young Cazes. "Turn left after three or four hundred meters and you'll come to the crossroads where the lookout is. Good luck."

Quartermain waited until he reached the intersection. Then he switched on his headlights and put his foot down. Almost before he knew it some outlying houses swam into view. Then, on the right of the road, he saw a man in a felt hat and black leather raincoat jump out of a parked car, leaving the door open. He braked hard as though intending to do a skid turn, then accelerated again. The man had to dive sideways at the last moment in order to avoid the Chenard's crumpled fender.

Quartermain roared through the little village at top speed and drove the next three kilometers with his foot flattened. The prearranged sign —two branches laid crosswise in the roadway—showed up ahead. He slowed, deliberately drove over them to wipe the slate clean, and slowed still more. Fifty yards farther on a big iron gate stood open. A woman closed it behind him as soon as he was inside. At the end of a drive flanked by plane trees stood what looked in the gloom like a big country house, and just to the right of the house Quartermain saw a flashlight wink on and off.

He pulled up beside Monsieur Cazes, who mounted the running board.

"I see you made it across the bridge. I'd never have believed it. That timber's as rotten as an overripe pear."

Quartermain grinned in the darkness. "So your son was kind enough to point out."

He drove across some parkland and through an open gate. Immediately beyond it was a stream, but someone had bridged it with planks, and he negotiated the obstacle without difficulty. Still under Monsieur Cazes's guidance, he zigzagged through an orchard and cut across an open field.

"A tractor will go over your tracks tomorrow morning," Monsieur Cazes explained. "Peasant cunning—isn't that what you city folk call it?"

Then came a barbed-wire fence with the strands conveniently cut and bent aside to let them pass, then two more fields in succession.

"Another job for the tractor?"

"First thing tomorrow."

"Pretty ingenious of you."

"I like to think so. Turn left here."

Quartermain found himself on a farm track. He had no conception of where it led to, let alone of its position relative to the main road. He was completely lost.

"Take the first turn on the right, then right again."

A minute later the Chenard drove into a barn. The double doors were swiftly closed behind it and a light went on.

"Switch it off. This is it."

There were eight men in the barn, three of them armed with blow-torches.

"They're going to cut your car up so small there won't be enough of it left to make a bicycle. Whom did it belong to?"

"A government official from Vichy."

"Serves him right, the swine. Come and look."

They emerged from the barn by another door and entered a house on the far side of the courtyard beyond it. Monsieur Cazes led the way to a room upstairs.

"Take a look," he whispered.

The window was shuttered. Peering through the slats, Quartermain found himself looking down at the intersection he'd passed less than half an hour before, now lit up like a film set by the glare of numerous headlights. The lookout was deep in conversation with another man in civilian clothes and several gendarmes. Even as Quartermain watched, the lookout and his civilian colleague detached themselves from the gendarmes and strolled past, just beneath the window. They were conversing in low voices, but the language was unmistakably German.

Back in the barn, Thomas was watching the progress of the demolition work. Monsieur Cazes nodded in the boy's direction.

"Think he can manage to walk half the night?"

"He can do anything he puts his mind to," Quartermain replied.

They trekked across country for the next three hours, guided by Monsieur Cazes and one of his sons. It was difficult going, what with the persistent downpour and the rugged terrain, but Thomas never lagged behind. "*Très bien*," he would say when Quartermain asked him how he was faring, "*et vous?*"

It must have been around seven in the morning when they came to a road. Their route thus far had taken them along rough tracks, through icy streams, up and down precipitous, rain-lashed hillsides, but never within sight of a house. They might have been four nocturnal shadows.

A couple of miles down the road, which was asphalt, they came to a shepherd's hut. There was a car inside.

"A fifteen-horse Citroën," said Monsieur Cazes. "Tuned to perfection, too. You won't find many cars around to beat it. It was the best I could do—I got it for half the money you gave me. The owner had it stashed away to prevent it from being requisitioned. The plates are false and the documents are made out in the name of Bjorn Olson. If you'd given me a bit more time I could have fixed you up with a Swedish passport."

"Another time, maybe," said Quartermain. "Thanks for everything. I'll pay you another visit once you've cleaned this country up."

"It shouldn't take much longer, but make sure we've finished the job first."

They shook hands.

"In you get, Thomas."

The boy got in without a word, but that might simply have been because he was exhausted.

Quartermain headed due east in the direction of Switzerland.

GREGOR LAEMMLE MADE HIS CALL TO HENRI LAFONT AT A STAGE when neither he nor anyone else had known for hours where the fugitives were or which way they were going. The probability was that they were traveling in a Chenard-Walker stolen in the vicinity of Nîmes, but that left numerous questions open. Were they making for Spain, had they turned back east, or had they managed to board some vessel outward bound from the Camargue for Catalonia or the Balearics, or even for North Africa? Alternatively, were they heading due north?

Laemmle not only plumped for the last theory but clung to it all the more fiercely because he had no evidence to support it. He still hadn't received—nor would he receive for another six hours—the message from the second-line lookout in Ardèche to the effect that a Chenard with a damaged fender had passed him heading west toward Cantal or the Dordogne, possibly intending to turn south for Toulouse and Spain. In other words, that the American had outflanked Hess's cordon in the north.

It was eight o'clock on the evening of November 10 when Laemmle got through to Lafont and stated his requirements.

"And you want all this by when?" the Frenchman asked. His falsetto voice was pleasantly modulated and easy on the ear.

"It's not much to ask."

"Oh, no?" Lafont emitted a high-pitched giggle. "It's nothing short of general mobilization."

"Money's no problem, you know that."

"I know you don't mind dipping your hand in your pocket—I've never had cause for complaint—but if I do this, it'll simply be because I like you."

"I'm flattered," said Laemmle. The odd thing was, he not only believed Lafont but reciprocated his sentiments.

"That fiasco down south was none of my doing. Your friend Hess insisted on dispensing with my services and recruiting a bunch of deadbeats from Toulon and Marseilles. Result: a messy massacre. You wanted the woman alive, I take it?"

"Correct."

"If I'd handled the operation she'd still be alive. Your friend Hess was clumsy, to say the least."

"He's no friend of mine."

Another falsetto giggle. "In that case I'll go further and call him a blithering idiot. Are you really sure they'll head northeast, the American and the boy?"

"Absolutely positive."

"They won't try crossing the demarcation line, surely?"

"Anything's possible, but it's my belief they'll try to get back across the Rhône."

"And make for Switzerland?"

"Yes." Laemmle shut his eyes. "There are eighteen bridges over the Rhône between Avignon and Lyon, not counting the towns themselves. I want three men and two cars watching each of them."

"Fifty-four men and thirty-six cars! Is that all?"

"No. I want backup teams covering four of those eighteen bridges— at Valence, La Voulte, Le Puzin, and Richemaure—because they're the likeliest crossing points. In addition—"

"Stop, you're giving me ulcers!" Lafont giggled again.

"In addition, I want a mobile reserve of three detachments stationed in the rear, ready to move as soon as the target crosses a bridge and the alarm is raised."

"That makes close to a hundred men," Lafont said eventually. "I'll have to get some reinforcements down from Lyons and Paris as well as up from Marseilles. How much of a reward are you offering?"

"As much as you think appropriate."

"Leave it to me—I won't cheat you."

"I know you won't."

"Strange how well we get on, you and I. Our backgrounds aren't exactly similar."

Loup Durand

"I share your surprise at the extent of our mutual understanding," said Laemmle, "but the surprise is a pleasant one."

"These men of mine," said Lafont, "are they to open fire?"

Laemmle considered this question, but only for the split second it took him to consign Joachim Gortz and his stipulation about Quartermain's survival to the devil.

"I want the boy without a scratch on him."

"And the American?"

"Accidents happen, I know, but it must be just that: an accident."

Lafont said he understood. He regretted that he couldn't take personal command of Laemmle's Maginot Line because of prior commitments. However, he proposed to entrust the operation to his nephew, Paul Clavié, and his principal lieutenant, Charles Cazauba. Both men would be leaving Paris within the hour.

"All the men you want will be in position between two and four A.M. tomorrow. That's the best I can do."

"It'll be quite good enough, *mon cher.*"

After some hesitation, Lafont came out with a request: could Laemmle get him promoted? He was only a captain in the German army and coveted the rank of major.

"Why not?" Laemmle replied benignly, though he couldn't see himself asking Himmler for a favor of any kind. "If *I'm* a colonel in the SS, anyone can be anything."

He hung up, had a good seafood dinner, surveyed the Canebière from his hotel balcony, and managed to doze for an hour or two.

It was a little past three A.M. when the phone rang. A second-line lookout in Ardèche reported that the Chenard, with a man and a child on board, had sped past him in a westerly direction. As far as Laemmle was concerned, that clinched it. Far too much time had elapsed between the first and second sightings.

"They must have gone to ground somewhere between the two cordons, Soeft, and they've only just set off again. Fetch me those maps." Laemmle studied them awhile. "Know what? They showed themselves deliberately. It was just a trick to get the police roadblocks moved farther west. They'll lie low somewhere, waiting for them to be shifted, and then they'll head northeast. Either that, or they've already set off across the mountains on foot. Then again, they may have found themselves another car, or a motorcycle, or a couple of bicycles. . . ."

Laemmle sat back with an air of decision.

"How many men do you have, Soeft? Sixteen? Get them moving in double-quick time. They're to cover all the crossroads in the east and northeast of Ardèche. I don't know exactly where the little imp will reappear, but you can bet he's making for the Rhône."

Where Lafont's men were already in position.

"I've got them, Soeft! I've almost got them!"

Unless the little imp had cooked up some other diabolical scheme. He wouldn't put anything past the boy. God, what a worthy opponent he was!

THOMAS WAS PORING OVER THE MAP IN THE GRAY LIGHT OF DAWN.

"We'll be coming to a crossroads in a kilometer or so."

"There are crossroads all over the place," said Quartermain. "So what?"

"Yellow Eyes must have moved his lookouts—he must have."

"Farther west, you mean?"

"No, east and north. He'll have guessed we were bluffing. It's obvious."

"Even if he has, they'll be behind us, not in front."

"We lost a lot of time walking. They've got cars—they may be ahead of us."

The Citroën was negotiating a series of downhill hairpin bends. Quartermain reacted swiftly when he saw a truckload of militiamen below him, coming the other way. He pulled off the road and concealed the car behind some bushes.

The truck crawled past them up the hill. It was the third they'd encountered, and all had been heading west.

"At least that's one point in our favor," Quartermain said. "They're shifting their roadblocks farther to the west."

"That was your idea."

"Thanks for the compliment."

Thomas looked up from the map and studied the American in profile. He's a strange person, he thought. Cool as a cucumber. Not stupid either—far from it. My plan was a good one, but he came up with some really bright ideas. Besides, he's an ace driver. He's got sharp eyes, and he does the right thing at the right moment without losing his nerve. He looks as if he couldn't care less, but he doesn't miss a trick. It's the same with Pistol Pete: just when you think he's failed to spot something and fallen into a trap, he escapes in the nick of time.

The other thing is, he's incredibly nice and kind. I've said some really nasty things to him—things that might have made him fly off the handle—but no, he . . .

Stop it!

Stop thinking like that or you'll start getting fond of him, and there's no point. He's as good as dead. He's still alive, of course, but he might as well be dead. Yellow Eyes will kill him, there's no question about that. Yellow Eyes hates the American, I know he does, because the American thinks he's my father. He'll tell Soeft to kill him just because of that—it's obvious, so why pretend it isn't?

Anyway, I'll be to blame for the American's death, because it's part of my plan. He's the piece I've got to sacrifice, and it's silly to get fond of one particular piece on a chessboard. . . .

The American was speaking, but he hadn't heard a word. The Citroën was still stationary.

Thomas said, "Shouldn't we be going?"

"We'll go, Thomas, but thirty seconds more or less won't make any difference. Do you think there'll be a lookout at the intersection down there?"

"There may be."

"Okay," said Quartermain, "let's assume there is. What do you suggest?"

"We drive straight past him—it's the only way. He won't catch us if you drive fast enough. This is an awfully good car."

Quartermain looked at him and nodded, but Thomas could tell that the other possible solution had occurred to him.

"Mm," he said. "The only trouble is, I'm not too used to this kind of thing. I don't have the training."

Thomas said nothing. What *could* he say? Quartermain gave another nod and smiled. He reached for the door handle.

"Will you wait here for me, Thomas?"

"Yes." He knows I'm sacrificing him, and he's being awfully brave about it. . . . "Yes, I'll wait here."

"Give me twenty minutes. If I'm not back by then, take off, okay?"

"Okay."

"I won't ask if you know where to go—I'm pretty sure you do. If you do go, take the binoculars and the map. Got some money?"

"Yes."

"See you, then," said Quartermain. He gave the boy a parting smile and strode off in his characteristically long-legged, loose-limbed way, limping a little as he went.

It gives me a funny pain in the chest to see him go, Thomas thought, but maybe he'll make it—maybe the American'll make it like Pistol Pete. I can't help feeling sad, though. Awfully sad . . .

QUARTERMAIN MADE HIS WAY DOWNHILL FOR THREE OR FOUR hundred yards until the densely wooded slope leveled off and the trees thinned sufficiently to give him a view of the road.

He stood very still, screened by some evergreen oaks, and peered through the foliage. The intersection was less than a hundred yards away.

No one to be seen. He breathed a sigh of relief.

His relief was short-lived. Closer scrutiny revealed the lookout, or rather, the hood of his car, which was just protruding from behind a small electrical transformer hut. Quartermain's pulse and heart beat a simultaneous tattoo. He was scared, he had to admit. How could he have imagined himself capable of what he planned to do? He would never pull it off.

And then, almost without knowing it, he was calmly, unhurriedly descending the slope and walking along the road. If there were two of them, he would wind up looking very foolish.

He tried to mesmerize himself with graphic recollections of Maria burning to death and the blazing, bullet-riddled figure of Javier Coll. It was odd, but the thought of Maria enraged him less than his vision of the Spaniard fighting to the end against all odds. He felt utterly lucid and self-aware—conscious of every last little movement his body made.

He drew level with the transformer hut and walked on.

Next, a double take: a turn of the head accompanied by the facial expression of a peaceful stroller who unexpectedly sights an old friend on a street corner.

There was only one lookout. He was sitting at the wheel of his car, watching Quartermain. Throwing up his hands with an air of delighted surprise, Quartermain went over to the driver's door and tapped on the window.

"Can you help me, please?"

The lookout stared at him, stupefied, but he wound his window halfway down.

"The thing is," Quartermain said, "I'd very much like to make the acquaintance of Yellow Eyes, otherwise known as Gregor Laemmle."

And he calmly extended his hand as though to remove a stray thread from the man's collar. Except that he gripped him by the throat, very fast and very hard, and brought his other hand to bear as well. Bracing one knee against the door, he hauled the man out of his seat. The upper part of the lookout's body slid through the window, but the rest of him jammed, obstructed by the steering wheel. Jesus, thought Quartermain, I'll never do it—he'll break my grip. He must be armed, and how that Soeft guy missed me the last time I'll never know. I won't be as lucky twice in a row.

He drove his thumbs into the muscular throat with redoubled force, but his adversary continued to struggle. Without letting go, Quartermain threw all his weight backward. The window broke and the lookout's entire body emerged like a cork from a bottle. Quartermain head-butted him smack on the nose, breaking it, as they fell to the ground in a close embrace. He could hear a kind of death rattle, but it wasn't issuing from the throat between his hands: it was his own stertorous breathing. Only then did he realize the extent of his crazy, demented urge to kill in memory of Javier Coll, a man he'd met only once.

To kill, too, for the sake of the boy whom these lousy bastards were hounding so mercilessly. . . .

Then it was over. The lookout went limp, tongue protruding, congested eyes upturned. Quartermain felt thwarted—he hadn't finished yet. He squeezed and went on squeezing in a cold fury until the cartilage cracked beneath his straining thumbs. He did so because now the visions assailed him without his having to summon them up: visions of Thomas numb with grief, sobbing and uttering plaintive little cries on account of a man or men like the one he'd just throttled.

Quartermain removed his hands, straightened up, and found that he was sitting astride his victim. He pulled the man's pistol from his shoulder holster and tossed it away.

You did it, he told himself. When it came to the moment, you did it. Anyone's a potential killer. . . .

He became aware that the road was only a yard or two behind him. Someone might pass by at any moment and see him. He hadn't given a thought to what he would do once the lookout was dead, but it was simple enough.

He opened the rear door and heaved the body inside. Then he remembered the gun. He retrieved it from the heap of gravel where it had fallen and laid it beside the body. That done, he got in behind the wheel and drove back up the winding road to the spot where he'd left the Citroën and Thomas.

If he was still there. . . .

He was, and he must have seen and recognized Quartermain at the wheel of the strange car, because he was standing beside the Citroën. He watched Quartermain extract the body and haul it through the undergrowth to the edge of a small ravine carpeted with brushwood. The lookout toppled into it headfirst and disappeared from view.

I should have searched the bastard, Quartermain thought belatedly. He tossed the man's pistol after him and returned to the Citroën.

"Get in."

"We ought to look in the glove compartment."

"Okay, you do it."

Quartermain got in, leaving the door open. The boy returned.

"It wasn't there—I found it under the driver's seat." He produced a yellow ID card printed in German and French. "It's a Gestapo card. His name was Heinemann. He also had some travel permits and things. They might be worth keeping."

"Get in."

Quartermain started up and backed out onto the road again. He was getting quite used to these cloak-and-dagger maneuvers, he reflected. Incredible, how calm he felt.

"You've got some blood on your face," Thomas said.

The intersection was deserted. They turned left and headed due north.

"COULD WE STOP, PLEASE?"

Quartermain pulled up beside a small clump of trees on the right of the road. Not far beyond them lay the Rhône.

Thomas got out and made his way into the copse. He turned and looked back at the car. He didn't want to relieve himself—he'd only said that to get the American to stop.

It's time I told him, he thought. I know what to say but I don't want to say it, especially not now. It was awfully brave of him to kill that lookout. He did it, but it made him feel sick. He hasn't said a word for the past hour, and his hands keep trembling. He's not like Soeft or Hess or Monsieur Cazes. They would kill someone without a second thought if they had to, but not the American. He's not used to it, of course, but that's not the real reason. He simply doesn't like killing people. When Grandpa Allègre had to kill a rabbit or a chicken he said he didn't have the knack, so Grandma Allègre wound up doing it for him, but the real reason was, it made him feel sick. . . .

Through the trees Thomas could see the big house he'd spotted from the car when they passed it a few hundred yards back. The gates were closed and so were all the shutters. It was obviously deserted—you could tell at a glance when a house was empty.

The house was set back from the road. It had two stories, and the shutters were an unusual shade of blue. Thomas debated whether to make a run for it there and then, but he dismissed the idea. The American would come looking for him, and besides, he couldn't just run off without a word. A piece you sacrificed didn't realize you were sacrificing it. The American was different.

He returned to the car and got in again.

"There's something I've got to tell you: I think the bridges will all be guarded."

"On Laemmle's orders, you mean?"

"Yes."

Quartermain shut his eyes. He's angry, Thomas thought. He's tired out like me, and he's still feeling sick because he killed that lookout, so he's angry. Angry in a quiet kind of way, though. That's how he is. . . .

"Sure you aren't crediting our friend Laemmle with supernatural powers?"

"No," said Thomas, "I don't think so." He paused. "After all, I wasn't wrong about the lookout. It was the logical place for him to be."

"And it's just as logical for the bridges to be guarded?"

Thomas didn't reply. It was pointless to state the obvious.

"Okay, so it's logical," Quartermain said. "Let's assume the bridges are being watched. How many are there?"

"Eighteen between Avignon and Lyons, plus the ones in Lyons itself."

"And you think the ones in Lyons are a better bet?"

"Yes."

Another silence. Quartermain rubbed his eyes and sighed. "All right, suppose you tell me exactly what you have in mind."

"We could try to cross at Lyons. The bridges in a big city are harder to check than bridges in the country or in little towns. That's logical, isn't it?"

"But Laemmle will think of that too, won't he?"

"Of course, but if he doesn't know I know he's watching the bridges he'll think we'll try to cross one without suspecting anything and then he'll be able to catch us, or maybe he'll think I've thought up a trick to get us across, or maybe he'll think I *think* he thinks I've thought up a trick and we won't try crossing any of the bridges because I know he knows, so it'll be a good place to cross after all."

"I didn't get a word of that," Quartermain said, smiling for the first time in ages. "Not a word. Would you like to repeat it and put in a couple of commas here and there?"

"It's obvious, though," said Thomas. Well, almost, he added to himself.

"Lyons it is, then?"

"We can try." Thomas yawned without even meaning to. "The only trouble is, I'm awfully tired. Hungry, too."

Quartermain shrugged. "No reason why we shouldn't stop awhile. It'll be a few hours before the lookout's relieved, with any luck. If his orders were to raise the alarm if he saw us go past, Laemmle will think we either haven't gone that way or we went that way earlier on, so he'll be looking for us someplace else."

"You can say some pretty complicated things yourself when you try," Thomas said.

"That's high praise, coming from an expert like you," said Quartermain. "Anyway, if the bridges really are being watched the way you think, there's no point in rushing into anything. We ought to give it some thought first."

"Besides, if Yellow Eyes and his lookouts don't see a sign of us they may think we aren't where we are. They may think we're heading west after all."

"Now that *does* strike me as obvious," Quartermain said with another faint smile.

"Me too."

"While you were pretending to take a leak I saw you looking at the house with the blue shutters. I noticed it too, while we were driving past. Think it's empty?"

Thomas nodded.

"In that case, let's go."

To Thomas, what happened then was like a repetition of that time on the beach at Port-Issol, when a huge wave filled his mouth and throat with seawater and rolled him over and over until he didn't know where he was and thought he was going to drown until Javier appeared and grabbed him by the arm and hauled him ashore.

Except that there wasn't any Javier now, nor would there ever be again. He would always be alone from now on, a lonely little boy with no one to look after him, and it wasn't fair, and there were times when he genuinely wanted to die because things just couldn't go on this way —*he* couldn't go on this way . . .

"Thomas," the American was saying. His voice had gone all soft and gentle. "Oh, Thomas!"

"Don't touch me, please. Don't touch me."

The wave had descended on him again, rolling him over and over until he didn't know where he was. It would be awfully nice if someone—not just anyone, but the American—took him by the arm as Javier had done. It was hard being alone, awfully hard, but what if he became fond of this American who understood him better than Javier, who was kind and cheerful even if he wasn't as tough? It would only bring the American bad luck like the others. They were dead, all the people he'd ever loved and been loved by, so the best thing was not to love anyone at all. He knew now what the wave was: it was his affection for the American and his utter inability to save him from the inevitable.

"I'm fine, monsieur," he said. "I'm fine. Just a bit tired, that's all." His nails had drawn blood, he'd driven them into his knees so hard, but the worst was over. The machine had taken charge again. "Shouldn't we make sure the house is really empty first? The people may come back—perhaps they've just gone shopping or something."

"We'll take a look," said Quartermain.

He turned the Citroën and drove back along the road to the wrought-iron gates. There was no answer when he rang the bell, so he drove on until he came to a lane that led to another gate, a wooden one secured by a padlock. Beyond it lay an avenue of plane trees with an ornamental lily pond in the middle.

"Wait here, Thomas."

He climbed over the gate and disappeared into the grounds. It was many minutes before he returned.

"It's empty, all right," he said. He opened the padlock with a key, then the gate itself, and drove inside. Having locked the gate behind them, he parked the Citroën in a garage to which he also produced the key. When Thomas asked where he'd found all these keys, he explained that he'd broken in by climbing onto a roof and removing some tiles, then searched around until he found a spare set.

"You forget I'm an experienced burglar, Thomas. Every house has a spare set of keys."

Although the place was deserted, the beds were made up.

"Get some sleep, Thomas." Quartermain smiled at him. "You first. We'll take turns keeping watch, like sentries."

Exhaustion triumphed over hunger. Thomas slept.

QUARTERMAIN'S EYES JERKED OPEN. THE SOUR TASTE IN HIS mouth was that of a sleeper prematurely awakened. He satisfied himself that the boy was still fast asleep, then got up. He must have dozed off. Any sentry who did that on active duty would be court-martialed.

It was half past noon by his watch. Going from room to room and window to window, he scanned the surrounding area through chinks in the shutters without seeing anything of note. The front rooms afforded a view of the road and, separated from the road by a few hundred yards of scrub, the river.

However they managed to cross the Rhône—even if they swam it or rowed across or leapfrogged it in a hot-air balloon—they would still have to find themselves another car for the drive to Switzerland. Except that. . . . Why in hell did he have this vague and ill-defined feeling that the boy had no intention of going to Switzerland, or certainly not in his company?

He returned to the room where Thomas was sleeping and promptly succumbed to the glow of affection that had never really left him throughout the past two days, even when he was throttling the life out of that German. That was his sole excuse and the reason for his almost total absence of remorse. The plain truth was, killing the man had given him pleasure, or if not pleasure, extreme satisfaction.

Feeling hungry, he went downstairs and rummaged in the kitchen and pantry. The results were less than meager, they were nil. Then he remembered Madame Cazes's sandwiches, which were still in the Citroën. All was quiet outside. Not suspiciously quiet but just as it should have been. If they simply sat it out here, perhaps Uncle Peter and Cousin Larry would march to their rescue with a U.S. infantry division.

He locked himself in again and went upstairs. Thomas was sleeping like a baby. The little face had lost some of its deathly pallor. The lashes were so long and dark that they might almost have been coated with mascara like those of Quartermain's female playmates at home. He'd completely forgotten about them. It seemed years since he'd left Vermont.

He ate standing up for fear of dropping off to sleep again. Just before they'd made their joint decision to bivouac in this house, a curious change had come over the boy. His eyes had filled with tears, and for one long minute he simply wasn't there in the car anymore: he was there without being there, probably overcome by another terrible recollection of the scene on the coast. He possessed a courage and resilience that many men would envy, Quartermain reflected, himself first and foremost.

The house resembled a miniature chateau. The doors were decorated with bosses and ornamental motifs, the locks with brass fleurs-de-lis that shone in the artificial twilight created by the closed shutters. White dust sheets covered all the furniture except in a few of the upstairs rooms. It was clear that someone lived here, or had done so until recently, but only in part of the premises. As weary as he was, Quartermain's imagination ran riot. Looking at the tapestries and portraits, testers and four-poster beds, he seemed to inhale the scent and sweetness of the warm, living flesh that had dwelt within these walls. Companionship was what he needed, but not here in these alien, ultra-French surroundings. In Vermont, perhaps, where Thomas and he would go fishing and hunting together, and Thomas would teach him to play chess infinitely better than he'd ever done before. . . .

Traffic could be heard on the road in front of the house. Peering through the shutters in the largest bedroom, Quartermain saw a strange convoy composed of five or six charcoal-burning cars and trucks piled high with a motley assortment of household goods. He was reminded of one of his rare visits to the movies. The newsreel had shown pathetic columns of refugees straggling along the roads of France in 1940.

The road was empty for a while after the convoy had passed by. Then another one appeared. Like the first, it was traveling from left to right, or north to south. Quartermain was still contemplating this spectacle when he heard a voice behind him.

"There's a woman in that bed."

Quartermain spun around—he hadn't heard Thomas come in—and stared at the lofty four-poster. Barely visible above the bedclothes and ensconced in a nest of lace pillows was a small gray head. The light was so dim, he hadn't noticed. He went over to the bed and flicked his lighter: not only was the old woman dead; her mummified condition suggested that she'd been dead for weeks, if not months.

"I think she must have starved to death," Thomas said. "I think she lived by herself and didn't have anything left to eat, so she went to bed to die."

"How would you know?" said Quartermain, unnerved by this calmly authoritative statement.

"The beds were made but all the doors were locked and chained. Maybe she was waiting for someone who never turned up."

Quartermain suddenly found the atmosphere oppressive. "Let's get out of here," he said, and led the way downstairs to the drawing room.

"Hungry?" he asked as he watched the boy tearing at one of Madame Cazes's ham sandwiches with his little white teeth.

"Did I sleep for a long time, monsieur?"

"A good six hours."

"How about you?"

"I slept for a bit. I dozed off in an armchair."

"You can get some sleep now. I'll keep watch."

"Personally, I think we should leave."

"There's no hurry. The longer they wait for us to cross, the less wide-awake they'll be. Yellow Eyes may begin to think he's wrong, and we aren't where he thought we were."

"Sounds logical," said Quartermain.

"It is." Halfway to Thomas's mouth, the thick ham sandwich stopped short. "Yellow Eyes used to make me slices of bread and jam at the hotel in Grenoble. I told him I didn't know how to butter my own bread. He didn't believe me, but he *wanted* to do it for me. Naturally he did, being a *maricón*."

"A what?"

"A pederast," the boy said calmly. "I once heard Tomeo use the

word about a man he'd known, so I looked it up in the dictionary." He
resumed his assault on the sandwich.

Quartermain was flabbergasted. "And you say Laemmle's one?
How on earth do you know?"

"You can tell, that's all. That's why I stayed with him when I
noticed him following me at Aix, and then in the train, and afterward
at Grenoble. He was protecting me from Jürgen Hess and the others.
Even now he knows more or less where we are but he won't tell Hess
or the gendarmes. He wants to catch me all by himself—*for* himself."

God Almighty, Quartermain thought. He's blithely telling me that
the Gestapo's chief sleuth is in love with him, and that he escaped by
deliberately exploiting the man's emotional attachment!

He went to one of the drawing-room windows and observed the
road again. Nothing could now be seen in either direction: not a truck,
not a car, not even a cyclist or farm cart. It was utterly deserted.
Quartermain had an unaccountable but irresistible feeling that something was up. First that miniature exodus of a few dozen vehicles at
most, now this sudden silence and lack of movement.

"I won't be long, Thomas."

He went upstairs to the attic and found the hole he'd made in the
lath-and-plaster ceiling. Lifting the tiles again, he very cautiously
poked his head out.

The rest of him emerged with equal caution. Stretched out on the
roof in the lee of a chimney stack, he swept the entire district with his
binoculars. Every potential hiding place—every bush, every little fold
in the ground—was scrutinized in the half-serious expectation of seeing Gregor Laemmle's lookouts converging on the house.

Nothing.

He could see for miles, though. The nearest house, a roadside cottage, was eight or nine hundred yards away. A man was at work in his
garden, alternately turning the soil and bending down to weed it in a
leisurely way. As Quartermain watched, he leaned on his fork and said
something to a woman on the cottage doorstep. No sight could have
been more reassuringly commonplace. In the distance was a town or a
large village, but no traffic could be seen entering or leaving it.

Quartermain transferred his attention to the farther bank of the
river and the main road beyond it. No sign of life there either. Minutes
passed before a lone bus appeared, heading south like the strange little
convoys he'd noticed earlier.

What the hell was going on?

THOMAS SHARED THE AMERICAN'S VIEW: THE LACK OF ACTIVITY *was* odd. He'd seen it for himself, not from the roof—the American forbade him to go up there—but from an upstairs window. Yellow Eyes might be responsible, but it seemed unlikely. He might be able to ban all traffic on the German side of the demarcation line, but not in the unoccupied zone.

"Anyway," said Quartermain, "it's one more reason for staying put. I don't like the idea of driving along in total isolation, just the two of us, not till I've found out why the roads are deserted. What do you think, Thomas?"

"The same as you."

Quartermain had found a checkers set and was busy scratching letters on the bottom of the men with a knife point.

"How do you say 'pawn' in French?"

"Pion," said Thomas.

"Fine, so they both start with a P." Quartermain went on scratching away at his makeshift chess set. "Did you play against Yellow Eyes?"

"Once, yes."

"You beat him?"

"Yes."

"Easily?"

"Yes."

"Is he as bad as all that?"

"I'm good, that's all."

"Who taught you?"

Thomas hesitated. "I taught myself."

"Somebody must have shown you the various moves."

The boy looked Quartermain straight in the eyes. "I'd rather not talk about it."

"Who else have you played? Javier Coll?"

"He didn't play. I played by myself."

"Think we could play with this homemade set?"

"I guess so."

They played two games in quick succession. Quartermain was checkmated in seventeen moves the first time, eleven the second.

"You're really good, Thomas. I could play you ten times a day for twenty years and never take a game off you."

"That's because you don't concentrate hard enough. You make some awfully silly mistakes."

Thomas instantly grasped, from the way the American looked at him, why he'd suggested playing chess.

"I learned to play back in 1930, Thomas. I've hardly ever played since, but I played quite a few games around that time. Always against the same person—the person who taught me. I only beat her once or twice."

"Let's talk about something else."

"On the contrary, I think it's time we talked about just that. She was the one who sent for me, Thomas, and that's an indisputable fact. You read her letter. It doesn't matter whether or not you think she was lying to me or whether or not I'm really your father. We'll probably never know, either of us. Sit down, boy! I could force you to listen, so don't make me."

Thomas complied. He sat back, gripping the arms of his chair in silent rage.

"I got to know her in August 1930, Thomas. You've inherited her eyes, but I've no need to tell you that."

The American talked on. Thomas tried hard not to listen, but he couldn't help himself. He listened with overpowering fury, but he listened. At first it drove him almost insane to hear a man—any man, even this one—recall how he'd held Her in his arms and kissed Her. He even considered killing the American as well as Laemmle, but the impulse waned and he began, despite his rage, to analyze every word of every episode in the American's story. He wasn't lying—too much of what he said accorded with what Thomas already knew, except that he hadn't known there'd been someone living with Her in Seville in that house She'd shown him. The American even mentioned the doves that used to roost in the eaves. No, he wasn't lying. It was going to be terribly hard to sacrifice him now, terribly hard to send him to his death. . . .

The American ended by describing their last few days together at the house near Sanary and their final farewell at the Marseilles station, where Javier had waved to him. Then he fell silent. Thomas avoided his eye. He felt completely lost—even the machine wasn't running smoothly. Everything was all mixed up.

The rumbling sound could barely be heard at first, but it swelled until it resembled an approaching thunderstorm. It was accompanied by another sound, a peculiar clanking, jingling sound, and it was coming along the road from left to right. In other words, from north to south.

Quartermain was the first to get up and look through the shutters. "Oh, my God!" he exclaimed, and Thomas quickly joined him at the window. Quartermain took him by the waist and lifted him up so that he could see.

And see he did.

"Well, my friend," Quartermain said, "I guess the so-called unoccupied zone has just been occupied."

Truckloads of steel-helmeted German soldiers, scout cars, motorcycle-sidecar combinations, tanks bristling with guns—the road was filled with an endless, ever-advancing column of vehicles. Even the Rhône looked puny beside that river of steel.

GREGOR LAEMMLE WAS FAR FROM OVERJOYED BY THE NEWS THAT Adolf's armies had entered the unoccupied zone. "Really, Soeft," he complained to his faithful lieutenant. "Have I ever asked Adolf for a helping hand? No. So why is he butting in? It's like an elephant playing skittles, as we say in French. I'm absolutely shattered."

He'd heard the news before the French did. Joachim Gortz had called him late the previous night. "You seem to be having some difficulty in recovering what you've lost," he announced in a more than usually maddening tone of voice, "so we've decided to send you some reinforcements. We may have overdone it a bit, but at least you'll have all the manpower you need."

The rest of what he said, which was in similar vein, only confirmed Laemmle's hatred of the man.

"And another thing," Gortz went on. "In the unlikely event that you haven't drawn all the obvious conclusions from what will start happening at seven o'clock tomorrow morning, I should point out that it will appreciably strengthen the hand of your colleague Marcel Magny."

Laemmle was about to ask who the devil this was when he remembered just in time that Marcel Magny was Jürgen Hess's pseudonym. It seemed that Berlin had widened dear Jürgen's sphere of responsibility and invested him with far greater powers. From now on he would be able to call on the occupation forces in any part of France.

"So you see, Gregor, if you have any means of recouping your losses, be quick or the competition will beat you to it. I'd remind you of my recommendations, which come from very high up. I'm only moderately interested in the smaller of the two packages—it's the big one I'm after. In any case, all the relevant orders have been issued. You and your eccentricities are my only worry. I'll pay you a visit before long—unless, of course, you have some news for me in the interim."

Being a financier, Joachim Gortz wouldn't have told anyone the time of day over the phone in case the operator was eavesdropping. But clearly this meant that Quartermain was to be taken alive. As for the boy, it would be better to nab him before Hess could lay hands on him.

As if I didn't know that, thought Laemmle. Having reviewed the situation during the next few hours, he felt more than ever convinced that he was right: quite unaware that they were heading straight for the German army, the American and the boy must be northward bound. They couldn't have crossed the Rhône or Lafont's mercenaries would have intercepted them.

True, the delay in sighting them again was a little too long for his taste. It was odd that Soeft's lookouts had seen and reported nothing from their posts on the outskirts of the mountainous, densely wooded region through which the fugitives must have passed.

"Are you sure your men were in position in time, Soeft? Really? Strange. . . ."

One thing was certain: this incursion by Adolf's troops changed at least one aspect of the problem and militated against the best of his strategic ploys. In the little imp's place, he would have scented the possibility that the Rhône bridges might be guarded and gone as far north as possible. Well, thought Laemmle as he watched a column of Wehrmacht tanks rattle past, at least the little imp would be unable to carry out his original intention.

"By this time, Soeft, he must have sighted the vanguard of our glorious army. He's certainly got the gall to think he can press on regardless, but I doubt if he will. He might get through on his own, perhaps, but not the American—I can't imagine *him* talking his way past the German military police without arousing their suspicions. Would he really sacrifice the American as one sacrifices a knight or a rook, let alone a queen, for the sake of final victory?" Laemmle broke off. "For pity's sake, Soeft, answer that confounded phone!"

Soeft did so, and the expression that then came over his face told Laemmle that something of importance had happened. He snatched the receiver.

"Would you repeat that, please?"

The voice at the other end informed him that a lookout was missing, together with his car. Traces of blood had been found at the spot where he'd been stationed.

Laemmle inquired the lookout's position and consulted the map. Instantly, he experienced the delicious thrill that a chess player feels when an opponent does precisely what he's been nudged into doing.

"They broke through just where I said they would, Soeft. What's more, a very surprising thing has happened: the American has killed his first man in cold blood. I'm amazed—I'd never have thought him capable of it."

But that was secondary. Laemmle did his sums all over again.

"It's as clear as daylight, Soeft. They haven't had time to get to Lyons—our motorized columns have cut them off—so they're bogged down somewhere. There are two choices open to them: head for Lyons just the same, or try to cross the Rhône. If they do anything else they'll bump into Hess. Didn't you tell me that he and his thugs had spread their net and were moving north? Yes, of course you did. Well, what are the odds? Will the boy throw himself into my arms at Lyons or try crossing the Rhône?"

QUARTERMAIN DOUBLE-LOCKED THE FRONT DOOR AND CAUGHT up with Thomas, who had gone on ahead to the garage.

"You never know, Thomas. I'm not going to chuck these keys away —there's just a chance we might need them again sometime. Look, I'll bury them here. Think you can remember the place?"

The boy nodded. It was three-forty A.M., but the night could have been darker. Whenever a gap appeared between the clouds drifting overhead, the visibility was quite good. Quartermain eased the Citroën very quietly past the lily pond and out through the back gate, which he chained and padlocked behind him. Then he drove along the lane that skirted the wall of the estate until he came to the main road.

"North it is, Thomas?"

"Yes, monsieur."

Quartermain turned left. He drove without haste, feeling strangely calm and resolute. He even thought he detected the kind of exhilaration he'd felt when preparing to schuss down a mountainside which fellow skiers had pronounced too steep for safety. All things considered, he was beginning to wonder if his easygoing exterior didn't conceal a streak of insanity.

"We should reach the bridge in thirty or forty minutes."

No reply.

"Tell me what books you've read, Thomas. At least that's one subject that shouldn't embarrass you."

"I don't feel like talking."

"All the more reason. Have you read *Treasure Island*? And *The Master of Ballantrae*? Yes? How about *The Weir of Hermiston*? No? Stevenson never finished it, which is a pity—I think it might have been his best book ever. It's the story of a manhunt and the relationship between the hunter and the hunted. Interested?"

"Yes, monsieur."

Quartermain's account of the plot had the desired effect. Thomas and he proceeded to discuss how they would have ended the novel in Robert Louis Stevenson's place. After that Quartermain embarked on an account of his own adventures in the Cévennes, though he hadn't ridden through them on a donkey like Stevenson.

They sighted the bridge at a distance of six or seven hundred yards. Quartermain pulled up and switched off his lights.

He wasn't surprised, on getting out, to find that the boy had followed suit. They made their way along the dark little streets in parallel, one on either side; they froze whenever they came to an intersection and signaled to each other. It developed into an enthralling game of cops and robbers.

You're playing your final card, Quartermain told himself. Strange how easy you find it to slip into the role of a child. You know you've only got a few precious minutes left together, that's why you want him to preserve the best possible recollection of you. . . .

He rounded the corner of a building and drew back quickly: the bridge was less than fifty yards away. There was a German armored car in the middle. As if that were not enough, two Volkswagen jeeps were parked near the mouth of the bridge in such a way that any driver wishing to cross would have to slow down and zigzag past them. More German soldiers could be seen on the other bank.

Quartermain and Thomas, peering around the corner, held a whispered conference.

"We'd never get across, monsieur, however fast you drove."

"I couldn't agree more. We'll have to try another bridge, but farther south. Looks like the Germans are occupying all the Rhône bridges as they go. Our only hope is to leave right now and drive like hell. If we overtake them soon enough we may find a bridge that isn't guarded yet."

Quartermain drove south with his foot hard down. The Citroën sped past the secluded house with the blue shutters, the lily pond, and the mummified old lady in the four-poster bed. Ten minutes later they passed a small German column halted on the left of the road.

Five kilometers farther on they passed a somewhat larger contingent, including a number of tanks. Here the Germans had set up a regular bivouac complete with camp fires. Soldiers stood beside the road, watching idly as the car roared by. Quartermain was struck by an idea that seemed worth pursuing: the more conspicuous they made themselves, the less suspicion they might arouse. He'd taken one of the cards found in the dead lookout's car and stuck it under his windshield, because it looked like a document designed for that purpose. He only hoped it wasn't a vaccination certificate or a membership card for the Baden-Württemberg Bowling Club.

The third column he overtook was on the move. Yielding to a sudden whim, he bestowed a friendly wave on the officer at the head of the convoy. Thomas, meanwhile, was lying flat in the back with a rug over him.

The next bridge was as heavily guarded as the first.

So was the one after that. Dawn was breaking, and the night's scattered clouds had merged into a uniform gray mass. Quartermain had passed a whole succession of convoys, one of them nearly a kilometer long. It was while he was overtaking the latter that a German motorcyclist drew level with him. The man glanced at the card under the windshield and shouted something unintelligible. Quartermain merely nodded back. It must have been an acceptable response, because the motorcyclist seemed satisfied.

A fourth bridge stood outlined against the paling sky with the town it served nestling on the far bank. Quartermain turned right onto some rising ground.

"We could try this one, Thomas. It looks good." He pulled up and stopped. "We're nearly fifteen minutes ahead of that last convoy."

He got out and trained his binoculars on the bridge. It was half a mile away and a couple of hundred feet below.

He heard the Citroën's door open and close, but he didn't turn around. Still scanning the environs of the bridge, he spotted a small German army truck with a driver in the cab. Another two soldiers were busy unloading some flimsy wooden barriers.

"I really like the look of this bridge, Thomas. I don't think we'll find a better one. So it's a simple choice: either we try crossing here or we go even farther south. The trouble with the second alternative is Hess. If you're right, and I think you are, he must be heading this way fast."

There wasn't a sound behind him now. Had the youngster taken off already?

"You still there?" said Quartermain.

"Yes."

"To be honest, I thought you'd gone."

"Gone where?"

Quartermain chuckled. He still had his back turned and his binoculars trained on the bridge.

Thomas was standing a couple of yards behind the Citroën. He'd thought of going, it was true. He could have sneaked off into the pine trees while the American's back was turned. Once there he would have run and hidden until the American gave up and left. He obviously knew he was to be sacrificed—he even approved of the idea—so no explanations were necessary.

"It's a bit irritating, trying to discuss a plan with someone I can't see because he's skulking in the background. The more I look at that bridge and the road leading to it, the less time I think we've got to spare. Come over here, please."

Thomas eyed the tall figure of the American, who still hadn't turned around. Don't be a fool, he told himself. If he wasn't willing to be sacrificed he'd have headed straight for the bridge with you in the car.

"What plan?" he asked, walking over to Quartermain.

"Don't act dumb. There's no time."

"I don't know if your plan is the same as mine."

"Like to bet?" Quartermain said lightly.

"You drive across on your own with a dummy beside you—some

branches or something, wrapped up in a rug—and the lookouts think it's me, so they take off after you. That leaves the coast clear for me."

"Not bad."

"What's your plan, then?"

"The same as yours, at least to begin with. I drive across fast so the lookouts go tearing after me. You watch the whole thing through the binoculars, which I'll leave you, and then you take off on your own. You probably won't cross the bridge at all."

"I won't head for Switzerland, you mean?"

"That's something I don't know for sure, but I doubt it. Once I'm gone, I think you'll head for your rendezvous."

"What rendezvous?"

"Your fall-back rendezvous with the invisible sniper. It could be someone else, but he seems the likeliest person."

He's guessed the whole thing, Thomas told himself. He's a whole lot smarter than I ever dreamed. . . .

"Listen, Thomas," Quartermain said, still peering through the binoculars. "I won't ask you where your rendezvous is. It's better that I don't know, and anyway, you wouldn't tell me. I just hope the man takes better care of you than I've been able to, that's all."

Thomas yearned to say something, but he didn't know what. In any case, his throat was too tight. Saying goodbye to the American was worse than his worst imaginings—far, far worse.

"I'm going to shoot across that bridge like a rocket," Quartermain went on. "I can see two men in a car, obviously lookouts, but there may be more. I think there are two at the left-hand exit from the bridge and another two a bit farther along. Have a look."

He handed the binoculars to Thomas, who took a long look.

"I can definitely see four," he said at length, "plus another two at the mouth of the street on the left." He spotted a car with a Bouches-du-Rhône license plate. It was empty, but there were two men braving the cold at a café table a few yards away. "That makes eight of them and four cars, if not more." He lowered the binoculars with a feeling of numb despair. "You'll be killed."

Quartermain laughed. "I'm Pistol Pete in person. Pistol Pete never gets killed, you ought to know that. He gallops through hordes of bandits blazing away, and the worst he ever gets is a measly little flesh wound in the left shoulder—or the right shoulder if he's left-handed. Only eight of them, you reckon? I'm disappointed. Forty would have been more my size."

"They'll kill you."

"You only say that because you've never seen me drive really fast. They may catch me in the end, though, in which case they'll find I'm alone in the car and start looking for you again. I'll try to keep them busy for as long as possible—I'll even try to fix it so they think you crossed the bridge with me and I dropped you off somewhere east of it before taking them on a wild-goose chase." Quartermain broke off. "Please don't look like that, Thomas. The less you worry about me the better your chances. Play your game of chess with Yellow Eyes and beat him—forget about everything but beating him. Okay, kid?"

Thomas had squatted down and was staring at the ground. He felt incredibly sad.

"Thomas?"

"Okay," the boy said. "I'll beat him."

QUARTERMAIN CAST A FINAL GLANCE AT THE DUMMY IN THE back of the Citroën, a bundle of pine branches swathed in a couple of blankets. It had better work, he thought.

The last German convoy they'd overtaken was less than a kilometer from the bridge. He handed the binoculars to Thomas.

"Just for argument's sake," he said, "what if you wanted to see me again? Would you know what to do?"

"Yes. Walk into one of your banks and ask them to pass a message to your Cousin Larry reminding him of your bike ride through Ardèche."

"You don't forget much, huh?"

"No, not much."

Quartermain studied the little face a couple of feet below his own. The boy was close to tears. The phenomenal shell his mother had built up over the years was on the point of cracking, and he, Quartermain, was weakening it still further with his melodramatic behavior. Thomas had never been in greater need of the training Maria had given him. Whether or not she'd destroyed his childhood was another matter, and one there was no time to go into now.

Quartermain settled himself at the wheel, conscious of the big gray eyes that were watching his every move. If you can't say something helpful, he thought, don't say anything at all. Just go. Leave him and hope he's as strong as you think he is.

He turned the Citroën and drove off.

He didn't know if Thomas was his son or not, and he never would. The strange thing was, he didn't care. He loved the boy like a son, and that was that. Hemingway always claimed that sentimental men were the first to die. If he was right, there seemed every possibility that he would die like a dog on some lousy French road, and no one would ever figure out what on earth he was doing there.

He drove downhill to the main road, where the convoy was already streaming past. Then he pulled out and slowly overtook it, smiling and waving to the German tank commanders as he went by.

The one comparatively intelligent thing he'd done in the past week was to write that letter and address it to the Paris branch of the Clan's bank, which was still going great guns—business being business—in spite of the fact that Germany was at war with the United States. With a bit of luck, the letter would eventually get to Cousin Larry.

He was twenty yards from the bridge when the head of the armored column started to cross it.

Not yet. . . .

He aimed the Citroën's nose at the roadway.

Be honest, you're scared as hell. You have been for a long time. . . .

THE CITROEN HADN'T MOVED. IT CONTINUED TO STAND THERE while the tanks rumbled past it. Thomas gripped the binoculars even tighter.

What was he waiting for?

Then it dawned on him. Of course! The American wanted the head of the convoy to draw almost level with the lookouts at the far end of the bridge. He wouldn't try to cross till the tanks were between him and the lookouts. Even if the lookouts saw him coming, they wouldn't open fire. It wouldn't be very wise of them to blaze away at him: the tank gunners might misunderstand and fire back. The American was being really smart.

Seconds ticked by. The tanks were taking an eternity to cross the confounded bridge. Thomas refocused the binoculars on the Citroën.

It still hadn't budged. The American was overdoing it—the Germans would set up a roadblock, and then it would be too late.

Now!

It was as if the American had heard his unspoken cry. The Citroën leaped forward. It was on the bridge now, and traveling so fast that the tanks might have been standing still as it skimmed past them.

Faster and faster it went. "You've never seen me drive really fast," the American had said, and he wasn't exaggerating. No one else could have done what he was doing. He crossed the bridge like a bullet from a gun, slalomed between the first and second tanks, came out on the other side, braked violently to avoid the German scout car at the very head of the column, and turned hard right. The Citroën slewed around in a rear-wheel skid but corrected it and roared off along the embankment.

Thomas picked up the lookouts in his binoculars. They were running around like headless chickens, not eight of them but ten or a dozen in five cars. The American had a lead of two or three hundred yards by the time they set off in pursuit.

Not that it would do him any good. Yellow Eyes must have foreseen a trick like that—driving across like lightning, and so on—and the whole district would be swarming with his men. Every road would be watched. Besides, he had the German army to help him now.

The American didn't stand a chance—not a chance, and they both knew it.

He straightened up, replaced the binoculars in their canvas satchel, then shouldered it by the strap.

It was up to him now.

She'd told him scores of times: to play any game really well, you have to be on your own.

Well, now he was.

FIVE

THE VOICE ON THE TELEPHONE WAS APOLOGETIC. "THAT AMER-
ican drives like a maniac. We thought we'd cornered him half a dozen
times, but he always managed to get away."

Paul Clavié, Henri Lafont's nephew and trusted lieutenant, started
to explain how Quartermain had eluded them, but Laemmle cut him
short.

"What about the boy?"

"He's with him, of course."

There was a trace of hesitation in Clavié's tone. Laemmle shut his
eyes and sighed. The man was beginning to exasperate him.

"What makes you so sure?" he asked mildly.

"I caught a glimpse of the boy less than an hour ago, just before the
American headed for the hills where he's hiding at this moment."

And where Clavié felt confident of flushing him out by dawn at
latest, especially now that the Citroën was badly damaged.

A glimpse. Icy fingers tickled Laemmle's spine.

"You should have called me long ago," he said eventually. "You've
been careering around the countryside for hours, yet you only conde-
scend to phone me now. Listen carefully, Clavié. It's not only possible
but probable that the American is creating a diversion. While you're
chasing after him, the boy may well be making off in the opposite
direction, either alone or accompanied by a leather-jacketed Spanish
bodyguard armed with a sniper's rifle. Have you got that?"

"Don't worry, monsieur." Clavier promised to detach forty of his men and ask his uncle for reinforcements from the French police. "If the boy's heading for Switzerland we can still cut him off."

"Do that." Laemmle cupped his hand over the receiver. "Soeft?"

Soeft, already studying a map, said that he would regroup his lookouts on the east bank of the Rhône and send them after the boy. He also proposed to—

"Just a minute!" Laemmle was completely at a loss. Had the boy crossed the Rhône or hadn't he? Surely he wouldn't have headed east or south, straight for Jürgen Hess? He didn't know what was best to do. "Soeft? Move only half your men across the Rhône. Leave the others where they are." He spoke into the mouthpiece again.

"Clavié? Where is the Citroën now?"

Clavié explained that after outmaneuvering his pursuers or ramming them so recklessly that his car was fit for the scrapyard, the American had taken refuge in a mountainous area devoid of roads.

"This time we've got him—he doesn't stand a chance. We know where he is to the nearest two or three hundred meters. If it wasn't dark we could spot him with binoculars."

Laemmle broke the two seconds of silence that followed with a savagery that surprised himself. "I want him alive," he said abruptly. "Alive, do you hear?"

Instead of hanging up, he jiggled the cradle and asked for Gortz's number.

"Joachim, I've reason to believe that the boy and the American have split up. That army of yours has completely destroyed my plans by crossing the demarcation line. Can you at least ask the military authorities to set up checkpoints on all routes to Switzerland east of the Rhône? No, not for the American, for the boy! We've got the American cornered, apparently. You scratch my back and I'll scratch yours. You shall have your American, Joachim, but whether you have him dead or alive depends on the boy's condition when I get him back. Do I make myself clear?"

Gortz asked if Hess had been notified. Laemmle ignored the question and hung up on him.

He was still in Lyons and had witnessed the city's occupation by German troops. It was a spectacle that had aroused precisely the same sense of outrage, of personal affront, as that which had possessed him when Hitler's legions went tramping along the Champs-Élysées. He felt despondent—infinitely more so than he did during one of his regular bouts of depression.

He'd failed, he could feel it in his bones. What new and diabolical scheme had the little monkey dreamed up now?

QUARTERMAIN RECOVERED CONSCIOUSNESS. HE WASN'T DEAD, that was pretty certain, or his hip and his neck wouldn't be hurting so much.

Nor would his knee. He opened his eyes, and a little of the reality of his predicament dawned on him. Branches were jutting through the shattered windscreen, fragments of which reflected the dying rays of the sun. Having extricated himself from the car with a supreme effort, he started crawling. The ground was densely carpeted with scrub, and his knee hurt even more than his hip, but he finally reached a clearer patch and scrambled to his feet. He was a couple of hundred feet below the summit of a steep slope dotted with clumps of bushes. The Citroën had plowed its way into one of these before coming to a halt.

Why hadn't they spotted him?

The silence was unbroken, the light fading fast. He was all alone. Could they have inspected the car, ascertained that Thomas wasn't in it, and left him to his own devices?

In fact, the Citroën would have been almost invisible to anyone at the top of the hill. Only its roof projected above the dense scrub into which it had plunged. Quartermain looked down the hillside. It seemed to end in a line of rocks, but it sloped away to the left.

How to proceed? On foot? With this knee, he wouldn't get a hundred yards.

An idea occurred to him—a crazy idea, but he didn't dismiss it out of hand. He was already examining the car. If he could free it, and if the engine would only start . . .

He toiled away grimly for the whole of the next hour. The Citroën had ended up with its rear end buried in the ground. The twisted bumper and the wheels had plowed up the soil. The front end was perched on a mound of foliage and splintered branches. The car wasn't pointing straight downhill. Using the crank handle, Quartermain cleared and dug two parallel furrows. He unearthed the bumper, then one rear wheel, then the other. Somehow or other he was going to have to pivot the car on its axis. It took him another good hour to uproot a whole clump of bushes five or six yards farther down the slope and stack this vegetation against the line of rocks at its foot, hobbling and gasping with pain whenever he put his weight on his knee.

Night had fallen long ago, but the light was sufficient for his purposes. He dug the heel of his good leg into the ground, braced his shoulders against a rear fender, and shoved. The car pivoted a few inches, then stopped: the twisted bumper had acted as an anchor—he hadn't dug deep enough. He excavated another furrow with the crank handle. This time, when he braced himself against the car, it really did move. The rear end slid sideways and lifted, but the hood remained buried in splintered branches. One last shove did the trick: the Citroën freed itself and coasted downhill for twenty or thirty yards until brought up short by the vegetation-cushioned line of rocks.

What if it refused to start? That would be all he needed.

But no, the engine sprang to life at the second attempt and ticked over imperturbably. Even one of the parking lights was still working. Fifty yards to the left the scrub thinned to reveal a track that skirted the flank of another hill, ran through a wood, and threaded its way between low dry-laid stone walls and banks of whitish soil. Quartermain crawled along in second gear for half an hour or more, apparently going nowhere, until he crossed a miniature pass and felt asphalt beneath his front wheels. He stopped and got out. All he could hear was the murmur of a nearby stream.

Could they really have called off the hunt?

If he hadn't already been aware of the excruciating pain in his knee, one step in the direction of the stream would have reminded him of it with a vengeance. He started hopping on one leg, then went down on all fours, or rather, threes. He groped his way across the grass to the water's edge and drank, feeling like a hunted beast. The night was very still, but they were lying in wait for him somewhere—at least, he hoped so. If they'd called off the hunt for him it would mean that Thomas was already in their hands, which God forbid. . . .

He dragged himself back to the Citroën, slid painfully behind the wheel, and drove on. After passing a handful of farmhouses, all of them in darkness, he came to a crossroads.

It was completely deserted. He drove straight on, not even bothering to decipher the name on the signpost. Another intersection loomed up after three or four kilometers. Again he drove straight on, his sense of unreality steadily mounting as he continued to traverse this desolate landscape with its darkened, shuttered, solitary farmhouses.

They couldn't have given up, but where were they all?

A kind of stupor overcame him. He even dozed off a couple of times and lost control of the car, which collided with various banks and bushes, but managed to extricate himself and drive on. He almost welcomed it when the road became tortuous because the added danger forced him to concentrate and kept sleep at bay.

At last he came to a village. A lone figure standing beside the road signaled to him to stop, but not in any urgent or peremptory way. Reassured, he pulled up.

"That car of yours is quite a sight," said the man.

"I had an accident," Quartermain explained.

The door behind the man was ajar, and through it he could see the interior of a country café.

"You ought to come inside for a bit."

There was something definitely odd about the man's tone and his air of faint amusement. Quartermain looked up and down the street. The village appeared to be a tiny place, but his remaining parking light was too dim to reveal much. He debated whether to put his foot down on the accelerator and make a dash for it.

"Any reason why I shouldn't drive on?" he said.

The man shrugged. "See for yourself." He raised his hand, and six pairs of headlights bathed the village street in a harsh glare. The cars were drawn up in line abreast—a bicycle couldn't have got past them.

"You ought to come inside," the man repeated stolidly. He opened the driver's door, or rather, yanked it half open. Unsurprised by the sound of tortured metal—the door was badly smashed—he stepped aside like a well-drilled chauffeur.

"If you insist," said Quartermain.

There were four men inside the café. Of the three who were standing, one was obviously the proprietor, whose bare feet and nightshirt suggested that he'd just been routed out of bed. The other two looked like just what they were: Gestapo thugs. The fourth man was seated beside a roaring stove. He was short, plump, sandy-haired, and very smartly dressed in a cream linen double-breasted suit which Quartermain could have sworn had been tailored in London.

"My name is Gregor Laemmle," said the fourth man, rising with a table napkin in his hand. "I'm sure you must be famished after your long drive, Mr. Quartermain. Will you do me the honor of dining with me?"

"A LITTLE MORE *FOIE GRAS*?" LAEMMLE INQUIRED.

"No. I couldn't."

"But I could, Soeft."

The man with the girlish face—Quartermain recognized him now—produced more *foie gras* from a big wicker hamper and served him.

"Some champagne, then?"

"No more for me," Quartermain said.

Laemmle smiled at him. "You're a most congenial companion, you know."

"Thanks for the compliment." Quartermain returned the yellow-eyed gaze without flinching. Conversation during dinner had centered on America and distinguished American authors in particular—Emerson, Thoreau, and Melville among others. Gregor Laemmle seemed to have an encyclopedic knowledge of literature and the arts, and there was no mistaking his exceptional intelligence.

"Most congenial," he repeated. "You'll laugh, but a couple of hours ago I was positively determined to kill you. Now I'm of two minds."

"Delighted to hear it," said Quartermain, grimly battling with his fatigue.

"Are you acquainted with Joachim Gortz?"

"No."

"He knows you. Or rather, he knows some cousins of yours."

"Who is this Gortz?"

"The man who has forbidden me to kill you. He claims you're worth more than Thomas."

Quartermain sipped the last of his champagne. "Who's Thomas?"

"Very amusing. Soeft, what's next on the menu?"

"Crayfish in aspic with truffles," said the man with the girlish face.

"Ah well, one must expect a few hardships in wartime." Laemmle treated Quartermain to a puckish smile. "It took me several hours to realize that the boy wasn't in the car with you, and that he hadn't even crossed the bridge with you—in other words, that he'd remained behind on the west bank. I was very poorly served by my subordinates, but still, I shouldn't have taken so long to grasp that Thomas had sacrificed you like the expert chess player he is."

Soeft produced two plates from the hamper and put one in front of Quartermain.

"Personally," said Quartermain, "I seldom play the game."

"Oh dear," said Laemmle, "I can feel that urge to kill you coming on again. You think I'm joking?"

"I wouldn't bet on it."

The yellow eyes glowed. "Proceed, Soeft."

Having put the second plate in front of Laemmle, Soeft made his way around behind Quartermain, who stiffened.

But Soeft's objective turned out to be the proprietor of the café. A gun appeared in his hand like magic. Thrusting the muzzle against the Frenchman's chest in the region of the heart, he fired twice. Then, as his victim started to crumple, he grabbed him by the collar of his nightshirt and put a bullet in his head.

"Quartermain?"

Quartermain had shut his eyes. He opened them to find the yellow gaze fixed on him.

"Quartermain," Laemmle repeated, "I feel a trifle better now that I've executed you by proxy, so to speak. The truth is, my nerves are on edge. The boy hasn't crossed the Rhône—he's done the only thing calculated to take me by surprise: he's heading south and west, straight for someone named Hess. I fear the worst, Quartermain."

The corpse lay sprawled on the floor a bare yard from the table, oozing blood. Quartermain eyed it with mingled horror and compassion.

"I fear the worst. With me he has every chance of survival; with Hess he has none, but he knows this and has taken the risk. He's a child, but what a child! You and I—yes, I even include myself—are poor creatures in comparison. Our minds have become dulled and blunted by education and experience, by the so-called rationality that comes with age. Thomas's mind is pure, cold, and implacable. He knows neither pity nor remorse. He dreams the impossible because he has yet to learn that the impossible exists. The extent to which a person is original and creative—revolutionary, if you like—depends on how much of his childhood he retains within himself."

"You're completely insane," said Quartermain, still staring at the body on the floor.

"Thomas is a boy of quite exceptional intelligence. Knowing that from the outset, as she must have done, she did all she could to make him what he now is: a monster by conventional standards. When I say 'she,' of course, I mean the woman who was his mother. She was also your mistress, it seems, which may possibly mean that you're his father. Possibly. I assume you still carry the letter she must have written you to persuade you to cross the Atlantic? Soeft will relieve you of it and I shall read it before destroying it. No, Quartermain, don't move! Don't try to touch me, still less kill me. Don't even think of it!"

All that broke the silence was the sound of cars starting up in the street outside.

"The only person I authorize to kill me is Thomas himself," Laemmle went on quietly. "He has promised to do so and I hope he keeps his word. Killing me would be a token of affection, so to speak." He smiled. "But I can't expect you to understand that. As for you, the fact that you think you're his father, and that he believes or would like to believe so—that fact is reason enough for me to hate you more than I can say. I dread to think what you'd have made of him if, by some terrible mischance, you'd managed to take him from me. You'd have destroyed him, Quartermain—you'd have turned him into an ordinary child: a trifle more intelligent than most, perhaps, but gentle, affectionate, and *ordinary*. That marvelous machine in his head would have been useless to him except as an aid to passing examinations and becoming the richest man in America. It turns my stomach to think of it!" Laemmle paused. "But you haven't touched your crayfish."

Quartermain rose and went to the window. He pulled the curtain aside. A convoy of cars was forming up with a big black saloon in the center. The battered Citroën had been removed and was nowhere to be seen.

"I don't propose to kill you after all, Quartermain—not yet, anyway—for one extremely compelling reason. It's quite possible that Jürgen Hess will catch the boy in the next few hours. That will leave two possibilities open. Either Thomas will be unscathed and I'll exchange you for him, or my charming associate will pluck out one of his eyes or tear an arm off—or, worse still, kill him, in which case you won't reach Gortz alive. And now, if you really don't want any crayfish, we'll be on our way. . . ."

THOMAS HAD PUT OVER FIFTY KILOMETERS BETWEEN HIMSELF AND the bridge, thanks to the bicycle he'd stolen from outside a church where some children were busy learning their catechism. The milk can suspended from the handlebars had proved invaluable. Sundry gendarmes had let him through, evidently in the belief that he was a local boy on his way to a farm to buy some milk. One of the silly fools had even asked him, jokingly, whether he wasn't going to turn his milk into butter by bouncing along the road like that. The can's additional advantage was that it had genuinely enabled him to buy himself some milk and drink it on the way.

I'm really sad, Thomas told himself as he pedaled along—really sad. I'll let myself think of the American, but only for a minute or two. After that I'll tuck him away in a corner of my head and bury him, like the Thing.

A minute or two, that's all.

I know She wasn't lying in Her letter—She never lied. She wouldn't have sent for the American unless he really was my father. Either that or She wished he was, which comes to the same thing. She chose him. She chose him, and there's nothing I can do about it.

And now he's dead—dead, dead, dead, like Her.

That's enough! Stop thinking about him. You're only hurting yourself for nothing—you aren't even looking where you're going. . . .

Darkness fell and still he pedaled on. Only another eleven kilometers, according to the map, but that was no reason to stop concentrating. On the contrary, he had to be doubly careful. More and more often now he stopped and hid in ditches or behind trees and bushes, when there were any. Eleven cars or trucks had passed him going one way or the other, plus three motorcycles and several cyclists.

And all the time his sense of foreboding, his "rat's instinct," became more insistent. He got out the binoculars a score of times and peered in all directions without seeing anything suspicious in the gathering gloom, but it didn't dispel his feeling that something was about to happen.

The feeling became so pronounced that he stopped and got off. The road, which was undulating but almost straight at this point, ran across a large expanse of open country interspersed with knolls and hillocks. But for the darkness, he would have been visible from a long way off. He had an urge to get back on his bike and pedal like mad for those last eleven kilometers, but it was silly to take risks at this stage.

He made up his mind at last.

He also made a terrible mistake: he hid the bike in the ditch, but not too carefully, telling himself that he wouldn't be gone for more than a minute. Then he jumped the ditch and made for a hillock some fifty yards from the road. The view from the top would surely prove his nameless fears unfounded.

The hillock culminated in a slab of rock. He scaled it and slowly scanned his surroundings through the binoculars, starting with the direction in which his rendezvous lay.

Nothing at all.

He looked left and right.

Nothing there either, apart from a bridge and some isolated farmhouses whose windows twinkled in the darkness.

And a few cars.

A pair of headlights drew nearer. He trained the binoculars on them and saw that they belonged to a bus, not a car. There were some passengers on board—ordinary-looking men and women. Nothing suspicious about that.

No sound came to his ears except the hum of the approaching bus. It was bound to pass the spot where he'd left his bike, but the driver and his passengers would be traveling too fast to notice it. Sure enough, the bus kept going. He was about to climb down off his rock when he saw another pair of headlights coming the other way.

Then it happened.

The black Citroën was illuminated by the headlights of the bus. Thomas not only recognized it, he recognized the driver as one of two plainclothesmen at a roadblock he'd passed hours before.

Worse still, the car was moving very slowly, and the two men inside were playing flashlights over the verges. Thomas grasped the truth at once. These were Jürgen Hess's men. He'd sneaked past the roadblock in the midst of a party of schoolchildren. The men must somehow have discovered that one of them had been a stranger who didn't go to their school.

They would see the bike!

He scrambled down off the rock and started running, then froze. It was too late: the road and the ditches beside it were already bathed in the glare of the oncoming headlights. He could have wept with rage at his own stupidity.

He retreated in a hurry. Instead of climbing the hillock again, he went around it. Then he looked back, already knowing what he would see. The Citroën had stopped at the crucial spot. One of the men got down into the ditch, picked up the bike, and showed it to his companion. "It's got to be him," he said in German. "He can't be far. You go and phone while I try to corner him. Leave me your flashlight."

The Citroën roared off. The man stayed put, sweeping the area with both flashlights at once.

Thomas just had time to dodge behind the hillock, but he didn't linger. He set off for the bridge, revising his calculations as he went. Eleven kilometers by road on a bicycle might have taken him half an hour. But on foot, by a roundabout route across country? He was too angry with himself to feel frightened in the least.

He started to run, but not too fast. Running fast was pointless when you had a long way to go, and he must have a good fifteen kilometers ahead of him.

The situation developed even more rapidly than he'd feared. Less than ten minutes later two cars appeared on his left, one of them with a mobile spotlight capable of ranging out several hundred yards.

Another three materialized on his right. More could be seen to his rear, and further reinforcements kept arriving.

Thomas had just crossed the bridge and was three hundred yards beyond it when a car loomed up ahead of him. His only recourse was to dive into an irrigation ditch. He was sweating hard after his run, but the water was terribly cold. He poked his head over the edge and saw a dirt road on the other side. Scrambling out, he darted across it just as more headlights veered in his direction. The next ditch was even deeper and full of equally icy water. He waded along it until he was brought up short by a massive drainage pipe. Then, after making sure that darkness had closed over him again, he climbed out, shivering. There were trees here, and the ground was thickly carpeted with dead leaves.

He'd gone a hundred yards, possibly more, when a string of lights appeared dead ahead of him. He dodged behind a tree. The lights seemed to have sprung from the very ground. Then he realized what they were: a line of beaters had just breasted a low hill—dozens of them. He hadn't a hope of slipping through the net.

He looked behind him, then left and right. No doubt about it: he was hemmed in on all sides.

Think! Think, dammit, don't cry!

"I HAVE A WHOLE THEORY ON THE SUBJECT OF CHILDHOOD," SAID
Laemmle.

There was no reply, of course, but he hadn't expected one. Quartermain was seated on his right in the big Renault Viva sports saloon,
which could carry eight and boasted an engine displacement in excess
of five liters. The American had been handcuffed. He was sitting there
with his head back and his eyes shut—he might even be genuinely
asleep.

They were now entering Lyons. An hour ago, when they passed a
German military post of appreciable size, Soeft had got out and shown
his ID. He returned after a brief conversation with the local commander, telling Laemmle that the reply to his inquiry would be awaiting him on arrival in Lyons. Soeft had four of his men with him, three
to guard Quartermain and one to drive.

They skirted the Rhône with an escort of eight cars manned by
Henri Lafont's mercenaries, four in front and four behind. It was a
clear night, and to Laemmle there seemed something almost funereal
about the convoy's leisurely progress along the riverbank. The boy's
fate hung in the balance.

In spite of the sublime sense of mockery on which he so justly
prided himself, Laemmle reflected, there was a definite streak of exhi-
bitionism in his makeup. His fundamental aim was to inflict as much
unhappiness as possible on this American, who was the only person
capable of understanding him. Apart from Soeft, of course, but Soeft
was about as important as a bellpull.

He turned his head and inspected Quartermain. He wouldn't go so
far as to call him handsome, although the hands were big and shapely,
the forehead was high, the jaw firm. Reports had credited him with a
certain resemblance to that Hollywood star named Gary Cooper, and
they weren't so wide of the mark. That was annoying in itself.
Laemmle would have preferred a nasal-voiced gum-chewer in a gaudy
necktie. He was disconcerted and exasperated by this lean, lanky, imperturbable man who had actually read Emerson and Thoreau—imagine!—and even had a touch of elegance about him. But he was far
more enraged by another resemblance he thought he detected: a resemblance to Thomas. There were similarities in the line of the forehead, the nose, the lips—in short, the profile—which seemed to support the theory that they were related by blood. He had to concede
that for the first time in his life, he cherished a profound hatred for
someone other than himself.

The Renault pulled up outside the German headquarters in Lyons. Preceded by Soeft, who paved their way by flashing various official passes, Laemmle went inside. A middle-aged officer pointed to a telephone on a desk. Laemmle snatched up the receiver.

"Yes, Jürgen?"

Hess announced that this was it at last: he'd caught the boy, or almost—it was only a matter of minutes now. He described the situation, which sounded quite straightforward. "We'll take him alive," he concluded.

"Thanks for keeping me informed," Laemmle replied, concealing his desperate apprehension beneath a veneer of sarcasm. "My dear Jürgen, your manhunt is certain to go down in the annals as one of the greatest military exploits of all time."

He emerged into the cold night air and returned to the Renault. Quartermain was looking at him; he could sense it as he calmly rearranged the rug over his knees.

"Let's go, Soeft. Oh yes, and kindly pour me a glass of Chartreuse. Will you join me, Quartermain?"

No reply. Laemmle pulled the rug up to his chin and shut his eyes. With a clarity that made him tremble, he pictured Thomas in the predicament Hess had just described. It almost made him weep.

THOMAS CHANGED POSITION FOR THE THIRD TIME. HE WAS WAITing for confirmation that he'd precisely determined the beaters' line of advance before deciding on the right place. It had to be flat and featureless, discounting any trees, of course. It must also provide routes that would automatically prompt the beaters to bypass it as they continued their search. He crawled until he found the ideal spot, a tiny gully filled with moist earth and an abundance of rotting leaves. Then he enlarged it, taking great care not to scatter the freshly turned soil, and scooped some leaves together in preparation for the finishing touches. Last of all he buried himself, legs and midsection first, chest next, then one arm, then his face, then the other arm.

It worked just the way it had for Pistol Pete when the Sioux were after his scalp and walked right past without spotting him. Pistol Pete had buried himself in sand, but the principle was the same.

The beaters came within a couple of feet of him. He heard them exchanging remarks in German and French, asking where the devil he could have got to, the little bastard, when they'd actually caught a glimpse of him in the distance.

The hue and cry receded. He didn't move at once for fear of stragglers, or in case someone turned and looked back. Perhaps they'd pretended not to notice him—perhaps they were forming a circle around his hiding place. Don't be silly, he thought, stop scaring yourself unnecessarily.

A minute went by.

He moved his head to and fro, very gingerly, to dislodge the earth and dead leaves from his eyes, but the confounded things clung and he was compelled to bring a hand up and brush them away.

It was dark. No lights of any kind, just noises in the distance.

He extricated himself with the utmost care, feeling chilled to the marrow. He was bound to catch his death. Having emerged inch by inch, he filled in the shallow grave and scattered leaves over it. If they came back and saw it they'd be bound to guess what he'd done, and he couldn't use the same trick twice. Flat on his belly on the damp ground, teeth chattering with cold, he surveyed his surroundings. He couldn't see much through the trees except a stationary circle of beaters a couple of hundred yards away. Not a hope of getting through— or was there?

He raised his head a little more. The hills were almost invisible now. If he could see them at all it was only because he had excellent night vision—the opposite of nyctalopia, night blindness; he'd looked it up in a dictionary at Sanary. Not even Javier had known the word.

All right, now he had to find some way of slipping through the cordon. He'd already thought of one, but it wasn't going to be easy. He could hear more cars driving up, and not only cars. It sounded as if Hess had sent for truckloads of German troops as well.

Almost in the exact center of the big circle of lights, he began to crawl. He hid behind a bush to avoid the beam of a spotlight. A moment later he rolled over into a dip to dodge another. They were stupid, he thought. If they swung the beams to and fro instead of keeping them relatively still, they'd have caught him long ago. The best way of all would have been to divide up the ground into squares and search them one by one. He would never have escaped detection then. They really were a bunch of idiots.

At last he reached the irrigation ditch beside the lower road, where most of the vehicles were parked. There must have been at least thirty of them, not counting trucks. The road itself was swarming with troops—he could see them coming and going in the glare of the head-lights.

He hadn't a hope of getting across, but that was fine with him—he didn't want to anyway.

Along the ditch he went, up to his neck in water—Ouch, was it cold!—but careful not to make the slightest splashing sound. German soldiers were standing within a few feet of him, so near that he could hear one of them talking about his parents' bakery at Kronach.

He'd gone forty or fifty yards when a new assortment of sounds reached his ears: the voices of dog handlers, the eager yelping and panting of their charges. *Dogs!* Fear engulfed him, accompanied by visions of Adolf the watchdog's yellow fangs at the villa near Sanary. He couldn't help it, he'd always been scared of dogs.

Dogs, just when he'd reached the mouth of the pipe! Damn, damn, damn! He cowered down even lower until the water immersed his chin, which instantly felt as if he'd dipped it in a bowl of ice.

He forced himself to think calmly. It was like a game of chess in which your opponent brought his confounded rook into play and you realized you'd be checkmated in six unless you dreamed up a defense. Concentrate, he told himself. Think!

Twenty seconds. He extended his arm underwater and touched the rim of the pipe. If he hid inside he'd be cornered. The dogs would crawl in after him. He wouldn't even be able to fight them off. He'd be trapped inside a concrete tube and eaten alive.

Another ten seconds of panic-stricken indecision. He felt tempted to shout, stand up, give up, but the urge subsided. He regained control of his mental processes and relaxed every inch of his body in the way that She had taught him.

That was better. He was thinking now, and thinking pretty well. The machine had restarted—he could almost hear it humming. With his eyes shut he reconstructed the position of every piece in the game he was playing against Hess: the line of cars and trucks on the two parallel roads, the soldiers standing guard, the beaters with their torches, the spotlights, and Jürgen Hess himself, a mere two hundred yards from where he now was, he the human quarry, up to his neck in a ditch brimful of icy water.

Two other factors: the drainage pipe and the dogs, especially the dogs. A farmer's wife had given him some food in an old shopping bag, and the bag must have been found with his bicycle. The horrible beasts would surely be given that to sniff. With his scent in their nostrils, they would unearth his hiding place and track him to the ditch, race along the bank to the mouth of the pipe, and start barking like mad.

After that, one of two things would happen—or rather, both things at once: Hess would have the fiercest dog unleashed into the pipe while men and more dogs were sent to guard the exits. That way, one set of fangs would be tearing at his legs while another did the same to his face. He'd be trapped like a rabbit in its burrow.

Very well, there was only one thing for it.

He removed his coat. It took him a full minute to do so without splashing, and all the time he could hear the clamor of the dogs drawing nearer. They sounded really pleased with themselves, the brutes.

Very quietly—there was a soldier with his back turned only six feet away—he rolled his coat into a ball and inserted it in the pipe. That done, he crawled in after it. One yard, then another, and he was stretched out inside. It was a really awful sensation, lying there with the concrete compressing his shoulders. He couldn't even raise his head.

It wasn't too bad to begin with, inching his way along, even though he couldn't crawl or spread his elbows or bend his legs properly, but it became harder and harder. Like a cork in a bottle, his body excluded any fresh air that might have followed in his wake. He felt he was suffocating. The pipe seemed to be getting narrower, the concrete closing in on him, the water rising until it threatened to fill the conduit to the very top. His sense of panic returned, a thousand times more potent than it had been when he first heard the dogs. It transfixed him like a shaft of lightning. He struggled, emitted a bubbling scream as his head went under. The coat wrapped itself around his face like some slimy, viscous monster—like an octopus squeezing the life out of him. The machine ground to a halt.

One . . . two . . .

The reflex had taken over: he'd started counting. Three, four, five, six, seven . . . He counted as She had taught him to, not simply reciting the numbers in turn but forcing himself to visualize them as well—to see them imprinted on his eyelids. A red one, a yellow two, a blue three, a pink four, and so on, but you had to memorize the colors you'd already used and never use the same color twice. Ordinary colors wouldn't do, either: they had to be geranium red, sunflower yellow, the blue of the Lalique vase in his bedroom . . .

Calm was restored. The cogs engaged and began to turn.

Already forty or fifty feet along the pipe, he resumed his slow advance.

The cork was well and truly embedded.

THE BIG RENAULT HAD JUST PULLED UP OUTSIDE A HOUSE ON the outskirts of a town—what town, Quartermain didn't know. The house was a palatial establishment set in its own grounds. "Kindly take note," said Laemmle, "that you're still alive and kicking—so far. This way, please."

Up some steps and into a hallway. In the hallway, doors leading off to the left and right and another door at the far end. Two men in German army uniform were standing guard at the foot of a marble staircase. Quartermain was conducted up it and into a spacious, luxuriously furnished bedroom. Another soldier was seated on a chair facing the bed with his finger on the trigger of a submachine gun resting across his thighs.

"Make yourself at home, Quartermain. You'll remain here until I'm informed of the boy's fate. Get some sleep—you look as if you need it badly."

Laemmle withdrew, followed by the ever taciturn and phlegmatic Soeft. Quartermain, handcuffed no longer, was left alone with his mute, motionless guard. He inspected the bathroom, found that it offered no ready means of escape, and returned to the bedroom. Both the windows were barred. He removed his shoes and stretched out on the bed. When he extinguished the bedside lamp, the only remaining illumination was a pinkish glow from a heavily shaded wall light. The effect was that of a photographic darkroom.

To begin with, all he could see of his guard was a dim figure seated some fifteen feet from the bed, but details took shape as the minutes went by and his half-closed eyes grew accustomed to the gloom.

Quartermain had feigned sleep for at least an hour before he detected a hint of relaxation in the sentry's posture: the man's breathing became slower and deeper. He slid off the bed and took a few experimental steps in the direction of the bathroom. The slow, regular breathing persisted, so he stealthily advanced on its source until he was only a yard away. There was a heavy glass ashtray on a table beside the door. He reached for it without a second thought.

The blow was delivered like a backhand volley. The solid block of glass connected with the man's jaw—possibly with the cheekbone as well. Quartermain had time to put the ashtray down and catch the gun before it fell with a clatter. Gently easing the limp body from the chair to the floor, he felt for the jugular: the man was out like a light but still alive. The key of the bedroom door was in the left-hand pocket of his uniform jacket. Quartermain turned it in the lock and cautiously opened the door an inch.

The landing was deserted.

He'd expected as much. After two such coincidences—a sleeping guard and a handy ashtray of adequate weight—it seemed obvious that Laemmle *wanted* him to escape. Perhaps he was looking for a pretext to gun him down, or perhaps Thomas hadn't been caught after all and he hoped to recapture them both at some fall-back rendezvous.

Quartermain limped out onto the landing and leaned over the banister. The two guards downstairs were chatting in low voices. All he could see of them was a pair of shadows on the marble floor.

Get going, Pistol Pete. . . . Momentarily reminded of Thomas, he was unsurprised by the glow of affection he felt.

Having tied his laces together and hung his shoes around his neck, he removed the key from the bedroom door and fetched a rubber mat from the bathroom. Carefully holding the key between two folds of rubber, he half-withdrew the plug of the bedside lamp from its socket and shorted it by laying the key across the prongs. There was a sharp click and the wall light went out.

So did every light in the house, as he found when he hobbled quickly out onto the landing again. Halfway down the stairs he heard someone pounding up them. Over the banister he went, clinging to the uprights in the darkness, then let himself dangle and drop. He landed silently, though it was all he could do not to cry out with pain, and groped his way to the door at the back of the hall. It led to the kitchen, which he identified by sense of smell alone. Negotiating it in the dark was a problem—he blundered into a table as he went—but he eventually sighted the pale rectangle of a glass-paneled door. The key was in the lock.

It was bitterly cold outside in the garden, but light enough for him to discern a boundary wall on his right. He scrambled over it and dropped into another garden, which he traversed at a limping run.

Two more gardens followed. He cut straight across them in the same way, determined not to waste a moment. His escape was a disguised trap, he felt sure, but he couldn't guess at its nature.

He paused to put his shoes on and then ran again as soon as he'd knotted the laces, heedless of the agonizing pain in his knee. He had no idea which way to go, but events decided for him: not far away to his right, a pair of headlights snapped on and caught him in their beam. Striding out like the middle-distance runner he'd been in his college days, he hared along a couple of side streets, dodged an oncoming car, and dived down a narrow alleyway, still convinced that he was doing precisely what Laemmle intended him to do. The alleyway debouched into an avenue. He skimmed a tram as it rattled past in the predawn gloom and skirted a row of darkened shop windows. Left, right, and left again. Still no sign of any pursuers. Could he be wrong after all—had his escape really taken them unawares?

Either way, he needed transportation of some kind. He tried the doors of several parked cars and wasn't surprised to find them securely locked.

He came out into an avenue, possibly the same one. Another tram was approaching. With a feeling of total unreality, he raised his hand: the tram rattled to a stop. He got in and sat down on one of the slatted wooden seats. His only fellow passengers were three morose-looking workmen and a woman with a poodle on her lap, but at the last moment two men in long black leather coats got in too. They were joined at the next stop by three more.

Another two got in at the stop after that. Loath as he was to admit defeat, Quartermain resigned himself to the inevitable. He rested his sweating forehead against the cold, damp windowpane. A hundred yards down the road a car drew level with the tram and kept pace with it. The face looking up at him from the driver's seat, only three or four feet away, was Soeft's.

Two stops later Laemmle himself appeared. He climbed aboard with surprising agility and sat down at Quartermain's side.

"What's this I hear? You've created an absolute shambles, so I'm told." The tram slowed to a stop. "This is where we get off, *mon cher.*"

Quartermain was hustled into the Renault and driven back to the house. A figure lay sprawled on the steps in a pool of blood.

"What gratuitous savagery," Laemmle observed. "You nearly decapitated the poor fellow."

A second man, also clad in civilian clothes, was lying in the hall with his throat cut in similar fashion.

"But the worst is yet to come, Quartermain. That unfortunate young kitchen maid! What could have possessed you to carve her up like that? Why didn't you simply knock her out? You're a positive Jekyll and Hyde. I'm amazed—I never knew an American millionaire could be so bloodthirsty."

Quartermain refused to climb the stairs, so they carried him up. The bedroom he'd left an hour ago was empty. The unconscious soldier had disappeared, the bed had been remade, and the bathroom's appearance had been modified by the addition of some feminine toilet articles he'd never seen before.

"Allow me to summarize the situation," said Laemmle. "Not content with having instituted a wholesale massacre with the help of some paid killers from Marseilles—purely in order to kidnap a boy whose mother refused to acknowledge that you were his father—not content with that, you strangle a member of the Gestapo, mortally wound a French plainclothesman attempting to apprehend you, and resume your flight, simultaneously hunted by the French police and their fraternal associates in the German army. At the end of your tether, you take refuge in this house but are discovered by its occupants, whom you proceed to kill in the most barbarous manner. It so happens that one of them was a soldier in our glorious Wehrmacht—a Polish conscript, but still, you couldn't have been more ill-advised in your choice of victim. You'd have done better to slaughter the population of an entire French town."

"Where's Thomas? What's happened to him?"

The yellow eyes gazed at him inscrutably.

"They've killed the boy," Laemmle said at length. His tone conveyed no emotion of any kind. "They drowned him like a rat. He's dead, Quartermain—dead. I hope the news pains you immeasurably."

Quartermain lunged at him. In the ensuing split second he grabbed Laemmle by the throat and squeezed, trying to crush the windpipe. He took one blow from Soeft, then two more. A pistol butt smashed his right wrist. He let go but continued to lash out with his left hand, lash out and claw at the yellow eyes. More blows rained down, fracturing his collarbone. He reeled across the room and collided with the chair on which the guard had been sitting. He tried to get up, but the pistol butt thudded into his ribs. From then on the blows descended with brutal, terrifying, methodical, monotonous regularity, breaking one bone after another. It flashed through his mind that they might not be intended to kill him, but he was scarcely capable of thought by now. He dragged himself across the floor with no aim other than to escape this monstrous hail of blows, passed out for a moment, caught a glimpse of Laemmle slumped on the bed with his face bleeding. Then the pistol butt descended again and he distinctly heard the crack of yet another bone breaking.

It was only then that he passed out completely. His one emotion, as he lapsed into welcome unconsciousness, was regret.

I'm dying, Thomas, and I didn't manage to save you. Sorry. . . .

THE DOGS HAD PICKED UP HIS SCENT AS EXPECTED. THEY TOWED their handlers to the shallow grave among the trees, then on to the ditch. They found the first shoe he'd dropped and, twenty yards along, the second. Yelping and whining hysterically, they reached the mouth of the conduit.

Jürgen Hess, who had hurried to the scene, bent down and yelled at Thomas, first in French, then in German, to come out.

No reply.

Hess proceeded to issue orders at the top of his voice. Boneheaded he might be, thought Thomas, but he certainly had an effective bellow. Some of his men were instructed to cover every access to this godforsaken drainage system, others to procure a plan of its layout from the local town hall, or wherever. Then came a final order.

"And stick a dog in there. If it chews the little bastard up a bit, too bad!"

The dog backed out of the conduit a few minutes later, three-quarters drowned but dragging the sodden coat behind it. Hess immediately regrouped his forces. "So he really is in there! Fetch some picks and start breaking up that goddam concrete, all of you. You can hack an arm off or poke an eye out, but I want him alive!" He added that he would kill the sonofabitch who killed the little bastard.

Thomas mentally cocked a snook at him. He'd waited, feeling like a block of ice, until his pursuers reached the mouth of the conduit. He himself wasn't in there any longer, having emerged at the other end and made his way along the ditch for a couple of hundred yards. Ducking below the surface for greater safety, he'd held his breath for as long as he could and swum the first few yards, and when he came up for air there was no one in the immediate vicinity. *It had worked*: the idiots thought he was still in there! He started to scramble out of the ditch but realized at once that this would be a mistake and got back in again. Although the water was shallower here, it still came up to his knees. He waded along for half a mile or more, shivering uncontrollably and almost weeping with the cold. His throat and chest were beginning to burn, but he kept going, because it was the only way to prevent those lousy dogs from picking up his scent again. Pistol Pete had used precisely the same trick in *The Pale-Eyed Sioux*.

When he thought he'd gone far enough he climbed out, crossed the dirt road beside the ditch, and ran another two hundred yards to the river. Here, to throw the dogs off the scent, he took to the water again. The current was very strong—it swept him out of his depth—and he had great difficulty in regaining the bank a mile downstream.

At last he set off for the hills that were his true destination. For an hour he ran and walked alternately until he could hardly breathe, his chest hurt so much. He felt hot and cold at the same time, and his eyes kept blurring. Almost without knowing it he stumbled and fell headlong. Although he was flat on his face in grass so encrusted with frost that it was almost brittle, he must have dozed off for a while before staggering to his feet again. He couldn't go much farther, that was certain.

He was coughing now, and every time he coughed it felt as if someone had shaved his throat with a cutthroat razor. The machine was still functioning, though—still giving him instructions: turn right, bear left, take that path—no, not that one, the other one, don't stop to rest or you'll never get started again. *Keep moving!*

He'd passed the two farmhouses at least ten minutes ago and was heading straight uphill. His legs were like pistons driven by the machine in his head—they obeyed without his comprehension or volition. The machine recited the directions Javier Coll had given him so many months before, playing them back like a gramophone: *Keep straight on after the river, Thomas. You'll see two farmhouses on your left. The first has round-arched windows like the windows of a church, the second is farther up the track and has a pigeon loft. Don't let anyone see you, just keep going. After a couple of kilometers you'll come to a sheepcote—a little one. The wall facing west has been reinforced with an iron brace in the shape of a cross, and the points of the cross are like fleurs-de-lis. . . .*

He tottered onward and upward, always upward, stumbling, cannoning off trees, lungs on fire, temples throbbing. When he came to the sheepcote he rested his burning forehead against the dank stone wall and groped his way blindly along it because he hadn't the strength to open his eyes again. His hand came into contact with some rough, rusty ironwork. He ran his fingers over it: sure enough, the arms of the cross ended in three points. *Don't take the track to the right, Thomas, even if the going looks easier. Carry straight on up through the trees till you come to a path. Beside it are two big rocks, one balanced on top of the other. Ever seen someone playing cup-and-ball? You have? Well, that's what those rocks look like: a ball resting in a cup. . . .*

The slope above the sheepcote was terribly hard going, all roots and tree stumps and muddy soil made even more treacherous by a layer of rotting leaves. He slid back two yards for every three he gained, slipped and fell with monotonous regularity. He had his eyes shut most of the time—his eyelids were too heavy—and the tears that streamed down his cheeks felt scalding hot. He wasn't disheartened, though. The machine kept ordering him to his feet, telling him not to be a baby, reminding him of Her and all She'd expected of him. He wasn't disheartened, just utterly exhausted.

No one can see you cry, he told himself, so why not let go a little? He cried, but he went on climbing. Then he fell yet again and slid back down the slope for several yards. Take a breather, he told himself—only for a minute, cross my heart and hope to die. Anyway, even if I do die, who cares . . .

The dogs!

He thought he was dreaming at first, but no, he could hear them coming nearer. Jürgen Hess must have caught on at last. Hess was on his trail again, and if he didn't move soon he'd be caught.

He moved. Before he knew it, he'd struggled to his feet and was making up the yards he'd lost. The damned machine didn't even congratulate him: it simply went on telling him what to do, ordering him onward and upward without caring that he was ill and exhausted and half dead with cold—without caring that he was just a little boy being hunted down by men with dogs and guns.

All at once the path loomed up, dead ahead, and beside it the rocks that looked like a cup-and-ball game. He'd steered straight for it in spite of everything.

Now for the defile. He hadn't understood at first when Javier said the word, which was unfamiliar to him. Javier explained that it meant a kind of narrow ravine or gorge—in Castilian, a *desfiladero*.

Well, there it was.

He set off. The defile certainly was a narrow one—he could almost touch both sides at the same time, just by stretching out his arms, except that he didn't have the energy left to raise his arms, only to put one foot in front of the other, and even then he reeled along like a drunk, cannoning off the walls, falling to his knees, scrambling up and staggering on. Something was clawing and biting the inside of his chest. He couldn't feel his legs anymore—he was almost incapable of keeping his eyes open.

When you come to the end of the defile, Thomas, you'll see a rocky slope with a little path running up it. . . .

The dogs were very close now. And he could hear men calling to each other in German and French.

He tackled the slope and promptly fell flat. He struggled on, crawling now, and hauled himself ten or fifteen feet up the slope. When the flashlight beams caught him he saw them but didn't understand, or refused to understand, what they meant.

"Get the little bastard!" Hess yelled in French. His voice sounded very far away—he might have been on the moon.

Thomas was back on his feet and climbing. Nothing could stop him now—nothing. It didn't matter that he fell over two or three times and cut his cheek on a jagged rock. He climbed on blindly, indifferent to everything—he'd even stopped feeling ill. *When you reach the top of the slope, you'll find another path running along the crest. That'll mean you're nearly there. . . .*

Hess again: "Wait a bit before you collar him. Throw a scare into him first—it'll serve him right."

Thomas heard a volley of rifle shots—he heard them but they weren't for real, they were like the gunfire in a Western. He went on climbing. Nothing and no one could stop him now. Bullets were pinging off the rocks overhead, showering him with dust and splinters. Hess's men were having fun. Then, as he groped his way to the summit, his outstretched fingers touched a leg instead of a rock. He swiped at the leg in an attempt to shift it. No one was going to stop him—no one! Rage overcame him. If he'd been a grown-up he'd have killed the man with his bare hands.

He continued to struggle furiously, lashing out with his fists and feet, when the man picked him up. And then: *"Tranquilo, Tomás, tranquilo . . . calma te, soy Miquel . . ."*

Still he struggled, murder in his heart. If he could only lay hands on a stone he would smash the man's skull—he might be little, but he would kill him all the same!

"Tomás! Soy Miquel!" The man who was holding him in his arms repeated the words again and again. *"Soy Miquel, Miquel! Calma te!"*

The Spanish words, the voice, the familiar timbre and intonation—all these began to penetrate his consciousness. He stopped struggling but remained on his guard. The machine commanded him to be wary: perhaps it wasn't the real Miquel—perhaps it was only Jürgen Hess pretending! He tried to open his eyes, but his eyelids might have been glued shut.

"Who was your *jefe*, Miquel, and where was he from?"

"My *jefe* was Javier, Tomás. He came from Sóller in Majorca."

Oh, my God, thought Thomas, it *is* him, it's Miquel the Invisible Man. I've made it—I've really made it!

"Have I really made it, Miquel? *De verdad?*"

"You're here with me. It's all over," said Miquel's voice, and Thomas could tell that he was crying. His whole body was racked with sobs—he was crying like a woman.

"Everything's all right, Tomás. Everything's all right—it's over now."

Still sobbing, Miquel bore him off on his back.

"CAN YOU HEAR ME, MR. QUARTERMAIN?"

He didn't react immediately. It seemed to him that the voice had been addressing him for quite some time—an unfamiliar voice speaking almost too perfect English with an impeccable Oxford accent.

"My name is Joachim Gortz, Mr. Quartermain. I've had business dealings with your family for over fifteen years."

Quartermain managed to open his eyes. He discovered that he was lying in a hospital bed. Judging by the taste in his mouth, his torpid condition had been induced by some form of drug.

"Do you understand what I'm saying, Mr. Quartermain?"

He blinked an affirmative. The man beside the bed, who looked fiftyish, had pink cheeks, blue eyes, and graying hair. He was remarkably well dressed.

"I realize that your fractured jaw prevents you from speaking," Gortz went on, "and believe me, I profoundly regret what was done to you. However, allow me to reassure you on one point straight away: I've managed to contact our friends in New York, and your family have been informed. From now on you'll be under my personal protection—more especially, under the protection of high finance. Your life is no longer in danger."

And Thomas—what had happened to Thomas? Quartermain vainly strove to move his lips, but it was as though Gortz had read the question in his eyes.

"Your young companion has disappeared, Mr. Quartermain. His pursuers have failed to recapture him. That's as much as I can tell you. I'm entirely ignorant of his present whereabouts."

Quartermain shut his eyes again. Every inch of him was sheer agony. Gortz's voice reached him through a mist of pain.

"I'm having you moved to Germany as soon as your condition allows. I intend to satisfy myself that you receive the best medical attention available."

THE DISCARDED RECEIVER LYING ON THE TABLE BESIDE GREGOR Laemmle had been vibrating with fury for several minutes. Laemmle himself was writing a letter, or rather, embarking on the fifth draft of a letter that would never be read, he knew, because it was addressed to Thomas: *Having spent so long trying to find her, I would give anything to have saved your mother's life. . . .* He was in Lyons, on the second floor of a riverside hotel overlooking the Saône or the Rhône, whichever. Who cared about such minor details?

He tore up his fifth unfinished draft and replaced the receiver, cutting short Gortz's interminable recriminations. What the devil was he complaining about? He'd got his American back alive—a bit the worse for wear, but alive.

A moment later Laemmle was smitten by the worst bout of depression and self-loathing he'd known in the fifty years of his existence to date. It was so bad, he took care not to venture too close to the window in case he couldn't resist the temptation to throw himself out —and even then he would probably have botched things.

He tried to read, but even his beloved Montaigne failed to distract him for long. When Jürgen Hess turned up two hours later he found Laemmle sitting there like a yellow-eyed statue, staring into space, with the book on the table in front of him and his arms folded over his paunch.

Hess recounted the story of his abortive manhunt. He described how his men had demolished an entire drainage system before discovering that the boy wasn't in it, how he'd then dispatched search parties in all directions, how one of them had picked up "the little bastard's" trail, and how they'd come within yards of recapturing him, only to be foiled by the intervention of a team of expert marksmen.

"Some of them spoke Spanish," Hess concluded. "Maybe all of them."

"A whole team, you say?" Laemmle smiled sardonically.

Hess explained that the Spaniards had laid down a murderous fire and melted away before his surviving men could get to them. He'd spent the last five days combing the area, but to no avail. He'd even extended the search as far as the Spanish border.

"I think the boy must be over the frontier by now."

It was awhile before Laemmle spoke. Eventually he said, "And you've come to enlist my help?"

Hess nodded.

Another silence. Laemmle's yellow eyes strayed to Soeft's immobile figure standing beside the door. Soeft would undoubtedly kill Hess on the spot if ordered to, but what would that achieve? He gave Hess an amiable smile.

"Tell me," he said, "what have you done with that woman Catherine Lamiel?"

"I've got her tucked up in a cell at Fresnes."

"Was it really Catherine Lamiel who betrayed Maria Weber to you?"

"She told us where the rendezvous would be, yes."

"How did you induce her to do that?"

By striking a bargain with her, Hess explained: Maria Weber in exchange for the lives of her brother and several other people.

"Did you keep your part of the bargain?"

No, they'd all been executed by firing squad.

"I want her dead, Jürgen. Kindly arrange to have her shot tomorrow morning or sent to one of those death camps your bosses are so proud of. Don't say no. That's the little favor I want in return for my assistance."

It wasn't fair that a woman who'd helped to burn Maria Weber alive and wrecked all his plans should go on living, Laemmle reflected. Besides, having her killed was an act of pure compassion. What sort of life could Catherine Lamiel have looked forward to in the unlikely event of her survival?

"Well, Jürgen, yes or no?"

"Yes."

"You'll have her shot?"

"Yes."

Laemmle closed his eyes. "Very well, my dear fellow, now be off with you."

Without opening his eyes, he raised a pudgy hand to fend off the inevitable question: how and when would he retrieve the boy?

"On your way, I said."

His recollection of the woman he'd just sentenced to death with such equanimity faded almost as quickly as the sound of Hess's receding footsteps.

"We leave tomorrow morning, Soeft."

They drove to Grenoble the next day and went straight to Barthélémy's, the greengrocer's shop in Place Sainte-Claire. Laemmle meekly took his place at the end of a queue of housewives. It was a school half-holiday, and two of the proprietor's sons were helping behind the counter.

Laemmle's turn came at last.

"I'd like a word with you," he said. "It's about Thomas."

The greengrocer not unnaturally disclaimed all knowledge of anyone called Thomas and couldn't imagine what he meant. Laemmle gave him a sympathetic smile—he'd taken a genuine liking to the big Majorcan—and suggested that he might prefer to talk in private.

"For your children's sake," he added.

With Soeft at their heels, Laemmle and Barthélémy circled the Place Sainte-Claire. Snow drifted down, muffling the sound of footsteps and traffic.

"I urge you to cooperate for your own sake and that of your wife, your three sons, and your brother, who drove Thomas to Annemasse in an attempt to smuggle him into Switzerland—oh yes, and your goats. I should add that I'm in a position to order the summary execution of two or three hundred people, let alone a few animals."

"I don't know any Thomas," the greengrocer insisted stubbornly.

Even Laemmle found it hard to smile at such obduracy.

"Javier Coll is dead," he said quietly, "and so are the other two Spaniards, probably Majorcans like yourself, who were guarding the boy at Aix. The sole survivor is the man who usually wears a leather jacket and carries a sniper's rifle. He and Thomas are now in hiding somewhere. Circumstances of a wildly improbable nature have invested me with the power of life and death, monsieur. Were you acquainted with a woman named Catherine Lamiel?"

"No."

"She was executed this morning at Fresnes Prison in Paris. Someone had to punish her, so I did—I simply gave an order to one of my subordinates. If I told him of the part you played in Thomas's escape some time ago—you, your wife, your sons, and your brother—he would exterminate you with the greatest pleasure, but not before he'd persuaded you to reveal the whereabouts of Thomas and his surviving bodyguard. You would talk, monsieur, believe me."

Barthélémy bowed his head. If he'd been alone in the world, a single man without a wife and children, he would have let them flay him alive rather than breathe a word about Thomas.

"But I don't propose to give you away," Laemmle went on. "To the extent that it depends on me, your own and your family's survival is assured. I should, however, like you to pass a message on. Tell Thomas three things. The first is that Catherine Lamiel, who betrayed his mother, has been suitably punished. Next . . ."

Laemmle braced himself for the first real lie he'd ever told in his life.

"Next, tell him the American is dead. The third thing concerns me. Tell Thomas I've resigned. I'm not playing anymore—I've laid down my king. Kindly repeat my words as accurately as possible, and tell him that I shall be dividing the remainder of my time on earth between Italy, where I own a villa at Fiesole in the name of Golaz-Hueber, and the Black Forest, which had the honor to be my place of birth. Can you remember all that?"

The greengrocer met his gaze without flinching.

"Fiesole near Florence or the Black Forest near Freiburg im Breisgau. He'll find me if he tries hard enough. And now, monsieur, you may return to your potatoes."

He was at Fiesole when the envelope reached him many months later. It bore a Barcelona postmark—not that this convinced him that Thomas was actually walking the *ramblas* of Catalonia—and it contained a one-line missive. Signed "T," it read: *I shall come, someday.*

QUARTERMAIN KNEW VERY LITTLE ABOUT THE PLACE WHERE they'd sent him apart from the name of the nearest town, Berchtesgaden, which he'd never heard of before, and the fact that it was in Bavaria. It was a kind of clinic in which he had three rooms all to himself—in fact, he seemed to be the only patient. If his physical condition had permitted, he would have been entitled to go walking in the grounds. For the moment he was confined to a wheelchair, though the last of his twenty operations had almost entirely restored the use of his left leg. He'd already managed to walk for the first time in seven months, but one lap around his bedroom on crutches was quite enough to exhaust a man who'd lost over fifty pounds. His personal nurse, a girl named Rosa Maier, was the daughter of a Viennese hotelier. She spoke fluent English, though Quartermain himself had picked up quite a lot of German during his convalescence.

Summer had come, and the panoramic view of the Bavarian Alps framed by his windows was bathed in glorious sunlight. Brief and sporadic at first, Joachim Gortz's visits had become more frequent. Two months ago, while Gortz was with him, Quartermain had received a phone call from Joe Sowinski in Zurich. Sowinski never at any stage mentioned Gortz by name. He referred to him simply as "our mutual friend" and assured Quartermain that he could trust him implicitly: "All the way, Dave, just like you can trust me." There followed a long dissertation on the following theme: since Quartermain was in Germany, why not take advantage of that fact to further the Clan's interests there? And not the Clan's alone. There were plenty of other interests to safeguard in these difficult wartime days. "After all, Dave, nobody *asked* you to go to Europe. We thought you were dead, and you would be if it wasn't for our mutual friend, so try to be reasonable. Anyway, what's all this about you kidnapping a boy?"

Quartermain hung up and turned to Gortz, who was smiling at him.

"What interests was he talking about?"

"You're a major stockholder and director of Banner Petroleum of New York, one of the biggest American oil companies."

"So?"

"What if I told you that Germany is desperately short of oil?"

"Germany happens to be at war with my country."

Gortz chuckled dryly. "I hope you don't propose to sing me 'The Star-Spangled Banner,'" he said. "We're talking finance."

"Let's forget any minor unpleasantnesses, you mean?"

"Precisely. In four or five years' time our countries will once more be standing shoulder to shoulder against the only real enemy, Russia. Your uncle and your cousins realize that, so we may as well cut a few corners now."

"I can't see myself ordering so and so many thousands of tons of oil a month to be delivered to Germany, however many corners I cut."

"We're not asking you to do anything of the kind. We've already received and are still receiving all the oil your company can reasonably be expected to send us."

Quartermain's jaw dropped. "I don't believe you."

Gortz cocked his head and stared at him curiously for a moment.

"I shall send you some files to look at as soon as you're fit enough to study them properly, but I can answer you now, in part. What interests—that was your question, wasn't it? Well, apart from your holding in Banner Petroleum, you're also a stockholder and director of Hunt Manhattan, one of the three biggest banks in the United States. Like several of its American and British competitors, it has continued to maintain a branch in Paris, even after Pearl Harbor and America's entry into the war. We still do excellent business together, I'm glad to say.

"Talking of banks, you must at least be familiar with the name of the Bank for International Settlements, which is based at Basel in Switzerland. Needless to say, my country totally controls it, and for a very good reason. Since December 1941, when the Japanese raided Hawaii, the German authorities have taken the precaution of depositing four hundred million dollars there, in gold. I should add in passing that this gold was extracted from the central banks of the Netherlands, Belgium, Luxembourg, Austria, and Czechoslovakia, as well as from the inmates of our concentration camps. The BIS itself was founded in 1929 by the president of our own central bank, Hjalmar Schacht. Its function was to maintain financial transactions in the event of an international conflict—transactions between belligerent countries, of course. Never fear, Mr. Quartermain, we aren't going to ask you to join the board—there isn't a vacancy in any case. At this very moment, a German banker directly representing Adolf Hitler is happily sitting around the boardroom table with fellow bankers from America, Britain, France, Italy, and who knows where else. Between financiers, the wartime atmosphere couldn't be more cordial."

There was another silence. Then Quartermain said, "Given that I wanted to locate the boy and get him out of France, what would have happened if I'd made a direct approach through my own bank—my family's bank, I mean?"

Gortz smiled. "A pity you didn't do so, Mr. Quartermain. Bankers can always reach an accommodation in such matters."

"What about Gregor Laemmle?"

"Someone would doubtless have persuaded him to abandon the hunt and redevote himself to philosophy at his country seat in the Black Forest. As for Jürgen Hess, he would probably have been sent to the Russian front."

"Would you have gone to the length of killing Laemmle?"

"No comment," was the only response.

Week after week and month after month from then on, Gortz's minions brought files for Quartermain to peruse and took away those he'd already seen. One of the men regularly explained that although he was at liberty to study these files *in toto*, he mustn't make any notes or extract and keep any document they contained.

Quartermain examined them with growing alarm, but not with disbelief; he didn't for one moment doubt the authenticity of this phenomenal mass of documentation. He learned, for example, that Adolf Hitler's rise to power had been largely financed and maintained during the 1930s by over half the financial establishments in Wall Street—and probably by himself, too, since he'd never troubled to find out what Uncle Peter and Cousin Larry were doing with his money. He also read that during the summer and autumn of 1942, a Frenchman named Pierre Pucheu had informed the Bank for International Settlements (and thus some carefully handpicked German financiers) that an Anglo-American landing in North Africa was imminent; and that this information, which had come from a Hunt Manhattan agent judiciously placed in the U.S. embassy at Vichy, had facilitated one of the most profitable financial transactions of recent years, if only because it prompted the immediate transfer of nine billion francs from Germany into the safekeeping of various Algerian banks.

A very full file on Joe Sowinski disclosed that a German conglomerate had been trebling his salary for nearly ten years. IG Farben paid him an annual retainer of fifty thousand dollars via the BIS, which credited it to a numbered account in Zurich.

Further files revealed the monstrous omnipotence of the said IG Farben, whose main board had formerly included Max Warburg, a German national but the brother of Paul Warburg, who was an American citizen and one of the founders of the U.S. Federal Reserve System. All the German armies were dependent on IG Farben because it supplied 100 percent of their synthetic rubber, methanol, and lubricating oils. It also supplied toxic gases. An appendix to the relevant file gave the names and locations of the IG Farben factories entrusted with the manufacture of Zyklon B, "currently used in the following extermination camps." The ensuing list of names—Auschwitz, for example—meant nothing to Quartermain.

IG Farben's office in Berlin NW 7 housed one of the most important Nazi counterespionage centers, Quartermain learned. "This office is headed by Max Ilgner and Hermann Schmitz, who are also on the board of the U.S. subsidiary, American IG, together with Henry Ford, Paul Warburg of the Bank of Manhattan, and Charles E. Mitchell of the Federal Reserve Bank of New York. "You're personally acquainted with those three gentlemen, aren't you, Mr. Quartermain? Remember, Mr. Quartermain, don't make notes or keep any of these documents, *bitte*."

Banner Petroleum's turn came next. Documents by the cardboard boxload were toted in and out of Quartermain's room for days on end. He discovered that the world's largest oil company had, by secret agreement, sold German industry the formula of isooctane, a tetramethyl-based additive essential to the manufacture of aviation fuel. "So you see, Mr. Quartermain, through the medium of banking operations and procedures of which you'll find details appended to this file, the British government is currently paying royalties to the German chemical industry in order to obtain the materials it needs to counter the Luftwaffe's attacks on its own capital city. Amusing, don't you agree?"

Quartermain further discovered that Banner had been supplying Hitler's Germany with oil—between fifty and eighty thousand tons of it monthly, according to Gortz—for more than three years. Arranged through its Venezuelan and Mexican subsidiaries, these consignments were carried initially by German tankers and subsequently by vessels sailing under the Vichy French or Panamanian flags. One "amusing" incident described in an appendix to the Banner file concerned a French tanker stopped by the Royal Navy but allowed to proceed after the State Department had intervened in response to protests from "your Uncle Peter's senators."

Hundreds of similar instances were listed, all of them fully supported by incontrovertible evidence.

As the weeks went by, Quartermain exchanged his wheelchair for a pair of crutches. Sometimes he even ventured a few steps with the aid of a stick. He went for walks in the grounds, though it took him twenty minutes to negotiate the stairs that led to his suite.

Autumn in Bavaria was a delight to the eye. "And so are you," said Rosa Maier, who had been sharing Quartermain's bed for the last three months.

He was, in fact, astonished by the sight of his own reflection in the bathroom mirror. The last few operations had worked wonders with his appearance. His voice betrayed the only minor change, the German surgeons having been unable to repair his damaged vocal cords completely. It was slightly lower in pitch and rather husky—"Very sexy," as Rosa put it.

And still he went on reading. A ritual had become established. Joachim Gortz's bookkeepers—how else to describe them?—turned up at ten each morning, five days a week. Having unpacked their files and laid them out on a long table specially installed for the purpose, they would watch in stolid silence as Quartermain read a document, then carefully replace it in the appropriate folder. At four in the afternoon precisely, they took their leave.

Quartermain had to undergo one last operation designed to restore his right hand to full mobility. He could now write again.

But he read on.

Other files submitted to him disclosed that Banner Petroleum and the family bank weren't alone in their underhand dealings. He and his cousins and Uncle Peter were far from unique. If every American guilty of connivance with the enemy were shot, Park Avenue would have been depopulated.

He immersed himself in a detailed account of the peculiar activities of the vice-president of the U.S. War Industries Bureau, most of whose energies seemed devoted to running SKF, the world's largest manufacturer of ball bearings. He combined his duties at Washington with his status as a U.S. director of this concern, one of his codirectors being a man named Rosen, a cousin of Göring's.

Quartermain, whose knowledge of the subject had hitherto been vague, became acquainted with the cardinal importance of ball bearings in wartime. Aircraft, submarines and surface vessels, tanks and trucks, trains and generators, ventilation systems and bombsights—none of these could dispense with ball bearings. A single Focke-Wulf fighter required four thousand of them.

Though Swedish in origin, SKF controlled the whole of the ball-bearing market in the United States through its interests in mines, blast furnaces, foundries, and subcontracting factories of all kinds. One of SKF's three principal centers was in Schweinfurt, Germany, another in Göteburg, Sweden, and the third in Philadelphia. The file submitted to Quartermain, which dealt exclusively with the Philadelphia operation, listed thousands of figures and contained fifty pounds of documents. It proved that at a time when the U.S. Air Force was doing battle in the Pacific and preparing to engage in Europe, it was partially grounded by a shortage of ball bearings—and this while immense consignments of these essential components were being regularly dispatched from the United States to Sweden, Spain, Portugal, and Switzerland: in reality, to Germany.

One Saturday morning, with the aid of a stick alone, Quartermain took only seven minutes to descend and reascend the double flight of outside steps leading to the grounds. He'd been at the clinic for exactly twelve months.

He was now reading a file on the world-famous Detroit automobile firm whose president and founder had received his Grand Cross of the German Eagle from Hitler's hands at the same time as the aviator Charles Lindbergh, and whose French factories had calmly continued to mass-produce motor vehicles, not only after the German occupation, but also since the United States entered the war. These factories not only supplied Hitler's armies with the trucks they needed but went so far as to manufacture components for the repair of Molotov trucks captured on the Russian front. "If the day ever comes when American and German motorized columns confront each other on European soil, Mr. Quartermain, your compatriot from Detroit will be able to congratulate himself on having supplied both sides with trucks. Business is business. . . ."

"MERRY CHRISTMAS," SAID ROSA AS SHE CLIMBED INTO QUAR-termain's bed on the night in question.

Two days earlier Quartermain had received an unusual visitor: a fellow American officially traveling in wartime Germany in his capac-ity as president of the Bank for International Settlements. A former Hunt Manhattan executive and personal acquaintance of Uncle Pe-ter's and Cousin Larry's, he expressed great confidence in the outcome of the war but refrained from divulging too many details about its current progress. On his way back from Berlin after conferring there with some of Hitler's top financial advisers, he came bearing gifts, including books, phonograph records, and three dozen Hollywood movies. "Joachim's going to fix you up with your own little projection room, David. He really spoils you, you've got to admit."

Quartermain's next reading matter was the file on TTT, which man-ufactured telephones and communications systems of all kinds. "I'm sure you're personally acquainted with the founder and president of TTT, Mr. Quartermain," Gortz had written in a covering letter, "since you're a major stockholder."

The TTT file was enormous—so enormous, Quartermain reflected, that a Senate committee of inquiry would have taken a year to wade through it. He retained only one or two essential points, for instance that one representative of the TTT empire in Germany was Walter Schellenberg, head of the Gestapo's counterespionage service; that TTT had for years made regular payments to Heinrich Himmler and his SS; and that it still retained very substantial investments in Ger-many. An appendix stated: "You will note that the telephone and radio networks used by Herr Hitler, his government departments, and the OKW, or Armed Forces High Command, are regularly serviced and updated by American-trained technicians in the firm's employ (cf. Items 2/137 and 2/224)."

Gortz's covering letter gave details of another interesting TTT in-vestment, to wit, a firm by the name of Lorenz, which was almost wholly TTT-owned. "In August 1939, a few days before German troops invaded Poland, Lorenz acquired a 25 percent stake in Focke-Wulf AG of Bremen, which manufactures fighters for the Luftwaffe. That stake has since been increased, so it might almost be said that

TTT coproduces fighter aircraft for both sides. The profits from TTT's operations in Germany are, of course, channeled through BIS under the supervision of that charming American banker who visited you recently. By the way, I've given orders for your private cinema to be installed as soon as possible."

"Convinced now?"

Gortz, back in Berchtesgaden again, had volunteered to accompany Quartermain on his afternoon walk, which was now a daily routine. The two men were strolling side by side through the grounds, the paths having been sufficiently cleared of the snow that had fallen in the first few weeks of 1944.

"I'm delighted to note such a remarkable improvement in your physical condition," Gortz went on. "Our surgeons have done you proud—you'll soon be able to dispense with that stick."

"Who compiled those files? It must have taken months of work, if not years."

"Who do you think compiled them?"

"Several Joachim Gortzes. Dozens of them, probably."

"Not as many as all that," Gortz said archly.

"You and men like you must have been taking out insurance for years, even since before the war."

"Your German is coming on astonishingly well, Mr. Quartermain. You might almost be mistaken for a Viennese at times." Gortz accompanied this allusion to Rosa Maier with a faint smile.

"Before we go any further," Quartermain said, "what news of the boy?"

"I don't have any. It's reassuring, in a way."

"What do you mean?"

"You know what I mean, I'm sure, but I'll tell you anyway. If the boy were still being hunted by someone, and certainly if he'd been caught, I should have heard."

"What about Laemmle?"

"No change since our last meeting. He's out of the picture."

"That leaves Hess."

"When last I heard, he was fighting the Russians with immense enthusiasm. May I call you David?"

"No."

"I'm on first-name terms with four of your cousins, including Larry."

No reply. Quartermain's short walk had exhausted him. He made for a bench that had been cleared of snow. Gortz sat down beside him.

"Mr. Quartermain," he said, "you must have given a great deal of thought to the reasons why I and certain other people set so much store by your presence here. Have you identified them?"

"I'm a hostage."

"That's something of an oversimplification."

"How goes the minor unpleasantness?"

"If you mean the war, Germany's in the process of losing it magnificently. It can only be a matter of months—to be pessimistic, a year at most."

"Your patriotism brings tears to my eyes."

"I take that as a compliment," said Gortz, lighting the Chesterfield in his glove-encased fingers.

"Know what I think?" said Quartermain. "I think you'd have packed me off to a concentration camp or simply had me shot if Germany had shown signs of winning. The worse the minor unpleasantness goes, the more I'm worth to you. You began by using me as an incentive to my family to step up its assistance to Germany. Now you're using me to pave the way for the reestablishment of lucrative commercial and financial relations once the war's over. My survival has become the test of your good faith and humane disposition."

"My personal insurance policy, you mean?"

"Exactly. What's more, you justify yourself in your own eyes by claiming to have the long-term interests of your country at heart, over and above any minor unpleasantnesses."

"Splendid," said Gortz. "So I'm a patriot after all."

"I don't like you, Gortz."

"I'm distressed to hear you say that, truly I am. To carry your argument to its logical conclusion, however, shouldn't you cherish an equal dislike for your own family?"

"That's my business."

"Granted. What else have you deduced about my intentions?"

"I think you may be planning to give me the dossier you and your friends have compiled about my family's interests, or a copy of it."

"It's an original thought."

Quartermain, both hands folded on the handle of his stick, studied the German financier in profile.

"I've even toyed with the notion that you may release me—or allow me to escape."

Gortz turned to look at him, and their eyes met.

"Really? Why should I do a thing like that?"

"I think you'll do it as soon as you feel absolutely convinced that the war is lost, and as soon as you know for sure that your Wall Street friends will be arriving in Germany on the heels of the Allied armies to get the country going again in double-quick time."

Still looking at him, Gortz started laughing.

"You've got a very fertile imagination, Mr. Quartermain."

"More fertile than you think. It's even occurred to me that your friends may be planning to hurry things along and prevent the minor unpleasantness from becoming too unpleasant by getting rid of Hitler."

That touched Gortz on the raw, Quartermain was genuinely pleased to note. The banker's eyelids flickered for a split second.

"I withdraw that remark. Strike it from the record," Quartermain went on. "If any such attempt is ever made, I'm sure your friends won't be involved—or rather, I'm sure nobody will ever be able to prove they were if it fails. I know you saved my life, Gortz, and I know you ran certain risks in the process. There must surely be people in Berlin, people in Hitler's immediate orbit, who'd hang you from a butcher's hook if they knew the kind of game you're playing."

"Is that a threat?" asked Gortz.

Quartermain smiled. "I guess I'm going to be able to escape quite soon," he said. "I seem to think Switzerland isn't too far from where we're sitting right now."

Gortz bowed his head in thought, then looked up again.

"It's possible, I only say possible, that you may find your way there sometime. If you do, you won't try to get even with me."

"Oh? Why not?"

"Because I'm just a common or garden banker—not important enough for you to regard me as a mortal enemy. The war will end and you'll forget all about me. I'm a pawn, nothing more."

"Your modesty does you credit, but I don't buy that. You helped to track the boy down."

"I helped to look for someone in possession of some access codes I'd been ordered to retrieve, but that's ancient history. Today I wouldn't cross the road to recover the funds secreted by old Gall. Circumstances have changed."

"Gall? Who's he?"

"A Frankfurt banker who jumped out of a window some ten years ago. He was the great-grandfather of the boy you call Thomas."

"If anything happens to Thomas, you and your friends can kiss the world goodbye."

Gortz shrugged. "Why so protective about a boy who may not even be your son? You'll never know for sure."

Rage welled up in Quartermain, astonishing him with its intensity. He hadn't realized until that moment how boundless and irrevocable his love for Thomas was. He struggled with his emotions for several long seconds.

"Now it's my turn," said Gortz. "I withdraw that remark."

"The boy's mother," Quartermain said. "Who was responsible for her death?"

"Jürgen Hess and Gregor Laemmle, but don't ask me exactly what part each of them played. Their versions differ."

Rosa Maier had just come down the steps with a rug over her arm. Sunday afternoon was drawing to a close and the air had already taken on a nocturnal chill.

"I underestimated you," said Gortz. "You were my prisoner; now I'm yours. My only excuse is that your family didn't have a very high opinion of you. Perhaps you've ceased to be the David Quartermain they used to know."

"Perhaps." Quartermain's tone was supremely indifferent. "How do you rate your chances, Gortz? Think you'll come out of this with flying colors?"

"I think so, yes. I'm working on it. Long live the world of high finance."

Rosa walked up to them.

"Time to go," she said.

Quartermain nodded. "Herr Gortz and I had just come to the same conclusion."

"MIQUEL?"

"*Estoy aquí.* I'm right behind you."

"Surely you've no need to go on hiding. There's no one around."

"The more I hide the less people see of me," said Miquel—or rather, said Miquel's voice.

"Very smart of you," said Thomas.

He smiled to himself. Miquel was really funny sometimes, with his craze for hiding. You'd think he was miles away—you'd think he'd lost track of you and start getting worried, but no, not at all, he'd be lurking there all the time, as quiet as a mouse—even quieter than Pistol Pete when he took off his boots and sneaked up on the bank robbers' camp. He was a terrifically good shot, too, the best in the world. Dr. Nadal—he had been born in Majorca too, but he'd lived in France for over thirty-five years—had wanted to see how well Miquel could shoot. "Would you ask him to give me a demonstration, Thomas? The night the Kléber group got away from that German patrol, I'm told he gunned down eight men in almost as many seconds —in the dark, too." Thomas doubted if Miquel would agree but promised to ask him. Miquel had naturally refused—he hadn't even budged from his quarters in the loft above the barn, where he not only slept but kept watch on the surrounding area. "Just to please me, Miquel," said Thomas, rather hurt by his refusal, whereupon Miquel had delivered a whole speech (at least twenty-five words—a regular miracle!). Javier Coll had advised him never to fire his rifle for fun, he said. An eye like his was a gift from God, and you didn't fool around with a gift from God. Thomas went on and on at him for weeks until he finally said yes. They both went off into the forest with Dr. Nadal and four empty wine bottles. Miquel had explained how he wanted the bottles set up: in pairs, one balanced on top of the other. Then he walked off, so far away that he looked like a dot and they could hardly see him. Dr. Nadal and Thomas only just had time to glimpse what happened when he opened fire, because the four shots were almost simultaneous. The first two bullets shattered the lower pair of bottles, the third and fourth caught the others before they could hit the ground. Dr. Nadal's face was a picture, and Thomas swelled with pride. After that, Thomas took a nut from his pocket and held it at eye level between his thumb and forefinger. The nut exploded without even grazing his fingers. All he felt was a puff of wind.

"Miquel?"

"*Estoy aquí.*"

There! Thomas hadn't heard or seen a thing, but Miquel had changed position. He was over to the left now.

"Don't you ever feel like going back to Spain?"

"*A Mallorca? Claro que sí!*"

"How old are you?"

"Twenty-three and a half."

"That's awfully old."

"Sí, muy viejo."

"Your fiancée, your *novia*—she must miss you a lot."

Miquel was no fool. He knew at once what Thomas was driving at.

"Estamos muy bien aquí, Tomás. We're fine where we are."

"But there are too many *maquisards* here, Miquel. One day the Germans will turn up. They'll send tanks and masses of soldiers, and Jürgen Hess will come with them."

Miquel replied that it was possible, but that he would see them coming first. That would be the moment for them to leave. There was no immediate hurry and no sign of danger. Thomas had been Dr. Nadal's nephew for more than a year now. Everyone was used to seeing him around—no one suspected anything. Miquel didn't speak at such length, of course: he uttered only four or five words. But Thomas grasped what underlay them.

Thomas walked on. Winter was on the way out, and the scents of the countryside were changing. It wasn't so bad, this place where they'd lived for the past year or more. He didn't want for much except books. He'd already read the three hundred French and Spanish books in Dr. Nadal's little library. Dr. Nadal himself was awfully nice— almost like a real uncle—and so was his wife, Aunt Mayo (her real name was María de Los Angeles, and she came from Majorca too). Then there were some other interesting people, the Berthiers for instance (that wasn't their real name either, but they were Jews, so they had to hide). Monsieur Berthier, who had taught mathematics at a school in Paris, was giving him lessons. Math was really easy—he'd completed a four-year syllabus in the past twelve months. Madame Berthier was teaching him French (as if he didn't know it already) and history and geography as well. Geography was all right, but history! Why should he care who murdered Henri IV? It wouldn't have surprised him to learn that the police were still hunting for the killer.

"Miquel, do you think Jürgen Hess is still after me?"

"No sé."

"What do you mean, you don't know? You'd be bound to know if his spies were in the neighborhood."

The other thing about Monsieur Berthier was that he played chess pretty well. He'd almost won two and drawn five of the hundred and twenty-three games they'd played so far, which wasn't bad for an old man of fifty-nine.

"Well, have you seen any spies or haven't you?"

Miquel's voice, which was somewhere on his right now, said he hadn't seen a soul, but that proved nothing.

Mind you, he'd been careful not to play too well against Monsieur Berthier so as not to discourage him. It wasn't only that, though. One of their drawn games had resulted from a loss of concentration on his part. He'd been looking over Monsieur Berthier's shoulder at Susanne's underpants. Susanne, Dr. Nadal's youngest daughter, was sitting in the red armchair pretending to read with her legs apart so he could see them. It was bound to put a fellow off, a thing like that.

"What goes on round here, Miquel?"

"In town? In town there's the German army, and the SS, and the militia, and the gendarmes, and the men of the French Gestapo."

"That makes a lot of them."

"Sí, Tomás, hace mucha gente."

Susanne was awfully sweet. She was quite grown-up—thirteen already—but awfully nice all the same. She'd let him look at her breasts almost at once, not that they were much, her little buttons. They weren't real breasts like Aunt Mayo's (*they* were huge), but with luck they'd grow a bit.

"You don't think it's too crowded around here?"

"No," Miquel's voice said firmly.

"I'm getting awfully bored, Miquel. I'd like to move on."

"Tenemos que esperar. We'll have to see."

Thomas hated the prospect of sitting out the war like a rabbit in a burrow, even if Miquel did keep assuring him that everyone thought he'd crossed over into Spain. Yellow Eyes knew he wasn't in Spain. He hadn't come looking for him because he didn't want to, that was the only reason. He obviously hadn't been lying when he'd told Barthélémy he'd laid down his king. Yellow Eyes had resigned. Maybe, but *he* hadn't. . . .

He crouched down. Although he could hear the sound of running water below, he couldn't see the river itself. The shooting pains in his head had returned, as they always did whenever he thought of the Thing and Yellow Eyes. They drove him nearly mad. Dr. Nadal had told him they were an aftereffect of his double pneumonia, but that was wrong. His head hurt because he wanted to kill Yellow Eyes, wanted him dead, wanted to be the one that killed him, wanted him to suffer. It was easy to say "forget," but he didn't want to. Sometimes, when his memory of the Thing was less vivid, he thought of Susanne and didn't feel so mean and almost lost his desire to kill Yellow Eyes. If he waited much longer it would be too late—he would have changed too much. Besides, he'd written to Yellow Eyes to say that he would come and kill him someday. It would be like breaking his word.

"Miquel, there's something I must tell you."

"*Sí, Tomás?*"

"A week ago I saw something with my binoculars. There were four men in a black Citroën. Three of them I didn't know—they were all in civilian clothes, but they were wearing black leather coats like the Gestapo, and there was a yellow card under the windscreen. I recognized the fourth one, though. He was on the road from Sanary to Bandol with the very big man, the one called Abel."

He heard a rustle of leaves. It was very rare for Miquel to make a sound when changing position. That proved he was alarmed—proved that he believed the lie he'd just been told.

"*Estás seguro, Tomás?*"

Thomas didn't trouble to reply. It wasn't true that he'd seen the one-armed man who looked like an Arab, but the bit about the four men in the Citroën was true enough. He'd watched them through his binoculars. Although he'd never seen any of them before, they were the same type of men as Yellow Eyes had employed at Sanary: Lafont's men.

The lie he'd just told wouldn't be enough to persuade Miquel to leave, of course, but it was like an opening gambit.

The game was beginning again.

He straightened up and walked to the brow of the hill. From there he had a view of the Corrèze, the river from which the region took its name, with the town of Tulle in the background.

GREGOR LAEMMLE HAD BEEN IN PARIS FOR THREE DAYS. HE WAS back from Italy after a lengthy stay at his house in Fiesole under the name Golaz-Hueber. He'd abandoned his beloved Tuscany for several reasons, by far the least important of them being what had happened in the south of the Italian peninsula. The British and Americans had landed there and were pushing north. They would undoubtedly get to Rome in the end, whatever the merits of the so-called Gustav Line, and any information or assurances to the contrary left Laemmle as cold as a block of Carrara marble.

He'd left Italy because, as the months went by, his obsession with suicide had grown stronger with every passing day. It had been his vague hope that the resumption of a privileged existence in the French capital would help him to recover, not a taste for life (that would have been too much to ask), but something in the nature of wry and cynical resignation. He should have known himself better: things went from bad to worse, and his obsession became steadily more insistent.

He moved back into his old apartment in the Rue Guynemer, overlooking the Jardin du Luxembourg, which had remained unrequisitioned. The first three days he devoted to his old routine pursuits. He toured the bookshops and spent an entire afternoon discussing Verlaine with a bookseller in the Rue Saint-André-des-Arts. He hardly ever left Saint-Germain-des-Prés, where he rediscovered an antique shop he'd patronized fifteen years before. Without coveting it in the least, and simply to convince himself that he was still alive, he allowed himself to fall in love with an Aubusson tapestry and bought it for an astronomical price.

On the morning of the fourth day the doorbell rang. It was Monsieur Henri Lafont, and his fragile edifice of calm and resignation collapsed in ruins: Lafont had come to talk about the boy.

"We located him quite by accident," he said in the fluting voice that held a certain appeal for Laemmle. "It's been two days now. I dropped in on the off chance—I didn't think you'd be here—but it's him sure enough, my men are absolutely positive. He's in Corrèze—I've got the address. You know how it is: we infiltrate those damned Resistance groups, bring up reinforcements, raid their bases, and so on. I do my best, but it isn't easy. Sorry, I'm talking too much—it's my nerves. I won't tell you all I've done for Germany, I get the impression you couldn't care less. The boy is another matter, of course. . . ."

Lafont smiled. His eyes had the absolute fixity of a big cat's. Studying him as he sipped his coffee, Laemmle found that Monsieur Henri had changed a good deal since their last encounter several months ago. There was something feverish underlying his talkative and self-assured manner, but it wasn't fear. The man was anything but afraid.

"Well," Laemmle said, "how is he?"

Lafont hesitated, then smiled again. He wasn't holding out for a better price, he explained. "I have all the money I want. That isn't why I came to see you." He fell silent, sipping the cognac-laced coffee

Soeft had brought him. At length he said, "So you're still interested in the youngster?"

Laemmle, cursing the mischance that had brought Lafont to his door, simply nodded. The feline eyes scrutinized him intently.

"You're a strange person, monsieur—one of nature's oddities. Me, I don't give a damn about anything, but you . . . Maybe that's what draws us together, the attraction of opposites."

"Get on with it. Is the boy in danger?"

"You might say that."

"The map, Soeft."

Laemmle spread it out on the table. Lafont indicated the Corrèze area.

"That's where he's tucked away, near Tulle. He's living with a Dr. Nadal, who's a Spaniard in spite of his name."

"Nadal is a Spanish name too," said Laemmle. You thought you'd heard the last of this business, he told himself, but you were wrong. Aloud, he said, "Who else have you sold this information to?"

"Sharp as ever, aren't you?"

"Who else?"

Jürgen Hess, of course. As ill luck would have it, Hess had just returned from the Russian front with a chestful of medals and the rank of Standartenführer, or colonel in the SS. He'd been reassigned to the Second SS Panzer Division, the Das Reich, at Bordeaux, but was still in Paris.

"He called me and arranged a meeting for tonight."

"How much does he know?"

"Only that I know the boy's whereabouts, that's all."

"A little more coffee?"

Lafont declined, rose, and walked to the door. He would be dead before the year was out, he said, but no matter; he'd packed ten times as much into his life as most men. Everyone had to pay up sometime, and he was ready to do so. He didn't know why he'd come—it was just a fleeting impulse.

He took his leave.

That afternoon Laemmle spurned the nearby Luxembourg Gardens and crossed the Seine to the Jardin des Tuileries, where he sat down on a bench. What he'd done and was in the process of doing would remain unique in the annals of German philosophy, he reflected, though it was ages since he'd credited philosophy with any validity at all. He was like a sailor who hated the sea but could no longer endure to live ashore. Hours later, a shivering old park attendant asked him to leave because the gardens were closing for the night. He emerged into the Rue de Rivoli and strolled along in the chill of the Parisian night, waiting for Soeft to pick him up as arranged.

Soeft duly appeared with the requisite information.

"Thank you, Soeft. I approve of this nice white car you've found us, by the way. White is the color of mourning in China—an admirable choice."

He took his place in the back and muffled himself up in rugs. He hadn't realized quite how cold he was.

"Let's go, Soeft."

Only a few days ago, on his way back from Italy to bid farewell to Paris, he'd been planning to return to his native Schwarzwald and put a bullet in his head or open his veins in a warm bath—he hadn't quite decided which. Thomas had been merely a memory, but now that memory had come alive again. . . .

QUARTERMAIN HAD CHOSEN TONIGHT SIMPLY BECAUSE IT WOULD be dark, and it was, devilishly so, judging by the view from the window where he'd been waiting for nearly two hours. He couldn't even make out the first row of trees in the grounds, only thirty yards from the main building, and there wasn't a sign of any sentries. They seemed to be conspicuous by their absence tonight.

It was one-fifteen A.M. when his escape began in earnest. The previous evening had followed an uneventful course. He'd dined at seven-thirty. Once the trolley had been wheeled out he'd loaded the projector himself and watched a second showing of John Ford's *Grapes of Wrath*. Rosa had tried to join him at eleven, but he'd begged off, pleading illness. At eleven-thirty he went to bed, switching off his lights.

The door to the grounds should have been double-locked, but only one of the locks had been secured, and that he easily dismantled with the screwdriver Rosa had procured for him weeks before.

The sentry box at the foot of the steps was empty. This wasn't an escape, he thought, it was more like a quiet stroll. He'd just reached the first line of trees when he stumbled over the body of a sentry: the man had lost his steel helmet and was lying there with blood oozing from the base of his skull. A mile farther on he came to the ornamental lake that was as far as he'd ever walked, leaning heavily on his stick to simulate an incapacity for prolonged exercise. He skirted the lake and crossed the wooden bridge over the stream, whose conformation had always reminded him of the Serpentine in London's Hyde Park.

It was then, if not before, that he distinctly sensed that someone was watching him. Undaunted, he bypassed a small hunting lodge that had been converted into a guard post. It was brightly lit, and more lights revealed that sentries were pacing up and down beside the main entrance to the grounds a couple of hundred yards away. The route that Gortz had cleared for him obviously didn't lead in that direction.

Quartermain veered left, hugging the shelter of some larch trees, until he came to the perimeter wall, which was a good fifteen feet high and topped with barbed wire. He couldn't be expected to clear that—Gortz must have devised an easier way out.

No patrols, no dogs. He followed the wall until he came to a farmhouse just inside the grounds. The body of a soldier lay sprawled outside the door—another of his victims. He was amazed at his talent for unarmed combat. The farmhouse, which abutted the perimeter wall, was deserted, and its back door opened onto a road beyond the wall.

He set off along the road but retreated to a path through the trees when a military vehicle passed without spotting him. Twenty minutes later—it must have been two o'clock by this time—he came to a small village.

He couldn't have failed to see the Mercedes. It was parked outside the village inn, which stood on the brow of a hill. He had only to release the handbrake and the car began to coast downhill without a sound, but not before he'd glimpsed a man's face at the window of the inn.

The ignition key was in place, of course, but he suppressed a fierce temptation to switch it on and let the Mercedes rip. When he finally did so it wasn't for long. He was more or less expecting what happened next. As the Mercedes rounded a bend, its headlights illuminated a roadblock: three cars were drawn up in line abreast with half a dozen men beside them.

He pulled up.

A man of medium height but massive build detached himself from the others. He was wearing a black leather coat and a brown felt hat, and his gloved hand was holding a Luger with the muzzle pointing at the ground. He strode up to the Mercedes and signaled to Quartermain to lower his window.

"Lie down on the floor," he said in English. "Be quick, please."

His tone was calm and businesslike. When Quartermain just stared at him, the muzzle of the Luger appeared.

"I won't kill you, but I wasn't forbidden to shoot you in the legs. Lie down, please."

Quartermain complied, flattening himself as best he could. It was only ten seconds before they started shooting. A burst of automatic fire swept the car, shattering the side windows and peppering some of the bodywork. Silence returned.

"You can get up now."

Quartermain did so. The roadblock was opening up. The submachine gunners had returned to their own cars. The big man climbed into the back of the Mercedes and sat down.

"Drive on."

"Where to?"

"There's another roadblock, a real one, a few kilometers down the road. Don't worry about the barrier—drive straight through it. A soldier may fire at you, but his rifle will be loaded with blanks. Anyway, if you're as good a driver as I'm told you are he won't have time to aim. You can drive as fast as you like from now on."

Quartermain, glancing in the rearview mirror, met a cold and inscrutable gaze. The big man's Luger was across his knees.

The Mercedes responded instantly and gathered speed. A few minutes later it smashed through a flimsy wooden barrier painted red and black, traveling far too fast for the three or four soldiers who were manning the roadblock to take aim.

"You drive remarkably well, Herr Quartermain."

They were now skirting a lake.

"Who killed those two sentries in the grounds? Did you?"

The dark eyes stared back at him, as impenetrable as ever. The Mercedes roared through a tiny, slumbering village and came to a crossroads. A signpost indicated that Salzburg lay to the right.

"Turn left here, please."

A series of lakes showed up on the left. They were still descending, but not as steeply.

"There's a guard post a kilometer ahead. Keep going."

Quartermain kept going with his foot flattened. He caught a glimpse of an illuminated building on his right and two uniformed figures standing outside with their arms raised in a derisory attempt to stop him.

"Are we in Austria?" he asked.

"We just crossed the border."

He was tempted to ask the obvious question—"What happens now?"—but he refrained. Joachim Gortz must have allowed for every eventuality. All at once he recognized the road he was speeding along: it was the Kitzbühel road. Memories of skiing there with Maria surfaced in his mind, but he thrust them aside. In any case, it seemed centuries ago.

"In a very short time you'll see a truck parked on the right of the road. Pull up behind it, please."

It was more of a van than a truck. The rear doors opened and a man got out. Without a word, he settled himself at the wheel of the Mercedes and drove off.

Quartermain got into the van at once, followed by the big man. The whole exchange had taken less than fifteen seconds.

The van turned out to be a security van for the transportation of banknotes. The only windows were a couple of barred loopholes. Two and a half hours of brisk driving took them past Innsbruck. They stopped at four checkpoints, but the driver's papers got them through without incident.

"I suppose the man who took over the Mercedes is laying a false trail?"

The big man's eyes were jet-black. He nodded.

"In the direction of Italy, maybe?"

Another nod.

The jet-black eyes had strayed from Quartermain only once. That was at the third checkpoint, when the guard commander showed signs of wanting to inspect the interior of the van with the Reichsbank emblem on the side. For a very short space of time, five or six seconds at most, the big man had turned to face the double doors, Luger poised, listening intently to what was being said outside.

That was time enough. The length of wire Quartermain had found on the floor of the van disappeared beneath his overcoat. He'd managed to tear his pockets sufficiently to work with both hands, and his long fingers were busy fashioning a noose.

THOMAS HAD CYCLED INTO TULLE TWO DAYS AGO. HE HADN'T even needed to invent an excuse, because Dr. Nadal had asked him to go and fetch some medical supplies. It wasn't by any means his first visit to the town. He'd already been there several times, but he looked forward to this particular outing more eagerly than usual. Resistance fighters regularly visited Dr. Nadal for treatment under cover of darkness, and he'd heard them boast that they intended to attack the town without waiting for the Americans to arrive.

Thomas wanted to gauge the enemy's strength for himself. Once he'd picked up the prescriptions from the pharmacy, he systematically inspected all the places the *maquisards* planned to attack in due course. He wheeled his bike past Gestapo headquarters at the Hôtel Moderne, past the Hôtel La Trémolière, which housed the German military police, past Champ de Fer Barracks, where the French militia hung out, past the Hôtel Dufayet and the Hôtel Terminus, both of which were said to be full of German officers (they were), and as far as Place de Souillac. There were plenty of Germans in evidence there too.

He had no premonition of danger save once, while passing the terrace of the Café Tivoli, where his "rat's instinct" sounded the alarm. A dozen men were seated at a table, drinking and laughing. He swiftly scanned their faces without recognizing any of them, but still, you could sense when someone was on the other side of a door even if you didn't hear him arrive or ring the bell or anything: you simply *knew* he was there. . . . He jumped on his bike at once but quickly called himself to order: pedaling off like a madman was a silly thing to do—it would only attract attention.

He'd just turned off down the Rue du Pont-Neuf when a minor incident occurred: he was stopped by some armed Gardes Mobiles who demanded to know what he was up to and why he wasn't at school. No problem: he produced a certificate signed by the local schoolmaster exempting him from school on account of mumps. Then a real gendarme arrived on the scene. "It's Dr. Nadal's nephew," he told the officious swine with their rifles and steel helmets. "I know Dr. Nadal—the boy's all right."

And he rode on.

That was two days ago. Thomas had almost forgotten his little jaunt, mainly because of Susanne, whom he'd finally persuaded to take all her clothes off in the barn yesterday evening.

But he recalled it now. One by one, his memory summoned up the faces of the men sitting outside the Café Tivoli.

Those were two of them, no doubt about it. Their confounded Citroën was parked several hundred yards away in a clump of trees set back from the road. They were just sitting there, smoking one cigarette after another with a casual air. They might have been admiring the scenery, except that their vantage point gave them an excellent view of the road leading to Dr. Nadal's house.

"Do you see them, Miquel?"

"Sí."

Thomas lowered his binoculars.

"Could you get them from here?"

"There's no point, Tomás."

Miquel was right—it was silly of him. Even if he'd killed them, scores of others would have turned up. He'd been spotted. They must have recognized him from the Tivoli terrace and were keeping him under surveillance. They could have come for him yesterday, but they hadn't done so because they were waiting for orders. They were Lafont's men. Now that Yellow Eyes had given up, that meant they were working for Jürgen Hess. That was it: Hess must be on his way. The hunt was on again. . . .

He crawled until he was well out of sight. Then he stood up.

"I think we should go back as soon as possible, Miquel. Where are you?"

"In front of you, now you've turned around."

"I didn't do it on purpose."

"No entiendo."

"I didn't mean to be spotted in Tulle."

He set off at a brisk pace. It might be only a matter of minutes.

"I didn't mean to, really I didn't. Or maybe I *did* want to be spotted, somewhere at the back of my mind. Anyway, it's all my fault, I should have ridden off more slowly or something. I'm sorry."

Miquel didn't reply. That was the annoying thing about Miquel: you seldom saw him and he seldom spoke. Thomas put on speed. The situation was clear as daylight. Hess would swoop on Dr. Nadal's house like lightning, and he was quite capable of slaughtering everyone there: Dr. Nadal and Aunt Mayo and the maidservant, not to mention the Berthiers and Susanne and her brothers and sisters. He might even kill the people in the neighboring farms. He must warn them.

He broke into a run in spite of the uneven ground, pausing several times to scan the surrounding area through his binoculars. Maybe Hess or Lafont's other men were already in position, awaiting his return. It wouldn't do to walk straight into a trap, he told himself. His powers of concentration had waned since he'd been in Corrèze. He was less wary, less alert. He ought to have suspected something as soon as the alarm sounded in his head outside the Tivoli. Instead, he'd calmly cycled home without a word to anyone. He'd gone soft, that was the trouble, and he hated himself for it.

Icy fingers clutched at his heart. He pictured Dr. Nadal and Aunt Mayo lying dead with their heads cut off like Grandpa and Grandma Allègre at Sanary, and all on account of him. Visualizing these horrors, he felt a resurgence of hatred, stronger than ever before. Would the nightmare never end? He'd lain low for too long—he'd played an exclusively defensive game. It was time to attack, time to—

Something had caught his eye. Dead ahead and two or three hundred yards off, a human figure was on the move. He flung himself down and leveled the binoculars, only to discover that it was Monsieur Berthier with his short legs, potbelly, and bald head. Monsieur Berthier was out of breath and sweating hard. Thomas looked to see if he was really alone—they might be using him to bait a trap—but no, there was no one else in sight. He stood up. As soon as Monsieur Berthier was within earshot he breathlessly announced that everyone was very worried about Thomas—they'd been looking for him for hours. Did he know someone called Barthélémy, who claimed to be a greengrocer from Grenoble? He did? Well, this Barthélémy had telephoned to warn him that he must go away at once. He'd left a message.

"Dr. Nadal wants you home as quickly as possible, Thomas. Are you all on your own? Isn't your friend with you?"

Thomas didn't bother to reply. Of course Miquel was around—Miquel was always around. He dismissed the question. There were far more important matters to consider.

"We'll go right away," he said, "but we'd better not go together. Would you mind going on ahead? I'll follow you. When we get to the house, you go in first. If everything's all right, give me a wave."

Thomas was watching through his binoculars when Monsieur Berthier entered Dr. Nadal's house twenty minutes later. He emerged almost at once and signaled that all was well, but Thomas warily completed his inspection of the area before entering in his turn.

Dr. Nadal was extremely alarmed. He didn't understand: how could a Grenoble greengrocer possibly know where Thomas was hiding? Who was this Barthélémy, anyway, and why did Thomas have to keep disappearing for hours on end?

"I'm terribly sorry," Thomas told him. "Please forgive me for being such a nuisance. Would you mind telling me what the message was?"

The message, word for word, ran: *The blond maniac knows where the little imp is and Pistol Pete is on his way to the Black Forest.*

Dr. Nadal shook his head. "It doesn't mean a thing to me. How about you?"

Thomas replied that he knew precisely what the message meant. The machine in his head was running at top speed. He asked if Barthélémy had had a Majorcan accent. Dr. Nadal looked surprised and said no.

"Then it wasn't him on the phone. Anyway, he doesn't know where I am. The only time he sent me a message he wrote to his family in Majorca and they passed it on to some other Majorcans in Toulouse." Thomas paused. "The little imp, that's me, and the blond maniac is Jürgen Hess, a German who's been after me for the last two years. If Hess knows where I am we'd better be quick—he may be on his way already. He'll come with soldiers. Miquel and I spotted two lookouts, but there are bound to be others."

"You must go to the *maquisards* at once," said Dr. Nadal. "You and Miquel. Your knapsacks are packed and ready. By the way, where *is* Miquel?"

"Outside somewhere, keeping watch." Thomas thought hard. "Look, you don't understand. I'm not the only one in danger. They won't leave you in peace just because I've gone. You must all get out of here too—you and Aunt Mayo and Monsieur and Madame Berthier. You must leave this minute."

The flat refusal in Nadal's eyes was mirrored in those of Monsieur Berthier. Thomas was infuriated by their lack of comprehension. What did they think? That Hess would thank them politely and go when he found that his bird had flown?

"I'm a doctor, I'm needed here," Nadal said stubbornly. "I've no intention of heading for the hills."

Monsieur Berthier said much the same: he and his wife were too old to contemplate such an idea.

Thomas could have howled with rage, but there was nothing to be done. Dr. Nadal was adamant.

"Do as I say for once, Thomas! It's all arranged: four of Kléber's men will be waiting for you at the Rocher de la Demoiselle. Now go!"

Night had fallen. Thomas slipped out of the house carrying the two knapsacks, Miquel's and his own. It saddened him beyond belief to think of the people he was leaving behind. Why, oh why, wouldn't they understand? He was so preoccupied with his own distress that he jumped when a dim figure loomed up alongside, relieved him of the larger of the two knapsacks, and gave his shoulder a friendly squeeze. Very softly, Miquel whispered that the house was already surrounded, so they mustn't make a sound.

As Thomas stole along at Miquel's heels, the machine in his head gave him a fierce telling-off. It mightn't have been Miquel who'd crept up on him unheard, in which case he would now be Hess's prisoner. Instead of losing his concentration and going soft, he would do better to model his movements on Miquel's. Miquel was a marvel: only five or six feet ahead of him, yet he couldn't hear a sound. He pitied any Majorcan wild boar unlucky enough to be stalked by Miquel.

Everything was falling into place. The machine had stopped telling him off and started thinking for him instead. First of all, it said, take that message: Yellow Eyes must have sent it, because he never wanted Hess to catch you and he still doesn't. Somehow or other he must have found out that Hess is on your track and decided to warn you. All right, but what about the second part of the message? *Pistol Pete is on his way to the Black Forest.* Can it really mean that the American's still alive after all, or is it just a cruel joke? Yellow Eyes used to be a professor at Freiburg. His house is somewhere in the Black Forest, and it should be easy enough to find, first because it must be a grand house —he's got pots of money—and secondly because you'd only have to go to Freiburg University and ask for Professor Laemmle's address. The American still alive? Is it possible?

Miquel had come to a sudden halt. Thomas followed suit. They were at the foot of a ravine overgrown with scrub. Total silence reigned, but it wasn't Miquel's ears that had alerted him, it was his nose. Thomas caught it too, now: a whiff of cigarette smoke. There must be some lookouts nearby. Thomas crouched down and waited. He didn't budge an inch, but his head was spinning like a top and his heart pounding so hard he was afraid it would give them away.

The machine was addressing him again. All right, it said, perhaps the message means that Yellow Eyes was lying the first time—perhaps the American really is alive. If he's on his way to the Black Forest he must be planning to kill Yellow Eyes, but not before he's made him say where you are. He's fond of you, so that would be logical. Maybe he's been in prison somewhere—maybe he's escaped or they've let him go, and Yellow Eyes is telling you on purpose. Why? Because then *you'd* have two reasons to head for the Black Forest too: to kill Yellow Eyes and find the American. A smart move, that.

It could be a trap, of course. The American may be dead and Yellow Eyes may simply be luring you into his den. That would be a smart move too: by warning you that Hess is coming he wouldn't have to hunt you down himself, he'd simply wait for you to come to him. Either way, he's a really strong player. . . .

Very slowly, Miquel straightened up and signaled that the coast was clear. They set off again. At the top of the ravine they came to a road. Two hundred yards along it and to their left they could just make out a line of stationary cars. They darted across the road and continued on their way. The Rocher de la Demoiselle was another half hour's walk.

You *will* go to the Black Forest—of course you will. He wants to see you again, and you won't disappoint him. You'll go as soon as you've done the other thing you have to do, and the time for that is now. . . .

"Miquel?"

The stealthy figure ahead of him came to a stop.

"Miquel, I've been thinking. We aren't going to join up with the *maquisards*."

Miquel waited. It was characteristic of him not to ask any questions.

"We aren't going to do that for two reasons. In the first place, we'd bring Hess down on their heads. He'd slaughter the lot of them—he'd call up tanks and guns and blast them out of existence. Joining them would be like condemning them to death. The *maquisards* aren't real soldiers. They talk too much. Look at the way they keep boasting how they're going to attack Tulle. If you plan to do a thing like that you do it, you don't broadcast it to everyone in advance. I don't trust them." Thomas paused. "Besides, I'm sick of running away from Hess."

Silence.

"*I* want to be the hunter now, Miquel."

Miquel melted into the darkness as though the earth had swallowed him up.

"Are you still there, Miquel?"

"Estoy aquí."

Although Thomas hadn't heard a sound, Miquel had changed position in a matter of seconds.

"The second reason is Dr. Nadal and Aunt Mayo and Monsieur and Madame Berthier. There's one way of saving them in spite of themselves, and that's to kill Hess. I don't think the other Germans care much about catching me—they've got other worries, what with the Americans landing in the south and the Russians wiping them out in the east. If we kill Hess, it'll be over for us."

Concentrate, said the machine. Say the kind of things that will convince him, and whatever you do, don't make the mistake of thinking he's stupid: he isn't. His mind doesn't work the same way as yours, that's all. . . .

"We can't go on running from Hess, Miquel—not from the man who killed Javier and Juan and Tomeo, and Grandpa and Grandma Allègre."

He didn't have to manufacture the catch in his voice as he said their names. His rage and grief were such that he could have wept.

"We can't let him go on living, not after what he did to Her. . . ."

There was a peculiar depth and intensity to the silence that followed. Thomas couldn't get another word out. Hatred bubbled up inside him like lava. He knew that only Hess's death—the death of a man he hated almost as much as he hated Yellow Eyes—could stem the eruption and restore his peace of mind. A wave of nausea assailed him, and for a moment the machine slipped out of gear.

Then the nausea subsided and the cogs meshed once more. No more spells of weakness, he told himself. It was all or nothing now.

He set off, but not toward the Rocher de la Demoiselle. He bore left, owl eyes scanning the darkness ahead. Tulle, he estimated, was three hours' walk away.

It would be too wonderful for words if the American was still alive, but he couldn't be. He'd been sacrificed, and that was that. It would be too wonderful, but why waste time on an impossible dream? Better think of Hess and how to kill him. All right, so he already knew how, but it still required more thought.

After two miles he came to a road. He waited for a convoy to pass: half a dozen truckloads of German soldiers escorted by a brace of armored cars. Still he crouched in the ditch, waiting. Another convoy might be following on behind, and there were open fields on the far side of the road.

He'd been wise to wait: a third armored car went by, closely followed by two motorcycle-sidecar combinations.

Nothing broke the stillness now, but he could sense a presence on his right.

"*Hola, Miquel.*"

"*Hola, Tomás.*"

He scrambled out of the ditch and set off across the fields, walking briskly but not running. Strength flooded into his limbs at every stride. He didn't have to play Tarzan or Pistol Pete, not any more: plain Thomas was good enough.

Tulle was now only two hours' walk away. With luck he would be there by midnight.

THE REICHSBANK VAN PULLED UP SHARPLY. THE BIG MAN OPENED the double doors at the rear and motioned to Quartermain to get out. He jumped down without thinking, a minor feat of acrobatics that seared his hip like a red-hot poker. A car was waiting for them, unobtrusively parked at the mouth of a farm track.

"Please get in."

The voice was utterly flat and expressionless. Quartermain got into the back and the big man got in beside him. The driver, an anonymous figure in the gloom, turned out onto the road and headed north, or so Quartermain guessed. That meant they were skirting the principality of Liechtenstein. He'd once stopped for a meal at the little capital, Vaduz, but that was seven or eight years ago and his recollection of it was vague. He couldn't even remember if the Germans had occupied the place.

The car twisted and turned along a succession of minor roads. For several minutes now they'd been proceeding almost at a walking pace, without lights, and Quartermain's nerves were on edge. Finally they pulled up. The driver got out and walked off into the darkness.

"Kindly take his place, Herr Quartermain."

The Luger made an infinitesimal gesture. Quartermain complied.

"Please drive on. There's a village a few hundred meters ahead. It would be better to avoid the main street—I'll direct you. The frontier isn't far now."

Quartermain surreptitiously produced his length of wire and enlarged the noose. He laid it across his lap, took the wheel, and eased the car into motion. Three bends later some houses showed up against the night sky.

"Take the dirt road on the left," the man behind him said in a low voice.

He skirted a hedge and a series of farm buildings.

"Now turn right, please."

He was in a narrow lane—a cul-de-sac from the look of it. The archway at the end seemed to lead nowhere.

"Don't worry," said the voice in his ear, "you'll make it—we checked the width in advance. Try not to touch the walls. You've only got two centimeters' clearance on each side."

He took five minutes to cover thirty yards and only grazed the wall once. The covered alleyway debouched into a street.

"First left, then first right."

Sheer tension had brought him out in a sweat. He juggled delicately with the clutch and throttle to keep his engine noise to a minimum.

"Straight on for two hundred meters, then turn right."

The houses on either side melted away. He crawled along a track flanked by fences and turned out onto an asphalt road.

"The police station is three hundred meters behind us. You may switch your headlights on, but don't accelerate."

Three minutes went by. The big man's voice had almost resumed its normal pitch.

"Good, now you can—"

Quartermain flattened his foot. The man behind him was thrown backward, but he righted himself and raised his gun. Quartermain braked and swung the wheel over simultaneously, putting the car into a violent skid. Letting go of the wheel, he slipped the noose over the man's head and pulled him across the back of the passenger seat with his right hand while his left grabbed the barrel of the Luger and wrenched it sideways. The car smashed through a fence, careened across a field, and was brought up short by an abandoned tractor. The next few seconds were chaotic. The driver's door burst open on impact, and Quartermain found himself lying on his back with his legs inside the car, still hauling two-handed on the wire noose. His adversary landed on top of him and seized him, too, by the throat.

With a strength born of despair, the American continued to haul away until the steely fingers relaxed their grip. The big man went limp and became a dead weight.

Horrified by his own handiwork, Quartermain extricated himself and staggered back to the road. He should have tried to salvage the car, he thought vaguely, but he walked on. The road was flanked by an alternation of hedges and fences. He'd just passed a farmhouse, which was in darkness, when a light shone full in his face. He thought it was a motorcycle at first, but it turned out to be a powerful flashlight with two men behind it.

"Who are you and where are you going?"

The questions were couched in German.

"I crashed my car," he said, knowing that his own German wouldn't have deceived a two-year-old child.

"Your papers, please."

He caught the glint of a rifle barrel trained on him. Dazzled by the light, he made out two uniformed figures. They were wearing forage caps, not steel helmets.

It all happened in a flash. He was still groping for words to explain that he'd left his papers in the car when another figure materialized on the right. There was a blur of movement, a choking sound, and the soft thud of two bodies hitting the ground. Quartermain bent down to retrieve the rifle that had fallen at his feet, but something prodded him in the shoulder. It was the muzzle of a Luger.

"I deliberately refrained from shooting you just now," said a familiar voice. "Stand back, or I may disobey orders."

Quartermain couldn't believe his ears. "I could have sworn I'd killed you," he said.

"I'm not that easy to kill."

The flashlight sought out each frontier guard in turn. There was blood everywhere.

"You're leaving quite a trail behind you, Herr Quartermain," the big man said dryly. "Help me to dispose of them, would you?"

He dragged one body to the side of the road and rolled it into the ditch. Quartermain took the other by the shoulders and did the same.

"From here on, we walk. It isn't far to the frontier. I won't hesitate to shoot another time, Herr Quartermain, is that clear?"

"As daylight," said Quartermain.

"Walk ahead of me, please."

"Who's paying you? Gortz?"

"My orders are to get you to Switzerland alive. Alive but not necessarily in one piece—that's up to you. Walk, don't talk. We'll be passing some farms, and there are plenty of frontier patrols around."

Quartermain went through hell in the next half hour. The big man steered him off the beaten track and across a series of waterlogged fields. He was at the end of his tether. Still recovering from the effects of months of surgery, his body had been overtaxed by the exertions of the last two nights. He fell several times, and only a prodigious effort of the will kept him going at all.

Then they came to a steep rise. Mustering the remainder of his strength, he climbed for forty or fifty feet before he collapsed. Half dazed, he still had sufficient presence of mind to shield his face with one arm.

"Get up, Herr Quartermain."

"Drop dead."

A massive fist seized him by the coat collar and hauled him to his feet.

"Keep walking, please."

He swung a feeble punch at the big man, who didn't even trouble to dodge it. The movement was enough to unbalance him. He went tumbling down the slope it had cost him such an effort to climb. His chin struck something hard, a tree stump or a rock, and he lost consciousness.

GREGOR LAEMMLE SAT PERCHED ON THE BOTTOM STEP OF A flight of stairs on the third floor of an apartment house in the Rue de Lisbonne, Paris. So as not to soil the trousers of his cream linen suit, he was sitting on the silk handkerchief that usually resided in his breast pocket. It amused him to think that he was acquiring a lavender-scented backside.

He'd now been waiting for over an hour. Soeft, meanwhile, had bullied the owner of the apartment upstairs, a retired industrialist, into giving him the run of his apartment and the use of his telephone. This meant that he could simultaneously stand guard and communicate with the outside world. His latest phone call, to a Tulle number supplied by Henri Lafont, had elicited the fact that Thomas was in hiding at the home of a certain Dr. Nadal. Lafont's men were keeping watch on the doctor's house but hadn't seen the boy emerge since his return just before nightfall. No, they hadn't spotted his elusive Spanish bodyguard either, but since they'd never yet set eyes on him they remained to be convinced that he existed at all.

Laemmle, of course, was preoccupied with thoughts of Thomas. For the first time in fifteen months he abandoned himself to the bittersweet joys of reminiscence like a reformed drug addict falling prey to his old addiction. The boy must have grown and might have changed a little, perhaps, but his voice wouldn't have broken yet. He would probably have acquired greater self-assurance, but he was still, thank heavens, at that delicious stage midway between childhood and adulthood. He would still be the same little gray-eyed imp, the quintessence of youth, the—

His reverie was interrupted by a discreet cough from the floor above.

"Yes, Soeft, what is it?"

"He just left the Hôtel Lutétia. He'll be here in ten minutes."

"Thank you, Soeft."

Laemmle returned to his musing. Let's assume, he thought, that the little imp has spotted Lafont's men and knows they've found him. If they haven't attacked they must be waiting for someone, but who? The blond maniac, of course. Thomas must realize that Hess is on his way to Tulle to direct operations. He must also realize, things being what they are, that Hess is the only man in the German army with a genuine interest in capturing him. Given that he knows all this, what countermeasures is he likely to take?

One would be to slip through the net as soon as possible and find himself another hiding place. He may already have abandoned the people who sheltered him just as he sacrificed the American, because he can't be unaware that Hess will vent his spleen on them. In that case, while I'm getting a stiff backside on these stairs, the boy may be tramping across Corrèze at this very moment in an effort to put as much distance as possible between himself and Hess.

It's odd, but I don't believe that. I know my little imp too well. He'll have dreamed up something else, something far more subtle, but what?

Laemmle paused for thought. Then he smote his plump thigh. "Good God," he muttered, "I wouldn't put it past him!"

"Soeft?" he called.

Soeft's head appeared over the banisters.

"Hess's first port of call when he gets to Tulle—where would that be?"

"Gestapo headquarters at the Hôtel Moderne."

"Thank you, Soeft."

Think, Gregor, Laemmle told himself. The boy's quite capable of heading straight for the enemy instead of turning tail. Why not? He's bound to have his mysterious marksman with him—the one who can drill an apple at several hundred meters. It sounds insane, but not when one knows the boy. The more I think of it the surer I am: he'll station himself on the roof of some building overlooking the entrance of the Hôtel Moderne, escorted by the Spaniard with the sniper's rifle.

You've guessed it, Gregor! You know where he is or will be in the next few hours. The choice is yours, and you don't have long to make up your mind. . . .

His yellow eyes widened. Such was his delicious, feverish, anguished state of indecision that Soeft had to call him two or three times.

"Yes, Soeft?"

"He's coming."

The stairwell light went on, almost blinding Laemmle after his long wait in the dark. Someone was taking the stairs two at a time with the athleticism of a man in peak physical condition. Jürgen Hess reached the landing, caught sight of Laemmle, and stopped dead.

"What are you doing here?"

"Waiting for you, my dear Jürgen." The black tunic of Hess's full-dress SS uniform was adorned with a piece of hardware that looked to Laemmle's inexpert eye like an Iron Cross of some superior grade. God forgive me, he thought, the man's a regular hero. "I wanted a word with you," he added.

Hess eyed him with disfavor. "I thought you were in Italy."

"I'm only passing through. May I come in for a moment?"

Hess opened the door of the apartment, which had been lent him, according to Soeft's information, by another hero currently doing battle with the Bolshevik hordes. Laemmle followed him inside.

"I don't have much time," Hess said. "I'm off again in a few minutes. Besides, I don't see what we could possibly have to discuss."

"The boy," said Laemmle. "We could talk about the boy."

Hess's ice-blue eyes studied Laemmle as he removed his shirt and army-issue vest. Laemmle felt half perturbed, half intrigued. How much more did he intend to take off?

"What boy?"

"The same old one, my dear fellow. The one you almost caught the November before last, only to make an utter fool of yourself by letting him escape. The one who has been hiding out in Corrèze with a certain Dr. Nadal, as Lafont informed you this evening. The one you're going to make another attempt to catch by boarding a military aircraft for Limoges just under two hours from now. All being well, you should make Tulle by two or three A.M."

Hess's face—a handsome face, Laemmle had to admit—remained absolutely expressionless. Soldiering in the steppes seemed to have injected a further dose of iron into his soul. He'd become harder and more mature—more knuckleheaded too, to judge by the dreary inevitability of his next question.

"How do you know all that?"

"I keep my ear to the ground."

He really *was* stripping! I'm actually going to see him in his birthday suit, thought Laemmle. If I were the type to swoon at the sight of a man's body—which I'm not—I should be quite excited by now. He followed his naked host into the bathroom.

"Get lost, Laemmle."

"May I remind you that I outrank you? I don't insist on your addressing me as Herr Oberführer, but no excessive familiarity, if you please."

The bathroom was a thoroughly uncivilized place. Decorated in a hideous, institutional shade of green—the paint was peeling, too—it contained a bath of dubious cleanliness, one of those horrible French bidets, and a lavatory. Bolted to the wall was a whole rack of dumbbells and one of those ridiculous rubber harnesses designed to be stretched in all directions as an aid to muscular development. Laemmle shuddered despite himself.

"Are you a body-builder, Jürgen? How bizarre—I had no idea."

"Get out before I throw you out," said Hess, vigorously spinning one of the taps. It dawned on Laemmle that he intended to take a cold bath—a cold bath! The man really was a maniac.

"You'll never catch the boy," Laemmle went on. "Not without my help, anyway. This operation you're planning—a 'raid,' isn't that the accepted term?—well, it's doomed to failure. You may slit a few throats, but that's all. The boy isn't there anymore."

No reply. Watching the muscular back as stone-cold water gushed into the bathtub, Laemmle saw it stiffen almost imperceptibly. That shaft went home, he thought.

"Think for a moment, Jürgen. Have you ever located the boy by yourself? Never. You always needed my help."

"I know damned well where the little bastard is."

To Laemmle's profound embarrassment, Hess swung around. Seeing the man naked from behind was one thing, but from the front! I've always been a puritan at heart, he reflected—puritanism is my fundamental characteristic. He smiled.

"You know where he *was*, you don't know where he is now."

"And you do?"

"Certainly. I know where he will be in two or three hours' time. Why not have your bath while it's still cold, Jürgen?" Laemmle almost blushed, he was so embarrassed by the intimacy of the situation, but he couldn't help being slightly titillated as well.

"Think, Jürgen. What will you do once you've slaughtered this Dr. Nadal and his nearest and dearest? Summon your armored division from Bordeaux and put all Corrèze to the sword? You wouldn't catch the boy with a dozen divisions. You had him surrounded by a couple of hundred men the last time, and he still got away. He'll do so again."

Hess decided to get in at last. He sat down, waist-deep in cold water, and gave Laemmle—who shivered involuntarily—a challenging stare.

"So where is he, according to you?"

"I think," said Laemmle, taking a dumbbell from the rack and bringing it down on the blond head, "I think he's waiting for you outside the Hôtel Moderne in Tulle, accompanied by a Spaniard armed with a sniper's rifle."

He struck again, painfully conscious of his clumsiness. The water in the bathtub became tinged with pink, but the dumbbell slipped through his fingers just as Hess, who was still alive, turned to look at him with an air of stupefaction. He'd wielded the thing like a woman, but it was true that he'd never so much as delivered a punch in his life, so he did have some excuse.

He snatched another dumbbell from the rack—a heavier one. The effects of the third blow were markedly superior: the skull caved in and the water in the bathtub turned red.

Another five or six blows reduced Hess's skull to a pulp. Laemmle was rather surprised—he'd expected his head to be harder. Examining the dumbbell, he discovered that it weighed ten pounds. That explained it.

The sight of the face, which was still slightly inclined in his direction, made him feel rather queasy. Sensing someone behind him, he turned to find Soeft standing in the doorway. The pistol in his hand was fitted with a silencer.

"You should have left him to me," said Soeft.

"There are some things in life one wants to do oneself," Laemmle replied.

Soeft relieved him of the dumbbell and replaced it in the rack.

Laemmle peered into the bathtub. "You're sure he's dead?"

Soeft nodded. "Absolutely," he said. He took Laemmle's arm, led him out on to the landing, locked the door behind them, and shepherded him down the three flights of stairs.

They made their unhurried way along the Rue de Lisbonne, Soeft still holding Laemmle's arm as if he were blind or mentally deranged —which he was, in a sense. He really did feel exceedingly odd.

"I've never killed anyone before, Soeft—not personally, I mean."

"Better wait awhile before you talk about it."

"You're absolutely right. I'm sorry."

The Rolls was parked in a forecourt. They got in, Soeft in front, Laemmle behind.

"You need a drink, Herr Oberführer. There's some Chartreuse in the cocktail bar."

The car moved off.

"That's the first time I've ever killed anyone with my own hands, Soeft. A curious experience. Not pleasant but not unpleasant either— more surprising than anything else. Is that the general rule? What do *you* feel when you kill someone?"

"Nothing, Herr Oberführer."

At the intersection of Boulevard Haussman and Rue du Faubourg-Saint-Honoré they were stopped by an ill-assorted quartet composed of two French gendarmes and two German military policemen with metal plaques dangling from chains around their necks. Soeft produced some papers and said a few words in German. The MPs stepped back and saluted; the Rolls drove on through the deserted streets of Paris.

"Pull up near some grass, Soeft. I think I'm going to be sick."

THOMAS WAS MAKING HIS WAY THROUGH TULLE WITH EXTREME
care, darting across streets when the coast was clear, hugging the walls
when it wasn't. The hectic excitement that had brought him thus far
was subsiding. He felt strangely calm and cold now, but that was all to
the good.

He had no idea where Miquel was, none at all, but he couldn't be
far away. Miquel was a shadow—no, not even that. Shadows were
visible. . . .

He was within two hundred yards of the Hôtel Moderne, or so he
estimated, when his "rat's instinct" stirred for the first time: a car was
parked alongside the curb with its lights off—a big black Citroën saloon. All right, so it was normal for cars to park beside the curb in a
town, but he didn't like the look of this one at all. For a start, it was
parked outside a haberdasher's, and who ever saw a haberdasher driving a car of that size?

He decided to make a detour. A pity, because he was almost within
sight of the Hôtel Moderne, but never mind. He turned off to the right
down a dark alleyway, making no sound at all. He couldn't even hear
his own footsteps, for the very good reason that he'd removed his
wooden-soled shoes and hung them around his neck by the laces. If
Aunt Mayo could see me wearing out my socks like this, he thought,
she'd spank me. . . . The alleyway extended for about thirty yards. If
he turned left at the next intersection, then left again . . .

He stopped short and flattened himself against the wall, peering into
the darkness: he'd just heard a man clear his throat. The sound had
come from the street on the left—the one he'd been planning to take.

There was someone there.

In a flash, his suspicious mind put the two facts together: a car in an
unlikely spot and a man around the corner. It was almost as if they
were expecting him.

Very well, he would check.

He stole across the street and melted into the shadows on the opposite pavement. An odd-shaped object was leaning against the wall
ahead of him. It wasn't until he was ten yards away that he identified
it as a handcart. Crouching in the shelter of the handcart, he got out
his trusty binoculars. Perhaps the sound had come from a bedroom
overlooking the street—perhaps he'd been imagining things. At last,
by following the line of every wall and house front in his vicinity, he
found what he was looking for: a pair of shoes protruding from a

doorway. Someone *was* there: a man standing motionless, not smoking, not moving his hands or feet, simply waiting.

In that case . . .

He checked another four streets in the next twenty minutes, and in each of them a man was barring his path.

His roundabout route was getting him nowhere, taking him no nearer the Hôtel Moderne, but what could he do? They'd cordoned off their lousy hotel, but not from the *maquisards* or they'd have posted more than one man in each street. From whom, then? Not from him, it wasn't logical: he hadn't known he was coming himself till an hour or two ago.

He tried various other streets with similar results. Most of the men were quite well hidden, but not all. He saw two standing plumb in the middle of the street as though taking the air—except that it was long past midnight and no one went for midnight strolls in a town swarming with French policemen and German soldiers. They obviously carried *Ausweise*, or passes entitling them to be out at this hour.

He didn't know what to do, and it was ages since he'd seen Miquel. Finally, at the end of one street, he sighted the Hôtel Moderne—not the front of it but the service entrance. Visible in the glow from two lighted windows was a sentry, a steel-helmeted German soldier with a tommy gun slung across his belly. It was the nearest he'd got to the hotel, which was only a hundred yards away, but he hadn't a hope of getting any nearer. He was exasperated by all these faceless figures planted in his path like trees; exasperated by Miquel, who was being altogether too invisible; and, last but not least, exasperated with himself for failing to solve a seemingly insoluble problem.

Maybe Hess was already in the hotel, maybe not. Either way, he couldn't have failed to hear a car drive up or drive off, and he hadn't heard a thing. The whole neighborhood was as silent as the grave.

One last street remained to be checked. He peered around the corner and jumped back quickly. The lookout was only a few feet away and facing in his direction. It was almost as if the man had known he was coming. . . .

Thomas beat a hasty retreat, steadying his clogs with one hand to prevent them from clattering together. Then he made a tour of all the streets he'd already checked and circled the hotel in the opposite direction.

That was when his "rat's instinct" really made itself felt, far more strongly than it had when he saw the big black Citroën. It wasn't just the telephone bell that so alarmed him, though it wasn't exactly usual for a phone to ring in the middle of the night. No, it was a combination of two other factors: first, that the sound emanated from a building he'd just passed, the plate on the door of which suggested that it contained nothing but offices; and, more especially, that it stopped abruptly—as if someone had picked the receiver up.

He had an instantaneous mental picture of a man lurking at a first-floor window, watching his every move. He'd spotted a total of nine men guarding the approaches to the hotel, not counting the one that must have been hiding in the Citroën, but there might be many more than that, all of them calling each other to report his latest position.

He broke into a run, but he'd gone only a few yards when the machine ordered him to stop panicking. He would only run straight into their arms.

He stood quite still, wondering where Miquel was. What if they'd jumped him—what if they'd strangled him without a sound? What if Miquel wasn't shadowing him after all—what if he, Thomas, was really all alone with a host of enemies closing in on him? He felt a little bit scared—not a lot, but a bit. The silent, deserted streets were getting on his nerves.

He backed into a doorway and tried the door, but it was locked. Just across the street from him—that was all he needed to cheer him up!—he saw a shop with a sign above it inscribed "Funeral Parlor." The interior was draped in black velvet and very dark.

And then something happened that brought his heart into his mouth: a pinpoint of light appeared—someone had struck a match—and the yellow flame illuminated a regular death's-head of a face with eyes like dark, bottomless pits. Very deliberately, the man stepped forward so that he was right up against the glass door. He gazed across at Thomas without expression, without moving, until the match went out, but even then he didn't budge.

He's trying to frighten you, that's all. . . .

Thomas emerged from the doorway. The street where he'd heard the telephone was on his right. He set off in the opposite direction, forbidding himself to run. The machine kept insisting that the man in the funeral parlor had only meant to scare him. Well, he'd succeeded!

He'd gone twenty yards when he heard a bolt slide back, followed by the faint creak of a door opening.

Don't look!

But he couldn't resist the temptation. Turning, he saw a man in a black leather coat and a felt hat standing motionless on the pavement with his hands in his pockets.

Don't run!

He backed away until he reached another intersection, where he started to turn right.

Another man was standing in the middle of the street, hands buried in the pockets of his black leather coat, face invisible in the shadow cast by his hatbrim—in fact, he mightn't have had a face at all. It was rather scary.

Thomas thought better of turning right and walked straight on.

A third man detached himself from a doorway. Another faceless, shadowy figure with his hands in his pockets and the same scary, expectant immobility.

The street on the left was empty. Thomas started along it, opening his mouth and inhaling deeply to counteract the thudding of his heart. He was as breathless as if he'd run for miles. A minute ago he'd been a little bit scared. He wasn't very, very scared, even now, but a lot more scared than before.

Footsteps were coming along the street behind him. You want to look? All right, look, but be calm about it. Show them you aren't afraid of them.

He swung around. The three men had set off after him, one on each sidewalk and the third in the middle of the roadway. They didn't look at each other: their unseen eyes were focused on him alone.

He turned and walked on until he came to another intersection. Sure enough, there they were: another two men indistinguishable from the first three, one in the street on the left, the other on the right. They didn't move, but he could sense that they, too, were about to follow him.

They were driving him like game. *Where are you, Miquel?*

But the machine promptly corrected him. It wouldn't be very smart of Miquel to show himself at this stage. He couldn't kill them all, and who knew how many of them there really were? Besides, he would wake the whole town if he opened fire, and that would bring a thousand soldiers hurrying to the spot.

Thomas emerged into a dimly lit tree-lined square enclosed by buildings with balconies adorning their facades. He recognized it as the Place de Souillac. Most but not all of the tables and chairs outside the Café Tivoli had been stacked for the night. One table and a few chairs were still in place on the terrace.

Some men were sitting there.

They stared at him, but no one stirred. What if he stayed put too? What would they do if he refused to take another step? Pretty damned silly they'd look if he did. . . .

God, am I scared!

He paused at the mouth of the square and looked around. His three shadows had also halted and were waiting some thirty yards behind him.

Very well, he thought. He started across the square, but even as he did so the side streets came alive with more shadowy figures in black leather coats: every exit was blocked. His chest heaved with the effort of fighting off the urge to run—the urge to weep, too, which was very strong now. He turned and looked at the handful of men on the terrace of the Tivoli. At long last, one of them moved. He raised his hand and pointed toward the railway station.

He felt like sitting down in the middle of the lousy square and letting them do their worst. It wasn't fair—he was only a little boy. Tears rose unbidden to his eyes, but the machine immediately rekindled his rage and hatred, resurrected the Thing and conjured up a vision of Yellow Eyes smiling derisively.

Yellow Eyes must have organized the whole thing. Who else?

He pulled himself together and set off for the station, which was ablaze with lights. Although no one should have been there at this hour, the ticket office was open. The man behind the counter, an elderly clerk with a white mustache and grizzled hair, looked at him oddly, almost pityingly, but said nothing. Thomas strolled out onto the platform in the faint, the very faint hope of crossing the tracks and disappearing into the darkness beyond.

Some hope! A couple of leather-coated men were leaning against the wall of the waiting room, hands in pockets.

So be it. He went inside again. The ticket clerk, who was still at his post, beckoned him over.

"I've got something for you, *mon petit*," he said in a voice as lugubrious as his face. He produced something from under the counter and held it out. It was a railway ticket.

"Where to?" asked Thomas.

"Mulhouse. There's something else. . . ." This time he proffered an envelope just big enough to contain a calling card.

"Thank you," said Thomas.

"The waiting room's over there. One moment." He handed Thomas a blanket. "The first train gets in at five-thirty. You'll have to change at Clermont-Ferrand and Lyons. I was also told to give you this."

"This" turned out to be a packet of sandwiches, half ham, half cheese.

Thomas shook his head. "I'm not hungry."

"Take them all the same. You may feel hungry in the night or tomorrow morning. I'll bring you some coffee in a minute."

"You're very kind, monsieur," Thomas said politely. "I'm much obliged to you."

He went into the waiting room and stretched out on a bench with the blanket wrapped around him. It was no use, though: he couldn't shut his eyes. His urge to cry had long subsided, but not his rage and hatred. His head was fuller of them than ever.

He lay with his back to the glass door that opened onto the platform, knowing that the two faceless men were standing there like statues, watching him. He banished them from his mind. They were merely pawns, merely dogs that did as they were told. Not even Hess counted anymore. Hess was nothing, nothing at all.

For the first time in well over a year he dredged up the pictures from the depths of his memory. They were terribly painful, of course, but he could endure them now. He could look at them without going crazy—unless he *was* crazy, which he might well be. He saw Her burning to death in the Hispano. The pictures were incredibly vivid, and he didn't skip a single one. Quite coolly, he scrutinized them again and again.

The ticket clerk put his head around the door.

"Asleep, *mon petit*?"

"No."

"Here, I've brought you some coffee."

"Not just now, monsieur, if you don't mind."

The man withdrew. Thomas suddenly remembered the little envelope. All it contained was a slip of white pasteboard, and neatly inscribed on it in capitals was the one word: "CHECK!"

All right, Yellow Eyes. Don't worry, I'm coming. . . .

Some hours later the waiting room began to fill up with people. They were ordinary travelers with lots of baggage, baskets, bundles—even live chickens. Some of them muttered about those "odd types" outside and speculated that they were Gestapo men waiting to arrest someone—*French* Gestapo men, which was a disgrace.

Thomas ate one sandwich, then another. There was no point in dying of hunger. Eating Laemmle's sandwiches wouldn't diminish his hatred for the man. He saw the ticket clerk beckoning to him and went over.

"I've still got your coffee," the clerk said as soon as they were inside his little office. The coffee pot was simmering on a stove in the corner. "I couldn't give it to you in front of everyone, you understand."

"Of course, monsieur. Thank you again. I won't forget your kindness."

The coffee was hot and sweet, just the way he liked it. Thomas sipped it gratefully. For some strange reason he felt like crying again—though the urge wasn't too strong this time, thank goodness—simply because the ticket clerk had been so kind. He couldn't think why, but he only cried over little things. Big ones left him dry-eyed.

"The train will be packed," the clerk said, just for something to say. "The trains always are these days. I really don't know what the world's coming to. . . ."

"I'll manage," Thomas said.

"Oh, you'll be all right," the clerk told him. "You've got a first-class ticket, and I've booked you a seat from Toulouse—and from Clermont-Ferrand and Lyons. It's quite close to Germany, Mulhouse. . . ."

It was the first time he'd asked an implied question about Thomas and the men in black leather coats.

"Very close," said Thomas. "There's a place called the Black Forest just across the frontier."

The clerk eyed him curiously. Thomas finished his coffee.

"Would it be possible for me to make a telephone call?"

It was Dr. Nadal himself who answered. He said he was fine—everything was fine—but you could tell he was choosing his words carefully and didn't want to say too much.

Thomas said he was fine too. It wasn't worth going into details, so he simply said goodbye and hung up.

The train pulled in ten minutes later. The ticket clerk had been right, it was jam-packed with people. Thomas lingered on the platform until he spotted them: four men in black leather coats, clearly waiting to see if he got in. He surveyed the platform with a studiously casual air to disguise the fact that he was looking for someone, but Miquel was nowhere to be seen. Nowhere.

Maybe he was already on the train with his rifle dismantled and stowed away in his knapsack, or maybe he'd hidden somewhere and was also waiting to board it at the last moment. He was definitely there, though—he had to be.

The stationmaster blew his whistle. As Thomas got in he saw the four men do likewise, two up ahead and two behind. They were obviously going to shadow him all the way.

His reserved seat was in a compartment already occupied by two German officers and a French couple. The wife was a fat, fur-coated woman with ring-encrusted fingers. Thomas sat down between her and one of the officers. When she demanded to know if he was really entitled to travel first-class he produced his ticket and stared at her fixedly until she looked away, disconcerted by his curiously cold, gray-eyed gaze.

One of his four shadows stationed himself in the corridor, well within view.

The train got under way.

Miquel had to be on board—he *had* to be!

"YOU WERE PAST WALKING SO I CARRIED YOU," THE BIG MAN SAID quietly.

Quartermain opened his eyes. Dawn light was streaming into the herdsman's hut where he lay on a straw-covered pallet. A smell of cow dung scented the mountain air.

"Where are we?"

"In Switzerland."

Quartermain's thoughts began to slot into place.

"I can remember falling, but that must have been hours ago. I can't have been out for as long as that."

The big man shrugged. "Perhaps I gave you something," he said calmly. His bulky frame was obstructing the only door.

Quartermain sat up. Aside from a couple of hundred assorted aches and pains, he didn't feel too bad. He struggled to his feet, swaying. Every muscle in his body was on fire. He took a few steps toward the door. The big man stepped aside to let him pass. Outside, foothills bathed in morning mist could be seen against a mountain backcloth.

"Whereabouts in Switzerland are we?"

"That's the Rhine down there. Liechtenstein's on the other side. We passed through there during the night, after crossing the Austrian frontier."

"What about those two guards? Am *I* supposed to have slit their throats?"

"Pure blood-lust, Herr Quartermain—there was no holding you."

"Do I have to stay cooped up in this cowshed?"

"Certainly not. You're an American citizen in possession of a valid passport. The Swiss have no quarrel with you. From now on you can come and go as you please."

"If I really am in Switzerland."

"You are. The nearest town is Sennwald, three kilometers away to our left. I can recommend the inn at the foot of the Hoher Kasten. You might even enjoy a trip to the summit—the view from there is superb. On a fine day you can see all the way to Lake Constance."

Quartermain tried pacing up and down. His muscles unknotted themselves and the stiffness in his limbs began to recede.

"Who's paying you?"

No reply. A few hundred feet below, skeins of mist were slowly unraveling themselves to reveal the Rhine.

"Why dump me here if I'm just an ordinary tourist?"

The silence behind him persisted. He swung around, but the big man was already fifty yards off and climbing briskly. He vanished into the trees without a backward glance.

Quartermain made for the valley below. He came to a track, then a road. Twenty minutes later he saw a sign marked Sennwald. The inn the big man had recommended wasn't open yet, and Quartermain could discern no signs of life through the colored panes in its gothic-style windows. He sat down to wait on one of the wooden benches outside, enveloped in a scent of geraniums from the window box behind him. Not long afterward he saw a car approaching.

It drove past, then braked fiercely and backed. Two men in dark city suits got out.

"Mr. Quartermain? Mr. David Quartermain? Welcome to Switzerland, sir. We're delighted to be the ones who found you first." It seemed that they were only two of thirty similar scouts patrolling the frontier in the Appenzell district alone. "We didn't know exactly where you would cross, or even if your attempt would be successful. Permit us to congratulate you on your escape."

They shepherded him into the back of the car, tucked him up in rugs and cushions, offered him coffee and sandwiches, produced a bottle of whiskey. He accepted the whiskey.

"Where are we going?"

"First we must telephone the good news. Then we drive to Zurich, where Mr. Sowinski is expecting you."

Joe Sowinski was waiting on the steps of the Hôtel Baur-au-Lac. He greeted Quartermain with a bear hug and led him inside.

"Am I glad to see you, Dave! It's just fantastic, what you did!"

"Why were those photographers clicking away at me like that?"

"All the U.S. wire services were there—even the British turned up. For Chrissakes, man, what did you expect? David Quartermain personally pulls off the most dramatic escape of the war, and you don't want the public told? The whole Clan's so proud of you, Dave—your uncle and your cousins are over the moon, especially Larry. Think you'll feel up to holding a press conference tomorrow morning?"

"Look, Joe," said Quartermain, but his attempt to stem the flood was futile.

"I've gotten together the best medical team in Switzerland," Sowinski gabbled on. "They're going to examine you to see what the Nazis did to you, how they tortured you and so on. Larry insisted on it—he wants a medical report detailing every last one of your injuries. No offense, Dave, but you look pretty good to me. A few pounds lighter, but that's all."

"Sorry to disappoint you," Quartermain said dryly.

"There's just one thing, Dave. We came to an arrangement with the press: they get their scoop, but only on condition they don't publish till we give them the word, even if it means waiting till the end of the war. If anyone helped you to escape from Germany, we don't want to put their lives in jeopardy. We thought of everything, see? Anyway, the war'll be over soon—we'll be in Berlin by Christmas, if not sooner. All this baggage is yours, by the way—I had a coupla dozen of your suits flown over from New York. About those medics: three o'clock suit you?"

"Look, Joe—"

"Up until now, the only member of the Clan I've been able to sell to the press is your cousin Winthrop, who joined the Marines after Pearl, but he hasn't done much aside from chasing pussy in Honolulu, so he isn't exactly good copy, whereas you—"

"Joe," Quartermain said evenly, "do me a favor and shut your goddam mouth." Sowinski stared at him in silence, then nodded.

"I get it. Nerves, huh? It's only natural, after being in the hands of those Nazis."

"I don't think I've come across a single genuine Nazi in the past sixteen months," said Quartermain, "or if I did I didn't notice. Joe, I urgently, repeat urgently, need all the information I can get on a boy age twelve or so, gray eyes, dark hair, first name Thomas, surname Lamiel or Weber or maybe something else. He could be here in Switzerland, he could be in Spain—either way I want to know. Hire as much help as you need, I don't care what it costs. Offer a reward. I'll go to a million dollars—ten million if necessary, it doesn't matter. I want checks run on every bank, every frontier post. The kid is or was accompanied by a Spaniard armed with a sniper's rifle—a fantastic shot."

Sowinski looked bewildered. "How come you're so—"

"What countries are still represented in Germany? Sweden and Switzerland? I want their diplomatic personnel questioned, I want them to use their good offices with the German authorities. If anyone needs paying, pay him, never mind how much." Quartermain paused for breath. "And another thing: it seems we maintain excellent connections with the world of German high finance, which backed Hitler for over ten years and is now planning to unload him. I want those folks to look for Thomas as if their lives depended on it. I'm telling you this now and I'll say the same to Uncle Peter and Cousin Larry as soon as I get a chance: I want that boy back alive—I want him more than anything else in the world—and he'd better be alive, for everyone's sake, because if he isn't I'm *really* going to give a press conference and describe how I *didn't* escape at all: how I was simply transported to Switzerland from one of the finest clinics in Germany. I shall also describe what remarkably favorable treatment I received and recite all I can recall of the contents of certain files made available to me by your friend Joachim Gortz—and my memory's excellent, Joe, believe me."

"But Dave—"

"Last but not least, get me all the dope you can on a former professor of philosophy at Freiburg University named Gregor Laemmle. I want to know his present whereabouts. He's a fairy around five feet six inches tall and on the plump side, sandy-haired, yellowish eyes. He has a bodyguard named Soeft. Soeft is pushing six feet, with blond hair and a face like a female wrestler. I want Laemmle alive too, Joe, but not for the same reasons. I also want five hundred thousand dollars in cash within two hours. And now, get out of here and get cracking—and tell your goddam medics and journalists to get lost."

Quartermain sat down and shut his eyes. He gripped his knees, trying to control the black fury that had been simmering inside him for weeks, if not months. The last few hours had brought it to the boil. His greatest mistake in life had been a failure to realize just how much weight he carried, even as a star of the second magnitude in the Clan's financial firmament. Well, he wouldn't make the same mistake twice.

Sowinski had already reached the door and grasped the handle. "This kid, Dave," he said, "is he really your son?"

"Yes," said Quartermain. "Really."

AT SEVEN THAT MORNING, HAVING GOT TO MULHOUSE, GREGOR Laemmle contacted Henri Lafont by phone. The news was excellent: everything had gone as planned. Lafont's high-pitched laugh came down the wire.

"My men aren't back yet. They aren't used to playing the nursemaid, but the youngster showed up in Tulle, just as you said, and they nudged him in the right direction."

"Did he catch that train, yes or no?"

"He did, and so did four of my boys with orders to see that no one gives him any trouble. He'll get to Mulhouse all right."

Laemmle strongly doubted if he would, but he didn't say so to Lafont. Speaking in French, he asked if the fifteen million francs had reached him safely and was assured that they had. He thanked Lafont for all his help and hung up, belatedly remembering that he'd meant to inquire about the invisible sniper. He wondered whether to make another call to the head of the French Gestapo—the French Gestapo, I ask you!—but finally decided against it. Leaving the post office phone booth, he went outside and got back into the Rolls.

"How much do we have left out of all that cash Heydrich gave us four years ago, Soeft?"

"In round figures," said Soeft, "seventy million francs."

As much as that? he thought. What the devil was he going to do with it? Aloud, he said, "First of all, Soeft, find me somewhere that serves a decent breakfast. Then get me a list of all the clubs and associations in the Mulhouse area."

Thomas must have been absolutely infuriated by my little calling card, Laemmle reflected as he sipped his hot chocolate. He'll have guessed it was meant to infuriate him, naturally, but that won't make him any the less angry. He'll come, if only on account of Pistol Pete. I told him the American was dead; now I've implied that he's alive. He'll come in order to discover the truth.

And in order to kill me, of course. That's his prime consideration. He'll turn up on my doorstep and raise his arm as he did at Grenoble when the Spaniard assassinated that apple. This time, I'll be the apple. Will he kill me outright or make me suffer first? It's nerve-racking, not knowing which. . . .

Soeft returned with a twenty-seven-page list covering everything from charitable organizations to bowling clubs. The three Laemmle selected were all anglers' clubs. Although he'd never done any fishing himself, he cherished a certain regard for anglers. They had, by definition, to be calm and peaceable types. It seemed improbable that blood-thirsty dreams could ever haunt someone capable of sitting beside a pond for eight or ten hours in the hope of catching a perch whose price at market he could earn in a twentieth of that time.

"Soeft, I want you to divide our seventy million francs into three equal shares and donate them anonymously to the three associations I've checkmarked. Off you go. You can pick me up later—we're in no hurry."

He'll come all right, Laemmle told himself again as he strolled through the town. I could always wait for him here in Mulhouse, but I very much doubt if he'll choose to come this way. Being his usual perverse self, the little imp will give Lafont's four thugs the slip and follow a route of his own. I originally thought of helping him to bribe his way across the frontier or finding some weird and wonderful means of providing him with false papers certifying that he was my nephew, but he'd have balked at that. I'm sure he'll get across the Rhine under his own steam. Oh yes, he'll come, and that will be the end of my story: fifty-one years of existence snuffed out by a beautiful boy with murder in his heart. . . .

Late that afternoon Laemmle and Soeft and the Rolls crossed the Rhine into Germany, the SS identity cards issued them so long ago by Heydrich having fulfilled their function for the last time. They headed for the Black Forest by way of Müllheim and Badenweiler and reached their destination at nightfall.

Laemmle's country seat, a half-timbered manor house with twenty-odd bedrooms, was brilliantly illuminated in defiance of the blackout regulations. His four family retainers, the youngest of whom was seventy-plus, had been warned to expect their master and greeted him by torchlight in the traditional manner.

The nearest farm was miles away, and the six windows of the library, which contained over nineteen thousand books, afforded a panoramic view that had rejoiced Laemmle's heart throughout his childhood and adolescence. He looked forward to seeing it again when morning came.

He paid a ritual visit to his mother's apartments, where nothing—not a single knickknack—had been moved since her death in 1924. Then he took a bath, a real Black Forest bath, in the porphyry bathtub she'd given him on his eighteenth birthday.

He dined alone, peacefully rereading Montaigne.

The long wait was nearly over.

"AND WHAT DO YOU WANT TO BE WHEN YOU GROW UP?" ASKED the German officer in the seat opposite Thomas.

"A terrorist," he replied in German.

The two officers laughed. In the preceding half hour Thomas had told them why he was traveling first-class, where he was going (Berlin), whose nephew he was (Ribbentrop's), who his grandfather was (the German ambassador in Madrid; that was why he spoke Spanish too—perhaps they'd like to hear a few words?), why he was going to Berlin (his mother was sending him to school there with a view to turning him into a good German), and why he was traveling alone (he wasn't; the man in the corridor was a Gestapo bodyguard—one of at least fifteen on board the train).

The idiots had swallowed every word, not least because of what had happened when those two Gestapo inspectors came down the train. They'd examined the papers of the fat woman and her husband—they even asked to see the officers' travel warrants—but he himself was totally ignored. He might have been invisible. It was really funny, the look on the others' faces.

The machine promptly issued a warning: All right, have a good laugh, but don't overdo it. Don't lose your concentration—and don't pull those officers' legs too hard, even if they are a couple of idiots.

Better think what you're going to do at Clermont-Ferrand and Lyons. Yes, you already know, but never mind: run through it again in case you've overlooked something. . . .

When they got to Clermont-Ferrand he shook hands with the two officers, who clicked their heels (he *was* Ribbentrop's nephew, after all), and boarded the Lyons train with his four escorts in tow. His original plan had been to escape through a lavatory window at the first convenient stop, but that was a silly idea and he discarded it. It was silly because of Miquel: how could Miquel be expected to follow him if he slipped away like that? The best place would be a big, bustling station where Miquel could lose himself in the crowd and follow him with ease. That meant Lyons. There wasn't a bigger place on his route than Lyons, so that was where he would escape.

He had entertained another plan, which entailed going to the lavatory seventeen times in quick succession, ostensibly because he was suffering from diarrhea. That would not only annoy his escorts but compel them to watch the lavatory window to the exclusion of all else.

He discarded that idea too, however. If he was to have any chance of catching them off-guard at Lyons, he would have to play the poor, disconsolate little boy, not the buffoon. He duly did so, either gazing sadly into space or shutting his eyes with a tearful expression as though crestfallen because he'd been spotted and cornered at Tulle.

He didn't budge when they got to Lyons, even though he knew full well that they had to get out and change trains again. He pretended to have fallen asleep, overcome by disappointment and fatigue. When the man in the corridor prodded him in the ribs, as he ultimately did, he gave a start and looked around him with a dazed expression. Very slowly and dejectedly, he emerged from the carriage just as a mob of would-be passengers were fighting to get aboard the Marseilles-Nice express on the other side of the platform.

Then he made his move.

He couldn't have been quicker. Having memorized the exact location of his four shadows, he managed to outflank one without being spotted and broke through the square they'd formed around him. It was like the fox-and-geese game he used to play with Grandpa Allègre —he invariably beat him—in which the fox had to evade the geese on the chessboard. He got back into the now empty Clermont train, sprinted along a succession of corridors, and reappeared at the last door of the last compartment. There he waited patiently until one of the four men caught sight of him. Feigning panic, he jumped down onto the platform, wormed his way through the crowd boarding the Marseilles train, and dived beneath it. He crawled along the track for a hundred yards and reemerged, but not before he'd seen and heard his pursuers' feet pounding along the platform. They were even stupider than he'd thought.

Nobody looked twice at him when he wriggled out from between the passengers' legs. Nobody, of course, but Miquel. Miquel would have stayed put, he felt sure, knowing that he wouldn't have slipped away without giving him a chance to follow. He stood still for a moment to enable Miquel to locate him properly.

Then he boarded the Clermont train for the second time and made his way to the sleeping car on all fours. Reaching up, he managed to pull a bunk out of the wall. He smashed the catches with one of his clogs so as not to be shut in, stretched out on the bunk, and pulled it up by the straps, first checking to see that the catches were really broken. They were, so he could push it down again whenever he wished. Lying there in the dark and commanding himself not to go to sleep, he proceeded to count up to thirty-six hundred at roughly one-second intervals. The fat woman had mentioned that it was two hours before the train from Clermont returned there, so an hour seemed a reasonable lapse of time. Overcome with impatience, he emerged on the count of thirty-five hundred and four.

There was no one in the corridor, but the platform was crowded again, this time with passengers storming a train bound for Paris. He waited another four minutes—time enough to count up to two hundred and fifty and satisfy himself that his shadows had disappeared. They had. The fools were probably combing the Marseilles train for him at this very moment.

He mingled with the crowd and made his way to the ticket windows, where he bought two tickets at each of two different windows, the first pair for Nevers, the second for Montélimar. "I'm traveling with my grandmother," he explained both times, "but she's got bad legs."

Then he emerged from the station at a run, dived down the first street he came to, and waited. He counted up to fifty, but no one appeared, not even Miquel. That was typical of him, though: he must have realized that it was a feint and stayed put. Miquel was no fool.

For one tiny moment a flicker of doubt assailed him. What if Miquel had really lost track of him? He banished the thought—he was scaring himself unnecessarily.

He returned to the station by another route but saw nothing untoward. For safety's sake he skirted the concourse instead of walking straight across it, still with one eye open for Miquel. If Miquel meant to be invisible, he was certainly succeeding.

There were masses of people queuing up to show their tickets at the barrier, but Thomas marked the inspector down as an observant type who would be bound to ask how he came to be traveling alone.

In that case . . .

He let twenty or thirty people go by before he settled on a pleasant-looking woman accompanied by two children. He waited for her to pass the barrier and presented his own ticket a few moments later. Sure enough, the inspector looked twice at him and opened his mouth to say something. Thomas promptly raised a hand in the direction of the woman with two children and gave tongue.

"Coming, Maman, coming!"

It worked, but in case the inspector was still looking he caught up with the woman, took her by the arm, and held out a thousand-franc note he'd swiftly extracted from his pocket.

"You dropped this, madame."

The woman looked at the money and hesitated for a moment.

"Thank you," she said. "You're a very honest little boy."

"And you're a very nice lady," Thomas replied, "I can tell. Your children look nice too. May I carry one of your bags for you?"

He walked along beside her for a while, then asked where she was bound for.

"Brioude," she said.

Thomas had never even heard of the place. "Goodbye, madame," he said. "I hope you have a really good trip."

He looked around for someone else, preferably an old woman who could pass for his grandmother, but couldn't see one anywhere. All right, how about a sister instead?

He found two prospects waiting for the train he planned to catch. One of them was a blonde with a bovine face, the other a very pretty brunette like a grown-up Susanne with breasts. He accosted the brunette.

"Look," he said, his nose on a level with her bosom, "I hope you don't think I'm trying to pick you up, but . . ."

She started to laugh and he knew he'd won. (It was the same with Susanne: make her laugh, and you were home free.) He spun her a yarn about how he was off to spend some time with his father, who was an engineer, and how his parents were divorced and what a bore it was shuttling to and fro between one parent and the other, and couldn't she say he was her younger brother if their papers were checked—no, not her brother but her brother-in-law or cousin because their names would be different. "My name is Thomas Nadal, by the way. . . ."

He went on to tell her about Susanne and the time he and Susanne had tried to milk a cow, and she laughed more and more, and by that time they were safely on board.

It was late afternoon and getting dark when the train pulled into Annemasse.

HIS FIRST STEP AT ANNEMASSE WAS TO GET OUT HIS BINOCULARS and inspect the school of Saint-François de Ville-le-Grand at long range. What he saw through the lighted windows immediately put him on his guard: the building was full of German soldiers.

He could only conclude that the priests had finally got caught, and that the Germans had moved in to prevent anyone else from sneaking into Switzerland by way of the school. Where did that leave him?

He debated the problem for a good fifteen minutes, munching his last remaining sandwich, before he came up with a provisional solution.

First he perfected his camouflage. Making his way back into the center of Annemasse, he bought a capacious shopping bag in which he stowed the binoculars and concealed them beneath a big bunch of leeks, these being all the grocer had in the way of vegetables. The leek idea proved even smarter than he'd thought. When a gendarme asked him why he was hanging around—what a drag it was to be only twelve!—he pointed to a brass plate on the nearest building.

"Maman's having a tooth out—that's why we're having leek soup for supper. I don't like leeks."

"That makes two of us," said the gendarme, and walked off.

Uneasily, Thomas noted that the shops were shutting up for the night. He'd been watching a hotel entrance for a while when he saw a couple and a child emerge. Their hurried, apprehensive manner was immediately perceptible, their single suitcase obviously heavy. They set off, but not toward the station. They walked to a bus stop and waited. Thomas, lurking in a shadowy alleyway, waited too. Twenty minutes later a bus turned up and the trio boarded it. Thomas sprinted for the bus and got there just as the driver was shutting the door. He bought a ticket and went and sat at the very back, his leeks prominently displayed. Nobody distrusted leeks, it seemed.

Looking out of the rear window, he thought he glimpsed a motorcycle following them. Miquel? Could Miquel have found himself a motorcycle? It *had* to be him. . . .

He'd heard the couple with the child ask for tickets to Tholonaz. When the bus stopped there, he got out first and walked off without losing sight of them. After a moment's hesitation they set off down a side road. A man emerged from the shadows and came to meet them. They were late, he said, and had they got the money?

They set off again with the man in the lead. He was obviously a smuggler of human merchandise. Thomas, who wouldn't have trusted him an inch, thought it foolish of the couple to put their faith in a man whose only interest was money. He shadowed them across a succession of fields until, quite suddenly, the darkness ahead was punctured by several beams of light: German frontier guards were on patrol with dogs and flashlights. Peering through his binoculars, Thomas made out a barbed-wire fence only a hundred yards away. It looked completely impenetrable. Why should the smuggler have guided his customers to this particular spot?

The machine's response was immediate: Why? Because he had no intention of smuggling them across! He might even get paid twice, once by the couple and once by the Germans for giving them away. That must be it.

Thomas continued to survey the fence until he found the gap he sought. The German patrol had walked straight past without seeing it —or rather, without *appearing* to see it.

He was terribly tempted to jump up, run over to the couple with the child, and warn them that it was a trap, but he resisted the impulse, because it was futile. He would only have been arrested too, and besides, he planned to make the most of the situation. A shame about the others, but that wasn't his fault. . . .

The smuggler was the first to rise to his feet when the patrol moved on. Beckoning to the other three, he led them to the gap in the wire and waved them through it into no-man's-land. "Keep going," his urgent gestures seemed to say, "everything's fine!"

Except that he'd hung on to their suitcase and feigned incomprehension when they asked him to hand it over.

Except that the patrol came doubling back and caught them before they could reach the Swiss side of no-man's-land.

Except that the woman wept, vainly begging the Germans at least to let her son across the border into Switzerland, and all three of them were prodded back through the fence at gunpoint. . . .

The smuggler had decamped with their suitcase, the swine. Thomas could see him slinking off, but he ignored him. He wasn't Pistol Pete, the scourge of evildoers and avenger of the innocent; his job was to get across this lousy frontier. Besides, Miquel must have seen the man too. . . . Still peering through his binoculars, he saw one of the frontier guards bend the wire back into place. "Well," Thomas heard him say, "that's that. We got another three of the *Schweinehunde*. . . ." And he strode off, chuckling.

Three minutes later Thomas himself slipped through the wire. He left the gap open for Miquel, who would be bound to close it behind him. Fifty yards beyond, on the far side of a small stream, he came to a second barbed-wire fence. This one, which consisted of a few strands strung between posts, presented little difficulty. Having noted the position of a Swiss patrol two hundred yards to his right, he squeezed under the bottom strand with ease.

He kept going for a whole hour after that, carefully avoiding all roads and cutting across vineyards. He mustn't stop concentrating just because he was in Switzerland, he told himself. It wasn't time for *that* yet, the machine warned him, but in vain: the Secret began to gush from his memory like water pouring through a hole in a dam.

No, not yet! Later!

It was useless, though: the Secret went on and on. That was what came of not concentrating hard enough.

All at once he heard a raucous voice challenge him in French with a Genevese accent and a man with a flashlight loomed up ahead. "You," he heard, "stand still or I fire! And put your hands up!"

Did that put a stop to the Secret? Not a bit of it; his memory continued to regurgitate facts and figures as if nothing had happened. He subsided into a crouching position, too exhausted to run—so exhausted that he could hardly keep his eyes open long enough to see that the man, a Swiss policeman, was only a yard away.

And then the policeman collapsed. His flashlight fell to the ground, rolled a couple of feet, and came to a stop with the beam focused on

Thomas's bare knees. He sat back, or rather, fell over backward, incapable of keeping his eyes open any longer. Somebody picked him up.

"*Estás bien, Tomás?*"

"*Estoy muy cansado, Miquel.* So tired . . ."

Miquel took him on his back again, the way he'd carried him so many months before. They'd better not hang around, he said. Swiss policemen didn't appreciate being hit on the head.

"Did he see you, Tomás?"

And still the Secret went on. Thomas was half asleep. Miquel shook him.

"Don't go to sleep, not yet. Did he see you?"

"Didn't have time to . . ."

Thomas clung to Miquel's shoulders with his cheek against the leather jacket.

"Don't go to sleep, Tomás. What's the telephone number of that Majorcan in Geneva?"

That did it: the Secret stopped at last. One drawer in his memory slid shut and another opened.

"There are three of them, Miquel."

He recited the three numbers. "Then I say 'Puerto de Sóller' and he must say he comes from Montuiri, not Sóller. If he doesn't, I hang up."

"*Muy bien,*" said Miquel.

"Miquel?"

Miquel laughed. "I'm still here."

"I was sure you'd followed me. Sure as anything."

"Naturally," said Miquel.

The Secret started again, but it got slower and slower, like a clockwork motor running down, until he finally fell asleep.

"EXCUSE ME, SIR," SAID THE YOUTH FROM THE RECEPTION DESK OF Zurich's Hôtel Baur-au-Lac, "but do you really want me to send this cable?"

Quartermain nodded. "What's more, I'll sue this place if a word of it is changed. Read it over to me, please—not the address, just the text itself."

" 'Dear Uncle Peter, dear Cousins Larry, James, Emerson, Henry,

Michael, Winthrop, Rodman, and the rest of you. If it wouldn't poison the fish, I'd tell you to go jump in the lake. Signed, David.' "

"Perfect," said Quartermain, proffering a thousand-franc note. "Get that off as soon as possible."

He waited until the youth had left his suite before reapplying himself to a large-scale map of the Black Forest. The location of the house had been ringed in pencil. He spread out the aerial photographs supplied by the Club Alpin and the cartographic section of the Swiss General Staff, together with the blowups that had been made for him overnight. The isolated house showed up as little more than a white blob, even under a magnifying glass, but it appeared to be a big place —twenty or thirty rooms—and three-storied.

The phone rang. Quartermain picked up the receiver, still studying the enlargements, and replaced it without a word as soon as he recognized Joe Sowinski's voice.

He ran over his calculations for the umpteenth time. The house was barely twelve miles from the Swiss border—more like seven or eight in a direct line—

The phone rang again, but this time it was the reception desk to tell him that his visitor had arrived.

"Send him up, please."

A minute later somebody knocked on the outside door and came in. Karl Zaugg was a wiry-looking Swiss in his late twenties.

"It's about a rather special flight," Quartermain explained. "I'm told you're capable of landing a plane on a mountaintop."

Zaugg looked from Quartermain to the map spread out on the table. He couldn't identify the area in question, because Quartermain had turned it over.

"That all depends on the mountain."

"You're reputed to have flown into German-occupied Yugoslavia and picked up some refugees."

"What mountain?"

"Money's no object," said Quartermain. "I already have the plane —I bought it here in Switzerland. It's a Fieseler-Storch. Are you familiar with it?"

"Yes. What mountain?"

Quartermain eyed the man, his mind already made up. He put out his hand and turned the map and photographic blowups over. Zaugg studied them in silence for quite a while. He was going to take the job, Quartermain could tell.

"It'll cost you fifty thousand dollars," he said at length.

"A hundred thousand. Fifty in advance, fifty when you get back."

"*If* I get back, you mean."

"You will. The worst they can do is intern you till the end of the war."

"The worst they can do is shoot me," said Zaugg, examining the aerial photographs.

"Officially," said Quartermain, "you'll be a Swiss pilot carrying out a test flight for a flying club based at Basel. The club not only exists but purchased the plane for me. During the flight you had a dizzy spell. It wasn't the first of its kind. A Zurich doctor will testify that he treated you for a similar condition two years ago. You strayed off course, overflew the German border without realizing it, and landed anywhere you could. You'll be interned, but representations will be made on your behalf by various organizations such as the Bank for International Settlements at Basel. They'll vouch for you."

"Will you be on board?"

"Yes, but I'll naturally make myself scarce as soon as we land. What happens to me needn't concern you. If I'm arrested I'll say I entered Germany under my own steam."

"I simply dump you there, is that it?"

Quartermain smiled. "And fly me back again, I hope. I'll need sufficient time to get from our landing place to that house on the map, spend an hour on the premises, and return. It all depends where you land."

"In darkness?"

"The darker the better."

"And I'd have to wait, maybe for hours, at the mercy of the German police?"

"On second thought," said Quartermain, "let's make it two hundred thousand dollars. May I offer you a drink?"

"Just coffee, thanks." Zaugg had focused the magnifying glass on a dark sea of pine forest and was picking out the pale patches that represented clearings.

Quartermain called room service and ordered coffee. The waiter brought it and withdrew. Zaugg's silence persisted. Eventually he said, "How soon do you need an answer?"

"There's no hurry—you've got all of five minutes. Oh yes, and I want to take off tomorrow night."

THE SECRET—OH GOD, THE SECRET! IT CHURNED AROUND INSIDE him like pent-up vomit. He was afraid it would escape again and flow away of its own accord, but luckily it didn't. Incredible how long he'd stored it up in his head without ever giving it a thought. He knew what had happened last night after he crossed the frontier: he'd been too exhausted, too relieved that his long journey was at an end. That was why it had started overflowing. It was only natural.

He had the same feeling this morning, only ten times as strong. This morning he was in Geneva. He'd called the Majorcan, and the Majorcan had brought him a new set of papers.

I'm Thomas Darder now, he told himself, a Swiss boy born at Geneva. The Majorcan's name is Jean Darder. He's my uncle—the last of my many uncles. He's a jeweler and watchmaker with a shop at 37 Rue du Rhône, and he's lived in the Place de Jargonnant for thirty years. He speaks French like a Genevese. He's forgotten most of his Castilian and all of his Majorcan, but She and Javier Coll knew what they were doing when they picked him—they never made a mistake. They weren't wrong about Grandpa and Grandma Allègre, or the colonel at Aix-en-Provence, or Barthélémy at Grenoble, or Dr. Nadal at Tulle. Looking back on things, I seem to have come an awful long way, but it's almost over now. I've reached the end of the road. That's why I've got this big black cloud hanging over me, and why the Secret is churning around in my head and doing its best to overflow. That's why I feel so trembly and feverish. . . .

Thomas was walking down the Rue de la Corraterie with Jean Darder at his side and the Rhône bridges visible below and straight ahead of them. He'd really made it at last—all his doubts on that score had vanished—and he couldn't have wished for a gentler, quieter, or more reassuring companion than this new uncle of his. Not counting the American, but he mustn't think of the American now. First he must do what he'd come to do. Afterward, yes—afterward he could think of the American as much as he liked. . . .

To fight off the Secret and hold it in check a little longer he thought of Her. It was the only way. He was with Her again in a multitude of places and under a multitude of circumstances; with Her when She'd taught him the Secret, making him repeat it and crying because She had to. And he remembered shaking his head and willing Her not to cry, and telling Her it didn't matter, he would never forget a single word, it was easy, he knew it by heart, he could even recite it backward. . . .

Well, here he was at last. He hadn't forgotten any of it—he'd done all that was expected of him, all She'd wanted him to do. . . .

They went into the bank. Jean Darder spoke to a member of the staff, and moments later someone emerged from an office, looked Darder and Thomas over, and said yes, they were expected, and would they kindly step this way. They climbed a white marble staircase to the mezzanine, where they were greeted by a black-suited gentleman with a silver watch chain adorning his waistcoat. He ushered them through a series of doors until he came to a double door whose four panels were faced with dark red leather.

"Go ahead, Thomas," said Darder. "I've done my part. Now it's up to you. Good luck." And he went, leaving Thomas alone.

Or rather, alone with the men. Thomas surveyed the room he'd been shown into. It was big and long and heavily curtained, with a long table in the middle and chairs all around it. You felt you were in a tomb, and that nothing you said in this room would ever escape.

The silence was almost deafening. All the men had risen when he came in. For one brief moment he felt a touch of pride: he was only a little boy in short pants, but all these important old men had risen to their feet at the sight of him.

There were eight of them—nine, including the stenographer in the corner. Some must have hurried to Geneva from Lausanne, Zurich, and Basel in order to be there on time. There had been ten bankers on Her list, but Jean Darder had discovered in the course of his late-night phone calls that two of them were dead. That was all right, though: She'd said that six would be sufficient.

He took a step forward. His head was empty save for the recollection of Her repeating, over and over, what he had to say and to whom.

"Please excuse me," he said in his clear little voice, "but before I begin I must ask you to identify yourselves."

He took another three steps forward and asked the first man to state his personal code number. The reply was in order. He turned to the next man, and the next, and so on until he'd finished. All eight replies were correct.

Now, Thomas . . .

Very, very calmly he announced that he was acting on behalf of

Maria Weber, his mother, and of Hans Thomas von Gall, his great-grandfather. He repeated this in German and English, just as She'd told him to.

He had a distinct feeling that he'd ceased to be Thomas and become Her—that She wasn't dead anymore because She was speaking with his voice. He asked the men to sit down and seated himself at the very end of the long table. A veil came down over his eyes and the black cloud enveloped him completely. There was a ringing in his ears like the sound you hear when you're underwater—he could even smell the seaweedy smell of Port-Issol. She was close beside him, listening with tears in Her eyes to make sure he left nothing out.

He didn't let Her down.

He recited the Secret in its entirety: surname first, then first name or names, then the surnames and first names of the respective heirs, the addresses and account numbers, the access codes, the sums involved, the dates when they were deposited, the names and addresses of the relevant banks.

Seven hundred and twenty-four times in succession.

Why? Because Thomas the Elder's list, the one he'd refused to divulge and died for, had comprised the names of no less than seven hundred and twenty-four clients, "and not even he could have carried all those in his head. Only you, *mon amour, mein Schatz*, with your amazing memory—only you can do that, and may God forgive me for what I'm turning you into. . . ."

He reached the end and fell silent. One of the men asked if he could repeat the particulars relating to Wilhelm Heinz Dreyer of Darmstadt. Thomas felt as if he were coming up from the deepest of dives. When he first heard the man's voice it sounded very remote.

He slowly turned his head. The figures around him took shape again. He stared fixedly and with mounting anger at the man who had spoken. He knew perfectly well what his white-haired questioner was up to: he was double-checking, trying to see if he, Thomas, had recalled everything accurately, that was why he'd made a deliberate mistake in one of the names.

"Dreyer, Wilhelm Hans, *not* Heinz," said Thomas. "Dreyer, Wilhelm Hans, Bahnhofstrasse 62, Darmstadt, Hesse; Dreyer, August Karl; Dreyer, Alicia Beatrix; Hausser, Edwina Margret. Address: 607 Harrison Avenue, Harrison, New York, United States of America. Account number 00050416113 KB, access code Venezia 11, RM117,886.00, August sixth, 1931—"

"Thank you, my boy," said the white-haired man, cutting him short. He shook his head. "My God," he said, "it's absolutely incredible. . . ."

Thomas's anger evaporated. It was only natural that he should have wanted to check—they all did, no doubt. It was only natural.

Only natural, only natural . . . The words echoed and reechoed in his head. The machine was malfunctioning a little. Hardly knowing where he was, he removed his hands from the table and rested them on his bare knees. He bent over, longing to rest his forehead on the dark, glossy tabletop and shut his eyes.

I'm empty now. . . .

He could feel the Eight Men's eyes upon him. They obviously couldn't get over the fact that a little boy had managed to memorize such a mass of detail and found it hard to believe their ears, but he couldn't have cared less.

The Secret was dead, so She was dead too. This time for good.

Oh, Maman!

He silently rolled the word around his tongue, allowed it to percolate his brain. It was a sweet and gentle word, but he'd seldom used it before—She'd told him not to do so because it might be dangerous, but that was all over now. He'd done all She expected of him and done it well.

He got down off his chair and walked out. Two or three of the Eight Men called after him in the nicest way: "Not so fast, young man, come back. You really are an exceptional little boy." I know damned well I'm exceptional, he thought, but do you think it makes me happy? It makes me awfully unhappy, if you want to know. . . .

Jean Darder was waiting for him in a room three doors along. He put his hand on Thomas's shoulder and said simply, "Come on, Thomas, let's go. It's over."

He said no more, but that was fine—he didn't have to. Jean Darder understood, because he, too, had loved Her in his way, like Javier and Juan and Tomeo, and Grandpa and Grandma Allègre, and the colonel at Aix, and Barthélémy and Dr. Nadal and the rest. They'd all loved Her, you could see it in their eyes. None of them had ever said so, but true love and things like that didn't have to be put into words. Every time you said them they lost a little something in the process. . . .

"Hungry, Thomas?"

"Not just now, thanks."

"Perhaps you could use a little fresh air?"

Thomas nodded. He knew it wasn't polite to nod like a donkey, but just for once . . .

They walked down to the Rhône and along the embankment, not for any particular reason, purely for the sake of walking. Thomas wasn't tall enough to lean on the parapet of the bridge they came to, so he contented himself with watching the river through the pierced ironwork. It was flowing awfully fast.

I've done all I came to do. I'm not worth anything to anyone, not anymore. . . .

"Is it really over, Uncle Jean?"

"Yes, really," said Darder, whose hand was still resting on his shoulder.

Minutes went by.

All right, I can think of the American now. It's a funny feeling, being able to love or grow fond of anyone I like without sentencing him to death. . . .

The machine had stopped completely, or had it? No, it had started up again. The wheels turned slowly at first, but they were gaining speed.

He asked Darder if he'd heard of the Hunt Manhattan Bank, and Darder said of course he had, it was one of the biggest banks in the world—everyone knew the name.

"Is there a branch here in Geneva?"

"I'm sure there is," said Darder. "We should be able to find it."

He didn't ask any questions. It struck Thomas that he could talk freely for the first time in years—the first time ever, in fact. He didn't have any secrets left, because he'd given them all away to the Eight Men. That was a funny feeling too.

"I want to find someone," he said. "An American called David John Quartermain. He once told me that if I ever wanted to see him again, all I had to do was walk into any Hunt Manhattan branch and ask for him."

"Does he work for the bank, then?"

"I think he owns it," Thomas said. "Not all by himself. He shares it with his cousins and his uncle and various other people, but he certainly owns a part of it. At least, that's what he told me."

He finally tore his gaze away from the river and looked up. Darder's eyes conveyed an unspoken question, but Thomas could tell that he was reluctant to ask it.

"You can ask me anything you like, now it's over."

"Have you seen this man lately, Thomas?"

"No, not lately. Not for ages."

"Did he help you?"

"Yes, but it's not just that."

For another few moments Thomas wrestled with the ingrained mistrust that had taught him never to say a word more than was necessary. Then, gazing down at the swirling waters of the Rhône, he overcame it and told Darder the whole story from beginning to end. Passersby kept streaming across the bridge behind them, but Thomas wasn't worried about spies and eavesdroppers. That was another thing of the past.

"This man Quartermain," Darder said at length, "he may have gone back to America. He may even be dead."

"I don't think so," Thomas said. "He isn't dead." It wasn't just the message from Yellow Eyes that made him so certain; the American simply *couldn't* be dead, and that was that.

"I already told you about the money, Thomas—the money that belongs to you, I mean. I don't know how much it is—my only job is to take you to some people who can tell you that—but I know it's a lot."

"That's not important for the moment."

"You also know that my wife and I would be not only willing but delighted to give you a home for as long as you care to stay with us."

"I know."

Thomas gave him a grateful smile, but it was no use, the machine continued to grind away. He knew what was coming.

"I'd like to ask you a rather personal question," said Darder.

"I told you, you can ask me anything you like."

"Do you think this man David Quartermain is your father, Thomas?"

He didn't reply, though he knew the answer.

"Could we go to the bank right away?" he said. "If it's not inconvenient, of course."

Darder stared at him for several seconds, then nodded.

The Geneva branch of the Hunt Manhattan turned out to be quite close. Thomas's head barely came up to the counter—he couldn't even see the bank clerk behind it. It really was high time he started growing. He resolved to work on the problem as soon as he had nothing better to do than attend some lousy Swiss school. He wanted to be at least as tall as the American, if not taller.

Meanwhile he climbed on the chair that Darder had fetched for him before discreetly retiring into the background. The bank clerk eyed him in some surprise, then looked down at the slip of paper he'd been handed.

"Please let Mr. Quartermain know that Thomas Darder of Geneva would like to see him a week from now. That's my address and telephone number. *Au revoir, monsieur.*"

"Why a week from now?" asked Darder as they left the bank together.

"Because he'd take a week to get here if he's in America, and because there's something I've still got to do."

QUARTERMAIN LEFT THE BAUR-AU-LAC TOWARD THE END OF THE afternoon, having been careful to ensure that no hint of his plans reached the ears of Joe Sowinski or anyone else. He left the hotel on foot as if intending to go for a stroll. It wasn't until he'd got beyond the Münsterhof and the old quarter of Zurich that he picked up the car he'd bought for cash. Zaugg had followed his instructions to the letter: the trunk contained a change of clothes, some walking shoes, a couple of coils of rope, a hunting knife, some binoculars, and a Colt .45 with four spare magazines.

He drove to Basel via Baden, Brugg, and Rheinfelden. In his pocket was a letter—Joe Sowinski would read it later—in which he stated that in the event of his death or disappearance, he left all he possessed to his son, Thomas David Lamiel, born at Lausanne on September 18, 1931. He was determined to mail this letter and did so the next day at Rheinfelden itself, less than an hour before the Storch took off.

Quartermain was in no doubt about the hazardous nature of his projected trip, if not its sheer folly, but he was still on the crest of the emotional wave that carried him all the way to Switzerland from the clinic near Berchtesgaden. He knew he wouldn't hesitate to kill Gregor Laemmle in cold blood once the man had told him where Thomas was. It was a novelty, his willingness to kill or even torture someone, but it didn't surprise him.

His one stop en route was at Rheinfelden. The plan was that Zaugg should land on a little-used road through the salt marshes, an area with which the Swiss pilot claimed to be thoroughly familiar, at four-thirty the following afternoon. If questioned, he would say that a minor mechanical problem had compelled him to land, but that he would be taking off again. He would indeed take off again, this time with Quartermain on board, and head for the Black Forest.

Rheinfelden. There were two towns of the same name, one Swiss and the other German, linked by a bridge across the Rhine. A small access road led to the bridge on the Swiss side of the river. Quartermain, surveying the spot through binoculars, made out the two frontier posts. The Swiss was a pretty casual affair, the German more heavily guarded. This seemed only logical, given that few people could have been desperate to abandon cozy Switzerland in favor of Hitler's Germany, whereas attempted escapes in the opposite direction were far more likely. One thing was certain: anyone would have a tough time getting back into Switzerland over this bridge, even in a tank.

He reached Basel less than thirty minutes later. Not knowing the city at all, he wasted nearly an hour finding Sulzerstrasse and the address Zaugg had given him. A young woman opened the door and invited him in. The sister of Zaugg's fiancée, she was a blonde of around thirty, not exceptionally pretty but intelligent-looking. She knew nothing about his forthcoming expedition.

"Karl phoned me, Mr. Wynn. Your room's all ready for you, and we can eat in an hour."

Quartermain, who'd chosen the pseudonym Wynn because it was the name of one of his friends, a San Francisco attorney who owned the finest ocean racer in California, suggested that they dine out instead. The truth was, he wanted to hear and speak some more German in the few hours he had left. Admit it, he told himself, you're just a little bit scared. . . .

They ate at a riverside restaurant, where, by an extraordinary and ironical coincidence, Quartermain gathered from their conversation that the diners at the next table were British and American representatives of the Bank for International Settlements. He didn't introduce himself, of course, and refrained from speaking a word of English. He practiced his German instead, but was appalled by his inadequate command of the language. If he was arrested in the Black Forest, twenty seconds' interrogation would be enough to unmask him.

The sight of the Rhine flowing past a few yards away made him wonder if it wouldn't have been easier to go by water. He might have sneaked across the frontier aboard one of the barges that seemed to ply between Switzerland and Germany in relative freedom. Recalling something he'd read in Joachim Gortz's gigantic file on Banner Petroleum, he looked for one of the petroleum barges—river tankers partly owned by himself—which Banner rented to the Nazi authorities. He didn't see one, but they must surely go via Basel. Where else would they take on oil?

What the situation boiled down to, in essence, was that he was about to infiltrate a country ruled by a madman, there to make mincemeat of someone before killing him, while simultaneously making millions out of the commercial relations existing between himself and that same country. How on earth had he ever come to such a pass?

His thoughts revolved around this question for hours after they got back to Sulzerstrasse. He tried to read a German novel for most of the night, and dawn was breaking by the time he fell asleep. The house was deserted when he woke. He lunched with a surprisingly good appetite. Afterward, having handed the house keys to a neighbor as requested by a note left on the kitchen table, he got into the car and headed for Rheinfelden.

Before leaving Basel, however, he bought four of the biggest available rolls of adhesive tape and some fine cord in case he had to bind and gag someone. He hesitated outside a gunsmith's shop, wondering whether or not to invest in a rifle. In the end he decided that it would weigh him down too much.

He drove through Rheinfelden and reached the salt marshes ten miles beyond. Some strange presentiment had made him glance at the Rhine bridge as he passed it. The rocky islet in the middle of the river, which bore the remains of an ancient castle, was shrouded in mist. What if Zaugg didn't show up? Fate would have decided for him. Did he *want* the man to show up, or was he merely scared sick?

But Zaugg was already at the rendezvous. Almost unrecognizable in his leather flying helmet and goggles, he was tinkering impassively with his engine while two or three Italian laborers from the saltworks looked on. It was now three P.M. Quartermain didn't approach the plane. He drove on to the local inn as arranged, ordered himself a large pot of coffee, and settled down with the book he'd borrowed from Sulzerstrasse, Robert Musil's *Der Mann ohne Eigenschaften*, which he'd enjoyed in an English translation but found hard going in German. Musil's bitterly ironic style was perfectly suited to the occasion. Quartermain's mood alternated between melancholy and grim determination. His sense that he would die in the next few hours was quite unequivocal at times.

A little before four-thirty, Zaugg walked in and ordered a beer. Ten minutes later, without even a glance in Quartermain's direction, he drained his glass and left.

Quartermain followed him out to the car. The light was already fading, and the forest on the far bank of the Rhine looked more somber and sinister than ever.

"The ceiling's a bit low, but we should be all right," Zaugg said quietly in his rather guttural English.

They unloaded the contents of the trunk.

"No rifle, Mr. Quartermain?"

"No, I decided against it."

"In your place I would have taken one."

"I'm the world's worst shot."

The workmen were still beside the plane. They made a few sarcastic remarks in Italian-accented German. Quartermain got in—after all, what did it really matter if anyone saw him now?

"Let's go," said Zaugg, switching on.

The takeoff was amazingly short. The Storch was hardly airborne before it banked to the left in a wide arc.

"I couldn't head straight for Germany—it would have looked suspicious." The plane's nose swung around until it was pointing north. "We're crossing the Rhine."

Quartermain, peering into the darkness, wondered how Zaugg could possibly know that. The most he himself had seen was a scattering of very dim lights—those of German Rheinfelden, no doubt. And then, close enough to make his flesh crawl, the tapering fingers of some pine trees reared up on the right.

"We're almost there," said Zaugg. "This isn't a flight, it's a flea-jump."

Except, thought Quartermain, that fleas don't often kill themselves when they land.

"Don't be alarmed," Zaugg went on calmly. "I'm going to cut the engine, but that's intentional. It's called a falling-leaf landing."

All that broke the sudden silence was a faint whistling sound.

"Now," said Zaugg.

The angle of descent increased a little. Pine trees glided past on either side like cliffs, black on midnight blue. The Storch hit the ground and rebounded into the air. A second impact, a little less violent than the first, followed by another rebound.

Then the plane was jolting along the ground, occasionally skimming it with one wingtip or the other.

At last it rolled to a stop at such a peculiar angle that Quartermain had to cling to the doorhandle to prevent himself from ending up on the pilot's lap.

"It's flatter than I expected" was Zaugg's only comment.

They both climbed out. The grass in the clearing was short, but the ground sloped away at an angle of more than one in ten. Quartermain wondered how they'd managed to land at all. He reached into the plane and pulled out the bag containing his equipment.

"Before you go, Mr. Quartermain, I'd appreciate some help. We must turn the plane so she's pointing in the opposite direction. We must also wheel her back out of sight from the air."

It took them nearly two hours. The Storch got away from them several times but was brought up short by the safety rope that Zaugg attached to various natural features as the little aircraft gradually neared the wall of pine trees behind them.

"There—I think that'll do. I'll cut some branches to camouflage her as much as possible. The police may have heard us go over—they may be looking for us right now."

Quartermain changed his shoes but decided to keep his suit on instead of changing into the dark slacks and sweater he'd brought with him. The night air was cold but not unbearably so. He was ready at last.

"Where exactly are we?"

They bent over the 1:50,000 map by the light of a small electric torch. According to Zaugg, the house was five or six kilometers south-southeast of them.

"That's as the crow flies. It'll be more than that on foot, I'm afraid. If I were you I'd make for this forest track and work your way along it rather than risk passing the house without seeing it. Do you have a compass?"

"No." Quartermain cursed himself for remembering everything but that.

"Here." Zaugg handed him one. "Take the flashlight as well. I have two more. Mr. Quartermain . . ." He hesitated.

Quartermain, who guessed what was coming, drew a deep breath.

"Mr. Quartermain," Zaugg said, "I shall wait for you as long as possible. To be honest, I'm not sure I'll be able to take off again. The odds are against it, but I'll try, and I must warn you: I can't guarantee to be here later than an hour before dawn."

"That's the most I could have expected," said Quartermain. "Thanks."

"Don't mention it," said the Swiss. He removed an ax and some shears from the Storch and prepared to cut some camouflage. "Do you know how to use a compass?"

Who does he think I am? thought Quartermain. Scott of the Antarctic? The truth was, he'd never so much as held one in his hands before. There were signposts even in the backwoods of Vermont.

"Of course," he said, shouldering his bag by the strap.

"In that case," said Zaugg, "good hunting."

Quartermain vaguely searched for some famous last words but failed to come up with any. He set off through the trees. When he turned to look after a hundred yards, the Storch and its pilot were entirely hidden from view. The silence was unbroken.

He had twelve hours at most in which to complete a round trip of twelve or fourteen kilometers and do what he intended to do, always assuming that he didn't spend the rest of his days vainly roaming the Black Forest or get himself shot as a spy in the interim. The other possibility was that Gregor Laemmle would kill him first.

He'd only gone another few hundred yards when he was compelled to stop, completely disoriented. Consulting his compass for the first time, he decided that south-southeast was probably to his left.

It was odd, but his doubts about the feasibility of the expedition, his misgivings and forebodings, even his fear—all these had vanished the moment the Storch taxied to a stop. There was no room inside him for anything but the extraordinary tenderness and affection he felt for Thomas.

Apart, of course, from his virulent hatred of Gregor Laemmle. He found the two emotions quite compatible.

SOEFT WAS STANDING MOTIONLESS IN THE DOORWAY OF THE LI-brary, staring blankly into the gloom like a blind man. His arms hung limp at his sides, and his lithe physique had all the formidable, feline strength proper to a born killer.

Just as some were born to make music or breed orchids, thought

Laemmle, watching him, so Soeft was born to exterminate his fellowmen. Never able to resist such ironical observations, especially in times of crisis, he returned to the book he was rereading, Robert Musil's *Die Verwirrungen des Zöglings Törless*. He had known Musil when the author was a librarian at Vienna and later in Berlin. They had certain attributes in common, but Musil, alas, had possessed a literary talent to which he himself could never aspire. . . .

The telegram, which a postman had delivered by bicycle three hours ago, was lying on the table beside him. He'd guessed its gist, or at least the identity of the sender, even before he opened it. He tipped the dumbfounded postman five thousand marks but left the envelope temporarily unopened. Instead, he returned to the library and waited awhile, masochistically reveling in his own uncertainty.

His thoughts returned to the late Robert Musil, who had at least left something behind in the shape of his books and the pleasure his readers still derived from them. It was profoundly unfair that he himself, being endowed with such a superlative intellect, should never have discovered what use to make of it despite fifty-one years of painstaking research. If God really didn't exist, Laemmle would have had to invent him at once, if only as a target for his recriminations. The sole purpose his intelligence had served was that of lucid self-scrutiny. It was as if he could see himself in a mirror, and the spectacle had become more and more intolerable as time went by. He was naked in that mirror, so he naturally caught cold and was susceptible to every passing ailment of the soul. . . .

He finally opened the telegram. It read: "I promised I'd come, and I'm coming."

A telephone call had followed two hours later, likewise from Switzerland. The cold, clear little voice had stated the time, place, and circumstances of their meeting.

"Soeft, go and ask the cook for another helping of chocolate mousse. And while you're about it, bring me a glass of Chartreuse."

I promised I'd come, and I'm coming. . . . The boy hadn't wasted any words. Laemmle pictured him in a Geneva post office, clambering on a chair to hand the clerk the text of his telegram, over which the cipher experts of Hitler's espionage and counterespionage services were doubtless poring at this moment.

He was so overwhelmed with love that he shut his eyes.

Soeft returned with his mousse and Chartreuse just as the record on the phonograph came to an end.

"More music, Soeft. Some Grieg, please." *Peer Gynt*—why not? Hours went by.

Eventually, still with his eyes shut, he said, "I intend to keep the appointment, Soeft. You may accompany me, but only on one condition."

QUARTERMAIN HAD LOST A GOOD TWO HOURS BECAUSE OF A large hill. Instead of skirting it as he should have done, he trudged straight up and over it, making surreptitious and sparing use of Zaugg's flashlight on the way.

South-southeast. He mouthed the words like an incantation, aching in every limb as if his multiple injuries of a year ago were determined to reassert themselves. South-southeast . . .

Startled by the sight of a light twinkling between the trees, he thought he'd reached his destination. For fear of dogs he approached it downwind, or so he thought, only to discover that the air was motionless—how could it be otherwise in the midst of so many trees?— and that there weren't any dogs. Besides, it wasn't a house, just a crude log cabin with one lighted window. He inspected it through his binoculars but could see no movement inside. Whatever it was, a hunting lodge or a gamekeeper's cottage, he decided to give it a wide berth.

According to his watch, five hours had elapsed since he left Zaugg and the Storch. It seemed unlikely that they would still be there when he got back—*if* he got back, to quote Zaugg's gloomy proviso.

He came to a stream—a narrow one, fortunately, but it was the fifth he'd had to cross. Or was it the same one? Had he been going in circles the whole time? He couldn't rule out the possibility.

South-southeast . . .

He bumped into the forest track—literally, because he tripped over a gully beside it and fell flat on his face. He sat down to rest for the first time since setting out. South-southeast was all very well, but the winding track ran due north and south at this point.

He decided to turn left. A minute later he sighted a building only a hundred yards ahead. Could it really be the small inn marked on the map?

The place was in darkness, but he made out a sign reading "Gasthof zum Blauen Engel." He'd done it, by God! Glancing at his watch, he saw he'd been walking for six whole hours. It wasn't much more than a kilometer to Laemmle's house, but he would never get back in time. Zaugg wouldn't wait for him, and rightly so. In his place, Quartermain wouldn't have made the trip at all. The man must have nerves of iron.

He was now on an asphalt road. No further need to consult the compass or a map—his memory would suffice from here on. He had only to bear right at a fork, and there the house would be, perched on the summit of a hill. The smaller building beside it might be a chapel, though the aerial photographs were inconclusive on that point.

He reached the fork and abandoned the asphalt road for a dirt road. The lights of the house showed up as soon as he rounded the first bend, far closer and brighter than he would have thought possible. Not only was the whole of the ground floor brilliantly illuminated, but lights of some kind had been switched on in the garden as well. Wartime restrictions obviously meant nothing to Laemmle.

He was still a couple of hundred yards away when he heard a metallic rumble: someone had opened a sliding door. His immediate reaction was to reach for the Colt in his belt, but it was premature. He stole on, keeping under cover. Why all these lights in the middle of the night? Could Laemmle be expecting him? Another few steps, and he was only fifty yards from the wrought-iron gates.

He just had time to dodge behind a tree: an old man bearing a pitch-pine torch was coming down the drive toward the gates, which he opened.

Then the silence was punctured by Laemmle's voice, the very sound of which made Quartermain quake with loathing.

"Not the Rolls, Soeft," he said airily. "Something more modest, if you please."

Quartermain reached the garden wall, which was only four or five feet high, and scrambled over it with ease. The old man had his back to him, one hand holding the gate open, the other grasping the torch like some elderly retainer in a costume drama.

Suddenly, from the building beside the main house—it was a converted barn, not a chapel—came the sound of a car starting up. Headlights transfixed the night and a Mercedes swung out onto the drive, accelerating rapidly. Quartermain reacted fast, but not fast enough: he raised his gun as the car sped past only fifteen yards from him, but his field of fire was obstructed by a tree trunk. The torchlight was just sufficient for him to catch a glimpse of Soeft at the wheel and

Laemmle in the back. The car's taillights disappeared from view in a matter of seconds.

Quartermain sprinted up the drive to the garage. The sliding door was still open, and parked inside were two more cars, one a white Rolls, the other a second Mercedes. He jumped into the Mercedes and switched it on. The engine caught the first time. Revving hard, he let out the clutch and roared down the drive. The old man, who was about to close the gates, leaped back with surprising agility when he flashed his lights.

He tore along the dirt road, but the other car was out of sight. Steady, he told himself. You didn't want to kill him outright anyway. If you'd fired and hit him you'd have destroyed your only chance of finding out what he's done with Thomas. . . .

He slowed a little. Two kilometers farther on he sighted the other car's taillights and slowed some more. Okay, he would follow the sonofabitch to the ends of the earth if necessary.

Soeft might have been part of a funeral cortège, he was driving so sedately. It was now three-forty A.M., and they were heading north. Just after four they entered a place called Kandern—less a town than a large village. Soeft pulled up, and Quartermain followed suit. Watching through his binoculars at a discreet distance, he saw Laemmle lean out of the car window and beckon to two men in uniform, who shook their heads in response to some question or other.

Soeft drove on, still heading north. Sooner or later they would come to a roadblock, Quartermain reflected. The odds against his survival were lengthening every minute. He'd stopped thinking about Zaugg and the Storch. God alone knew how he was going to extricate himself from this lousy country.

They passed through a village called Schliengen, still at the same sedate speed, and turned left onto a wider road.

A roadblock! Quartermain's heart skipped a beat. A soldier waved Soeft down. Quartermain pulled off the road and killed his headlights. He trained his binoculars on the roadblock just in time to see the guard commander examine some document or other and snap to attention with his right arm raised in the Hitler salute.

Soeft drove on again. He might almost have been stationary, the car was traveling so slowly, but the distance between it and the roadblock steadily increased. Quartermain shook with rage. The bastard was getting away.

And then, just as his hopes were fading, they revived. Not more than two hundred yards beyond the checkpoint was a building with a swastika flag flying over it. The Mercedes pulled up outside, and this time Laemmle himself got out and went in.

If they drive on, Quartermain told himself, I'll crash the barrier and take my chances.

Minutes went by and nothing happened. A quarter of an hour passed, then half an hour.

It would soon be daybreak. Zaugg had probably taken off already. What a fool he'd been not to get to the house five minutes earlier!

An hour.

The traffic, military vehicles for the most part, was increasing. He ducked down every time someone drove past, but this seemed an insufficient precaution. Reversing the Mercedes for a hundred yards, he backed it a little way down a side road. Shades of Ardèche.

He got out and continued to observe the building from behind a hedge. A few minutes later Laemmle finally reappeared, chatting to an officer whose Hitler salute he acknowledged with a gesture so studiously casual, so unmistakably derisive, that Quartermain might almost have admired it in someone else.

And then, just as he was about to put his foot down and charge the barrier at full throttle, a miracle occurred: Soeft made a U-turn. He was coming back! He negotiated the checkpoint and drove unhurriedly past the mouth of Quartermain's side road.

The two cars headed south. An hour later, when it was after seven and broad daylight, Soeft led the way into another town and parked. The two Germans got out and engaged in some kind of argument. Soeft, after shaking his head repeatedly, gave a resigned shrug and got in behind the wheel again.

Laemmle walked off by himself.

Quartermain got out and followed some two hundred yards behind. He passed Soeft unseen, screened by a passing truck, and lengthened his stride. The gap between himself and Laemmle steadily narrowed. Not only was Laemmle walking at a leisurely pace, but he even paused in front of a shop window to pat and smooth his sandy hair.

Thirty yards ahead on the opposite side of the street, Laemmle turned right. Quartermain crossed over and did likewise.

He almost stopped dead for a moment: the street that lay before him led down to the Rheinfelden bridge, only a few kilometers from the spot where he'd taken off the evening before, and Laemmle was heading straight for it.

Straight for the frontier post. . . .

THOMAS HAD BEEN IN BASEL SINCE YESTERDAY EVENING. WHILE traveling there by train he'd opened the third drawer in his mental filing cabinet. The first had contained the Secret, the second the American.

The third was reserved for Yellow Eyes.

He hadn't made the trip alone. His companion on this occasion was a brand-new "cousin" named François, Jean Darder's son. François was very old—thirty-one at least—and he had a wife and two boys, one of whom had been quite ill indeed as a baby. It was She who had saved his life—She'd even summoned a doctor from France to help the Swiss doctors treating him—so François's devotion to her memory was unbounded. "We all loved your mother, Thomas. There's nothing I wouldn't do to repay her for what she did. . . ."

It was the same with the Eight Men who'd listened to the Secret. Several of them had called to say that if Thomas needed anything, he had only to ask. He'd taken them at their word. That was how he'd managed to send the telegram to the Black Forest and put a call through to the same destination on arrival in Basel.

He'd almost wept, everyone was so helpful, until he realized that he owed all these kindnesses to Her: it was Her memory that had opened so many doors to him.

For a while, as the train sped toward Basel past the beautiful lakes and mountains and everything, he'd listened to François talking about his job—François worked in a bank, and one of the Eight Men was his boss—but little by little the shutters came down again and he reapplied his mind to Yellow Eyes and the best way of checkmating him.

Once and for all, this time.

And then he had a good idea—the best one possible, under the circumstances. . . .

Everything had gone right when they got to Basel last night. The chessboard was set out just as it should have been: the hotel rooms, the telephone call to the other side of the Rhine at precisely the time he wanted, François allowing him to concentrate, the ringing in his ears that meant he was ready. Strange how calm and cool he felt, now that the time had come. It was just like a game of chess, when you played the last few moves that would checkmate your opponent whatever he did. . . .

Now, having left Basel at six-fifteen A.M., he was pedaling along on the bicycle François had obtained for him. François had watched him go in silence. He was awfully worried, you could tell, but he hadn't said a word.

Six-fifteen was early enough—he wouldn't take all that long to cover the seventeen kilometers, though the weather could have been better. There were clouds in the sky—low clouds that changed color as the light grew stronger. Gray at first, they turned to violet in a way that probably meant rain. The heavens might open at any moment. He cycled through Birsfelden and the Hard Forest.

All right, all right, he told the machine in his head, it's useless telling me to keep calm and stop thinking about Yellow Eyes. I can't concentrate any harder than I'm concentrating right now. Be cool, calm, and merciless—that's what She always used to say. Well, I'm all of those things and more. . . .

It was true: he didn't even have to summon up or cultivate the ferocity he needed—it was there in full measure, but it was a calm sort of ferocity.

He'd reached the outskirts of Rheinfelden. Three minutes past seven: that gave him another twenty-seven minutes—time enough. He toiled uphill to the park, standing on the pedals. There was the bridge, and the rocky island, and the two Rheinfeldens, and the two frontier posts, one at either end of the bridge. He leveled his binoculars and studied the peaceful faces of the Swiss and German soldiers on guard.

Then he focused the lenses on a church tower. The clock said seven twenty-one. Nine minutes to go. He resumed his observation of the frontier post.

Still nothing.

He surveyed the streets leading to the bridge, one by one.

He shut his eyes for a while, then opened them.

He was there!

A bareheaded figure in a beige raincoat, Laemmle slowly and calmly walked up to the German frontier post. The steel-helmeted soldiers turned when they heard his footsteps. The guard commander stepped forward and saluted.

He must have warned them he was coming and told them to let him through, Thomas reflected. He may also have done something else, though. Take care, you know how strong his game is. He may have made some move you weren't expecting. . . .

If so, what?

I don't see it, I really don't. . . .

He got back on his bicycle and set off for the bridge.

It was an easy downhill ride.

"CERTAINLY, HERR PROFESSOR," SAID THE GUARD COMMANDER, "we were warned to expect you." Gregor Laemmle noted the use of his university title with wry amusement. So he'd finally been demoted from the rank of Ober-whatever, and about time too. He smiled at the guard commander, who was well into his fifties and looked like a tired old dachshund.

"Would you have such a thing as a cup of coffee in that hut of yours? I still have eight minutes to kill before my appointment in the middle of the bridge."

"It's only ersatz, Herr Professor."

"That would be very welcome."

He cradled his mug of coffee substitute in both hands and sipped it, gazing at the line that marked the exact center of the bridge and, consequently, the frontier. He'd already forgotten Soeft and their last little tiff about Soeft's proposed course of action. Now that the moment had come, nothing else mattered. He felt profoundly peaceful, extraordinarily serene. Dear old Socrates would have been proud of him. . . .

His heart beat no faster when the boy appeared on the other bank. Thomas's presence was simply in the natural order of things. Like any event too long awaited, it had lost its power to startle him. He was now in that strangely trancelike state which doubtless preceded the great sleep of death. . . .

He handed his half-empty mug to the guard commander and thanked him in a more than usually bland and mellifluous voice. Then, having waited for the barrier to be raised, he walked out onto the bridge. His senses were peculiarly alert to the sound of the Rhine flowing beneath him, the church clock striking half past seven, the mist that was rising from the water, the low canopy of violet-tinged cloud.

But his eyes, of course, were on the boy, who had passed the barrier on the Swiss side and was advancing toward him. They came to a halt on either side of the halfway line, face to face and barely a yard apart.

"Good morning, Thomas."

"Good morning, monsieur."

"You've grown."

"Not a lot, but I'm going to from now on."

"Did you find the American?"

"Yes."

The big gray eyes were not only inscrutable but cold as ice. Laemmle smiled.

"I assume you got my message at Tulle?"

" 'Check,' you mean? Yes, I got it."

For one brief moment Laemmle's eyes left the pale little face and scanned the high ground overlooking the Rheinfelden bridge on the Swiss side of the river.

"What's his name, Thomas?"

"Whose name?"

"The invisible sniper's. Surely you can tell me at this stage?"

"I'm sorry, monsieur, I don't know who you mean."

"What was it you wanted me to know?"

"That I've won, monsieur. While you were hunting for Her and holding me prisoner, all the codes were in my head. I got to Switzerland and passed them on the way She told me to—*and* I found the American again. You've lost."

"I admit it, Thomas: I've lost."

"You're checkmated."

"I know I am."

Thomas acknowledged this admission of defeat with a nod, and Laemmle was suddenly afraid that he would turn and walk off.

"Thomas? Don't go just yet. I too have something to tell you—two things, in fact. The first is that I know how greatly I attract you, because we possess the same brand of intelligence. We're very much alike, you and I . . ."

Not a flicker of expression, thought Laemmle—no reaction at all. He must have grasped that I'm deliberately pushing him to the limit.

"The second thing, Thomas, concerns your mother. In my opinion she *deserved* to be burned alive for having made you what you are. She was insane, Thomas."

The boy bowed his head and, in one movement, started to turn on his heel.

"Utterly insane, Thomas. She never really loved you."

Thomas completed his about-face and set off for the Swiss frontier post. All that betrayed the extraordinary violence of his rage and detestation was an almost imperceptible hunching of the shoulders. Laemmle watched him go. He'd said all he could. If the boy still hadn't made up his mind, what more could he do?

Thomas had already gone ten yards when Gregor Laemmle's heart stood still and an indescribable sense of relief and joy stole over him. The boy paused and turned, very slowly, with a look of merciless hatred in his gray eyes.

"Very well, monsieur."

He set off again. Laemmle just stood there, waiting.

He'd done it after all. . . .

QUARTERMAIN FROZE WHEN HE SAW THE BRIDGE. HIS FINGERS relaxed their grip on the butt of the Colt as he watched Laemmle walk on. It was pointless; he would never hit him at this range.

He swiftly retreated to the corner he'd just rounded and kept watch on Laemmle from there. The sandy-haired little man in the beige raincoat was talking to a grizzled German NCO. One of the soldiers handed him a mug. Quartermain saw him smile as he sipped the steaming contents, but his eyes kept straying to the far end of the bridge as if in expectation of something or someone.

Someone? Oh, my God!

Thomas had just appeared. Quartermain would have recognized that diminutive figure anywhere. The boy had walked up to the Swiss frontier guards, who were saying something to him. He nodded and walked on.

They were going to meet in the middle of the bridge!

Quartermain reached for the binoculars concealed beneath his overcoat but stopped himself just in time. It would have been sheer folly in the middle of a German frontier town, especially as his Savile Row clothes were already attracting curious glances. He retreated a little farther, looking for a roof from which he could see the bridge and both banks. Besides, he wanted to confirm his hunch that Thomas's Spanish bodyguard was safely in position.

A sudden, instinctive association of ideas sent an icy shiver down his spine: *Soeft!* He broke into a run. The Mercedes, still parked a hundred yards along the street, was empty. Panic-stricken, he looked up at the surrounding roofs. The man might be anywhere—anywhere at all. He stopped short, willing himself to think faster, striving to put himself in Soeft's place. To the amazement of several basket-laden housewives, he rotated on the spot with his head thrown back. That small apartment house seemed the likeliest bet. If he was wrong—if he got there too late—he would never forgive himself!

He sprinted along a passage and up two flights of stairs to a landing —a dead end, from the look of it. Then he spotted a half-open door. Beyond it lay another flight of stairs. Taking them two at a time, he came to a corridor with several rooms leading off it. Panic-stricken or not, he continued to think logically: the bridge had been on his right when he entered the building, so it must now be on his left. He tried one door after another. Soeft wouldn't have locked himself in—he wouldn't have had the time. The third door swung open to reveal an empty room with a window overlooking the bridge—Quartermain even caught a glimpse of Laemmle, alone for the moment, starting out on his brief walk to the midway point.

Quartermain dashed out again. The fourth door resisted, like the first two. He was about to give up when something caught his eye: this door was different from the rest in having a security lock. He shoulder-charged it and the panel splintered sufficiently for him to feel a jet of cold air on his face. Wrenching wildly at the wood with both hands, he created a hole large enough for him to insert one arm and manipulate the lock. The staircase beyond was more like a ladder, and the door at the top was open. He raced up it and very nearly dashed out his brains on the pavement three floors down: a tiled roof sloped steeply away at his feet. Hanging on to the doorframe with one hand, he drew the Colt. Where was the bastard?

Soeft was less than twenty yards from him. Stretched out flat on his stomach, he was calmly engaged in loading a rifle with a telescopic sight. Quartermain grasped the Colt two-handed and aimed at the back of the blond head.

Two seconds went by.

Quartermain lowered the gun. One shot, and he would be cornered like a rabbit at harvest time. If he was going to kill the man, he would have to do so silently. With the Colt in his right hand, he pulled off his shoes and crept cautiously across the tiles. A chimney stack obstructed his view for part of the way. By the time he rounded it Soeft had raised the rifle to his shoulder and was settling himself into a firing position.

From where he stood, Quartermain could see that the muzzle was pointing straight at Thomas, now walking across the bridge toward Laemmle.

Soeft's forefinger wasn't on the trigger yet; it was slowly, delicately caressing the trigger guard. Quartermain watched it like a hawk. As soon as it touched the trigger he would fire and be damned to the consequences. . . .

The gap steadily closed. Quartermain was within three feet of his objective when the prone figure swung around with incredible speed. A split second later he found himself looking down the muzzle of the rifle.

"I recognize you," Soeft said in French.

"I'm glad," Quartermain replied.

The red lips curled in a smile.

"You can't use that gun." Soeft nodded at the Colt, which was now only inches from his face. "Everyone would hear. The town's full of soldiers."

"That," said Quartermain, "was a detail that hadn't escaped me." And he buried the hunting knife in his left hand hilt-deep in Soeft's throat.

The sniper's rifle escaped from Soeft's convulsively twitching fingers, slid down the roof, remained poised on the edge for a moment, and plummeted into space. Soeft was dead by the time it landed in the street below.

Unbalanced by his own momentum, Quartermain had ended up on all fours. He gulped air, desperately trying to catch his breath.

And now get out of here!

His brain gave the order but his limbs refused to obey. It took him what seemed eons even to stand up.

Get out of here—that rifle will have given the game away!

Dazedly he looked across at the bridge. Thomas had just started to walk off, but Quartermain could sense that he would turn around.

Thomas did so. He said two or three words, then turned on his heel

and walked off again. There was something curiously stiff about his
bearing.

For God's sake get going!

Quartermain made his way back to the top of the little staircase and
started down it, but the temptation was irresistible. He looked back at
the bridge, this time using his binoculars. Thomas had just passed the
barrier on the Swiss side. The binoculars presented a perfect close-up
of his incredibly piercing gray eyes. He raised his right arm as if
saluting Gregor Laemmle for the last time. Laemmle, meanwhile, continued to stand there in the middle of the bridge, absolutely motionless.

Quartermain saw no more. He could hear footsteps hurrying along
the corridor below. All his reflexes back in working order, he snatched
up his shoes and ran across the roof. Someone yelled at him to stop.
He cleared one gap with relative ease—the alleyway beneath couldn't
have been more than six feet wide. Then he scrambled up one side of a
roof and slithered down the other, missed his footing, and just managed to catch hold of the gutter. He was gripping his shoelaces between his teeth, but one shoe escaped and landed at the feet of a
passerby, who promptly looked up and saw him dangling there. The
gutter held. Precariously, he worked his way along it to the upright of
a wooden balcony and slid down it to safety. More and more cries rent
the air, but not in his immediate vicinity. He pushed open some french
windows, tiptoed across one empty room, then another, emerged into
a corridor, and dashed down the first flight of stairs he came to.

Outside in the street a man shouted something and tried to grab him
by the sleeve, but he fiercely shook him off and ran on.

FIVE OR SIX YARDS BEYOND THE BULKY FIGURES OF THE SWISS
frontier guards, Thomas raised his arm.

For one second, no longer, he leveled his forefinger at Gregor
Laemmle, who was watching him steadily. Miquel would understand.

Then he turned, walked over to his bicycle, and got astride it.

He wanted you to kill him. . . .

He must have gone at least two hundred yards before the shot rang
out.

A single shot only.

He veered off the road, dumped his bicycle beneath some trees, and extracted the binoculars from the saddlebag. Frontier guards, German and Swiss, were running across the bridge toward Laemmle's supine form. Thomas could clearly see his face. It was quite serene. But for the neat red hole between his eyes and the welter of blood on the roadway beneath his head, he might have been asleep.

He wanted me to kill him. . . .

Thomas rode on into Swiss Rheinfelden. Some children passed him on their way to school. He dismounted and walked along with them. A little girl asked if he was a new boy, and he wanted to tell her yes, he came from Zurich, and his father and mother had just moved here.

But he couldn't get a word out, and the little girl and her companions stared at him open-mouthed.

I must watch my eyes, he told himself. I must take care—I'm sure I look like someone who's seen the devil. Oh, Maman, I did it because of what he said about you. He couldn't be allowed to go on living after that, so what else could I do? He wanted me to kill him, Maman, so I killed him, but now I feel awful and I want to cry. . . .

He roamed the streets of Rheinfelden and hid for a while in a recess behind a wash house. He leaned his head against the wall but couldn't shut his eyes, let alone cry.

It isn't true I'm like him—it just isn't true. He only said that to make me angry. He said it on purpose and I knew it, but I got angry all the same. I'd have killed him myself and now I'm ashamed. . . .

He slid to the ground and rested his cheek on the cobbles, but it was no use willing his eyes to shut or shed tears, no use at all.

It would wear off. It was hard at the moment, but it would wear off. *I'll never kill anyone again—it's too horrible. . . .*

It did wear off a little bit. He got up, hanging his head so no one would see his eyes, and walked along the street to a main road, and there was François Darder waiting with a car. François put an arm around him and patted his head. He didn't say anything, just made him get into the car and drove him back to Geneva.

"THERE'S NO NEED TO HIDE ANYMORE, MIQUEL."

"*No estoy seguro*. Someone may have seen me on the riverbank."

"I don't think so. Come and sit beside me."

"Better not, Tomás."

Thomas gazed across the park's well-tended lawns at the Lake of Geneva. Miquel had turned up without a sound. He might be sitting on a bench on the other side of the shrubbery or he might simply be standing there—it was impossible to tell.

He's leaving—Miquel's leaving and going back to Majorca, that's what he's come to tell me, but he can't bring himself to. He won't be there behind me with his gun anymore, not ever again. . . . I ought to be glad: for once, someone I love isn't dead. He'll go back to Majorca and see his *novia* again and they'll get married and have children and he'll never go short of anything for the rest of his life—She will have seen to that. I ought to be glad, but it really hurts, him going like this. It's almost like a pain in the chest.

"Miquel," he said in his clear little voice, managing to sound quite matter-of-fact, "I think it's time you went back to Majorca."

"You may still have need of me, Tomás."

"No, it's over. *Seguro.*"

"*Estoy muy triste, Tomás.*"

"Why sad? You want to go home, don't you?"

"*Sí. Claro que sí.*"

"Well, then. Go back to Majorca, marry your *novia*, and build that house of yours. There's nothing to be sad about. What did you do with the rifle?"

Miquel said he'd thrown it in the river. He also said he'd never liked killing people—never, and he never wanted to do so again however long he lived. It was simply that God had made him such a good shot —Javier was right—but it would be better if he never touched a gun again. Of course he'd be glad to see Majorca again, but he was sad to be leaving Thomas all the same. . . .

It was a tremendously long speech by Miquel's standards, almost certainly the longest he'd ever made, and his voice sounded really strange by the time he finished.

"Don't cry, Miquel," Thomas told him. He was having trouble with his own voice because he knew that it wouldn't take much to make him cry too. It was odd how weak he'd become now that the fever had left him at last.

"Don't cry, Miquel—please don't."

Luckily, a couple came strolling along the path at this moment. The man and his wife were smartly dressed but very old—so old that Thomas wouldn't have been surprised if their ages added up to a couple of centuries. They took tiny little steps, and the man, who was leaning on a stick, wore funny things made of gray cloth over his boots. They looked at Thomas as he sat there on his bench, alone except for some birds pecking up crumbs from the bun he'd been eating, and he could tell what they were thinking, as clearly as anything: they were thinking that he was a nice-looking little boy with a lock of dark hair falling across his forehead, and that it must be wonderful to be eleven or twelve and sit in a Geneva park, peacefully feeding crumbs to the birds.

Little did they know. . . .

He politely inclined his head as She had taught him to. The lady smiled, the gentleman raised his hat, and on they walked, wrapped in the aura of a bygone age.

"I'll come and see you in Majorca, Miquel," Thomas said. "What's your *novia*'s name? You've never told me."

"Catalina."

"I'm sure she's very pretty."

"Sí, es muy guapa," Miquel replied.

That did the trick, thought Thomas. He hadn't forgotten her name at all, he'd merely pretended to. Miquel had mentioned Catalina's name twice, once at Sanary, the first time they'd gone swimming together at night, which was nearly four years ago, and once in Corrèze. He never forgot things even when he wanted to. A pity his memory was so good, but still, it had worked: Miquel wasn't crying anymore.

"You're going away, Miquel, so there's no need to be too careful. If you won't come to me, I'll come to you. We can't say goodbye without looking at each other—it's crazy."

He got up very quietly so as not to frighten the birds, but by the time he'd rounded the shrubbery there was no one there.

Miquel had gone, invisible to the end. That was the way he was, and nothing would ever change him. Besides, perhaps he was right to be careful. The Swiss police had questioned Thomas after Rheinfelden, and although he'd said he knew nothing about the dead man on the bridge, it was clear that they didn't altogether believe him. If it hadn't been for the Eight Men, matters might well have gone further.

He left the park, walked along the Quai Wilson and the Quai du Mont-Blanc, and retraced his steps across the Rhône. Maybe Miquel was still behind him somewhere, maybe not. He was suddenly overcome with fear at the realization that that was over too: his unseen friend would never again be hovering in the background, ready to protect him. By degrees, his fear gave way to a positively unbearable feeling of loneliness. The Darders were awfully nice people, but there was no one he could really confide in. If he fell into the Rhône and drowned he would die twice over, once in the normal way and again because not even a cat would remember him after a day or two. You *really* died when no one still remembered you with love or suffered from heartache at the very thought of you. That was why She wasn't really dead. She would die when he did, not before. . . .

He walked down the Rue du Rhône to Jean Darder's shop, a terrifically smart shop with twelve or fifteen assistants. As soon as Darder saw Thomas he beckoned him over with a look on his face that spelled bad news and showed him into the back office. Waiting inside was someone Thomas had never seen before, a big fat American. You could tell he was an American just by looking at his necktie.

You could tell something else, too, the moment Darder left the room—you could tell it from the American's tone of voice and the look in his eye. He said his name was Joe Sowinski.

"You did a real fine job, you and your mother. Dave's dead and it's all your fault. He had a crazy streak, okay, and he sure as hell had the worst head for business in the States, but we loved the guy. Maybe you loved him a little too, kid, but I doubt it. With that poker face and those owl eyes of yours, you don't look like you love too many people. The Clan and me, we dug Dave out of Germany and smuggled him into Switzerland three days ago, but he took off again, the damn fool —he went looking for you in Germany. Christ Almighty, he hadn't been gone an hour when we heard you'd turned up at our branch in Geneva.

"If it was up to me, kid, I know damn well what I'd do with you, but I've got my instructions. Dave's uncle and cousins have decided to settle fifteen million dollars on you. They don't think you're his son, naturally, but Dave did, and they reckon that's worth fifteen million."

Thomas stared at him. He'd guessed that Yellow Eyes had a final move up his sleeve and he'd wondered what it was. Well, now he knew.

"When did Mr. Quartermain leave for Germany?" he asked.

"Four days ago."

In other words, the day before he'd killed Yellow Eyes. Everything was as clear as daylight now.

"Thank you for offering me that money, monsieur, but I can't take it. I don't want any money at all. All I want is for you to go away as soon as possible. I'm sorry to have to tell you this, monsieur, but I think you're a very stupid man."

Only a few days ago he would have been tempted to ask Miquel to kill this man in the hideous necktie. Miquel might have refused, but he'd have asked him anyway. Things were different now. Sowinski's face had gone purple and his mouth was opening and shutting like the gills of a stranded fish, but he couldn't care less. Nothing mattered anymore. It was funny how calm he felt, almost as if he were dead inside.

Sowinski stomped out and Darder came in.

"How did it go?"

"All right," Thomas replied, smiling faintly. "I'm rather tired, Uncle Jean. I think I'll go back to the Place de Jargonnant and read on my bed for a while."

"Would you like me to come with you?"

"No, thanks. Really not."

He walked off down the street, and it was funny, he couldn't even feel the pavement beneath his feet. He could hear the sounds of the city, but they were very far away. It was like when you were ill in bed and things went on as usual outside. Look at the way he'd boarded this tram: he'd got on for no particular reason, without really meaning to. He didn't have much idea of what he was doing, to be honest. It had never happened to him before. Maybe he was going mad. . . .

It had to be a dream—what else could it be? Anytime now he would see Yellow Eyes sitting opposite, smiling at him, even though he was dead. . . .

It was a dream, he told himself again, so he didn't turn his head. He just looked down at the hand that was resting on his knee: a big, lean hand with long, long fingers. And then he heard the American speak —the real American, not the other one.

"Well, kid, we had a little trouble meeting up again, but we made it after all, didn't we?"

"Thomas?"

"Yes, monsieur."

"Is your invisible friend still around? I hope he isn't watching me through that scope of his."

"His name is Miquel Enseñat, and he's gone back to Majorca to see his *novia*. He isn't here anymore."

"I can't stand Joe Sowinski," Quartermain said cautiously. He felt like someone threading his way through a minefield. The boy was clearly on edge, and every word he uttered might send him toppling. He mightn't be gambling with his life, not now, but a considerable part of it hung in the balance. After all, he still didn't know if Thomas was prepared to be his son. . . .

"I can't stand Joe Sowinski," he repeated, "and I'd rather not know what he told you at your new uncle's store." He would find out in due course, but not now. In his present nervous state, he might have beaten Sowinski's brains out with one of Hunt Manhattan's gold bars.

Thomas didn't move. His wide gray eyes were staring into space.

"We could always talk about Zaugg," said Quartermain. "Zaugg is a pilot. More Swiss than Zaugg you can't get. He's slightly less cool than an ice cube. He camped out in the Black Forest for three days and nights, waiting to pick me up. When I asked him why, all he said was, 'Why not?' "

"What were you doing in the Black Forest?"

"Nothing special. Ever tried finding your way through a forest? I invented my own personal method. You can't help walking in circles anyway, so that's what you do: you walk in circles on purpose. It's a foolproof system. After three days you're sure to bump into an airplane with a Swiss pilot waiting to take off. The important thing is, the Swiss pilot must have some chocolate on board—which he's bound to have, being Swiss—because a person starts to get mighty hungry after three days without food."

Quartermain had never taken his eyes off the sharp little profile. His heart was in his mouth. If it wasn't panic he felt, the resemblance was amazing.

"Soeft," Thomas said abruptly. "His name was Soeft. He wouldn't have let Yellow Eyes die without trying to save him. You killed him, didn't you?"

Don't use that as a lever, Quartermain told himself. Don't even think of it.

"Never heard of him," he said, trying to inject as much sincerity into his voice as possible.

"He was tall and fair-haired, with very red lips."

"I don't know who you're talking about, Thomas. As for killing someone, I'm no Pistol Pete."

"I know," Thomas said, "you're an ordinary man."

Quartermain felt stifled. He drew a deep breath.

"Is that a good thing or a bad thing, being an ordinary man?"

Thomas didn't answer for a while. Then he said, "A good thing—a very good thing, actually."

Jesus, thought Quartermain, why are my eyes so moist?

"I'd like to meet your Monsieur Zaugg someday," Thomas said. He still hadn't turned his head and was staring into space as fixedly as ever.

"That can be arranged, Thomas."

"I'd be happy to go and see him with you, monsieur."

For want of anything better to do with them, Quartermain buried his hands in the pockets of his raincoat.

"Thomas," he said, very gently, "do you really have to go on calling me 'monsieur'?"

No answer.

"You could call me David, for instance."

"I could," said Thomas.

"But you don't care to?"

"Not really."

Silence.

"What do you suggest, then?" Quartermain's nails were digging into his palms. "Look, could we speak English for a bit, the two of us? Maybe you could think of something English to call me."

"Like what?"

"Like anything at all," said Quartermain. "Like Pop or Dad or Daddy."

An even longer silence.

THE DAM'S BREAKING. IT'S NO USE, I CAN'T HOLD IT BACK. IT didn't happen even when She died, but this time it's too strong for me. That proves the fever's gone for good and I've turned into an ordinary, normal boy. Yellow Eyes was wrong about me: I'm not the least bit like him. He was crazy to say that—he only said it to hurt me. Maybe it was his way of telling me he loved me, but I've never wanted that kind of love. . . .

Who cares if everyone sees me crying? It doesn't matter a bit, because this is the end of one story and the beginning of another. The main thing is, I'm not alone anymore. . . .

The sob welled up inside him like a mighty wave. Then it broke, carrying all before it. Thomas wept without moving for a while. At last he leaned over and rested his cheek against Quartermain's shoulder. He went on crying, but it was a good feeling.

"I'll call you Daddy," he said. "Is that all right with you, Daddy?"

About the Author

LOUP DURAND began his career as a novelist at the age of forty-two. Under a pseudonym, he has written a number of French best sellers. His novels have won prizes and been translated into twenty different languages. *Daddy* is Durand's first novel published under his real name in America.

About the Translator

J. MAXWELL BROWNJOHN is a widely acclaimed translator and screenwriter whose best-selling translations include *The Night of the Generals* and *The Boat*.